ROBERT BLAKE
General-at-Sea

Miniature of Blake by Samuel Cooper

J. R. POWELL

ROBERT BLAKE
General-at-Sea

*

COLLINS
ST JAMES'S PLACE, LONDON
1972

William Collins Sons & Co Ltd
London · Glasgow · Sydney . Auckland
Toronto · Johannesburg

First published 1972
© J. R. Powell, 1972
ISBN 0 00 211726 6
Set in Monotype Imprint
Made and printed in Great Britain by
William Collins Sons & Co Ltd Glasgow

Contents

Illustrations

Maps and Plans

The author wishes to thank the following for permission to reproduce maps and plans: 1 Brigadier Peter Young; 6, 17 and 18 Messrs. Longmans; 14 and 21 Brigadier Lucas Philips.

Preface

THE aim of this life of Robert Blake has been to try and place him against the background of his own times, both at home and abroad. For it is thus that his life best can be seen in its true perspective; to let him interpret himself through his own words, and to view him through the eyes of his contemporaries, both friend, comrade, royalist or foreigner; to listen to their spoken accounts of him; to set his portrait within the frame of his own period. I have therefore given the references to the various documents and authorities which I have used. As far as I know the authors of previous lives of him have not done this. For though Blake modestly says but little of himself, his greatness and personality spring to life in the words of those who either served with, under, or against him.

In London is a block of flats, each block being named after a great English admiral, save one, Robert Blake. This ignorance of him may be due to the fact that it is nearly fifty years since the last life of him appeared. This book, it is hoped, may supply the vacancy.

To the Navy Records Society I owe an incalculable debt for the information contained in their various volumes: the same is true of the Society for Nautical Research. Especially in the articles of Dr R. C. Anderson, my old friend and ever-generous helper, on 'The Royalists at Sea'. He has pioneered the way and smoothed my path. To Mr C. D. Curtis' life of Blake I am much indebted for information about the Admiral's fore-bears and early life: also to Miss N. F. Heane Ellis for her account of the reduction of Jersey, in her 'Channel Islands and the Great Rebellion', printed by the Societe Jersiaise in 1937: and to Doctor V. A. Rowe for her most valuable chapters on naval administration in her *Sir Henry Vane the Younger* (1970). I need hardly add that the Thomason Tracts in the British Museum still remain a mine of hidden treasure. Finally I am indebted to my friend and fellow Navy Records Society editor Mr E. K. Timings for much valuable advice and criticism.

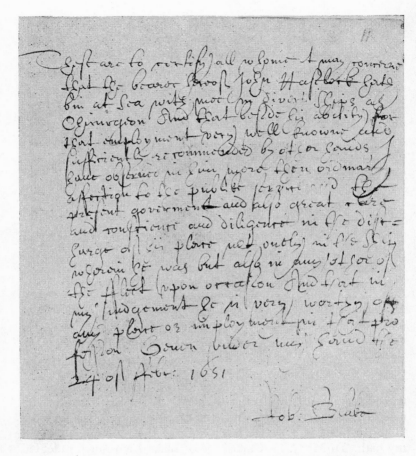

Blake's testimonial, written in his own hand to his surgeon John Halstock:

These are to certify all whom it may concerne that the bearer hereoff John Halstock hath bin at sea with mee in divers ships as chirurgeon. And that beside his ability for that employment very well knowne and sufficiently recommended by other hands I have observed in him more than ordinary affection to the public service and the present government and also great care and conscience and diligence in the discharge of his place not onely in the ships wherein he was but also in any other of the fleet upon occasion. And that in my judgement he is very worthy of any place or employment in that profession. Given under my hand the 24th of Febr. 1651.

Rob: Blake

CHAPTER I

The Appearance of the Blakes

*

THE first two Tudors had turned the minds of Englishmen towards the sea, and showed them that their future lay upon the ocean. By the time of Elizabeth, a race of merchant sea-captains had arisen, bold, daring, adventurous and unscrupulous. Such men were Frobisher, Drake, Hawkins, and Grenville. They sought to clip the wings of the King of Spain by allowing him to collect his gold and silver, and then liberally helping themselves to his 'excess profits'. In so doing they prepared themselves for the defeat of the Armada.

To join them came the Blakes. For the spirit of mercantile adventure had spread to the gentle Quantock Hills, in which they were bred. In 1552 Humphrey Blake died at Tuxwell Manor, in the village of Spaxton, at the foot of those kindly slopes.[1] He came of a family of small farming gentry. He had three sons, John, Thomas and Robert, to the last of whom he left his property, situated at Bishop's Lydiard. Robert however was an adventurous soul, who desired a larger sphere than that of rural life. He boldly moved himself to Bridgwater, and started a shipping business – probably because he saw that it was the trade of the future. He prospered and became the owner of four vessels, the *Mayflower*, *Nicholas*, *James* and *White Hart*. This last ship he shared with William Nicholls.[2] She, however, had the misfortune, in 1580, to be seized and plundered of her cargo, worth £1,200, by the Macleans of Mull. Though her owners sought redress from the King and the Privy Council of Scotland, they got nothing.[3] Otherwise he was successful, for he won the respect and confidence of his fellow-townsmen, who elected him mayor in 1574, 1579 and 1597. In 1584, 1586 and 1588 they also elected him to represent them in the Commons. For the anarchy of the former days of the Wars of the Roses had been forgotten, and the new middle-class had begun to stir, though rather nervously, for Elizabeth knew how to rule. Even when she gave way she made it seem rather the bestowal of a royal favour than a yielding. Perhaps it was, as Kipling once wrote, 'the eternal naughty boy in every man hung his head before the eternal mother in every woman'. For the middle-class had sufficient sense to recognise the Queen's qualities.

Robert married a wife, Margaret Symonds, by whom he had a son, Humphrey, who in turn was to be the father of the future Admiral, Robert Blake.[4] In 1592 Robert died, leaving Humphrey some £8,000, according to John Oldmixon (1673–1742), a dubious historian. He was the Collector of Taxes at Bridgwater in 1718, and wrote a life of Robert, purporting to be by 'One bred and born in the Family', one Thomas Bear. But Oldmixon wrote in the reign of George the First, by which time legend, as with all great men, had gathered round Robert Blake. Oldmixon was incapable of distinguishing between fact and legend. As he was entirely uncritical he seized avidly upon legend, which he quoted practically verbatim from printed sources, as if they were his own discovery. Most of these were incorrect and unsupported by exact evidence, and contradicted by Blake's silence upon the events of which Oldmixon wrote. He was in fact a mere snapper-up of unconsidered trifles. These he fathered upon Thomas Bear, whom he presented as Blake's personal servant at sea, and who became Mayor of Bridgwater in 1702. Yet it is remarkable that Blake, who never forgot anyone who had served him faithfully, while he left bequests to three of those who had served him at sea, bequeathed nothing to Thomas.[5]

In addition to inheriting a prosperous business, Humphrey married a well-off wife, a widow, Sarah Williams, who brought him the estate of Plainsfield, near Overstowey, adjoining the Blake property at Tuxwell. This had been granted to her father, Sir Henry Williams, by Henry the Seventh, in return for his support during the rebellion of Perkin Warbeck. In addition she brought to Humphrey estates on the north side of the Parrett, at Puriton, Woolavington, Catcott and Bawdrip. Humphrey thus moved up in the social scale, for in the Heralds' Visitation of Somerset, he is described as *generosi et armigeri*, a person of some local importance. He was a member of the 'Company of Merchants trading into France, and the Dominions thereof', and his ships engaged in the Bordeaux wine trade. As the Borough Port Books show he was busily engaged with lading other ships than his own with wine, grain, iron and cloth: a man of many interests indeed.[6]

Humphrey took his bride to his house in Dampiet Street, which now forms the Blake Museum. From here he proudly bore his first-born son, Robert, for baptism at St Mary's Church on 27 September, 1598. On the plaster of the walls of the Blake home are still to be seen, roughly scratched, the drawing of a seventeenth-century ship, which pious imagination would like to attribute to young Robert.

Eleven other sons and daughters followed, of whom Humphrey, William, George, Samuel, Nicholas, Benjamin, Alexander, Bridget and an unnamed daughter, survived. Robert, the eldest, thus early learned a youthful leadership. Supported by the steady Humphrey he must have had to subdue the petulant, self-opinionated, impetuous Benjamin. With the keen eyes of observant youth he must have watched the building of a ship, and the fashion of its masts, sails and ropes. For the garden of his home ran down to the banks of the muddy, meandering Parrett, as it made its way to the Severn Sea. A turn to the left would bring Robert and his brothers to the old stone bridge, and beyond it to the quayside. Here they must have listened to the tales of some rough old mariner of how the Bridgwater ship, the *Emanuel*, under Captain Newton, had sailed with Frobisher, in 1578, to seek the north-west passage. Of how she got into the ice-pack so that, when she got free, her stern was so beaten in that she could hardly keep afloat: only by making 500 strokes in half a watch at the pumps was she saved. Of how again in Bear Strait she was in great peril, 'but by good hap found a way out into the North Sea', and so eventually got safely home.[7] More stirring still the tales of Robert Cross, of Spaxton, near Tuxwell, who, in 1588, fought in the *Hope* at the defeat of the Armada, in which the *Bark*, of Bridgwater, also fought.[8] And how, in 1592, Cross in the *Foresight*, had captured the *Madre di Dios*, a rich Spanish carrack, laden with specie, ebony, silks, satins and tapestry, which brought him £2,000 as his share of the booty. Had not too a Palmer of Fairfield, in the Quantock country, sailed round the world with Francis Drake, reaching home in 1580. Here was stuff to thrill the Blake boys as they listened breathlessly as their imaginations were set afire.

More soberly Robert got his education at King James's school.[10] Though it has long vanished, it was one of those Grammar schools, to which England owes a debt that never can be calculated. For they provided a sound classical learning with a background of true religion and godliness. Moreover such a community built for itself that intangible tradition that influenced its scholars for life. Here were produced the future local leaders, who were to form a powerful body in the approaching struggle against absolute monarchy. Robert is said to have shown a literary bent, especially towards the classics. He learned to write and speak Latin fluently, so that later on he was able to correspond in that tongue, the language of diplomacy, with foreign statesmen. This classical training helped him to write English clearly and simply. Thus his dispatches reveal him as a man of action, accustomed to go straight to the heart of the matter, with the ability to express himself in apt phrases and few words. He knew exactly what he wanted to say, and said it with ease and lucidity. The dispatches, too, bear the stamp of modesty that is characteristic of the truly great man, and they are inspired by the great tradition of his country's service. So there shines through them the integrity of a brave and devoted soul. It is not surprising therefore that he reveals but little of himself, though happily at intervals there flashes out the natural man who, with dry humour, cannot conceal his ironical irritation with those who would solve his present difficulties with a stroke of the pen, from the safe distance of an office stool.

With his rise in the social scale his father, in 1615, sent Robert, at the age of sixteen, to St Albans Hall, Oxford. Here he failed to gain a scholarship at Christ Church, and migrated instead to Wadham College. This had been founded by Dorothy Wadham, in memory of her husband, Nicholas, of Somerset. Of Blake's life here only hearsay evidence remains. It is said that besides angling and fowling, he was addicted to the strange sport of snaring swans. Anthony Wood, the author of this tit-bit, was however inaccurate enough to attribute to Robert, verses written on the death of the historian Camden, which were in fact the work of his brother William, who had joined Robert at Wadham.[11]

Clarendon, who never met Robert personally, writes of him: 'he was well enough versed in books for a man who intended not to be of any profession, having sufficient of his own to maintain him in the plenty he affected, and having then no appearance of ambition to be a greater man than he was. He was of a melancholy and sullen nature, and spent his time most with good fellows, who liked his moroseness and the freedom he used in inveighing against the licence of the times and the power of the Court. They that knew him inwardly discovered he had an anti-monarchical spirit, when few men thought the government in any danger'.[12] This is partly true, for Blake was never personally ambitious. Yet it hardly seems likely that he was morose or sullen, for he mixed freely with, and was welcomed by, his fellows. Free expression of views has always been a feature of college life, and its exchange taught men to respect and tolerate each other, however much they differed. For among the members of Wadham were Charles Doiley and Nicholas Love, both ardent Parliamentarians, while Charles Dymoke and Francis Blewett were Royalists. As for his anti-monarchical spirit, this may have been expressed by all the members of the college in indignation when, in 1618, James the First tried to foist upon Wadham, as a fellow, Walter Durham, contrary to the Statutes, since the vacancy had already been filled.

In the following year, 1619, Robert stood for a fellowship at Merton. The Warden, Sir Henry Savile, is said to have rejected him on the ground that he was not tall enough. Oldmixon, who relates this, records his height as five foot six, but there is no reason whatever to believe this.[13] He also declared he was a woman-hater, but in his letters Blake sends his humble respects to both Desborough's and Mountagu's wives.[14]

One ironical fact remains to be recorded. Each commoner, on his admission, was required to buy a piece of plate for his own use during his residence, though, when he left, it became college property. Blake bought a fourteen ounce silver salt-cellar. In the inventory of silver 'lent' to the king for his use in the Civil War, this was included and melted down.[15]

In 1618 Robert took his B.A. degree. A little later he seems to have returned home. His father was in failing health and, on 19 November, 1625, he died. His estate is said to have been in a parlous state and encumbered with debt. In reality his Will shows that he left about £8,000, a large sum in seventeenth century values, of which the majority went to Robert, though five other sons and a daughter were provided for. His widow was left his house, since she was provided for by her marriage settlement.[16] What had happened was that the shipping trade had undergone a slump. The Blakes were now well-off, in the place of being wealthy. Robert and Humphrey took over the business, while Nicholas carried on the trade with France and Spain from Dunster and

Minehead. James the First had made a Treaty with Spain in 1604, by which Englishmen could no longer trade with those parts which were under Spanish influence, while privateering was made a capital offence, nor would James issue Letters of Marque. Above all the immunity of English crews from the activities of the Spanish Inquisition ceased. It was a Spanish sea-trade victory. In his desire for peace the King had conceded everything without getting anything in exchange. He even laid up his men-of-war in the Medway, without their masts, guns or crews. The mercantile marine became an easy and attractive prey for the Moorish pirates of North Africa. They infested the Channel and even entered the Thames. Between 1609 and 1619 they captured 446 English vessels and enslaved their crews.[17] In 1640 the Mayor of Exeter reported that they had landed, and carried off women and children from the streets of Penzance.[18] By blockading the Thames they forced the city merchants to pay heavily for allowing their ships to enter or to go out. Small wonder was it that the shipping trade had slumped.[19]

Charles the First found a solution in the building of the Ship-Money fleet, which secured comparative safety round the English coast. Ironically enough most of the vessels, together with those built by James the First, were to pass into the hands of Parliament and of Blake. Some of them even furnished him with flagships. Since Parliament refused to grant Charles any money, for eleven years, from 1625 to 1636, the King ruled without it. To get supplies to carry on his war with the Scots the King was driven to recall Parliament. To this Robert was elected as the member for Bridgwater. Since it only sat for three weeks, and was therefore known as the Short Parliament, it is very doubtful if Blake ever took his seat. In the New Year the Scots defeated the royal troops, and took Newcastle, so that once more the King had to summon Parliament. Blake however lost his seat to Edmund Wyndham, a Royalist. This was probably due to the fact that when the Long Parliament met, its members were practically unanimous in their hostility to Charles's government. But as yet the attack on the hereditary power of the Crown had not then developed. It may well have been felt that Wyndham's influence throughout the county was wider than that of Robert. The Long Parliament asserted its power by abolishing the Courts of Star Chamber and of the High Commission, and by impeaching the King's strong men, Laud and Strafford. Charles retaliated by going down to the

Commons to arrest the leaders of the opposition, only to find that they had fled to the city for refuge. Baffled in his attempt the King left London for York, only to return six years later as a prisoner. One strange fact deserves notice. Though Pym lived at Cannington, three miles from Bridgwater, their names have never been linked together. Possibly Pym regarded him as too insignificant a person with whom to consort.

Yet even in their comparative obscurity the Blakes had clashed with authority. They were members of the Church of England, which suited Robert's soberness. Humphrey was churchwarden of St Mary's, whose Vicar was John Devenish, a stout Puritan, well suited to the town's religious convictions. Laud, at the time Bishop of Bath and Wells, censured Humphrey for having connived at what Laud considered to be certain irregularities in the conduct of the services. In Humphrey's defence Elizabethan precedents were quoted and embodied in a remonstrance sent to Laud. Robert is said to have signed this document. Though the story is vague it is consistent with the attitude of those who were opposed to the royal methods of administration.[20]

Robert's religion was a simple one, which deepened throughout his life. By belief he was a Presbyterian. A very real religious note sounds throughout his dispatches. But they are free from that extravagant wealth of verbiage that was characteristic of the period. The language of Sion was absent, for his religious sentiments exhibit his natural reserve. When he does express them it is with simplicity and economy of phrase, which is all the more convincing. He was to show himself as a simple seaman who had experienced God's wonders in the deep, both of the ocean and of his own soul. Thus when called on to command a fleet, he conceived of himself as a man selected of God for great purposes, which he was therefore bound to carry out. Such 'checks', as Providence saw fit to lay upon him were the result, not of a mistaken purpose, but rather of his own unworthiness. The reality of this faith inbred in him that devotion to duty that rings throughout his letters. Even towards the end, when it grows clear that the sick, tired and dying man holds on only by sheer effort of faith and conscience, he is sustained by his trust in his God.

To return to his early life there remains the problem which has been termed the 'fifteen missing years'! i.e. what he was doing between his rejection for the Merton Fellowship and his election

to the Short Parliament of 1640. Much research has met with no
definite result. Many ship owners were accustomed to make
voyages in their own vessels, and Blake was probably no exception.
This, the late Professor Lewis has suggested to me, is the explanation of the lack of information about Robert during the missing
years. The explanation gains support from the nature of Robert
himself in his later years. He was a man who had to satisfy himself
personally as to the smallest detail. Thus at Porto Farina in 1655
he had soundings made as to the depth of the water, while at the
same time he took note of the range of the Moorish guns, before
he made his attack.[21] In August of the same year he went below
personally to satisfy himself that it was impossible to run out the
lower tier of guns.[22] This attention to detail surely supports the
conjecture that he must have voyaged in his own vessels so as to
satisfy himself of their sea-worthiness, and of the ability of their
captains and crews, and as to the conditions of trade at ports
abroad. Since Humphrey, his brother, later became a Commissioner
for Prizes, it is possible that he undertook to deal with the office
side of the business, leaving Robert free to supervise the sea-going
matters. Moreover previous writers have failed to notice the naval
careers of many of the Blakes. His brother, Benjamin, reversed
the usual custom attributed to naval officers, by leaving his little
farm and going to sea. In 1650 he commanded the *Assurance*
frigate off Lisbon. It is inconceivable that he could have done
this without some previous experience at sea. Is it not possible
that he accompanied his brother in voyages in the firm's business?
Robert's nephews, Robert, John and Samuel, also held naval
commands, as did two other young relatives, Thomas and William.
Is it fanciful to picture their uncle introducing them to the sea
by a voyage in his own vessels?

A story which may well confirm this theory comes from a Dutch
newspaper, the *Hollandsche Mercurius*. It relates how, in 1652, when
Blake fell in with the Dutch herring fishery fleet, he took a Dutch
skipper aboard and asked him where he lived. The answer was,
'at Schiedam'. To which Blake replied, 'I lived there for five or
six years in my youth.' He then set the skipper free with his catch.[23]
The Schiedam records however contain no mention of Blake's
name. After the first battle off Dover, in May 1652, Tromp wrote
to him to ask him to return some captured Dutch ships, 'for
friendship's sake', which may seem to imply they had previously

met. This might seem to confirm the Schiedam story, but Blake's angry refusal gives no support to it.[24] Tromp, however, may have been referring to their meeting off the Scillies in 1651, when Blake was about to reduce the islands.[25]

Mr C. D. Curtis discovered that a Robert Blake was admitted to the Freedom of the Borough of Dorchester, in Dorset, in 1629 on the payment of a fee of £20. This showed that he was a 'stranger or foreigner' as natives were admitted for a trifling sum. In 1630 he petitioned the Privy Council, as he had freighted the *Texel* of Middelburg in Holland with masts, deal and timber for Weymouth. On her arrival there the authorities had refused to allow her to unload, 'by reason of His Majesty's late Proclamation prohibiting the importation of such commodities in any other but English bottoms.' Robert declared that the cargo was urgently needed at Dorchester, and that he was ignorant of the prohibition, and he humbly begged for the return of his goods. Unfortunately the petition is in a lawyer's hand, without Robert's signature. Nor can his signature be found in the minutes of the Dorchester Freemen. Even the Bridgwater Records contain no mention of Robert between the years 1625 to 1640.[26]

In 1917 Mr C. R. Barrett claimed to have made a startling find. He believed that Robert spent ten years from 1629 onwards as a merchant in Morocco, after having been in command of the merchantmen *Phoenix* and *Golden Hind* in London. He had acted as a factor, or agent, for the old Barbary Company. In this capacity he brought fifteen redeemed captives to Captain William Rainsborough, when he visited Sallee in the *Leopard* in 1637. In 1638 he returned to London, where the Privy Council acquitted him of charges of improper dealings in Morocco, brought against him by Captain William Bradshaw. He then returned as factor for the new Barbary Company, only to have fresh charges brought against him, of which he was again acquitted. Mr Barrett thus claimed he had solved the problem of the missing years. But this claim was torpedoed, appropriately enough by the late W. G. Perrin, the Admiralty librarian. He examined a letter signed by the Barbary factor, which was in the Coke manuscripts in the possession of Lord Walter Kerr. It was instantly apparent from the writing that the two Roberts were separate persons, as their signatures were so widely different that it was impossible for them to have been written by the same hand.[27] The *coup de grâce* was

finally administered by the late Sir Charles Firth. He discovered
that on 2 November, 1643, a Robert Blake, 'a fellow who had
been a merchant in Barbary – releasing English', had been hanged
by Prince Rupert, near Abingdon. He had somehow managed to
become a groom of the King's bedchamber, and his papers revealed
that he was about to betray the King and his two sons to the Earl
of Essex.[28]

But there is still a natural explanation for the lack of information
about Blake's early life. The Civil War, with its disruption of
ordinary living may very well have obliterated from men's minds
such slight memories of Robert Blake as they had. The past had
faded out against the much more vivid present. Bridgwater had
been besieged, and the Blakes had been scattered. Great and
changing events had filled men's minds to the exclusion of the
memory of the old life, which had been so different that it was
almost inconceivable that it had ever existed.

Yet in that vanished life Blake had learned to plan and make
decisions, to judge and understand men, so that he came to handle
them with tact, consideration and firmness; while they, too, learned
that his word was his bond. In his voyaging he had gained an
experience which he stored up and never forgot. With the coming
of the Civil War he was called with his fellows to move out of a
small world into a much larger one. Yet it was in that smaller
world that his character had been shaped, had grown and developed.

CHAPTER 2

Blake makes his Appearance at Bristol

*

ON 22 August, 1642, Charles raised his standard at Nottingham and the Civil War officially began. But long before this hostilities had been in progress. On 22 April the King had failed to secure the Arsenal at Hull, which was filled with arms for use against the Scots. His attempt to remove the Earl of Warwick from the command of the fleet had also been frustrated, and in July he lost the use of the navy. In the west the Marquis of Hertford, in his attempt to execute the royal Summons of Array, had been driven off by Alexander Popham and Sir John Horner, and forced to take shelter in Sherborne Castle, in Dorset. Blake is said to have been either a lieutenant or a captain in Popham's regiment of foot, though both Wood and Oldmixon relate that he raised a regiment of dragoons, or mounted infantry.[1] But all records point to the fact that he served with the foot.

Unfortunately the earliest direct evidence is that in March 1643 Blake was one of the twenty-six members appointed by Parliament, to form a Committee for the Sequestration of the Estates of the Royalists in Somerset. But this may show that he was already regarded as a person of rising importance in the county.[2] Oldmixon hints that Edmund Wyndham forced him to leave Bridgwater, but it seems most unlikely that Robert, a man of action, would have been content to serve merely upon a committee.[3]

Of his military experience there is no record until July, 1643, when he appears as in command of a company garrisoning Prior's Hill Fort at Bristol. Yet his selection for this important command suggests that already he had made his mark as a bold and efficient leader of men. Mr Hepworth Dixon, the first of Blake's biographers, declares: 'he was in almost every action of importance in the western counties, fighting his way gradually into military notice. He distinguished himself in the sharp encounter at Bodmin; and gained the confidence of Sir William Waller by his conduct on the fiercely disputed field of Lansdown. Detached from the army to strengthen the garrison at Bristol, he missed the disastrous defeat at Roundway Down.' Unfortunately he gives no authority for these statements, and none can be found to support them.[4]

To understand the course of events it is necessary to epitomise them briefly. The King left York for Shrewsbury to recruit his forces preparatory to an attack upon London, the nerve centre of the Parliament, and its source of wealth. Thus he hoped by one decisive stroke to end the war. The Parliamentary Commander, the Earl of Essex, advanced to Worcester to stop his advance, but Charles slipped past him, and Essex moved after him. At Edgehill the King turned to meet him and, after a battle, Essex had to retire to Warwick. Charles advanced to Oxford, and paused there to rest his troops. Essex, taking a northerly route, reached London before him. On 12 November the King encountered Skippon, with the London Trained Bands, at Turnham Green. Outnumbered by at least 10,000 men, Charles had no choice but to retire to Oxford, followed by Essex, who took Reading, and so barred the way to the capital.

Meanwhile Sir William Waller, after capturing Portsmouth on 7 September, was given the command of the Western Association and made his headquarters at Bristol in February, 1643.[6] He then secured Gloucester, and barred the way to South Wales, the King's principal source of man power. Then, in May, he made Bath his centre.

In February, the Queen escorted by Tromp, the Dutch admiral, brought over from Holland a convoy of arms, money, officers and artillery. Tromp forced Batten, with four ships to retire from Bridlington, and the Queen landed her supplies on the 28th. Almost at once she sent off forty wagon-loads of arms and munitions, with 300 barrels of powder, which reached Oxford on 15 May. In August, 1642 the Princes, Rupert and Maurice had sailed from Holland and joined the King.

In Cornwall Sir Ralph Hopton, after defeating Lord Stamford at Stratton on 16 May, advanced into Devon. Then, after leaving a force to contain Plymouth, a Parliamentary stronghold, he moved into Somerset. At Chard he was joined by Prince Maurice and Lord Hertford, who had been sent by the King to join him, since he knew the Cornish army was short of cavalry and powder. The combined forces now secured Dunster, Taunton, Bridgwater and Wells, and so secured the line of the west. Then they advanced on Bath. At Lansdown they encountered Waller, and drove him back to Bath on 5 July. Next day their powder wagon exploded, partly blinding Hopton and, in their turn, they had to retire to Devizes. Here Lord Wilmot came to their aid. This enabled them to meet Waller and to rout him utterly at Roundway Down, on 13 July. On the same day the Queen joined the King at Oxford, bringing with her 3,000 men, nine guns and a hundred wagons of arms and munitions. This valuable reinforcement determined the King's Council to seize the opportunity to complete the conquest of the West.

On 18 July Rupert was sent to join Hopton's army. With him were three brigades of foot, two wings of horse, nine troops of dragoons and a train of artillery. On the 23rd he reconnoitred the City of Bristol from the height of Durdham Down. The defences ran from the Water Fort, on the River Avon, north to Brandon Hill Fort, and then on to the Windmill Fort. Between these two there was a dangerous re-entrant angle, with its apex at Washington's Breach. Just inside this line was a small work, called the Essex Fort, which, however, was partly hidden. From the Windmill Fort the line ran on to St Michael's Hill redoubt, or the Fort Royal, which contained a battery. Then it continued slightly eastward to Coulston's Mount Fort, and on to Prior's Hill Fort. Here the line turned south to Stoke's Croft and so on to the River Frome, and crossed this to Lawford Gate. Then it ran due south to the Temple Gate, crossing the Avon at Tower Harratz. At the Temple Gate the line turned at right angles to Redcliffe Gate and the Avon. The forts were connected by an earthwork some five feet high, and three feet thick at the top. Outside there was a six foot broad ditch, five feet deep, though in some rocky places it was very shallow. The forts themselves were self-contained, with dry ditches and palisades round them, with artificial glacises thrown up in front of the walls to protect them from cannon fire. Rupert had some 20,000 men to dispose of, and he placed the Cornish army, under Prince Maurice, Lord Hertford and Hopton, on the south side, near the Temple Gate. The remaining troops, under his own command, were assembled on the Gloucester side.[5]

The garrison was commanded by Nathaniel Fiennes. It consisted of 300 horse and 1,500 foot, with the townsfolk in addition, and some 100 guns. Waller had, however, denuded the garrison of 1,200 foot, whom he had taken to Roundway Down. Fiennes's

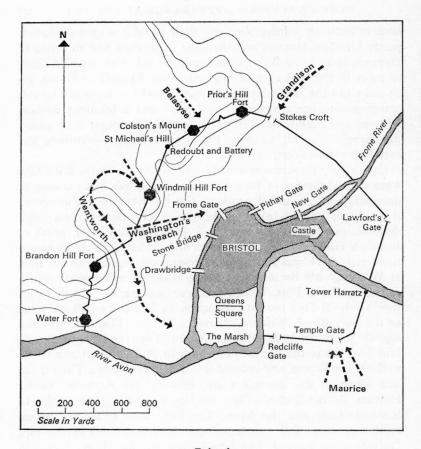

Bristol

task was almost impossible, for Bristol itself lay 'in a hole'. On the Gloucestershire side it was commanded by high ground which, if captured, would make the city untenable, unless the citizens were prepared to endure a fierce bombardment, which was most unlikely. The city proper was defended by a wall with bastions at various intervals, and by the rivers Avon and Frome forming a moat around it.[7]

Blake, at Prior's Hill Fort, was at the apex of the outer line. It had two tiers of loopholes, and had been built to mount thirteen guns, of which, however, only three were in position, while the

Fort itself was unfinished. On Sunday, 23 July, news came to Rupert that eight ships, including the *Fellowship*, the *Hart* and the *Tenth Whelp*, which were lying in the Kingsroad, were willing to come over to the King's side. Next day they did so, thus giving Charles the nucleus of a small fleet. Rupert at once summoned the City. At the same time he positioned his troops and batteries. Colonel Wentworth, on Durdham Down, had placed two guns between the Water Fort and Brandon Hill Fort. Occasional shots were exchanged, but the twelve-pounders restrained the sallies made from Brandon Hill, whose guns did little hurt. Colonel Belasyse, whose brigade was next to Wentworth, planted another two twelve-pounders some half cannon-shot from the Windmill Fort, while he had a watch on Colston's Mount. Lord Grandison erected one of his two demi-cannon near Prior's Hill Fort, selecting some rising ground by a stone stile behind a hedge, some 140 yards distant from the fort. He also had an eye to Stokes Croft. When night fell all remained quiet until midnight, when Grandison fired two guns at Prior's Hill Fort. Blake at once replied with case shot and musketry, as he expected an alarm. "Twas a beautiful piece of danger', wrote De Gomme, who fortunately kept a journal of the siege, 'to see so many fires incessantly in the dark, from pieces on both sides.'[8]

Prince Rupert, next morning, crossed the river to confer with the Cornish commanders. He was himself in favour of an immediate assault, rather than to sap. Maurice on the other hand preferred a close investment so as to starve out the city. His scaling ladders were too short, while to storm would prove costly to his already scanty troops. Rupert however won the day. The attack was fixed for the morrow. All ranks were to wear green without any band or handkerchief at the neck, so that they could not be confused with the foe. Directly any part of the line was forced, part of the stormers were to fill the ditch with the debris from the breach, so as to make a passage for the horse and foot. Maurice was to attack the Temple Gate with three brigades: Colonel Buck on the right, Slanning in the centre and Major-General Bassett on the left. Wagons were to be driven into the ditch to form a rough bridge while faggots and scaling ladders were to be held in reserve.[9]

Rupert returned and in the evening he conferred with his own commanders, to whom he gave a free hand as to their attacks.

The enemy was to be kept awake all night by alarms. A general assault was to begin as soon as Grandison's two demi-cannons fired the signal. During the night, says De Gomme, they 'tore Prior's Fort shrewdly: they answering again with three pieces, still shot over us. Mr Busye, our skilful Cannonier, was slain and one of their three pieces was silenced.'

Next morning, Wednesday the 26th, before the signal for the attack was fired, the over-eager Cornish troops began the attack on their own, rushing forward about 3 a.m. Rupert grasped the situation at once, and had the signal given. He held his horse in reserve, so as to be able to check any sally by the foe, and to support his foot. Thus they would be ready to enter the line, directly the infantry had opened the way for them. Grandison ordered a lieutenant, with fifty-six musketeers to attack the line on the right of Prior's Hill Fort, while another, with fifty more, assaulted Stokes Croft. Colonel Lunsford, with 300 men followed, but the Croft was so well defended that he was forced to draw off towards Prior's Hill Fort. Here another 250 men came up 'to pistol-shot and push of pike with the defendants, through the bars', and threw hand grenades into the works, while Captain Fawcett fastened a petard upon the gate, but only broke two or three of the bars without making a gap wide enough to enter. For over an hour the fight continued. Then, as De Gomme observed, 'plainly both works and line were so well defended, that ours being able to do no more than give a testimony of their valour', the attack had to withdraw. Once again Grandison led his men up the hill. The soldiers 'very cheerfully fell into the very ditch of Prior's Fort with him'. Unfortunately no scaling ladders had yet come up, 'by reason the assault began sooner than was concluded by the orders', and the troops had to huddle beneath the walls. Here shot and stones from the fort rained down upon them, together with musket shot from both the line and other forts, so that once again they were forced to quit. Some ran down the hill, 'others along the line, but some stood to their arms, firing very gallantly'. Sir Ralph Dutton, who had charged right up to the fort, pike in hand, went down to bring back his pikemen, 'being fallen off from the Fort'. With Grandison's aid he persuaded them to return, only to be driven out once more. Colonel Lunsford, who had found an enemy ladder in the field, carried it as far as the palisade, only to discover that it was too short, and he too had to retire.[10]

Grandison now mounted his horse and for the third time rallied the retreating men. Once again 'they obeyed very willingly, following up to the very ditch'. Blake, with the instinct of the born commander, realised that this was the psychological moment, as he saw the tired enemy clambering wearily up the slope. This was the exact opportune moment for a counter-attack, and to change from defence to offence. Sallying out into the ditch, he met the weary stormers disorganised by the climb, before they could reform, and at push of pike drove them back. Grandison was wounded in the leg, and had to hand over command to Colonel Owen, who was then shot in the face. The unexpected loss of both of their commanders so disheartened their men that they broke into a confused retreat headlong down the hill. Their leaders went to have their wounds dressed, and their men joined up with Belasyse's brigade.[11]

He, too, had failed in his attack on the Windmill fort, for he had been held up at the ditch through lack of scaling ladders and faggots. His men too had to take shelter under a stone wall. Some of them began to retreat, but Rupert met them, and led them back personally, having his charger shot from beneath him as he did so. He remounted on a fresh horse and brought them back up to the Windmill Fort.[12]

The ground between that Fort and Brandon Hill Fort was so uneven and thick with furze bushes that Wentworth's troops fell into disorder. As they pushed on up the re-entrant between the two forts, a very heavy fire forced them to run, as best they could, close up to the works so that they could get into dead ground. Here they would be invisible, from both forts, so they hurled hand grenades over the line and stormed the works. The defence broke and streamed back towards the city. The stormers using their halberds, partisans and even their bare hands, frantically tore a breach open. Through this gap Lieutenant-Colonel Littleton galloped along the line with a blazing fire-pike in his hand. With terror-stricken cries of 'wildfire' the garrison bolted like rabbits.[13]

Fiennes had posted Major Hercules Langrishe here with his horse to support the foot. But he could not persuade his men to charge. Soon 300 Royalists had got into the gap, but before they had time to reform properly, a troop of Fiennes's own horse charged them, but were beaten back by some Royalist musketeers, that lined a hedge. Once again they charged but some Cavalier officers ran up to them with lighted fire-pikes, and both horses and riders bolted in terror at an attack for which they had no ready defence. Fiennes was fatally handicapped by the fact that he had no reserve, beyond his scanty cavalry, which could deal with any force that breached his line. Once that was pierced at any point, he could neither prevent the opening from being widened, nor also the whole line being rolled up from the flanks. It was simply impossible to hold a line that was some five miles long.[14]

Meanwhile on the other side of the Avon, Maurice and the Cornish had fared badly. The ditch was found to be too deep for the carts, which were to have formed a bridge, to be driven into it. The scaling ladders and faggots, either because of the suddenness of the attack, or else by some mistake, had been left behind. After half an hour's hot fighting, they were driven off by bullets and stones, and had to take refuge in the hedges. Buck was killed, and Slanning and Trevanion both mortally wounded, while the loss among the soldiers was very heavy.[15]

The time was now somewhere about 4 a.m. Wentworth's men, in trying to avoid some enemy horse, ran towards the Essex Fort, whereupon the defender took panic and fled, and the fort fell. Wentworth then made good his position until Belasyse's brigade came up. This enabled Wentworth to advance to College Green, where he seized and manned the cathedral and two nearby churches. Next he moved on to the quay. From here it was possible, at low tide, to cross over the river to the city. Belasyse, in turn, supported by horse, under Major-General Aston, advanced upon the Frome Gate. Here, 200 women led by Dorothy Hazard, had blocked up the way with earth and sacks of wool. The defenders sallied out covered by fire from the windows behind them. For two hours a desperate fight raged. On Christmas Steps, Lunsford was shot through the heart, and Belasyse was severely wounded. Then, just as the weary stormers had begun to flag, some of Grandison's men came up, and forced their way through the Gate into the town.[16]

By this time Rupert had posted himself at Washington's Breach, both to receive reports and to watch the operations. Directly he saw that his troops had reached the suburbs, he sent across the river to order Maurice to send him 1,000 men to storm the Frome Gate. Maurice sent him 200, and followed himself with 500 more. But before they could arrive Fiennes had asked for a parley, and

Rupert agreed to suspend firing for two hours. A meeting then took place at 'a garden gate, right against the Essex Fort'.[17]

It was agreed that the garrison should march out the next morning with their arms. They were not to be plundered, and their wounded and sick were to be carried away in carts. Rupert's troops were not to march in till after 9 a.m., after the garrison had withdrawn. Their cannon, ammunition and colours were to be left behind. Finally the inhabitants were promised protection from plunder, violence and wrong.[18] By some oversight neither Blake at Prior's Hill, nor Husbands at Brandon Hill, were notified. They therefore refused to surrender unless Fiennes sent them orders to do so. Clarendon states that Rupert threatened to hang them, and that only after the garrison had left did they hand over the forts. Rupert allowed them both to march to Warminster, probably after he had learned the real reason for their refusal.[19]

The fall of Bristol gave the King the second city in the Kingdom, with a trade to Ireland, the West Indies and Spain. In addition he acquired the nucleus of a navy. Yet the price of its capture was costly. Rupert had lost 500 men, and many of his chief officers, while the Cornish army had lost practically all its foot, with most of its leaders. As a fighting force it had perished.[20]

But it is probable that the city would have yielded to a short siege. For the citizens were depressed by Waller's two defeats. Fiennes had no military training and no commanding personality. He had told the inhabitants that he believed that Bristol could not be defended for more than a week, and that without a miracle it must surrender. Small wonder that he did not inspire them with any confidence. He was tried by Court-Martial and sentenced to death. Essex however commuted this harsh judgment and he lived. He had done what he could in an impossible situation.[21]

The King's Council deliberated upon their next move. Rupert wanted another attack upon London, but at length it was decided to besiege Gloucester. This would not only complete the conquest of the Severn valley, but its bridge would open the road from South Wales to Oxford, over which the Welsh recruits could move. There was much to encourage the Council. The Earl of Carnarvon had just overrun Dorset, capturing Dorchester, Weymouth and Portland. Only Exeter, Plymouth and Lyme still held out. Maurice, therefore, with the old Western Army, moved back into Devonshire, in the hope of securing these places.

Blake had encountered Rupert for the first time. Although he could not have foreseen it, he was to meet him again, but next at sea. He was promoted lieutenant-colonel in recognition of his service at Bristol. For ten months he vanishes again. Oldmixon tried to fill in the gap with a heart-rendering tale. He relates that, on his way to Lyme, he burst into Bridgwater and was driven out. His brother, Samuel, who was at Paulet, four miles north of the town, had learned that an Array-Captain was crossing the river at Combwich. He met the officer and was killed. The news was brought to Robert, who merely observed, 'Sam had no business there'. He then retired to the Swan Inn, and burst into tears with the words, 'Died Abner as a fool dieth'.[22] After which he was never known to refer to the matter again. Apart from the fact that to go to Warminster by the way of Bridgwater would have taken Robert through royalist country, there remains the singular fact that, on 1 October, 1644, Samuel was one of the defenders of Taunton, for his signature appears on a document sent by Robert to Wyndham, refusing to surrender the town.[23] Oldmixon thus gets the credit of composing the first of the legends about Blake. There were to be many such, but none so heart-searching as this. Possibly this is why it endured so long. Probably Oldmixon confused this with Blake's abortive attack on Bridgwater on 1 March, 1645. But there is no mention of Samuel in the affair. It can be dismissed as legend, despite Oldmixon's efforts.

Blake's figure was to become well known, though Bristol marks his first real appearance. According to Anthony Wood, he was short and thick set, which accords with Oldmixon's description that he was some five foot six.[24] His features have been preserved in the portrait now at Greenwich, by Samuel Cooper, and that, also at Greenwich, called the Pelly portrait. Both these resemble each other, though they show a man older than Blake was at Bristol. They picture him with thick dark hair, flowing down well over his shoulders, below his neck, with features inclined to heaviness. A high broad brow over dark eyebrows, confirms the intelligence of the eyes, perhaps the most revealing part of the face. For they are wide open, with a concentrated look, as if they were summing up the person or problem with which they were faced. The nose is straight and shapely, with full nostrils. Below the clean shaven mouth the upper lip is curved, meeting the lower one in a firm straight line, with its corners also firmly set. Both the jaw and chin reveals a marked determination.

The portraits show a serious minded man, full of character, who will carefully consider what has to be done, and who will then set about it with resolution, determination and tenacity. Though it is not the face of a rash man, its concentration reveals a man who will boldly exploit an opportunity. Obviously a man of action, whose intensity of purpose will tolerate neither inefficiency nor negligence. Though a leader who will expect and enforce discipline, he is neither cruel nor revengeful, but rather capable of generosity. A man therefore of human understanding, whose sense of fairness will ensure that justice is done. A quality that men will instantly recognise and trust, and to which they will respond by faithful and loyal service. It is, too, the face of a well-educated man, which humbler folk used to sum up as 'a perfect Gentleman', by which they meant they could trust him absolutely, for they knew he would never stoop to, nor tolerate, any mean action, but would do his very best for them. Above all there is a hint of a sense of humour, both in the eyes and mouth. That saving grace which redeems danger and difficulty and lightens men's hearts from despondency and fear by a jest. Yet beneath all there is the spiritual quality of a man who was to show himself as the very soul of the towns he defended as a soldier, and of the fleet he was to lead to attack and victory, in the narrow seas around England and in the wider waters of the Atlantic and the Mediterranean. This sprang from a simple and very real religion. The God whom Blake worshipped and from whom he derived his strength, was not the fierce and jealous God of the Old Testament. For so many of the Puritans had bound themselves solely to the Lord of Hosts; they stopped at the Old Testament and never progressed to the New. Blake, with his guiding star of service, found in the New Testament that gracious, human, understanding figure, who had come to serve men, and to devote His life to that purpose. From that figure he drew the strength to face hardship and infirmity. He believed in the God revealed to him, because he saw in His life, so much that resembled his own. And in the inspiration he found the courage, resolution and human understanding he needed. As he could make these qualities his own, so he fitted himself to lead.

CHAPTER 3

Blake Defies Maurice at Lyme

*

JUST as Gloucester was reduced to three barrels of powder, the King was forced to raise the siege. For Essex, with the London Trained Bands was approaching by forced marches. Charles then tried to stop Essex's return to London, by giving him battle at Newbury. At that moment his powder ran out, and he had to retire to Oxford, while Essex returned in triumph to the capital.

In Ireland Ormonde, by the King's order, had made a Cessation of Hostilities, and twelve regiments, mostly foot, were sent over to England. Most of them landed at Chester and joined Colonel Byron, while others were landed at Minehead and Bristol, some time in October. This was counter-balanced by Pym who, by agreeing to take the Solemn League and Covenant, had persuaded the Scots to send an army to invade England.

In the north the two Fairfaxes, after some successes in which they took Wakefield, were routed by Newcastle at Adwalton Moor on 30 June. They fled to Hull, where they were in time to prevent Hotham, the Governor, from betraying the port to the King. Adwalton was offset by Lord Willoughby's capture of Gainsborough on 20 July, which cut Newcastle's communications with Newark. As Cavendish, Newcastle's cavalry general, was still in the field, Meldrum and Cromwell were sent to support Willoughby. At Gainsborough they met and defeated Cavendish, who was killed. Then unexpectedly they found themselves confronted by Newcastle's entire army. They were forced to retire. On 30 July Gainsborough was lost and soon after Lincoln also. To meet this danger, in August, the army of the Eastern Association was formed, with the Earl of Manchester in command, with Cromwell under him.

On 19 January the Scots crossed the Tweed. Pym had trumped the King's Irish ace. Newcastle had to move to Sunderland to watch the invaders. Sir Thomas Fairfax was now free to deal with Byron and, on the 25th, he routed him and Byron fled to Chester. On 11 April the Fairfaxes had taken Selby, so that Newcastle, as his rear was exposed, had to retire to York where, on the 10th, he was besieged by the Scots and the Fairfaxes.

To retrieve the desperate situation in the north, Rupert was sent to take over from Byron. On 19 February he made Shrewsbury his headquarters. Already Newark, the focal point of the King's communications with the north, was in danger. On 6 March it was invested by Sir John Meldrum. By the King's order Rupert moved to its relief. On 21 March he routed Meldrum, with the loss of all his guns, ammunition and muskets. Rupert then rejoined the King at Oxford on 25 April.

In the south things had gone badly for Charles. On 29 March Waller had beaten Hopton at Cheriton, and forced him to abandon all Hampshire and retire to Oxford. Here his forces were absorbed into those of the King, who was enabled to garrison Abingdon, Wallingford, Banbury and Reading.

In the west Exeter had fallen to Prince Maurice on 4 September and Dartmouth on 6 October. He then sat down before Plymouth, but the arrival of reinforcements by sea compelled him to raise the siege, leaving Colonel Digby to contain it.

It was decided to put into operation the plan that probably originated with Rupert. The King was to manoeuvre round Oxford with his horse, always refusing battle. The enemy would not be strong enough to overrun the fortresses, nor would they dare to advance into the west, and leave Oxford in their rear. Maurice would complete the conquest of the west, so as to be ready for an advance on London. Rupert was to relieve York and then, jointly with Newcastle, to defeat the Fairfaxes and the Scots, and so to advance on the capital.

The Royalists had a strong line of forts in the west. They ran from Dunster, Bridgwater, Taunton, Chard and Langport, so that the capture of Lyme would complete them. From Lyme raiding parties made their way into the heart of Devon, Somerset and Dorset. Its capture was a necessity. Nor was the Parliament any the less alive to its importance, but they had to bestir themselves if Lyme was to be held. For Maurice was now moving through the western counties. Blake was selected as the most likely man to inspire the defence, and thither he made his way to take up his first independent command.

Maurice had distinguished himself as a soldier at Ripple Field, Lansdown and Roundway Down. He was overshadowed by his brilliant brother, Rupert, and he lacked his power of inspiring men. Like most of the Royalist leaders he was inclined to despise his foe. He had little sense of strategy. Moreover he was by no means robust in health. At Exeter he had nearly died of influenza, and he was probably still suffering from its after-effects. It was a constant joke among the parliamentarians that his army was led, not by Maurice, but by his ghost. He may therefore have lacked the drive and energy necessary in a commander, if the siege was to be pressed to a rapid and successful conclusion.[1]

He decided to capture the contemptible little place, as it lay in the way of his advance, little doubting that he could do so in a day or so. Indeed the Royalists boasted that they would take it before breakfast. They seemingly had good grounds for their optimism. Lyme had been planned to meet an attack only from the sea. All its guns pointed thus. To meet a land attack Lyme was neither strong by nature, nor by military art. The defences were slight, consisting mostly of blockhouses of turf, some ten feet thick, hastily thrown up, and joined to each other by a rough line. The town lay in a 'hole', overlooked on three sides by the surrounding hills.

The plan shows the defences. The perimeter of the line was scarcely a mile, and the greatest distance from the sea was some 500 yards. For the greatest part of its length the line lay on a reverse slope, while a lane 'being deep and hollow the enemy may march without danger, five or six in a breast, home to the line'.[2] This was defended by the west, or Marsh's Fort. It was difficult of access, so that its defenders were hard put to it to reach it in safety, and they had to make a ditch and bank 'that they might walk the more securely'. Only this fort and Davey's had much field of fire. Once either fell the town was doomed.

Blake rarely forgot a lesson. Bristol had fallen because the line was too extended to hold with the number of men available. But it was impossible to contract it without exposing the city to the enemy fire. Here, to protect the town from artillery fire, it would have been of so vast an extent as to be out of the question. With the soldier's eye Blake saw that the steep decline of the ground to the shore would partly neutralise the enemy artillery, and enable a contracted line to be formed.

Colonel Ceeley, the Governor, was the titular commander of the town. He was a simple merchant, but a man of strong principles

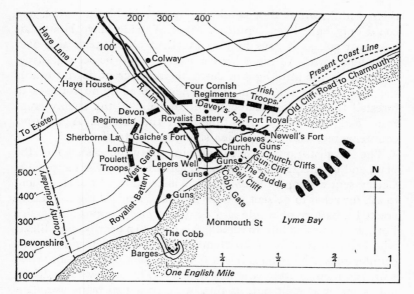

Siege of Lyme, Conjectural Positions

and character. Nominally under his command were some 1,100 soldiers, many of whom had served under Blake at Bristol. Colonel Were claimed to be next in command, but it was Blake's outstanding ability and strong personality that made all men acclaim him as the real leader.

Maurice's army was made up of men from Cornwall, Devon and Ireland, who were probably English troops sent over. It may have amounted to 6,000 men in all, with an excellent train of artillery.[3]

From the outset it was clear that the real defence of Lyme was based upon the command of the sea by the Parliament, which enabled the town to be supplied with provisions and soldiers, without which it must have fallen. Maurice took a considerable time to realise this fact.

On the afternoon of 20 April, 1644, Maurice was sighted on Rode Hill. In the evening he advanced 'in a breast' about a mile in length, and both sides greeted each other with shouts. Were, who had arrived before Blake, had posted some thirty men each on Colway and Haye Houses, a mile distant. Blake probably had

them withdrawn as they would be more valuable in Lyme, and
could only have been captured. Maurice made Haye House his
headquarters, as it gave him an excellent observation post over
the whole town. All night his camp fires could be seen glowing.
At 3 a.m. in the fitful light of dawn his forces crept down towards
the west end of the town. The defence fired some cottages to
forestall them, but, under cover of the smoke, the enemy crept
from hedge to hedge, shooting from the ditches. A vigorous
counter-attack was made which slew some forty of them.[4]

The Royalists now began to move into position, as shown on the
plan, and by the 22nd, Lyme was isolated except by sea approach.
Ceeley sent a sloop to Poole to let Waller know of the siege, and
to ask for relief to be sent both by land and sea.[5] At night Maurice
erected a battery of whole and demi-culverins, opposite Marsh's
Fort, which forced him to remove his guns to a nearby spot. Blake,
who believed that the best defence lay in attack, determined on a
counter-move. Next morning at 6 a.m. he sent out Captain Wood
with 100 men to attack the new battery. The enemy were driven
out, a gun was split but, as they were trying to bring away the
others, the Cornish, moving down to take up their post, drove
the sortie back. The Royalists had lost 100 men killed, while their
colours and thirty-five men were captured, for the loss of eight
men wounded, including Wood. By this action Blake had inspired
his men with belief in themselves.

For the next few days Maurice pushed forward his line to within
pistol shot, and raised a new battery in Colway meadow, which,
when it opened fire on Gaiche's Fort, so damaged it that two guns
had to be removed and mounted on a fresh platform. Two minor
sorties were made. One from the west which resulted in the killing
of sixteen of the enemy, and the capture of some arms. In the
other a few men, without orders, sallied out from Gaiche's Fort,
routed fifty of the enemy and captured muskets, shovels and pick-
axes. On the 25th another battery was raised 'in a lane within
pistol shot of our West Fort'. The gate was at once barricaded with
twelve foot of earth and stone to strengthen it. Unfortunately
Captain Marsh was killed by a musket shot which came through a
port hole.[6]

On the 27th Grenadoes, or a kind of bomb, were fired from the
Colway battery without doing much harm. A new battery was
raised on the east side, as Maurice had come to the conclusion

that here the town was most vulnerable. It caused a good deal of alarm, as it was feared that Davey's Fort, 'the stay of all', would be made impossible to hold, and it was strengthened with eight feet of earth. Though the new battery made little impression on this fort, Captain Newell was driven out of his fort at the extremity of the line.[7]

Meanwhile the Committee for Both Kingdoms had written, on the 27th, to Warwick detailing the distress of the town, and its importance for the shipping in the west. They urged him to send supplies by sea and, at the same time, they wrote to Waller and commended the town to his care.[8]

On Sunday, the 28th, Maurice launched his first great assault. The stormers rushed forward, with trumpets sounding and drums beating, only to be greeted with volleys of case-shot which effectually checked them. The horses strove to force them forward by slashing at the unfortunate foot with their swords, but all to no avail. Some sixty were slain, and the attack was broken off. The foot had no stomach for hurling themselves against unshaken defences. So loud was the cannonade that Captains Somaster and Jones, of the *Mary Rose* and the *Anne and Joyce*, bringing supplies from Portsmouth, heard it off Portland. Anxiously they crowded on all sail to come to Lyme's relief. In the nick of time they arrived, which 'begat new life in the almost tired soldiers'. Supplies and munitions were landed. Next day 100 men were sent ashore to aid in the defence. Fire arrows, for the first time were shot into the town, though by a miracle they did no damage to the thatch, with which practically the whole town was roofed. A sortie of soldiers and 'the bold seamen', was made on the west. A gun was spiked, some sixty of the enemy were killed and a few made prisoner. For the next four days peace prevailed, due to the tempestuous weather, which caused some anxiety for the shipping lying in the Cobb.[9]

On 5 May the Committee wrote again to Waller, enclosing a letter from Ceeley, begging for the relief of the town. As they had heard that Waller had 300 men ready to go there, they urged him to send them off. If they went by sea they might be detained by contrary wind, so they considered it advisable that he should send a considerable body of horse and dragoons by land as well.[10] On the same day Rupert set out from Oxford to go to Newcastle's relief, now cooped up in York. Hardly had he left than the King evacuated Reading in order to add 2,500 men to his army. It was a bad move, for on the 11th, Essex entered the town.

On the 6th, Lyme was enveloped in a thick sea mist, and the garrison stood anxiously to arms. But, to their surprise, as the day wore on to the afternoon, the enemy lay silent in their posts. So, lulled to a false security, most of the defence took the opportunity, about 7 p.m., to leave the line to sup. At this instant the enemy, who had probably calculated that this might happen, launched an attack at three different spots. Under cover of the mist, which deadened their approach, they got within pistol shot before they were discovered by the scanty sentries. Seeing how few the defenders were, the enemy rushed forward with the cry, 'Fall on, fall on, the town is ours'. The sentries gallantly stood their ground, calling out, 'Come on you rogues, we are ready to receive you'. The sudden outburst of firing brought back the defence instantly, pell-mell to the line again. After an hour's hard fighting, the attack was beaten off, the enemy abandoning their scaling ladders, hand grenades, 200 muskets and pikes. Over eighty were slain, including Colonel Blewett, who had been an undergraduate at Wadham with Blake. So decisive was the repulse that the enemy remained silent for the rest of the night.[11]

Next day Maurice requested an armistice to bury the dead, asking for Blewett's body, which was accorded, despite Maurice's refusal to exchange Ceeley's brother-in-law, Harvey. More generously Ceeley had Blewett's body enshrouded and coffined, and sent it, under Blake's charge, to the west to be handed over. As this was being done, Blake asked if the Royalists had any order to pay for the coffin and shroud. When they answered, 'no' he replied, 'Take it, we are not so poor but we can give it you'. Previously at the parley he had told the enemy representative, 'Here you see and behold how weak our works are: they are not things wherein we trust: therefore tell the Prince that, if he desires to come into the town to fight we will pull down ten or twelve yards, so that he may come in in a breast, and we will fight with him.' The taunt implied that the Royalist attack was so futile that he would make it easier for them.[12] To this characteristic Blake touch, the retort was that they would come in where they would, and to their best advantage. Already Blake had inspired the defence as its life and soul. His commanding personality gave courage and resolution to all, together with his outstanding ability and skill. The vigour of his defence, which allowed the enemy no time to consolidate, which answered bombardment with cannon fire, attack with sortie, all bear the marks of Blake's military genius. His very first sortie had given his men belief in themselves, and had built up their morale to the highest pitch.

On the 8th Maurice divided his army into two, 'which kept us in perpetual alarms all the afternoon and evening' but Captain Cock, in the *Mayflower* came in, and 'afforded us some relief both with men and provisions'. Two days later the enemy began to advance their approach very near the line on the west. Somewhere here, between the West Fort and Gaiche's, Blake made his head-quarters, so that he could observe the whole line. He sent out a party by night and drove the enemy farther off. On the 11th 300 men, sent by Waller, came in in six vessels, escorted by Jordan in the *Expedition*. As they landed men at the Cobb Gate, they were heavily fired upon. However a demi-cannon was landed from the *Mayflower*, which enabled the defence to reply to the heavier metal of the enemy on equal terms. Next day fire balls, or heated shot, were fired into the town, but did no harm.[13]

The arrival of reinforcements awoke Maurice to the necessity of dealing with them. He decided to shift his batteries. Under cover of darkness he moved his batteries from Colway to Holmbush Fields on the west. Here his guns would command the Cobb, or harbour, and also enfilade the flank of the town, while the batteries on the east would do the same. Lyme would be at the mercy of a cross fire. The unusual silence of gun fire led Blake to suspect that something was afoot. So he sent out a party on the east side to probe, as he believed this was the weakest spot. But it was stronger than he thought and the party was forced to retire. Another party at midnight fell upon a working party, building a breastwork. The enemy was taken by surprise, and some were killed while shovels and mattocks were carried off in triumph, a the cost of three men wounded; but the removal of the guns w still undetected.[14]

After three days silence, on 17 May, 16 guns from the new w battery opened an unexpected heavy fire on the Cobb, damag the ships lying there, and keeping up a continual bombardm To answer this surprise *Blake* decided upon a sortie on the for the next day. Just before dawn the Royalists on the called out asking when they might expect another attack.

defence, who had 120 men ready, dashed out. They entered the Fort Royal, took twenty prisoners, destroyed a brass gun and took ammunition and arms and retired. At the same time Blake made his sortie in the west, but the enemy ran away. At night, work was observed on a battery on the west. Thirty men were sent out; twenty workmen were killed, shovels and pickaxes marked with a crown and the initials C.R. were carried off as prized souvenirs. With the loss of two men the sortie retired. On the 20th in the morning 'the enemy came by Colonel Blake's quarter and approached near the Cobb'. An adventurous boy crept on to the Cobb itself, and stole a ship's colours from her stern as the crew slept. Next day the enemy improved their position by entrenching themselves on the west, near the shore by the Cobb, while their battery poured many great shot into the harbour. A half moon breast was erected against Gaiche's Fort, and the approaches there drawn nearer.[15]

The ascendency had clearly passed to Maurice. For it was plain 'hat, active as the defence had been, it had not been able to -event new batteries and positions from being taken up. This was bably due to the fact that troops had to be retained on the east iew of a possible attack there. But a new disaster was in store. he 22nd, under cover of the new west battery, a force was bled to rush the Cobb. A small vessel, unloading at the Gate, showed that the west battery now commanded that). Worse was to follow, for at 7 p.m. sixty men dashed the Cobb itself, and hurled wildfire among the barges . As the roaring flames and smoke shot upwards, the to their boats and escaped, leaving behind some barges. At this threat to their very existence, a fierce , led by Captain Pine, and probably organised by the new battery and the musketeers who held it . But the enemy, elated by their success, drove y slashing at them from horseback with their ers were forced to retire and Pine was mortally ips might be got again, but such a man was

n now seemed desperate, for unless aid came Warwick, who had an instinctive gift for right place at the right time, was on the sighted to the east. Was it a merchant

Adversaries at Lyme.
Prince Maurice (top)
after a portrait by
Dobson; the Earl of
Warwick, an etching by
Hollar

IE RIGHT HONOᵇˡᵉ ROBERT EARLE OF WARWICK BARON

Prince Rupert by Lely

fleet passing down the Channel? But at the masthead of the leading
vessel, the *James*, flew Warwick's standard. With him came six
warships. He anchored out of range to the east and, in the evening,
Blake and Ceeley rowed out to confer with him. Powder, clothing
and food were landed, and the sailors even sacrificed a fourth
part of the bread ration for the next four months, while it was
agreed to land 100 men.[17]

Before this could take place Pine was buried. As the coffin was
lowered into the grave, a salute was fired all round the town in
his honour. This sudden fire alarmed the enemy. They opened
fire, damaging roofs, houses and chimneys. The chief target was
Marsh's Fort, and the cross fire from east and west came into
action for the first time. A breach was made in the fort, but the
defence filled it in, and in so doing dug themselves into a ditch,
safe from the guns. Thus the musketeers were able to step up, and
make good the breach. Two attacks were launched from separate
places, 'very thinly'. They were led by three captains, and scaling
ladders were brought up. Again the foot broke, and were twice
driven back by their horse, only to retreat again. Blake and Were
were in the thick of the fight. Blake was slightly wounded in the
foot and Were in the stomach. One captain was killed, another got
back safe to his lines, while the third, Aston, was captured. The
fight had been severe for the 'town had its greatest loss as yet',
twelve men being killed.[18]

It was agreed with Warwick that he should send the *Expedition*
and the *Warwick*, with all the ships' boats, towards Bridport and
Charmouth, so as to draw off the enemy troops. At the same time
a sortie was planned from the West Fort.[19]

On the 29th the plan was put into execution. As a gun from
Davey's Fort gave the signal, the naval expedition set off. All day
long four or five troops of horse, with some hundreds of foot kept
company with the ships. Great shot from the vessels forced the
enemy to build a breastwork by the shore for their own defence.
Warwick says the enemy thought that men had been taken out of
the town, intending to land them, either to get provisions into the
town, or to fall upon Maurice's rear.[20] Confirmed in their belief
that troops had been withdrawn from the garrison, the enemy
waited until the ships were well away to the east. Then they seized
their opportunity to go in, as the defence weakened, for the kill. It
was exactly the right moment, just as the sortie was still being

assembled. Under cover of a fierce cannonade, they came on, 1,000 strong, with scaling ladders, and breached the line near the West Fort. The seamen, under fire for the first time, wavered and gave signs of breaking. Edward Moizer, their colour bearer, 'being a stout man both of person and courage', waved his flag and rallied them to their duty. He stood in the breach and never gave a foot of ground, until the staff of his flag was shot off with two or three of his fingers. He coolly handed the colours to another with the words, 'Take you the colours, while I go to the surgeons to get dressed'. His courageous action probably saved Lyme, and he was rightly recommended for promotion. Warwick, watching from the *James* says that from 6 to 8 o'clock 'there was a continual peal of small and great shot, so that the town seemed to be all on a flame'. Three times the enemy, in a body of 1,000 attacked, only to be beaten back. The third was the most violent. It, too, failed, and by 9 p.m. there was a general silence. The stormers lost 400 men, and the defence six or seven. This was due to the enemy bullets burying themselves in the thick earth of the breastworks. In that life and death struggle even the women had taken part, filling the bandoliers of the soldiers. One is said to have fired fifteen muskets at the foe, though whether she was more dangerous to friend or foe history does not relate.[21]

Sobered by their defeat the enemy lay quiet until the next afternoon, when they shot fire arrows into the town and destroyed four houses. It was suggested that the houses should be stripped of their thatch, but unfortunately no such step was taken. Next morning, 1 June, twenty houses were set alight. By sheer good luck the wind blew away from the town or else the thatch, dry from the hot weather, must have caught like wildfire and the town burnt to the ground. Amid a storm of small shot the townsfolk frantically endeavoured to get the fire under. Two maids bringing up a pail of water had the one her arms and the other her hands shot off. Then, just as the fire was subdued, the wind shifted and blew towards Lyme.[22]

Both Maurice and Blake had failed to put themselves in the enemy's place, and to make the obvious inferences. Maurice was convinced that men had been taken from the garrison to go with the boats, and that he had only to attack a much weakened garrison for Lyme to be his. Blake was equally convinced that the naval expedition would draw off so many troops that his sortie would meet with little resistance. Thus it was, just as his men were assembling, the enemy anticipated him by an unexpected attack.

On 1 June Warwick wrote to the committee suggesting that 500 horse and 500 dragoons could best raise the siege, as he knew that while he could supply Lyme by sea, only relief by land could raise the siege. Accordingly a message was sent to Essex to bid him speedily to send a party to relieve Lyme, or to request Waller to march into the west.[23]

The King was himself in difficulties. To avoid being besieged in Oxford by Essex and Waller, he cleverly, on 3 June, slipped past Essex and made his way to Worcester. Here, on the 6th, he found himself in very great danger of being surrounded by Essex, Waller and Massey. He was at Essex's mercy, who might have ended the war by a single stroke. But Essex could never see the war as a whole, but only from his personal point of view. Incredible as it may seem he and Waller agreed to separate. Essex would relieve Lyme while Waller watched the King. He was jealous of Waller, who regarded the west as his own sphere. The Devon and Cornish gentry had persuaded Essex that, after relieving Lyme, all he had to do was to march into the west. By cutting off Charles's main source of supply, he would do more to end the war than by fighting pitched battles. So Essex was about to abandon his true objective, the defeat of the King.

On 6 June an incident occurred which affords one of those human touches so characteristic of Blake. At the relieving of the town Guard there was an exchange of gunfire, and one of the gunners, Richard Squire, had his arm shot off.[24] He must have attracted Blake's notice for, on 3 April, 1649, he sent for him with Jonathan Pooke and James Pelsor, to come aboard his ship, the *Triumph*. Faithful service was never forgotten by Blake. It is in these personal relationships with his men that the quality of the great commander is revealed, and by which the loyalty with which they served him was inspired.

On the 12th Warwick wrote again. No relief had been heard of, and the enemy in some places was within a pike's length. As there were many sick ashore he had to keep his seamen there. The enemy had fired 100 great pieces of shot laden with the shanks of anchors, bars of iron and cannonballs heated red-hot. A house full of ammunition had been fired and some other houses. But the previous experience of the inhabitants had taught them to be ready, and they had pails of water prepared to deal with the situation.[25]

On the same day the leisurely Essex had lumbered his way to Blandford. Here the horrified orders of the committee reached him. After sending a sufficient force to relieve Lyme, he was to return to Oxford with his main body to renew his main objective. His answer was astounding. Waller was unfit to relieve Lyme, but he was in a good position to besiege Oxford. He would therefore march on to Lyme. He closed, 'If by following your orders the west be not reduced, Hopton's army recruited and Lyme lost, let not the blame be laid upon your Lordships' innocent but suspected servant'. In face of this insolent disobedience the committee was helpless.[26]

On the 13th Warwick sent for Blake to consult about landing more seamen for some design against the enemy. In the afternoon some sixteen or twenty seamen, without orders, made a sortie near Davey's Fort. They beat the foe from their breastworks, took a prisoner, and were forced to retire. The prisoner gave the news that the enemy were about to raise the siege. As for the last five days great and small shot had been poured into the town; this was welcome news indeed. That night Lieutenant Faire and his Ensign, with twenty-two of his men, came into Lyme. He said that relief was not far off, and that Maurice was preparing to raise the siege. Many more were prepared to desert as soon as they had the opportunity.[27] So Warwick, at 6 or 7 a.m. sent three ships, with boat-loads of men, towards Charmouth, under the pretence of landing.[28] Sporadic shots were still being fired into the town, and a piece of hot iron fell on the bed of Robert Newcombe, where five of his children were lying, but only one was slightly singed.[29]

About noon the enemy were seen to be taking down their tents and drawing off their guns. Captain Davey fired continually on them, and sent out a party which drove them into their great battery. Horse and foot were sent down from Colway to save the cannon, and the party had to withdraw hastily. Warwick's seamen landed and marched up into the country, driving off the horse and foot that came to meet them. The country men, now free, told them that troops under Essex or Waller were advancing and that Maurice himself had withdrawn about 5 p.m.[30]

Next morning Warwick's boats brought the news from the town that the enemy were raising the siege, and that fire had been opened on the enemy ine, to which no answer was made. A party then entered the works and found them empty.[31] At noon Warwick went ashore. He was amazed at the strength of the enemy works compared with the slightness of the defence. 'The courage and honesty of the officers and men were their sole defence.' Hardly an undamaged house remained.[32] Hugh Peters, Warwick's chaplain, preached at the Thanksgiving Service. His texts were remarkable: 'Who remembered us in our low estate, for His mercy endureth for ever:' 'And they had no children because that Elizabeth was barren, and they were both well stricken in years'. It is hoped that the sermons were not the final trial the people of Lyme had to endure.[33]

So after twenty-six days the siege ended. The town had lost six score men, while the enemy is said to have lost two or three thousand. Indeed they confessed they had lost more men than before either Bristol or Exeter. Jessop, Warwick's secretary, says they lost over a hundred officers and twenty-five gunners.[34] Maurice's reputation suffered severely, and he retired hastily to Exeter. He could console himself by the fact that he had lured Essex away from his real objective, the King. But on the other hand he had allowed Blake to pin him down at Lyme and, by so doing, he had ruined any prospect of an advance on London.

The siege had played an unexpected part in dislocating the plans of both sides. Essex, flushed with success, was confident that his decision to relieve Lyme had been justified. Now, by the advice of a Council of War, called by himself and Warwick, he decided to advance into Cornwall, with Warwick promising to bear him company with his ships by sea. Writing to the Speaker of the Lords, Essex declared that Warwick had assured him, 'the Western Counties would flock in from all parts to our body, in case I advance with my army further west, Plymouth men will take the field with 2,500 horses and foot, and fall upon the rear of the enemy, whilst we charge them in the front'.[35] So the country was to be stupefied by the spectacle of the two chief commanders on both sides about to march to disaster. Essex was to lose his army at Lostwithiel on 30 August, while Rupert, after relieving York, was to be routed with Newcastle at Marston Moor on 2 July with the total loss of all their foot.

From his first independent command Blake had emerged as a leader of distinction and of determination. He had shown tactical ability, personal courage and the power of inspiring his men. He had refused to allow the enemy to drive him into the town, and at the critical moment he was to be found at the point of danger, directing and leading the defence, which won him the trust and response of his troops. Even when taken by surprise he had remained cool and collected, keeping the defence well in hand. By making his headquarters almost in the front line, he upheld the morale of both troops and townsmen. Moreover from that spot he was able to observe both the enemy and his own works, and so he was able to deal with any situation as it arose. His flexible mind could adapt itself to any change of attack the enemy might adopt. Thus the shift of assault from the east to the west made him realise that the key to Lyme was not Davey's Fort, but Gaiche's, and the West Fort. For once these fell the Royalists could pour troops down the road or down the valley of the Lim into the town. His one mistake seems to have been the overlooking of the defence of the Cobb.

From the siege he learned and stored up in his brain many valuable lessons. If raw men, either soldiers or seamen, were to be put under fire for the first time, they must be stiffened by experienced troops, if disaster was to be avoided. In amphibious operations, the working together of troops and seamen must be well co-ordinated. These lessons he was to apply later on at the Scillies and at Jersey. Above all the siege had shown him both the ability and the limitations of a fleet; what it could and could not do. It could supply but it could not raise a siege. That must come by land. At Lyme, owing to the steep nature of the ground, the ship's guns were powerless to defend it. The severity of the siege developed his powers both of tactics and of leadership. At the very outset, by successful resistance to the enemy, Blake had raised the morale of his troops. For this always must be inspired by the leader. Here it was his strong character and personality, with his simple religious faith that was able to supply it. The Committee for Both Kingdoms, Essex and Warwick, had noted him as a man of the future. His defence had revealed qualities by which he could turn weakness into strength, threatened danger into opportunity, and resolution into success. Thus, six years later, when he entered upon that sea career by which his name is ever to be remembered, he was to hold, as stoutly as Warwick had done, to that domination by sea which was to grasp his foes in a grip of iron.

CHAPTER 4

Blake Holds Taunton

*

AFTER the relief of Lyme, Were urged Essex to send 1,500 horse in pursuit of Maurice's disheartened troops. But he refused on the ground that his cavalry were completely worn out. Only by great exertions did Blake and Were persuade the leisurely Essex to move his army from Dorchester to Chard. Here a Council of War was held, at which presumably it was decided that Blake and Sir Robert Pye should seize Taunton, while Essex pursued his leisurely way into the west.[1]

On 2 July they appeared before the town. As Maurice had withdrawn 800 men from the garrison for the siege of Lyme, Colonel Reeves, the Governor, was left with only 180 men with which to defend it.[2] After an uneventful siege of about a week, he was compelled to surrender, and was allowed to march off to Bristol. Here he faced the inevitable Court-Martial, and was condemned to death. However, he managed to escape and joined the Parliament side. Later on he was to meet Blake again, this time at Kinsale. In the castle much booty was found; a culverin, ten small guns, much bullet, two tons of match and some provisions were left to the victors. Blake at once busied himself in raising troops, in order to send foot to Essex and a troop of horse to Waller.[3]

Meanwhile the King, taking advantage of the absence of Essex, fell upon Waller and defeated him at Cropredy Bridge on 29 June. Then, hearing that Major-General Browne, with 4,500 men, was marching to join Waller, Charles retired to Evesham. Waller's men, however, demoralised by defeat, began to disintegrate, while his City brigade raised the cry of 'Home, Home'. Browne's Trained Bands from Essex and Hertford caught the fever and mutinied. They even attacked Browne and wounded him in the face, so that he withdrew to Reading, while Waller threw himself into Farnham. His woeful experience prompted him to write to the Committee for Both Kingdoms: 'an army compounded of

these men will never go through with your service, and until you
have an army merely your own, that you may command, it is in
a manner impossible to do anything'.[4] From this suggestion the
New Model Army was eventually to emerge.

Elated by success a Council of War, on 7 July, advised the King
to pursue Essex, who had now reached Devon. Charles welcomed
the proposal, as he was anxious for the safety of the Queen. She
had moved from Exeter to Falmouth, in view of the threat caused
by Essex's advance. On the 14th she sailed for France, cleverly
eluding Batten's ships, which were on the watch for her. On the
12th the King set out on the march that was to end in the destruction of Essex's army at Lostwithiel, on 1 September. Essex himself
deserted his army for the safety of Plymouth, while his troops
were allowed to march to Portsmouth. This disaster for the
Parliament was compensated for by the defeat of Rupert and
Newcastle at Marston Moor on the fateful day of 2 July. Newcastle
fled overseas, while Rupert collected some 6,000 horses and made
for Chester. Here he left Byron, and went to Bristol where he
arrived on 27 August.

After unsuccessfully attempting Plymouth, the King marched
on to Chard. From here, on the 27th, he sent 3,000 men, levied
from Devon and Cornwall, to join Sir Edmund Wyndham, the
Governor of Bridgwater, Blake's successor in Parliament with
orders that he was to 'restrain Taunton'. Obviously he did not
want the town to be attacked, as this would commit him to a
constant furnishing of more troops for this purpose.

The importance of Taunton lay in the fact that all the main
roads in Somerset converged upon it. The highway from Bristol
and Bridgwater entered it from the east, where it was known as
the East Reach, leading on into East Street, to the middle of the
town. From here it passed out on the west by the castle for
Exeter and Plymouth. The other main road approached the town
on the north-west from Minehead, and entered North Street after
crossing the river Tone by a stone bridge. The western approach
was adequately covered by the castle, while the Tone defended
the town from any attack from the Minehead Road. The eastern
approach, however, was defenceless, save for a wooden gate,
situated where the East Reach passed on into East Street. It then
joined North Street at a right angle.

Blake at once recognised that the vulnerable point of the defences lay at the East Gate. This would obviously be the spot at which to expect an attack. He therefore had two lines of trenches constructed outside the Gate, while stakes and palings were cut down to form barricades across East Street inside the Gate. He also brought up several pieces of artillery from the castle, and posted them so that they commanded the approach up the East Reach.

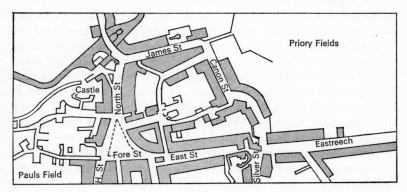

Taunton

Nearby houses, including the New Hospital, known as Pope's Almhouses, were prepared for defence by musketeers. Other houses which, if captured, might enfilade the defences, were pulled down. A little later, near the centre of the town, defences were built. Two earthworks were thrown up near St Mary Magdalen Church. One was known as the Vicar's House, naturally in the grounds of the Vicarage, and the other as the Maiden Fort. From the graceful tower of the church observation could be made of the surrounding countryside, while the church in itself was a strong point. Still another entrenchment was thrown up in the market place, before the East Gate of the castle.

The Castle was the corner-stone of the defences. It had a strong Norman keep, and was surrounded by an inner and outer moat, with massive walls extending on each side of the Gatehouse leading to the inner Bailey, and ending, east and west, in strong drum towers. Moreover there was a drawbridge. There were four main streets; East, Fore, North and High streets. All were narrow. The town was surrounded by small fields, with high thick hedges, and garden walls, for Taunton was not a walled town. Unlike Lyme no

R.B.–D

high walls commanded it. The steep ascent of the graceful Quantock Hills were some eleven miles to the north. Blake therefore decided that a restricted defence, which had served him so well at Lyme, would do equally well here. Especially as he had the castle as his base, to which he could retire in case of necessity.

The siege can be divided into three phases. The first took place when Wyndham arrived before the town early in October. He surrounded it at once, placing cannon from Bridgwater on a small hill, a mile east of the town, from which he could bombard the East Gate. On the west he planted some guns from Exeter, so as to command the castle.[5] Despite the King's orders he had come to the conclusion that he must stop the foraging raids of Blake's horse, which Clarendon describes as becoming 'a sharp thorn in the side of all that populous county'.[6] He began with an attack upon the East Gate, to which Blake replied with a sally on the enemy's quarters to the north. In this he captured some eighty prisoners, with some commanders among them. His horse 'pursued the chase of them a great way'. Wyndham, again despite the King's orders, made another attack which was also beaten off. A third assault, however, broke through into the town itself. After fierce fighting Blake was driven back into the castle. From here he wrote to Wyndham to say that if he wished the prisoners to be fed, he must send in provision for them, as he would not starve the garrison to do so. But he undertook to see that the food should be given solely to the captives. This Wyndham refused to do. He would not even allow the townsfolk to buy any food lest they should give it to those in the castle, which was likened to 'making all Somerset starve to make Taunton Castle surrender'.[7] But Wyndham can hardly be blamed for taking severe measures to achieve his purpose.

Meanwhile Parliament, alarmed by the disaster to Essex, and by the probability that the King would advance eastwards before Essex's army could be reformed, ordered Manchester and Cromwell, with the army of the Eastern Association, to march south to join Essex and Waller. They united near Newbury but, as Essex lay sick at Reading, the command devolved upon Manchester. On 27 October battle was joined. Only nightfall saved the King from defeat. He was allowed to slip away in the darkness, while the foe were asleep, and got to Oxford. As a result the parliamentary Generals quarrelled bitterly. Waller and Cromwell accused

Manchester of incompetence. The problem was ultimately solved by the passing of the Self-Denying Ordinance, and the creation of the New Model Army, under the sole command of Sir Thomas Fairfax.

Amid all this turmoil Taunton's fate might well have been forgotten. But the West Country members, led by William Strode, called attention to its dire straits, and obtained promises that its relief should be set in hand.[8] Colonels Holborne, Vandrusque and Ludlow with 1,200 horse and foot, were ordered to march from Chichester to Taunton. For there was the additional danger that Wyndham's forces, if he was successful, might join the King's gathering strength at Oxford. Wyndham's troops must be detained from so doing. But not until 4 December did Holborne begin his march. This led to the fear that if Taunton was lost, other garrisons might surrender in despair of being relieved.[9]

By 8 December Holborne arrived at Dorchester. Here he was joined by contingents from the local garrisons, under the command of Sir Anthony Ashley-Cooper, a former Royalist. In no generation would this young gentleman have been termed modest. He had supreme confidence in himself and, by his strong personality and assumption of leadership, he practically took over the command of the expedition. The news of his approach was smuggled in to Blake, who instantly told the garrison the good tidings, and asked them to fast for one day a week, to enable him to hold out until the relief came. Such was his inspiration that they offered to do so for 2 days instead, so long as they had health in their bodies.[10]

Wyndham also got the news, and at once sent in a summons from Orchard Portman, where he had made his headquarters. He offered Blake a surrender upon terms in the hope that the place would yield before the relief came. Blake, with his customary irony, expressed his surprise that it was thought possible to 'prevail over us by a mere paper project, either by threats to affright us from the duty we owe to God and our Country, or by artificial persuasions to induce us to a Treaty so dishonourable, so unwarrantable'. He ended, 'these are to let you know that, as we neither fear your menaces, nor accept your proffers, so we wish you for the time to come to desist from all overtures of a like nature to us, who are resolved to the last drop of our blood to maintain the quarrel'. The letter was also signed by Samuel Blake, his brother, and by Samuel Perry, his lieutenant-colonel.[11]

Upon Blake's refusal Wyndham advanced to Chard to meet Holborne, or perhaps rather Ashley-Cooper. But his men refused to fight and instead retreated to Bridgwater, leaving behind them prisoners, 100 arms, hay, oats and provisions.[12] On the 14th the relief entered Taunton. It was characteristic that Cooper wrote the dispatch and not Holborne. He described the keeping of Taunton as 'almost a miracle, their works being for the most part pales and hedges, with no line about'.[13] With the relief came 2,000 muskets, and forty barrels of powder. In addition Popham's horse and nine companies of foot were added to the garrison.[14]

As there was no advantage in shutting up so large a force within the town, without causing great difficulties to provision it, Holborne wisely withdrew to High Ham, near Langport, where he could command the country round, and also maintain his communications with Dorset.

Now began the second phase of the siege. For Hopton made an attempt to re-open it. At once Holborne returned, drove him off and also broke through Wyndham's quarters and began to attack Bridgwater. In a hot skirmish he took one of the works, with some prisoners and ten horses. But, as he had no reserve, he was forced to withdraw. On his way back he again fell upon the enemy's quarters, and took 150 horses, before returning to High Ham.[15] As Clarendon wrote, 'the garrison of Taunton, with that party of horse and dragoons which relieved it, commanded a very large circuit, and disturbed other parts of Somerset'.[16] How true this was is shown on 7 March, when Blake sent out 500 horse and foot, under a Scot, Captain Wem, to attack Bridgwater. They arrived early in the morning, marched boldly up to the works, and found the drawbridge down, so unexpected was their arrival. The alarm was instantly raised and a hot skirmish ensued, when Wem 'did much good execution upon the enemy, killing and wounding many'. He was however unfortunately killed himself, whereupon the defence brought up a gun, and the attackers were forced to retire to Taunton.[17] It is very probable that many such sallies had taken place, and that Taunton was now detaining many of the royal troops.

The Prince of Wales was sent to Bristol to form a Royalist Western Association. Goring was appointed their commander. He was a brilliant cavalry leader, who had put to flight half the allied armies at Marston Moor. He was however unreliable, independent, quarrelsome and a confessed drunkard. Though he treated his men well, his discipline was lax, so that they earned the hatred of the countryside by their cruelty and looting.

The growing strength of the Royalists made Holborne's isolated position perilous and accordingly he withdrew to join Cromwell, who was with his horse at Cerne Abbas. From here both of them fell back on Waller at Devizes. Once again Blake had to uphold the parliamentary cause in Somerset almost alone.[18] That cause was entangled in the turmoils of change. For, in March, the Self-Denying Ordinance was passed, and the New Model Army was being organised and trained by Fairfax and Skippon in the Windsor Meadows.

At a Royalist conference at Wells it was decided that, if the position in Somerset was to be firmly established, Taunton must be secured. So on 11 March Goring appeared before the town. He ordered Sir John Berkeley the Governor of Exeter, to bring him all the troops he could spare, while Grenville, who was besieging Plymouth, was to come in person with the bulk of his forces.[19]

The same jealousies and quarrels that had bedevilled the generals of the parliamentary armies now beset the Royalist commanders. Grenville would only move when the King himself ordered him to do so. Leaving behind him 2,000 foot and 400 horse to continue the siege, he marched leisurely towards Taunton.[20] News then came that Waller was advancing into the west 'with a great body of horse and dragoons and some foot'. The siege had to be suspended. Goring requested the Prince of Wales to order Grenville, who was now close to Taunton, to carry to him his 2,200 foot and 800 horse to join in the operations against Waller. But Grenville refused upon the ground that his men would not stir, and also because he had promised the Commissioners of Devon and Cornwall not to advance until Taunton was taken. This he expected to do speedily.[21]

Goring moved into Dorset and attacked Waller with some success. But he was unable to follow up his advantage, owing to the lack of Grenville's troops. Grenville, now at last before Taunton, was confident he could capture the town if 600 men were added to his force. Clarendon wrote that the capture of the town would mean that 'there would be an army of 4,000 horse and 5,000 foot ready to be applied to any service they should be directed to'. With this in mind the Prince wrote to Goring, who was now at Wells, since Waller had retired to Salisbury, to suggest that he should leave his foot and artillery with Grenville, while he, with his horse, should sweep across the Wiltshire Downs and harass Waller. This would cover the siege operations against a possible relief. It was left to Goring to decide whether he should go with the horse, or return with the foot and guns to Taunton.[22]

Goring answered in 'a short and sullen letter' that as he was commanded he had sent his foot and cannon to Taunton, and his horse to other places. But, as there was nothing left for him to do, he had gone to Bath to recruit his health. As he himself had previously suggested the proposed operation, it only goes to show how serious the trouble had grown among the Royalist leaders.[23]

This breathing space enabled Blake to re-organise his defence. In view of another impending siege he realised that he must now extend the perimeter of his line, instead of, as at Lyme, contracting it. His flexible and adaptable mind could adjust itself to a new situation. He saw that his troops must be given more room in which to manoeuvre. He therefore strengthened his outworks and built a series of barricades, one behind another, behind the East Gate. Thus he would not depend solely upon withdrawal to the castle. So he ensured that, if the East Gate fell, the enemy would have to storm East Street, barricade by barricade and house by house. He also sited a new work at the ruins of the Priory.

Strangely enough, in view of his tactics at Lyme, where he had withdrawn isolated garrisons into the town, he manned Wellington House, some five miles east. This belonged to Alexander Popham, his old commander. It was an astonishingly unwise move, for it deprived him of men who would have been of far more use in Taunton. It may have been due to a sense of loyalty to Popham, but sentiment has no place in war, and Blake for once neglected to stick to his last.

Grenville began his operations by sweeping the country round bare of provisions. By 10 April his troops had entrenched themselves within musket-shot of the 'still imperfect line'. By labouring night and day incessantly they 'close begirt the town' with twelve fortified guards, and 'constructed four several approaches'.[24] Reinforced by Goring's foot and artillery, they were able to cover the construction of their works with a continuous fire of cannon and musket-shot. This they did 'with such restlessness of importunity, volley upon volley, until the town seemed besieged by a wall of fire'. But Blake's obstinate defence still held on.[25]

Grenville himself had undertaken the siege of Wellington House. As he was giving orders to a gunner he was hit by a bullet, fired from a window, and so badly was he wounded that he had to be carried away. Sir John Berkeley took over the command. After several fierce attacks the garrison were almost overpowered. So, seeing there was no prospect of holding out, or of getting relief, they blew up the house, together with their powder, and surrendered. The enraged foe put fifty to the sword, and made 150 prisoners, captured 200 arms, and two drakes. According to Grenville, who was jealous of Berkeley, the latter had disobeyed his orders, by burning the remains of the house to the ground.[26]

This fresh siege of Taunton greatly alarmed the Parliament, who determined that its relief must be their first care. Fairfax accordingly was ordered to march from Windsor, with such regiments of the New Model, as were already trained. Once again they committed the folly of dividing their forces. For Charles was still strong at Oxford. To add to their folly Cromwell, on 20 April, was ordered to go to the west of Oxford to try and intercept the King's artillery. This was about to be sent to join Maurice at Hereford, preparatory to his moving to the relief of Chester. By making a broad sweep Cromwell gathered up all the draught horses he could find, and so prevented them from being used to haul the King's cannon. The King's plan was thus frustrated. On 30 April Fairfax set out. But on the 24th Charles had ordered Goring, with 3,000 horse, to join him at Oxford, with the result that he was now stronger there, and weaker in Somerset.[27] He was thus true to his policy of restraining Taunton, and of concentrating his forces. This changed situation awoke the Committee for Both Kingdoms to the blunder that they had made. At once they ordered Fairfax to abandon his march, and to move to Oxford to watch the King. So, on 7 May, when his new orders reached him at Blandford, Fairfax set out. He left the regiments under Colonels Weldon, Graves, Floyd, Fortescue and Ingoldsby, in all about 5,000 men, to go to the relief of Taunton.[28]

Here Hopton had replaced Goring and, on 25 April, he made an experimental attack, which was beaten off. But it was nevertheless realised that, as he had diverted the water from the town, he meant business.[29] A short lull ensued, which Blake utilised to build a great defensive work outside the East Gate, 'upon a small square by it'.[30] On 6 May, the first determined attack was made. The Vicar's house, on the east side, was lost as the defenders were beaten out by the continual play of the cannon upon it. Next day, Wednesday the 7th, 300 shots were fired in a bombardment of culverins upon the new defensive work outside the East Gate. It was very severely battered, and a wave of stormers moved forward to secure it. They were met with stones and scalding water rained upon them by Blake's men until they were driven back, after a bitter struggle.[31]

Next day Hopton learned of Fairfax's arrival at Blandford. He realised the danger he stood in, of being caught between this new force and Blake's troops at Taunton. Accordingly he decided he must withdraw to Bridgwater, Borough and Langport, to await the return of Goring, which he was expecting, though he was completely ignorant of his whereabouts. But, as his batteries were well placed at the four approaches, he resolved, before he moved, to attempt another general assault.[32]

He cleverly organised a sham fight with blank cartridges between two parties of his own men. By this ruse he hoped the defence would jump to the conclusion that the relief had arrived, and that they would sally out to support it, and so get caught in the ambush he had prepared for them. But Blake was not to be taken in and the trick failed as he kept his men within the town.[33] At 7 p.m. Hopton launched a terrific attack all round the town. The East Gate outwork was lost, and the East Gate was stormed, and by a fierce assault an entrance was forced. But the long East Street which ran uphill from the Gate was so narrow that even against great numbers a few men could hold it. By this time the stormers were so weary that they could make no further advance. Nevertheless Hopton had mastered the whole of the East Reach, and a great part of the line. His men even got possession of the West Gate and a small fort beside it, which protected the entrance. But they found themselves opposed and harassed by a guard, who were sheltered behind some entrenchments and barricades, thrown up purposely to protect it. After very hot fighting the enemy were driven out again.[34] Some of the defenders, seeing that some of their strongest works were lost, showed signs of losing heart, but the others encouraged them still to stand firm. All then resolved to make use of all possible shelter, even of the garden hedges and banks, and so to maintain their defence stubbornly to the bitter end. The foe, in the hope of terrifying the garrison, now fired part of the town they had taken, some 100 houses. But the wind blew back the smoke in their faces, and little harm was done. This act so enraged the defence that they concentrated their forces, and made a desperate resistance, determined, despite all hazards, to hold on to what still remained in their keeping.[35]

By the 9th Weldon, by forced marches, had arrived at Chard. Here news reached him that, if relief did not come swiftly, Taunton would be lost. Instantly he sent off a messenger to give notice of his arrival, and that the firing of ten guns would announce his approach. The messenger appears to have got into the town on the same day, for as neither side wore uniform it was not difficult to smuggle messages in, so alike were friend and foe.[36]

At the same time Hopton got intelligence that Fairfax was in no condition to march, though he did not know that he was now on his way to Oxford.[37] He therefore resolved in a final attack to complete the taking of Taunton. His men held all the barricades as far as the solid brick buildings of the New Hospital in East Street. They made another furious onslaught with shouts of, 'you Roundhead rogues, you look for relief, but we have relieved them, and Goring is coming on; we will not leave a house standing if you do not yield'.[38] A continual bombardment, to which no reply could be made, went on for eight hours. Hand to hand fighting took place, and several charges were made by Blake's horse and foot, led by Captain Mounsel, who was pulled from his horse and captured. From the house musketeers kept up a harassing fire, but house by house and barricade by barricade fell to the weight of the enemy numbers as they battered their way up the street, firing the wooden dwellings as they went. 'Nothing was heard but thunder and nothing was seen but fire'. Gradually the heavier weight of numbers and of the guns told severely upon Blake's weary and almost worn out men. At last they were driven back to the triangle of works round St Mary's Church, the Market-place and the fort known as the Maiden, and the castle, in which the homeless inhabitants had taken refuge. The outwork at the Priory had also fallen. Such was the situation at 6 p.m.[39] Both sides, who had been fighting since noon, had fought themselves to a standstill. A pall of smoke from the burning houses hung ominously over the seemingly doomed town.

Yet courage rose with increasing danger, and the defenders were resolved to fight it out to the last man. They grimly reminded one another that they had given the foe 'showers of lead, which filled the trenches with their filthy carcases, making them exchange the height and fury of their gallantry for the humility and silence of death'.[40]

Early in the morning next day Hopton sent in a summons, offering Blake honourable terms if he would surrender. He answered that he had four pairs of boots left, and that he would eat three of them before he yielded. The answer matched the moment, and was repeated with zest by the troops. Rightly so, for Blake was the very soul of Taunton. He refused to take a demand for surrender as serious, but turned it aside with a jest.[41]

A report from the Royalists bore unwilling tribute to his inspiration. 'The Governor of the place was yesterday slain by the breaking of a gun to which he was giving fire: and we hope will hasten a parley, for with him we conceive the malice of the place died, his name was Blake, a renegade from us'. Not only was it untrue, but once again the ghost of the Blake of Morocco had materialised.[42]

Yet the town was hard pressed. The thatch had been torn from the roofs and mixed with grain to feed the horses, and match had been improvised from bedcords.[43] Powder and match were reduced to such as were in the soldiers' bandoliers and in their muskets.[44]

There were enemies too within, for two men and a woman were caught in the act of trying to fire the town. The flames were put out and the men were cut to pieces by an angry mob, while the women dealt with their female accomplice. Before they died they confessed that they had received £10 for the deed, and they gave the names of fifty more traitors. These were arrested and imprisoned for correspondence with the foe, while a few were hanged.[45]

Meanwhile Hopton was confused by conflicting reports of the approach of the enemy, and he sent away three of his guns. Then came news that the relief had retreated in some disorder, whereupon Hopton recalled his cannon. For he had already, on receiving Blake's answer, made another somewhat half-hearted attack, and again without any success.[46]

On 8 May the King held a Council of War. Here it was debated whether to march north as Rupert, anxious to avenge Marston Moor, had advocated; or, as Goring desired, to fall upon Fairfax and the New Model. The rivalry was fierce, and Charles weakly decided upon a compromise. He would march north, gathering troops as he went, while Goring, with his 3,000 horse, was to take command again in the west. Like the Committee for Both Kingdoms he committed the fatal mistake of dividing his forces. The proper objective should have been Fairfax, who was now approaching Oxford.

At Chard, Weldon, in view of the desperate plight of Taunton only sixteen miles away, was on the march. His men had already trudged 112 miles in ten days. They urgently needed rest and their boots were almost worn out. Weldon however called upon them for a final effort. The officers set an example and marched beside the men, while the strictest discipline was enforced, and theft was punishable by death. On the 10th Orchard Portman, 2½ miles from Taunton, was reached. Weldon's arrival greatly impressed the country folk, accustomed to being plundered, when they found that such was no longer the case.[47]

Next day, Hopton in desperation threatened that if the town did not yield, he would take it by storm, and put the whole garrison to the sword, with the exception of seven men. Blake drily replied that if he would send in their names, he would send Hopton their bodies, another quip his men relished.[48] It was his last jest at Hopton's expense, for already a party of Weldon's horse were in contact with the Royalists to the south. In the belief that the newcomers were the whole of Fairfax's army, Hopton, at 4 p.m., raised the siege and withdrew to Bridgwater. In his withdrawal he blocked the road between Taunton and Trull by felling trees across it, and by lining the hedges with musketeers, partly to cover his own withdrawal and partly to hinder any advance.[49]

Hopton's withdrawal indicated to Blake that relief was at hand. 'Ever valiant and vigilant', he mounted St Mary's tower. With a 'prospective glass' he could glimpse, away to the south, the parliamentary infantry toiling towards Trull. Without waiting for the sound of the promised guns, even if they could have been heard, he rushed down from the tower to bring the glad news to his troops.[50] He then led them out himself in pursuit of Hopton, but the exhausted soldiers could not keep up with the flying foe, though they killed some stragglers and made a few more prisoners, before utter weariness compelled Blake to bring them back. In the enemy quarters were found 1,000 arms, barrels of powder, pioneer tools, ammunition and provisions, besides many wounded men. Taunton's loss was estimated at 100 dead and 200 wounded, while two-thirds of the town, including most of East Street, had been burned.[51]

Weldon's weary and foot-sore men were struggling. Their horse could not aid them by charging and dislodging the musketeers, owing to the thickness of the hedges. A halt had to be made for the artillery to come up. Small wonder that they took twelve hours to cover the distance. But when the sun rose on the 12th, the enemy had vanished.[52] With his men marched nearly off their legs, Weldon entered Taunton 'in the nick of time' as the town had only two barrels of powder left. His entrance was greeted with wild enthusiasm, while the country folk gazed 'with wonder on the works and on the men who had so stubbornly defended them'. A Thanksgiving Service was held at which the Reverend Thomas Welman rightly bid the congregation to 'give thanks unto the Lord, who remembered us at Taunton, for His mercy endureth for ever'. Parliament recognised Blake's services with a grant of £500, with another of £2,000 for his men.[53] Bonfires were lit in the streets of London, which must have celebrated the fact that Hopton was said to have lost between 500 and 1,000 dead.

But Taunton's trials were not yet over. For Goring was back at Bath, and on the 17th he joined Hopton on King's Moor, near Martock, so that their combined forces now numbered about 11,000 men. Their plan was to encircle Weldon for the latter, after putting supplies into the town, had withdrawn to Ilminster. He had no wish to be confined within the narrow limits of Taunton. Here he found that to go east he must force a bridge over the Parrett, or march back over the Blagdon Hills. This was 'an uneasy task' in view of Goring's horse. He therefore posted a rear-guard at South Petherton to hold the bridge, which apparently had been overlooked by the enemy.[54]

Goring believed he had shut up Weldon between 'narrow passes' which would prevent him taking either of his moves. In this effort to trap him Goring's two parties of foot in the darkness fell upon one another near South Petherton bridge, and fought for two hours before the error was discovered. Weldon had lined the hedges with musketeers so that Goring was unable to pursue him in the narrow winding lanes, and Weldon regained the safety of Taunton.[55]

In view of Fairfax's advance Rupert persuaded the King to move into the Midlands, so as to draw Fairfax away from Oxford, and

to order Goring to send 3,000 horse to join them at Market
Harborough. But Goring refused to obey on the ground that he
expected to reduce Taunton in a few days. If he left before this
was achieved the west would be at the mercy of the rebels, with
the added danger that they might march in his rear, and so bring
as great an addition to the enemy forces, as he could bring to the
King.[56]

Goring now approached Taunton cautiously, and the third phase
of the siege began. Not until 30 May did he establish contact with
Weldon's horse which were encamped on a large common, a mile
beyond the town. To relieve the food situation Weldon was as
anxious to get out as Goring was to keep him in. For the next
three days hot skirmishes took place. Weldon's men were so short
of ammunition that the front rank had to use their swords, and
the rear the butts of their muskets. Goring is said to have lost
800 men to Weldon's 300, but by his superior numbers he forced
Weldon back into the town and endeavoured to surround it.[57]

About this time powder was landed at Lyme and horsemen,
pretending to be Cavaliers, smuggled it into Taunton.[58] Ingoldsby,
hearing Goring was holding a Council of War, took the opportunity
to fall on it and kill many 'considerable persons'. But by 8 June
Weldon wrote to the Commons declaring that if relief did not come
speedily, he would be in great straits for ammunition and supplies.
Blake also wrote to the same effect. Goring had offered him a
parley, which he scorned even to accept. Rather than deliver up the
town he was resolved to feed upon the horses, and to fight it out
to the very end.[59]

On the 9th Goring, after a peremptory command from the King
drew off two or three thousand of his men, mostly all horse from
the siege, 'which our forces perceiving sallied out upon them, and
were received by the enemy'.[60] The besieged claimed to have gained
a circuit of six miles, but another account says 'the Royalists do
so keep in our men that if relief come not speedily they will be
forced to break through, and leave that well-affected town to the
fury of the enemy'. It adds, however, that Goring's foot were
deserting, 'owing to the hard duty laid upon them, and that 200
had done so in a single night'.[61] Whether Goring was about to
send his horse to the King can never be known. Clarendon, who
was biased against Goring, for all his faults a good general, wrote
'he grew more negligent in it than he had been; suffered provisions

in great quantity to be carried into the town through the midst
of his men: discouraged and neglected his own foot so much that
they ran away and gave himself wholly to license, insomuch that
he... was not seen abroad in three or four days together... suffered
his guards to be more negligently kept, that his quarters were
beaten up often, even at daytime'.[62]

On 14 June the situation suddenly and totally changed. The
King was utterly defeated at Naseby, with the loss of all his foot,
guns, and baggage. With 4,000 horse he retreated to Hereford. His
one chance was to have marched into Somerset and united with
Goring. Instead he retired to Raglan. The absence of Goring's
horse may have contributed to his defeat, for they might have
changed the result. As Clarendon wrote: 'Blake's obstinate resistance disappointed all our hopes both of men and of money in
that great county'. It had kept 5,000 foot and 4,000 horse pinned
down.[63] The King had rightly ordered Taunton to be 'contained'.
Instead his generals had allowed themselves to be committed to a
siege to maintain their prestige. A clamour on the parliamentary
side demanded the relief of Taunton. This had led to a division
of their army: only at the last possible moment had Fairfax's
troops been diverted to attack the King. Blake's tenacity had pinned
down a much larger proportion of the King's troops than Parliament had employed either to hold the town, or to relieve it.

Fairfax did not pursue the King's beaten army. Instead he
decided that Goring was the more dangerous. By so doing he
could also relieve Taunton. Together with Cromwell, after covering 113 miles in a week, they reached Marlborough. To avoid the
towns held by the enemy, they decided to approach Taunton from
the south. After assuring the Clubmen, the countrymen who had
banded themselves together for protection against the ravages of
both sides, that he 'would keep good order'[64] Fairfax moved to
Beaminster. Here on 4 July he got the unexpected news that
Goring had raised the siege of Taunton, and had advanced
towards Yeovil. For he had no wish to be caught between Blake
and Fairfax. At Crewkerne, next day, Fairfax met the Taunton
commanders. It was a most important conference, for Blake met
Fairfax and Cromwell for the first time.[65] The latter must have
been impressed with his personality, determination and ability,
and marked him down as a man worth the remembering. Inspired,
too, by the sight of Taunton's valiant defenders Fairfax's men

shouted out that they were willing to march all night to its relief.[66]
Goring had occupied a line from Langport to Yeovil, but the troops at Yeovil fell back without fighting on the 7th, and Goring was forced back to Langport. That night he fell back towards Bridgwater.[67] He cleverly deluded Fairfax into thinking that he was marching towards Taunton, and hoodwinked him into sending 4,000 men down the Taunton road. When battle was joined on the 10th his force was separated ten miles from Fairfax, with three rivers in between. Goring was thus at full force, while Fairfax had 10,000 men out of his 14,000. But, by a series of brilliant and resolute tactics, Goring was sent reeling back to Bridgwater, with Fairfax in full chase. Goring abandoned the town to its fate, and made for Barnstaple. Fairfax at once invested the town, and on the 22nd it surrendered.[68]

The King, roused at last by Goring's defeat, went to Cardiff, with the object of sending his troops across the Bristol Channel to join Goring. But he found that the twenty-six Welsh barques, hired for this purpose, had been captured off the Islands in the Channel, known as the Holms, by Admiral Batten, who had been warned that this was about to happen.[69]

Reporting the capture of Bridgwater on the 24th, Fairfax wrote, 'the King is expected this night at Bristol, if the news of Bridg-water stay him not: his greatest hope seems to be in the Clubmen – if the King had had the time to have got out his forces and these numerous Clubmen, we must surely have left it'.[70] Fairfax was rightly concerned, for the Clubmen were gathering in threatening numbers. Before he could move into the west, they must be cleared out of the way. There was an added danger that Rupert might move down from Bristol to join the Royalists in Sherborne Castle. As Taunton was now free Blake was sent ahead to meet the Clubmen. He drew up a form of submission to Fairfax. They were to be ready to join him, and so to help to end the war speedily.[71] But they refused. They intended they said to go 'a middle way – to join with neither side and not to oppose either side until – we see who are the enemies of that happy peace which we really desire'. Fairfax refused to treat with them, and on 4 August Cromwell broke them at Hambledon Hill.[72] Fairfax, with the aid of the Mendip miners, captured Sherborne on the 15th.[73] He lost no time in moving on to besiege Bristol, leaving Blake with a troop of horse at Bruton to guard against a possible attack from the south-west.[74] Once again Bristol proved impossible to hold, and Rupert, with great common sense, surrendered it on 10 September. In fury the King stripped him of all his posts, and ordered him to leave the Kingdom. With Maurice he did so, but both men were to encounter Blake again; this time at sea.

Blake now returned to Taunton to supervise the rebuilding of the town and to relieve the distress of the sufferers from the siege. This was largely met out of the fund provided by the sequestration of the local Royalist estates. At the most critical moment, when all seemed lost, with his cool courage he had steeled his men's resolution by meeting danger with a jest. By his quips at the enemy's expense his delighted troops had made his humour their own. He had been the soul of defence and the spearhead of attack. Yet perhaps the most important outcome of the siege lay in his meeting with Fairfax and Cromwell, for both men had marked him down as a future leader.

CHAPTER 5

Dunster and After

*

ON 5 August, the King left Cardiff and marched north in order to join Montrose in Scotland. He was encouraged to do this as Montrose had won two more victories, at Alford on 2 July, and at Kilsyth on 15 August. The recent Royalist defeats might yet be redeemed. Charles therefore readily responded to a call from Chester, now hard pressed by its besiegers. He successfully entered the city, only to see, from the Phoenix Tower, his army smashed to pieces under its walls on 24 September. All hopes of joining Montrose had to be abandoned when the Scots leader met with disaster at Philiphaugh on 12 September. Charles returned to Oxford, still optimistic. For Lord Astley still had some 3,000 men in Worcestershire. So, in the hope of raising a new army, the King ordered Astley to join him. But when Astley was overwhelmed at Stow-on-the-Wold in the following March, Charles was powerless.

With the news of the King's disaster at Chester ringing in his ears, Fairfax resolved to complete the conquest of the west. He sent Cromwell into Hampshire where he was to capture Devizes, Winchester and Basing House. By 19 October Fairfax had stormed Tiverton and had driven Goring before him into Devon. Here Goring handed over his command to Lord Wentworth, a worthless soldier, who was also addicted to the bottle, and retired to France. In Somerset only Dunster Castle still held out for the Royalists. Its owner, Luttrell, impressed by the King's victories in 1643, had surrendered the place to Colonel Francis Wyndham at the end of that year. It had played no part in the Civil War, but its importance now lay in the remote possibility that troops from Ireland might be landed at Minehead, nearby, for the King's service. More important was the fact that it was a possible threat to Fairfax's communications.

To counter this Fairfax selected Blake, together with Colonel Sydenham, to command a field-force to deal with Dunster. He had obviously been impressed by Blake's ability, while his local knowledge would stand him in good stead. Blake had with him some 600 men and some small field pieces. He made his head-quarters in a 'strong house' now known as the Luttrell Arms. By 6 November he had completely blocked up the castle. He expected Dunster to fall almost at once since, owing to a drought, it was short of water and of provisions.[1] Wyndham himself was doubtful whether he could hold out for another three weeks. Indeed he had written to the Royalist commander in the west to this effect, stating, however, that only the recent rains had enabled him to do so.[2] Blake therefore sent in repeated summons to surrender, each time to be met with an abrupt refusal. He therefore pushed his approaches and batteries forward gradually, only to find that his small guns could make no impression upon the stoutly built walls.

Meanwhile, in reply to Wyndham's appeal for help, a party of foot was sent to Bideford, to be sent by sea to Dunster. Horse, too, were got ready to march by land to protect them upon their arrival. But when the foot got to Bideford, they found that they were not to get the pay promised them, and that they were also expected to serve for more than the twenty days agreed upon. So they promptly deserted and ran away.[3] When Fairfax learned of the design, he posted a party to command the road, and to check any repetition of such an attempt. Early in December another party made a like attempt, only to be met by the parties guarding the Tiverton and Crediton roads, who turned them back.[4]

Blake, after the failure of his guns, now adopted Fairfax's methods at Sherborne and started to undermine the walls, prob-ably with the aid of Mendip miners. Again he sent in a summons, accompanied by a threat to storm if it was refused. Wyndham, secure behind his stout walls, replied that he held to his former intention to keep his charge to the utmost, so that he was and would ever be '*semper idem*', always the same. Blake, mindful of the heavy losses the Royalists had sustained at Taunton, resolved not to expend the lives of his men in a storming operation, and instead persevered with his mining.[5]

By the end of December Fairfax had occupied Crediton, and was now joined by Cromwell, who had completed his task in Hampshire. On 9 January, Cromwell surprised Wentworth's horse at Bovey Tracey, south of Exeter, and drove them in wild panic into Cornwall. Just previous to this, on 6 January, some 1,500 horse had been sent to Blake, possibly to prevent Wentworth's cavalry from attempting to relieve Dunster. Blake stationed them some five miles from the castle, on the Exeter road, with orders to keep a sharp outlook.[6] In a desperate attempt to hold together a rapidly disintegrating army, the Royalist council, on the 15th, appointed Hopton to command it. With only 2,000 foot and 3,000 horse he undertook the thankless task loyally, and moved to the relief of Exeter, now beset by Fairfax.[7]

Blake methodically pushed forward his approaches and batteries to places where they could play on the walls to better effect, and continued to sink his mines beneath the castle. He did not, however, spring them. It can hardly have been that he wished to avoid mutilating the castle, one of the glories of Somerset; rather surely because he realised that the explosion must be followed up by a storm, costly to the lives of his small force. Dunster, he believed, ultimately was bound to yield from starvation, as relief seemed to be out of the question. But Fairfax thought otherwise. As he was about to enter Cornwall, he had no intention of leaving behind him an unsubdued garrison in his rear. Especially as there was still a fairly strong Royalist force in Barnstaple. Accordingly he ordered Blake to spring the mines.[8]

So, early in January, Blake did so. The result was disappointing. One mine either failed to explode, or was not sprung. The enemy had discovered what was going on and, by counter mining, had rendered the second harmless, while the third, though it exploded well, only destroyed part of the castle wall, 'causing more noise than execution'. It made a considerable breach, but in an inaccessible spot, very difficult of approach, so that a storm was impossible. Blake wisely did not attempt it. The defence however was now feeling the effects of the blockade, for provisions were running very short, while their guards could only be maintained by doing double duty.[9]

Four days after Hopton had taken command, Fairfax stormed Dartmouth, which put an end to Hopton's hopes of relieving Exeter. Instead he moved into North Devon, hoping to turn Fairfax's flank, and concentrated his troops at Torrington. Fairfax's apprehensions were now justified for Hopton sent 1,500 horse and 300 foot, under Colonel Finch, from Barnstaple to relieve Dunster. On 5 February he threw into the castle four barrels of powder, thirty cows and fifty sheep. At his approach Blake wisely withdrew his forces into 'the strong house'. Either the 1,500 horse, watching the Exeter road, had been withdrawn or else Finch had cleverly by-passed them by using the north road by Minehead.[10] He wasted no time in attacking Blake, but instead he destroyed his works and approaches and then withdrew. Blake promptly carried out his usual tactic of falling upon his enemy's rear, only to get himself into difficulties, from which he had some trouble in extricating himself. Indeed he had to withdraw with some loss. However, he soon resumed the blockade, in the belief that he would soon be reinforced by Fairfax.[11]

Nor was he wrong: for on 13 February, Fairfax smashed Hopton at Torrington, forcing him to struggle back into Cornwall with very few men, no baggage and no artillery. On 13 March, Hopton gave up the useless struggle, and disbanded his army. On 13 April, Exeter yielded, followed shortly afterwards by Barnstaple. Fairfax then moved east and, by 8 April, had arrived at Chard. Here Blake met him, presumably to get further instructions, leaving Captain Burridge in command. It was resolved to confront Wyndham with an overwhelming force, and Blake returned, taking with him Skippon's regiment of foot.[12]

In his absence, on the night of 16 April, the defence called out to Burridge to know if it was true, as some of his men had told them, that Exeter and Barnstaple had fallen. Burridge replied by suggesting that both sides should give hostages, while they sent to get intelligence. If the report was untrue, he would forfeit his life, provided that if it was confirmed, they would agree to surrender. This 'wrought so much' upon the enfeebled garrison that they reopened talks, and again asked for leave to get intelligence. But Burridge, who knew that Blake was now returning, told them to have a little patience, and Blake himself would answer.[13]

On the 17th Blake arrived. He at once drew up Skippon's regiment in two strong bodies on a hill facing the castle. Then, in accordance with Fairfax's orders, he sent in another summons. Wyndham asked for a parley and, on the 19th, he surrendered. He had only lost twenty men. The terms were generous: the garrison were to keep their arms, horses and furniture, and were to march away with drums beating and colours flying, to Oxford, or to their homes, without being molested. Wyndham was to take with him all his private property, while that belonging to his wife was to be sent to her: prisoners on both sides were to be released: the castle, with the arms, ammunition and furniture of war, which amounted to six cannon and 200 stands of muskets, were to be delivered over for the use of 'the King and Parliament'.

In his report Blake justified his terms as due to the 'exemplary clemency' of Fairfax. He added that, 'it might have been obtained upon other terms, if the price of time and blood had not prevailed above other arguments'. He ended by observing that, 'the place was strong and of importance for the pass of Ireland'.[14] He had rightly exercised his quality of patience by waiting for a result, which was inevitable, as the King's cause was now hopelessly lost. By treating a gallant foe with generosity, he had shown his respect for his courage, so that the parting with his enemy was without any bitterness of spirit. His chivalrous nature rose up in resentment at any vindictive treatment of a fallen foe: in 1647 John Question, a surgeon of Dunster, was fined £100 for taking the Royalist side. This was, however, reduced to £10, in consideration for the services he had rendered to Blake's 'sick and wounded soldiers'.[15] There can be little doubt that Blake had personally intervened on his behalf, for the case may have come under his notice as one of the members of the Commission for the Sequestration of the Estates of the Somerset Delinquents. In the same year he had drawn Fairfax's attention to the fact that Bridgwater had been required to pay one third of the taxes for the Hundred of North Petherton. Since a third of the town had been burnt to the ground during the siege, he represented that this was an 'inequality' and Fairfax at once reduced the tax to one eighth.[16]

While he had been engaged at Dunster, Blake had been elected as the member for Bridgwater, but naturally had been unable to take his seat until May, 1646. After taking the oath he met Edmund Ludlow, and they entered the House together, 'which I chose to do, as assuring myself, he having been faithful and active in the public service abroad, that we should be as unanimous in the carrying it on within those doors', so wrote Ludlow. Together with nineteen others, they took the Covenant on 24 June.[17] On 27 November Parliament voted that Blake's regiment, with others, should be disbanded, as the Civil War was over. Blake may well have felt that his military career was ended, especially as the Self-Denying Ordinance required him, as a Member of Parliament, to resign his commission. Now, as Governor of Taunton, civil duties alone remained to him, for parliamentary duties seem to have had but little attraction for him.

At Westminster the victors soon split into two bitterly opposed groups, the Presbyterians and the Independents. Although Blake was not to be personally involved, the result of the quarrel was to determine his future career. For the soldiers were strongly Independent, or congregational, in religion. They were thus an obstacle to the settlement of ecclesiastical matters on strictly Presbyterian lines. Moreover the cost of keeping up the army was enormous. The Presbyterians, who controlled the parliamentary Government, proposed to solve the problem by sending six regiments to Ireland, and by disbanding the rest. But the soldiers' wages were heavily in arrears, and the six refused to move without pay. To add to their stupidity the Presbyterians laid down that no officer, unless he was a Presbyterian, was to be employed, while the men were not to petition either their officers or Parliament itself.

But the army had won the victory for Parliament. With no hopes of redress, it naturally turned its mind to active resistance. It formed a body, termed the Agitators, formed of two representatives from each regiment. Cromwell, however, was alive to the danger of the loss of army control. He would solve the problem thus: the King, the fount of authority, must act with the army. Cornet Joyce, on 4 June, 1647, seized the King and brought him to Newmarket, the army headquarters. In alarm the Presbyterians voted the payment of arrears. The army advanced to Royston and the Commons replied by appointing a Committee of Safety and by empowering the city to raise troops. This was met by a demand to dissolve Parliament and for toleration for the Independents. It was angrily rejected, and early in August the army entered London. They impeached Holles and five other members of the Commons, who fled on the 16th. The Independents thus gained control of the Commons, of the Admiralty Committee and of the Committee for Both Kingdoms.

The six members, armed with passes from both Speakers, had sailed for France. But they were stopped and brought before Batten in the Downs. He set them free and they reached France.[18] The Committee for Both Kingdoms sent for Batten, as an informer had declared he had heard him say that he feared the army would not deal fairly with the King.[19] When he met them on 17 September he resigned his commission under threat of having a charge brought against him.[20] Probably he feared that his secret correspondence with the Scots, in which he promised to throw the weight of the navy against the Independents, had been discovered. On 8 October the Commons voted that Colonel Rainsborough should command the fleet, which would thus be under their control.[21] He was the only man among them with naval experience, even though he had left the navy for an army command.

The Independents themselves now split into two groups. One religious, led by Fairfax and Cromwell, which hoped to bring the King to accept the verdict of war: the other, led by Rainsborough and including Radicals and Levellers, was politically militant. They proposed a single Chamber, elected every two years, manhood suffrage, without any property qualification. To Cromwell this spelt anarchy and he strongly opposed it. The simpler Levellers suggested that the King should be shot and Cromwell knocked on the head.

At this point the King managed to escape from Hampton Court on 5 November, only to have to surrender himself to the Governor of the Isle of Wight. The problem now was, not the control of the King's person, but of the army. The climax came on 15 November. At a meeting of the army at Ware, two Leveller regiments, in defiance of orders, appeared with copies of the Agreement of the People in their hats; Rainsborough tried to force one on Cromwell. Cromwell ordered them to be removed, but was insolently refused. Whereupon, with sword drawn, Cromwell charged their ranks. Panic seized the troopers, who tore the papers from their hats, begging for mercy. One ringleader was shot upon the spot. Cromwell and Fairfax had mastered the army. The Lords, when they received Fairfax's report, voted that Rainsborough, in view of his mutinous conduct, should not go to sea.[22]

But the combination of hot gospel and cold steel had spread alarm. The Leveller threat to property had brought over to the Royalist side the city merchants and the Presbyterian gentry. A strong Royalist tide had set in throughout the country. To combat this the army must be re-united. At an army meeting at Windsor, on 2 December, Rainsborough after being outvoted, confessed his errors, abandoned mutiny and promised to avoid such for the future. Fairfax pardoned him and wrote to the Houses to ask that he should be allowed to command the fleet. The Lords again refused [23] but the Commons contemptuously ignored them and sent the Admiral to guard the Solent and the King.[24]

On 27 December the King made a secret agreement with the

Scots Commissioners by which, if Parliament refused his request for a personal treaty, they would invade England. He hoped to unite the Royalists, the Presbyterians, the Scots and the property owners and win them to his side. The Independents, early in January 1648, dissolved the Committee for Both Kingdoms and replaced it by a committee of their own, named Derby House, after its place of meeting. The Scots members then left for Edinburgh, where they strove to bring over the nation to the King's side.

The seething discontent suddenly burst into flame. In South Wales, Colonel Poyer refused to hand over to Colonel Fleming, as his troops were to be disbanded without pay. Laugharne's men mutinied and joined him. Early in March 1648, the mutineers fired their first shot and the second Civil War began. Cromwell was ordered to suppress it and on 2 May he set out.[25]

Batten, angry at his treatment, had placed his agents in the fleet. On 24 May, Rainsborough reported that two ships might refuse to sail northwards with a convoy. On the 27th he observed a commotion on his ships in the Downs and, on trying to go to his flagship, his lieutenant refused to allow him aboard. The *Swallow*, *Satisfaction*, *Hind*, *Roebuck* and *Pelican* had also mutinied.[26] Three weeks later they gave their reasons: Parliament had granted commissions to sea-commanders in their own names, leaving out the King: several land-men made sea-commanders: the insufferable pride, ignorance and insolence of Colonel Rainsborough, the late Vice-Admiral, alienated the hearts of the seamen.[27] Derby House acted swiftly, for the regaining of the fleet was vital to them. Without it they might lose all they had fought to gain. They threw over Rainsborough, for they had no use for failures, and re-appointed Warwick as Lord High Admiral,[28] since he was the only man who could win back the fleet. But he, too, was not allowed to board the flagship.[29] The unrest had spread to Essex and Kent too. Fairfax marched there, and defeated the revolters at Maidstone,[30] and followed them into Essex, where he broke the revolt by the capture of Colchester in September. Colonel Rich invested Walmer, Deal and Sandown Castles.[31] Cut off from supplies, the rebel ships sailed to Holland to place themselves under the command of the Prince of Wales.[32] Here they were joined by Batten in the *Constant Warwick*, the fastest sailer of her day, of which he was part owner.[33] He had made a secret journey to Portsmouth, but had failed to suborn the mariners there.[34] However he was

knighted and made Rear-Admiral with Lord Willoughby of
Parham, a former parliamentarian commander as Vice-Admiral.

On 11 July Cromwell had crushed the revolt in South Wales by
the capture of Pembroke. Almost without a pause he marched
north and routed the Marquis of Hamilton, who had won over
the Scots to the King's side and invaded England, at Preston
on 16 August. This victory practically ended the Second Civil
War.

At this point Blake reappears. He had been ignored by the
Independents, who had left him in obscurity as the Governor of
Taunton. Batten spoke of him as one of the persons of the greatest
eminence, that had done their best service, but had been ill-
requited for it by the Independents. Writing to Derby House,
from Bridgwater, on 2 September, with other members of the
Committee for Somerset, Blake reported: 'an enemy design to
raise forces in the Western Counties'. But the committee was
alert and had their 'voluntary listed horse and foot ready at an
hour's call'. Colonel Alexander Popham had garrisoned Bath with
120 horse and 200 foot. This prevented the Royalists from seizing
the city, but they had enrolled many followers, and were busy
raising many others for the King's service. As soon as their names
were known, Blake would forward them. He already knew of one,
Colonel Slingsby, 'who was to have had large commands in this
design. We find likewise that many of that party have furnished
themselves with good horses in a posture of readiness for any
design'. The committee had therefore 'enlisted 600 horse, but not
well armed and of foot nigh 2,500, the latter most ready and willing
men for any employment'. But arms and money were badly
needed, and they did not know how to get them. They had hoped
to place this burden upon the 'neuters and malignants' but found
it impossible. The 'faithful town of Taunton' had in it 800 well-
armed men and a newly raised troop of horse, but in raising
these they had had to borrow money, 'as far as our credit will
extend'. So they asked for authority to borrow more, even for as
little as two months' pay. If Popham's troops were to do 'effectual
service' they must be paid. The lack of funds was preventing
'honest men from enlisting'. As there were still pockets of resistance
they would use 'all warrantable means to disarm the enemies horse
and foot'.[35]

By readiness and prompt action Blake and Popham had pre-

vented the infection from South Wales from spreading. By holding
Somerset in check they had rendered any risings in Devon and
Cornwall hopeless. As there was still trouble to be dealt with, this
may be the reason why neither of them was nominated to try the
King. Their presence was vital in the west. But there were others:
Blake was always generous to a defeated foe and averse to the
unnecessary shedding of blood. He was never an extremist. The
dubious Oldmixon may furnish the clue. He records that Blake
had said that 'he would as freely venture his life to save the King,
as ever he had done to serve the Parliament'.[36] In a highly distorted
form this may reveal his dislike for any revengeful treatment of the
King. Indeed Professor Laughton considered that Blake deemed his
execution to have been a blunder. As the Court to try Charles
was clearly expected to return a unanimous verdict, it may have
been thought unwise to summon Blake, since as a man of known
and firm convictions, he might well have voiced his disapproval
of the proceedings. That there were such persons is shown by the
fact that fifty-five members, though they were not bold enough to
voice their opinions, either declined, or excused themselves from
sitting. It is, of course, conjecture, though it appears to be in line
with what is known of Blake's character.

Somewhere about 24 July, the Prince of Wales came into the
Downs with about eleven ships. Derby House urged Warwick to
attack him. But as he did not know which ships he could trust, he
posted himself at the mouth of the Thames as the best strategic
position.[37] Here he hoped a squadron of ten ships from Portsmouth
would join him. The Prince, too, was in a difficult position.
Obviously the blockading of the Thames and the seizing of merchantmen as prizes, would ruin Parliament economically, alienate
the citizens from a government that could not protect it and provide
the Prince with a means to pay and provision his fleet. More
obviously the city merchants, whose ships were to be seized and
sold, would become enemies instead of friends. This had to be
avoided at all costs. A compromise, by which the seized ships were
freed upon the payment of a ransom, merely angered the seamen,
who accused Batten of putting the money into his own pocket and
depriving them of prize money.[38] A landing to drive off the forces
investing the castles ended in a disastrous defeat.[39] Cut off from
supplies the Prince sailed for Holland, but the seaman insisted on
entering the Thames to deal with Warwick. Here a sudden gale

forced both fleets to anchor just as battle seemed imminent. In the night the Prince, with no provisions left, sailed for Holland, actually passing through the Portsmouth ships.[40]

Not until 19 September did Warwick follow them. He anchored four miles below the revolters. He should have attacked at once, when he could almost certainly have achieved his object. For the Dutch, conscious they were sheltering a combatant fleet, boarded him to proclaim their neutrality. Instead of demanding the return of his ships, Warwick weakly consented to commit no hostile action, unless he was first attacked.[41] On the 29th, Tromp with sixteen ships, came in to enforce this one-sided neutrality.[42] Batten now resigned and returned to England under an amnesty. Willoughby 'besides his being without any experience of the sea, was weary of it, and would by no means continue there; and the seamen were too much broke loose from all kind of order to be reduced by a commander of an ordinary rank'.[43] Before he left Batten had arranged for the *Constant Warwick* to go over to Warwick, which she did on 8 November, and the *Hind* followed her on the next night.[44] On the 15th, Derby House wrote to congratulate Warwick, adding that they did not doubt 'you will improve all opportunities to finish what remains of the work before the winter makes it impossible for your Lordship to continue there'.[45] On 9 December they got a rude shock, for Warwick had sailed for the Downs, arriving there on the 23rd. His reasons were the fear of being frozen in; the difficulty of getting supplies; the danger of his seamen deserting to the Royalists, as some had done already.[46] Amazingly no frigates were left to keep watch on Rupert. Fortunately for the Royalists a kindly small-pox had seized the Prince of Wales at the Hague and cleared the way for Rupert to take command.[47] By way of contrast he was all life and energy, sending out raiding parties, who returned with a rich harvest.

Warwick's failure had its effect upon his crews. They grew disheartened by the sense of frustration. The enemy fleet was still intact, whereas their fleet was split. They had lost confidence in themselves, and in their leader.

So it was that Rupert, on 20 January, with three flagships and four frigates, boldly seized the opportunity of an open and un-guarded sea, to sail for Ireland.[48] On the 30 January the King was executed and the Commonwealth was born. A Council of State of forty-nine members took over, and from them a committee, known as the Admiralty Committee, took over the duties of the Lord High Admiral. For on the 20 February Warwick was dismissed.[49] Like Rainsborough he had failed, and the hard-headed Independents had no use for such. Now there was a gap in actual naval command. Never had the English Navy sunk so low.

CHAPTER 6

The Pursuit of Rupert

*

FOR three days the Council of State deliberated as to the choice of a man to command the navy. With Rupert at large at Kinsale a man of action and decision was essential. Yet among the existing captains no one stood out, with the possible exception of Penn.[1] Even he, though he had been exonerated, had been suspected of corresponding with the Royalists. It may well be that the council turned to the two men who had mastered the late rebellion, Fairfax and Cromwell, for their advice. They may have suggested the names of the men who, by holding down the west, had set them free to go north and east. These two men were Blake and Alexander Popham. Edward, his brother, had served in the Ship-Money fleet, and had commanded a large vessel in 1639, so he was selected to command the fleet. The fact that he had been absent for nearly ten years from the fleet probably counted in his favour, as he would be an unknown quantity to the seamen.

Presumably Popham was asked whom he would like for a colleague and named Blake, who had served in his brother Alexander's regiment. He must have been well acquainted with his special qualifications as the owner of a merchant shipping business, in which he had gained experience by sea and by land. Blake was admirably fitted to undertake the administrative work of a Navy. Both Fairfax and Cromwell knew him well. Cromwell, a shrewd judge of men, recognised, in Professor Lewis's words, that he 'appeared to possess all the qualities (including sea-experience) plus the inestimably important ones of superior character and intellect'. 'His letters' he adds 'reveal a really well-educated cultured mind, and a strong, intelligent, attractive personality'.[2] With his natural modesty Blake expressed surprise at his appointment as 'extremely beyond my expectations as well as my merits'. He consulted Edward Popham and by his 'counsel and friendship' he resolved to accept.[3]

The third appointment was that of Richard Deane. He had made sea voyages in his youth and was a relative of Cromwell, as well as being his staunch adherent. He had been Controller of the Ordnance, and had commanded the guns at Naseby and Cromwell's right wing at Preston.[4] His selection was probably due to Cromwell, whose experience in the Civil War had shown him the increasing importance of artillery. With his flair for seeing things as they were, he may have recognised that a ship was neither a regiment of horse nor of foot, but a mobile floating artillery unit. A gunnery expert was therefore essential to the navy.

So, on 23 February, the three 'Commissioners' were ordered to take command of the fleet.[5] They made an ideal trinity: Popham, who would lead the fleet to fight: Blake, who would organise: and Deane to supervise the artillery. The ships were ready to their hand. Some of them built by the first two Stuarts, large, strong and powerful, survived to fight in 1672. They had been added to in the Civil War by building, by the purchase of armed merchantmen and by captured prizes. Moreover Charles the First had built and repaired the dockyards.

But this was not their real problem. It was one that few naval historians seem to have noticed or written about. Yet it was the most important, immediate and difficult. For it was not a material but a human one. They had to restore to the fleet unity, morale, discipline, loyalty and above all, belief in itself. They had to gain the confidence of the seamen and to be regarded, not as the agents of a suspect Government, but as trusted leaders.

By 16 March they were hard at work at Westminster.[6] But on the 24th news came that five of Rupert's ships were off the Scillies, at the mouth of the Channel. They had taken the *Culpepper* and the *Ark*, and other merchant ships 'richly laden' and returned to Kinsale with five prizes.[7] Such news stung the Council into instant action. Popham, with such ships as were available was ordered to sail west. He hoisted his flag in the *Charles*, only to be detained in the Downs by convoy duty. Not until 16 April was he able to sail.[8] With him went the *Assurance, Constant Warwick* and *Increase*.

This left Blake and Deane to cope at Westminster. On the 21st Blake revealed his method of dealing with the revolters. He ordered that the master and seamen of the *Elizabeth Hoy*, which had 'voluntarily come into Falmouth' after deserting from Rupert, were to be set free for that very reason. Conciliation rather than revenge was to be followed.[9] On 14 April he had already got into personal touch with the seamen. He found that there were two 'obstructions wherein the mariners seem to be much unsatisfied'. The first relating to ships going to Ireland to trade with the rebels, which did not carry contraband goods, had led to uncertainty as to whether they were prize or not. Yet the instructions were to capture all such vessels. The seamen, who had taken these ships were very 'much discontented, and tell us that we promised them encouragement and that without delays – if there be not a sudden declaration how judges may proceed and what we may lawfully take'. The second was due to the lack of Commissioners for selling prize goods, so that the sailors did not get the money due to them. Unless 'the above mentioned inconveniences be not remedied before our being on board, we shall hardly keep that good opinion among the mariners which we hope we have in some measure obtained'. Blake's willingness to meet the seamen and his ability to listen to and understand their grievances, must have impressed them favourably. His strong personality convinced them that he was a man of justice, and that he would see that it was done.[10]

He and Deane were dealing also with every kind of detail for getting the fleet to sea: men, commanders, provisions, flags, grapnels, sails, surgeons, small arms, pistols, hatchets and guns. Supplies of provisions were also arranged for at London, Plymouth, Portsmouth, Pembroke and Yarmouth. Nothing seems to have escaped their notice.[11] Nor did Blake forget those who had previously served him well. For he sent for Jonathan Pooke, Richard Squire and James Pelsor, who lived in Lyme, to come to Chatham and enter themselves on his flagship, the *Triumph*, and he ordered that their conduct money should be paid to them.[12]

Popham now was on his way to Plymouth. Here he was to join Moulton, who was in the *Leopard*, with the *Bonaventure*, *Elizabeth* and *Thomas*: too small a force to deal with Rupert's raiders. On the 19th Blake and Deane embarked on the *Triumph* at Tilbury and sailed to the Downs, which they reached on the 20th.[13] Here they found fresh trouble. Unrest had broken out again among the seamen, probably stirred up by a remnant of the revolters. For the Levellers were causing trouble in the army. Some of the regiments, ordered to go to Ireland under Cromwell, had refused to sail unless the demands of the Levellers were met. These included the re-appointment of the Agitators and the General Council of the army, so that the rank and file should have an equal voice with the officers in deciding the political action of the army. Apparently some of the seamen had refused to sail on the same grounds. Hugh Peters, Cromwell's chaplain, was sent down to preach to the mariners. The 'seamen, courageous and daring, say they will never forget his sermon'. He even went aboard the ships, 'and asked them whether they were well resolved to their voyaging against the Prince's ships, and to comply with their Admirals. At once they cried out as one man, that they would live and die with the Admirals'. In some ships they had a Protestation drawn up by way of engagement, which all signed with great unanimity and cheerfulness, to go against the revolted ships.[14] Yet some were apprehended who were charged with endeavouring to make use of the army against the Parliament.[15] The Admirals, too, after coming on board, prepared an 'engagement the better to discover the mariners affections, which we with all the officers had sub-scribed'. This so delighted the seamen that 540 of them on the *Triumph* signed 'voluntary'. This was then sent to the other ships, and also forwarded to the north and to Popham's vessels.[16]

Sir George Ayscue, in the *St Andrew*, with the *Victory*, was sent off with provisions for Dublin, Chester and Liverpool. With him went the *Hercules*, which was to join Penn at Portsmouth.[17] On 5 May the Generals (to give them their title of Generals-at-Sea) sailed in company with the *Phoenix* and the *Nonsuch*, and reached Plymouth on the 12th.[18] Badiley was left behind to manage affairs in the Downs. At Plymouth they were met by Popham and Moulton with the good news of a spirited little action.

For, on 5 April, Rupert had sent out Sir Henry Stradling, in the *James*, as the commander of a squadron consisting of the *Charles*, *Roebuck* and *Thomas*. He was to sail for the Scillies, and there to put ashore provisions and soldiers, and to return within twenty-one days. Rupert's hope was 'to see Scilly a second Venice – for if the worst come to the worst, it is but going to Scilly with this fleet, where, after a little while, we may get the King a good subsistence and I believe we shall make a shift to live'.[19] Stradling was to fight any foe he should meet, and any prize that was taken was to have its hold spiked down to prevent embezzlement.[20] The ships were to keep together. In dark or thick weather every ship was to have a light on the poop, and Stradling would carry two. If a ship was hailed it was to answer 'Charles the Second', to which the hailer was to reply, 'York'.[21]

On the 20th, off the Scillies, Popham met the *Elizabeth*, which had lost contact with Moulton's squadron in the fog two days before. She had fallen into the midst of Stradling's ships in the dark. After giving them two broadsides, she had managed to get clear of them. Popham, taking her with him, that night met Moulton, some forty leagues off Land's End. Moulton had taken the *Thomas*, and had manned her with his own men. Next morning Popham, with the *Charles, Elizabeth, Constant Warwick* and *Increase*, steered north, while Moulton with the *Leopard, Bonaventure, Assurance* and *Thomas*, steered south. On the 25th, a dozen leagues off Scilly, Popham heard a gun, which he took to be the *Elizabeth*, as the fog was very thick. An hour later, the *James* loomed up out of the murk. Popham had only the *Constant Warwick* with him, but he at once fired at the foe, who, without replying, tacked away from him, and escaped. Though Popham had lost sight of her in the fog, he instantly made after her. Then, after half an hour, he suddenly ran into the *Guinea* (renamed the *Charles*). An hour's fight followed and her captain, Allin, surrendered. Popham took her with him to Falmouth, entering the port on the 27th.[22] The *James* and *Roebuck* got safely back to Kinsale, the *Roebuck* having taken a prize, the *George* of London, on the way.[23]

The Generals now sailed for Kinsale, which they reached on 21 May. With them were the *Triumph, Charles, Leopard, Hercules, Garland, Adventure, Constant Warwick, Nonsuch, Elizabeth* and *Increase*. They found Rupert in harbour with 13 ships: the *Reformation, Convertine, Swallow, James, Blackmoor Lady*, a Scottish frigate, the prizes *Ark* and *Culpepper*, the *Washford* frigate, the *Roebuck*, with the *George, Ambrose*, and *Charles*, small ships with about ten guns each. The fleet was manned by 600 seamen, many of whom were prisoners anxious to desert. Rupert therefore went to Waterford and Wexford to get more mariners, whom he attracted by the offer of prize money.[24]

Next day, the 22nd, Popham sailed in the *Adventure*, first to tell Ayscue to send his two best ships to Kinsale, next to go to Plymouth to bid Moulton to join the Generals, and finally on to London to report to the council on the state of affairs. The *Phoenix* was to ply in western waters after Moulton had left. Popham was to 'represent the posture of the enemy' and 'to ask that money and provisions may be sent to them with all speed'.[25] Ayscue complied by sending the *Lion* and the *John*, but it is uncertain whether Moulton joined them.

On the same day some fishermen came out of Kinsale and from them some intelligence was obtained. They were sent back to tell the town that they might fish without molestation, but this Rupert refused to allow. Next day seven seamen, who had been prisoners, managed to escape and join the fleet. On the 24th the foe began to build a small fort 'upon the point near the entrance into the bay, and drew some guns into it'. As it was suspected that 'in the darkest time of the night' some ships might steal out by

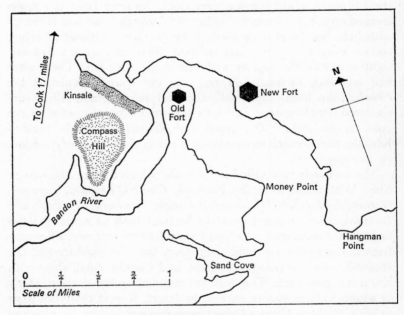

Kinsale, October, 1690

the shore and get away, the fleet stood in and anchored near the bay. The *Rebecca*, with the ship's boats was sent in to lie at the bay's mouth to keep watch, and to report the motion of the Royalists. But on the 28th a storm sprang up, and by 1 June it 'blew hard westerly with much sea'. With the danger of being dashed to pieces upon a rocky coast by the angry Atlantic rollers, the Generals were forced to leave. They had to cut their cables, abandon their anchors and to make for Milford Haven, to avoid being driven into St George's Channel. From there they sailed again for Kinsale, only to be forced by 'strong weather' to anchor under the shelter of Lundy Island on 6 June.[26] Back they went to Milford. Here, on 13 June, they wrote to the Speaker. They had been absent for ten days from Kinsale. With them were the *Triumph, Charles, Leopard, Lion, Garland, Hercules, John* and *Elizabeth*. They, with the first opportunity, would endeavour to get back to Milford. If the foe had gone they would 'follow him wherever he shall go'. They had warned Moulton and other ships, 'to defend themselves and oppose the enemy, in case he should be gone out and recover the Channel'.[27]

By the 20th they were again before Kinsale. Here they piously observed 'that that Providence which hath kept us by ill weather hence, hath by the same kept all the revolters still in here'. The same number of Rupert's ships were still there. Their desire was 'the reducement of that perfidious crew, which are sheltered in this harbour'.[28] On the 23rd Ayscue wrote to the Speaker. He had sent the *Nicodemus* to the Generals with some news, and he suggested that some forces should be landed in Munster, which would force Inchiquin, who was besieging Dublin with most of his army, to withdraw. This was the only way to relieve Dublin. He asked that this should be communicated to the Council of State, 'for I conceive it of great concernment'.[29]

On the same day the Generals wrote to say that they were in sight of the enemy, and that they had intelligence that they intended, their vessels being clean, either to escape by night or to fight. By keeping Rupert in, they hoped to ensure the safety of the Newfoundland trading ships. Two days later, they wrote again to Popham. Deane was going to Plymouth to get supplies in which they were of great want. They had drawn lots to decide who should go. As Ayscue could spare no help from Dublin they had also to watch Waterford and Wexford.[30] On the 31st Deane wrote from Plymouth: 'Colonel Blake sends me word that all Rupert's fleet is gone back to Kinsale Town, and that they keep only five of their best sailors to run away with: but whether it be a deceit to embolden us to draw off our great ships that they might wholly escape, I know not'.[31]

The monotony of blockade, which made it fortunate that Blake, with his gift of patience, was still in command, was broken on 5 July. The night before Rupert, in a shallop of 23 oars, escorted a frigate of nine guns, rowed by sixteen oars, to the harbour's mouth. Next day Ball, in the *Nonsuch*, sighted her and gave chase. At four in the afternoon, he came up with her and took her. She was the *Teresa*, formerly known as the *Wexford* frigate, commanded by Captain Darsey. On board were Colonel William Legge and Sir Hugh Wyndham, who were carrying dispatches from Rupert to Charles Stuart. As she was newly tallowed she was added to Blake's fleet. Reporting this, Blake wrote that he was disturbed by 'clamours' coming from the north coast, arising from the need to protect shipping. It was impossible to give complete satisfaction, 'especially from the fleet in this place, from whom so great performances are expected, as was lately hinted at in a letter from the Council of State'.[32] However, on the 7th, he was cheered by the arrival of the *Elizabeth* and *Nonsuch*, who brought in a Dutch man-of-war of thirty guns. Three days before she had been at Scilly, and was laden with thirty bales of silk, intended for Kinsale. The blockade was proving very effective.[33]

The Council of State now determined to conquer Ireland. With this purpose in view, Cromwell sailed from Milford Haven with thirty-five ships, bound for Dublin. He was, as Peters observed, 'as seasick as any man I saw in my life'. This was on 13 August. Next day Ireton, under the convoy of Deane, followed him with eighty transports for Munster. They got as far as Youghal, and then changed course for Dublin. Deane says that this was due to a shift of wind.[34] It is more probable that it had been hoped that the Governor of Youghal would hand the place over to the Parliament. Apparently at the last moment he was prevented by Johnston, 'Inchiquin's creature' from so doing.[35] It was then proposed to reship some of Ireton's regiment and attempt Youghal from the sea. This was abandoned, partly from military reasons, and partly from the risk of encountering heavy weather in September.[36] Instead Deane proposed to send Ayscue from Dublin, where Deane had arrived on 23 August, to Kinsale, so as to set free 'two great ships' to join Popham in the Channel. However, on 1 September, he sent Ayscue instead with the *Andrew* and the *Bonaventure* to join Popham.[37] This may have been due to information intercepted in a dispatch from Rupert, dated 22 July, to Ormonde. Rupert told him that he had decided to sail, either in

the middle, or at the latter end, of September, and then he would
be fully provisioned. It would be a fit time, 'since the enemy dare
not venture so far from their own coasts and we, by reason of our
safe harbours, and short voyages between the coast of Spain and
France and those parts, shall be able to cross the whole Trade
through both Channels; and every south and westerly wind, which
shuts them up in their harbours if they were ready, shall bring
big ships from the southern and easterly ports into our lap'. This
letter seems to have reached London some time in August.[38]

Blake was still off Kinsale, but owing to the leaky condition of
the *Triumph* and the *Victory*, he had to send them home, shifting
his flag to the *Lion*, on 16 September.[39] He now got an unexpected
offer. This had been anticipated by Deane on 23 August. In
Dublin he had obviously been in conversation with Cromwell. For
he wrote to Popham: 'I perceive that my Lord Lieutenant will
write to the Council of State to move for Colonel Blake to be
Major-General of the Foot. I wish we may have as honest a man
in his room if it be so.'[40] Writing to Popham, on 16 September,
Blake told him he had an offer from Cromwell, 'inviting me with
much affection to be his Major-General of his foot, and telling me
he had written to some friends in London to obtain it. It was a
great surprise, greater than that of my present employment'. He
told Popham that he had resolved to refuse it, and begging him to
use his influence to persuade the council not to confirm the offer.
If it was confirmed he proposed to retire, 'and in private to
contribute the devoutest performances of my soul for their honour
and prosperity'.[41] The council, on 2 October, wisely told Blake to
make his own decision.[42]

Blake was never personally ambitious and his refusal to hitch his
wagon to the rising star of Cromwell simply sprang from his
desire to serve the Commonwealth as best he could. His task at
sea was still unfinished, and he wished to complete it. He accounted
it 'an especial happiness to be able to serve them in that conjunction
which they have already placed me'. As a soldier he may have felt
he was merely a camouflaged civilian. As an Admiral the commercial shipping merchant passed naturally to the highest post in
the sphere he had chosen for himself. He was at home upon the
sea, and his flexible mind easily adapted itself to the change from
a merchantman to that of naval command. Though this took place
when he was fifty, to alter Sir Humphrey Gilbert's words, 'he was

nearer to heaven by sea than by land'. Already he was conscious that the seamen had responded to his leadership, as he restored to them their morale, discipline and belief in themselves.

By 26 September, Blake's fleet had been reduced to five vessels: the *Lion, Garland, Elizabeth, Nonsuch* and *Guinea*. The *Leopard* and the *Adventure*, with his brother Benjamin's ship, the *Paradox*, had been sent to the Downs, as they were now unfit for service in such stormy waters. News had come that Drogheda had been captured.[43] Once again tempestuous weather forced him back to Milford, since he dared not risk the loss of a single ship upon that rocky and dangerous coast. Here he was to be found on 16 October. Once again he had to shift his flag, this time to the *Guinea*. With the *Nonsuch* he prepared to return, leaving behind the *Lion* to act as a guardship.[44]

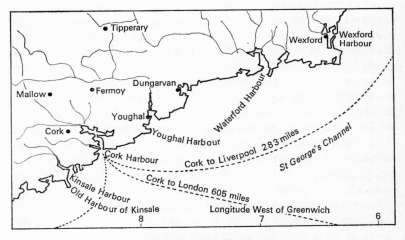

Southern Ireland

Meanwhile Cromwell had advanced swiftly southwards to Wexford, where he arrived on 3 October. Ireton, with 20 transports, with artillery and provisions, came in on the 7th. The landing of these decided the fate of the town. After a bombardment on the 11th, the castle was betrayed to Cromwell, and the town fell into his hands.[45] Wexford's fall gave Rupert furiously to think. He realised that he was in imminent danger of being hemmed in by

land by sea. If he was to save his fleet he must instantly get away
to sea. The going over of the English garrison of Cork to the
Parliament on 17 October, finally decided him. As Deane wrote,
'Rupert, three days after Cork declaring for the Parliament, in
great haste sailed from Kinsale with seven ships'[46]. These were the
*Constant Reformation, Convertine, Swallow, Blackmoor Lady, Mary,
Scot*, and *Black Knight*. The *James* and the *Roebuck* were left
behind, and were captured at the fall of Kinsale. He owed his
deliverance to the stormy weather, which had driven Blake to
Milford on 16 October.

Presumably the news of Rupert's escape must have reached
Blake at Milford, as he returned to Munster. For Deane, who
had returned to Milford, wrote on 27 October that 'my partner
Blake is on the coast of Munster with the *Guinea* frigate and the
Nonsuch'.[47] Deane had been escorting some twenty vessels, carrying Cromwell's battering guns, bread and ammunition. He lay off
the Bar of Wexford harbour on 29 September, but bad weather
had prevented the landing of any supplies.[48] He had then returned
to Milford, and apparently took Blake's place. Wexford and New
Ross in County Wexford had both fallen to Cromwell, and the
Guinea lay at Waterford.

On 16 October the English garrison at Cork suddenly turned
out Major-General Stirling, the governor, and then paraded the
streets, shouting 'out with all Irish, and in with all townsmen that
are English'.[49] The news reached Cromwell somewhere about 30
October. He asked Blake, who was with him at Ross, to sail there
in the *Guinea*, taking with him Mildmay in the *Nonsuch*.[50] Blake
sailed from Waterford on 30 October and reached Cork on 5
November. Colonels Townsend and Reeves, the former Governor
of Taunton, who had joined the Parliament, came aboard with other
released prisoners. Blake had got in safely, though he was fired
at by the fort at the harbour's mouth, which was still in possession
of the Irish. This fort had prevented Townsend, who was to have
taken the news to Cromwell, from getting past it by sea. Blake put
both colonels on the *Nonsuch*, and sent them away to Ross. With
them he sent a letter to Cromwell to give him an account of what
had happened, and of the present state of affairs in Cork. He told
Cromwell that he had sent to Milford for the *Lion*, or other ships
of force to come to him and to lie in the harbour. He himself was
going to the town 'to confirm the resolutions of the soldiers and

townsmen' who were expecting some relief from the army commander. Just as he was finishing his letter, news came that Youghal
had again declared for the Parliament, and that Johnston 'who
formerly betrayed them' was a prisoner there. He also sent the
good news to Popham. In Cork 440 horse and 1,000 foot had come
into him and daily more came in.[51]

In the meantime the *Garland* came into Waterford Bay with a
great prize. Cromwell put on board Colonel Phaire, with 500 foot
and £1,500 and sent Phaire to Cork. Off Dungarvan they were
held up by a contrary wind, but here they met the *Nonsuch*, with
the colonels aboard, who gave them the news about Youghal. At
once Phaire altered his course and went up to Youghal. Here the
mayor came aboard, and agreed to yield up the town. Phaire then
landed his foot, and after settling matters in the town, left 200
men and marched overland with the rest to Cork.[52] Cromwell
now appointed Blake, Deane, Lord Broghill and Sir William
Fenton as Commissioners to manage matters in Cork, which was
to be made a victualling base in the place of Milford Haven.[53]

Where Rupert had gone was still unknown, but the intercepted
letter of 22 July had revealed that he might cruise off the coasts of
France and Portugal. He had realised that to make the Scillies his
base would force him to face the full concentration of the Parliament's fleet. Popham however thought he might cruise at the
mouth of the Channel, with the Scillies as his base. So he sent off
the *Leopard, Entrance,* and *Adventure* to lie off Land's End, while
the *Bonaventure* was sent to reinforce Blake and Deane in Irish
waters.[54] Deane however had guessed Rupert's intentions for, in
a letter to Popham, dated 8 November, he suggested that he had
probably gone 'for the Straits to meet the vintage fleet coming
home'.[55] His guess was correct for, on 9 November, it was known
that Rupert was on the Portuguese coast.[56] The Council of State
therefore wrote to the Generals to consult together how best to
deal with the new situation.[57] On 5 December Popham and Blake
met at Portsmouth to discuss the position. It was decided that, as
Deane was sick, Blake should command the fleet to be sent against
Rupert.[58] Blake then returned to Kinsale on 10 December to
arrange with Penn for the security of the port. Cromwell had
desired that a ship of force should lie in the harbour 'for counten-
ancing the inhabitants in their trade and security of the harbour'.
Penn was to remain for this purpose in the *Lion*, till he should

receive other orders from Colonel Deane.[59] Blake was relieved by
Deane towards the end of December, and went to Portsmouth.[60]
On 10 January he was in London conferring with Popham. They
made the quaint request for trumpeters to be provided 'and
particularly a complete noise for the ship appointed for us'.[61] This
would suggest that neither of them was musical. Blake then
returned to Plymouth to await and supervise the fitting out of his
ships. On the 17th he received his instructions. He was to 'pursue,
seize, scatter or destroy, all ships of the revolted fleet, and all other
adhering to them'. If foreign ships were to support Rupert, he was
to attack them also: but 'that so after the fight ends, in case you
may happen upon any foreigners, there be not made any slaughter
of them in cold blood, but that they may be kept and used civilly
as prisoners of war'. He was also given authority, in case of need, to
impress any English merchantmen available. The sale by Rupert of
any of his ships was to be regarded as void, and was not to consti-
tute a bar to a demand for their restitution.[62]

Blake had carried out his task well. Despite all difficulties he
had patiently held on to the monotonous task of blockade, and he
contained Rupert within Kinsale. He and Deane, by their control
of the sea, had enabled Cromwell to advance southwards. By
prompt action Blake had exploited the revolts in Cork and Youghal.
'Had we not come hither' wrote an observer 'at the very time we
did, within a few days their Admiral, with some more, had gone
to Waterford and Wexford to join with those frigates, and then
we must have danced a wild-goose chase after them, or else the
merchants in all probability would have suffered much by them,
but the wise Disposer of all things ordered it better in his
Providence'.[63]

CHAPTER 7

The Pursuit moves to Portugal

*

On 1 March, 1650, Blake sailed from Cowes.[1] His fleet was composed as follows.[2]

	Guns
St George, Flagship, Captain Thorrowgood	56
Leopard, Captain Moulton, senior, Vice-Admiral	56
Entrance, Captain Badiley, Rear-Admiral	46
Bonaventure, Captain Harris	42
Adventure, frigate, Captain Ball	40
John, Captain Saltonstall	30
Assurance frigate, Captain Benjamin Blake	32
Constant Warwick, Captain Moulton, junior	32
Tiger frigate, Captain Peacock	36
Providence frigate, Captain Pierce	30
Expedition frigate, Captain Wheeler	30
Signet fireship, Captain Rose	3
Tenth Whelp fireship	8
William Ketch	6
Patrick Ketch	6
Total	453

With Blake went Charles Vane, younger brother of Sir Henry, who was appointed Envoy to the Portuguese King, for the Council of State and obviously did not want to enter into hostilities with him. Though unrecognised by the King they hoped to gain their object by diplomatic means instead. Blake anchored in Cascais Road on 10 March. The King had promised Rupert protection and allowed him to anchor in Oeiras Road. His Ministers, headed by de Miro, realising how vulnerable their shipping was to a hostile fleet, urged Rupert to embark 'and with all brevity hasten his departure'. But Rupert ignored this broad hint until it was too late.[3]

Blake at once sent his lieutenant with a letter to the King, with

another from the council. Blake piously observed that it was
obviously 'the work of some special Providence' that Rupert had
been detained until his arrival. He was sure that the King could
have no objection to 'the extermination of the nefarious tribes of
pirates', which for so long had preyed upon English commerce,
contrary to the 'common advantage of Nations'. This would
justify any action and would be to the 'advantage of his kingdom
and nation'. He asked accordingly that he might 'freely use your
port, without placing any obstacle in the way'. He ended by
declaring that he would never do anything 'in the least degree
inconsistent with the friendship between the two Nations or which
might give just grounds of offence to the King'.[4]

Next day, after a Council of War had 'craved direction from the
great God', it was decided to go up and engage the enemy.[5] Blake
may have recalled Warwick's fatal delay at Helvoetsluys when he
first arrived there. Boldly Blake led the way, followed by the
Bonaventure, Leopard and *Entrance*. As they approached St Julian's
Castle it fired eleven shots at them, and Fort Bugio four. All
missed. Then, just as the ships came between the two forts, it
suddenly fell calm and they had to anchor in a dangerous position.
An Aide-de-Camp arrived hurriedly from the King to explain that
the forts had fired without orders from the King. But he complained
of the attempt made by the fleet 'in offering to come in without
leave'. He urged that the fleet should move farther to seawards,
to which Blake objected 'as very inconsistent to the accommodation
and security thereof'. Four days later the Aide-de-Camp returned
and pressed for the ships to go out of sight of the city. If this were
done he would try and get the King to order Rupert to depart.[6]

Meanwhile Vane, on 18 March, had made a successful agreement
with the King. Blake was not to pass beyond the castles without
the written leave of the King, though in case of stormy weather
he was to be allowed to anchor in Oeiras Bay. In this case he was
not to attack Rupert without the King's permission, except for
the purpose of self-defence. All soldiers and seamen were to be
kept aboard their ships to avoid friction, though some might go
into the city to get supplies.[7]

On the same day Blake, who presumably had seen a copy of the
proposed agreement, weighed anchor and moved into Oeiras Bay,
'foul weather appearing'. He had taken advantage conveniently of
the stress of weather clause. He anchored two miles below Rupert,

who lay under the shelter of Belem Castle, ten in number with some fireships. 'Many of his men run ashore, some whereof are come to us, his chief expectation is of assistance from France – for by information of some come from Toulon, four frigates of good sort and many men are coming to him'.[8]

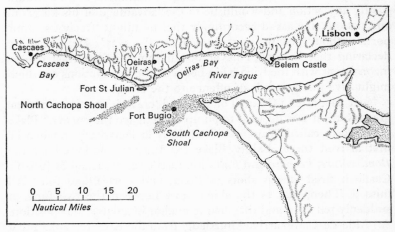

Lisbon

Rupert's fleet was composed as follows.[9]

	Guns
Reformation, Rupert's flagship, Captain Kettleby	52
Convertine, Prince Maurice, Vice-Admiral	46
Swallow, Sir John Mennes, Rear-Admiral	40
Second Charles, Captain Marshall	40
Captain Eustace's ship (the owner or Commander)	
Black Prince, Captain Goulding	36
Scot, Captain Langley	30
Henry (*Roebuck* renamed) Captain Barnaby Burley	30
Mr Hargrave's ship (owner or Commander)	30
Hopeful Adventure, Captain Michel	30
Mary, Captain Sir John Mucknell	24
Black Night	14
Total	372

On the 23rd, another Envoy arrived to ask that a person of quality should be sent ashore to treat. A Council of War, held on the same day, chose Vice-Admiral Moulton. He was to present four demands. First the surrender of Rupert's ships: secondly, if this was refused, to demand permission to attack him where he lay: thirdly to request that both fleets should be ordered to leave together: fourthly, if this was refused, to demand 'the freedom and privilege of the harbour and to ride where we shall find most safety for our ships'. Lastly he was to make it clear that Blake's sole object was to reduce or destroy Rupert's fleet, 'with no evil purpose in the least measure to His Majesty's kingdom'. The last clause was the only one in the King's power to grant. It was so framed as to leave the King a loophole to save his face. For the freedom of the harbour meant that Blake could remain in the river for so long as he saw fit. And it was adroitly worded so as to avoid an actual rupture, so that negotiations could still continue.[10]

The King realised that he was being manoeuvred into a new position. For the freedom of the harbour tacitly involved the recognition of the Commonwealth, and the disavowal of Rupert. As a King he regarded the Commonwealth as an undesirable upstart: as a practical politician he respected the power of its fleet. Accordingly he tried to play a temporising role, with an inclination to the side of Rupert. But Blake was not to be fooled.

On the 20th he wrote to Vane. It was evident to him that the King would do all he could in favour of Rupert, especially as he knew that another fleet was preparing in England to join Blake. By his message to Vane it was clear that his purpose was 'to contribute what he can to the increase of Rupert's strength and to the lessening of ours'. Blake and his Council of War therefore desired that Vane should speak plainly to the King or his agents, and press him for a 'clear and positive and universal answer to our propositions, and to let them know that we should take it far better at his hands that he did openly declare for Rupert, than by such indirect policies, to undermine us – and to lead us along by the nose with an opinion of his neutrality – as we may clearly perceive by that order given to his forts, the contrary was intended'.[11]

The wretched King's difficulties were increased by the pressure from his own subjects. For Rupert was busily engaged in ingratiating himself with them by his liberality to all. He also applied himself to the clergy, whose pulpits rang loudly with denunciations of the Commonwealth, declaring 'how shameful a thing it was for a Christian King to treat with rebels'.[12] The Royalists now tried to persuade the King to insist that, on their putting to sea, Blake should not be allowed to follow them for three days. Vane in his turn persuaded some English merchants to beg the King to send both fleets to sea, but this came to nothing. The King now showed his inclination to side with Rupert by giving orders that no more English men-of-war should be allowed to enter the river. Vane at once pointed out that this meant that Blake could receive no reinforcement, while Rupert could be joined by ships of any other nation.[13]

Hardly had Vane made his protest than it was justified. On 5 April two French men-of-war, of forty and thirty-two guns, entered the river and anchored by mistake among Blake's ships. Their captains then boarded the *George*, under the impression that she was Rupert's flagship. Blake demanded from them an undertaking that they should not join Rupert. On their refusal he took possession of both their vessels. The French Envoy promptly protested, and the King sent Vane a peremptory order to secure their immediate release, and Blake thought it best to comply. So, after two days detention they proceeded up the river and joined Rupert.[14] As yet Blake had no direct authority to make reprisals on the French. He felt himself obliged to a strict observance of diplomatic niceties. He refused to be provoked into any precipitate act which might put him in the wrong. He had, also, Vane's position to consider. Not only might his negotiations be compromised, but also his personal safety. The Portuguese had shown signs, though slowly, of meeting his demands which an unwise action might frustrate. His correspondence with the King, which seems to have vanished, must have been sizeable. A bill, sent in by Thomas Williams, Blake's trumpeter, on 6 April, amounted to £6.16.0. for nineteen visits ashore.[15]

On 13 April, a fight took place between some of Blake's men, who had been sent ashore to get water, and a party led by Rupert himself. The Princes declared that the men had come in an attempt to kidnap them while they were hunting. Some of Blake's men were killed, others wounded, and some taken prisoner. In the afternoon Rupert followed this up by sending a Portuguese boat, laden with oil and fruit to sell to the fleet. They came alongside the *Leopard*. The men in the boat, two Negroes and an Englishman, disguised as a Portuguese, sold a cask of oil. As it was being hoisted aboard, the Englishman in his excitement spoke in English. This aroused instant suspicion, and he was seized. On examination the cask was found to contain 'a bomb-ball in a double-headed barrel, with a lock in the bowels to give fire to a quick-match'. Another account says it was to be operated by a string, 'to be pulled by the boatmen, so that it would take fire and blow up the ship'. The prisoner confessed that he had been promised £100 to plant Rupert's infernal machine.[16]

Vane at once claimed that this incident constituted an act of hostility, and that Blake was 'thereby set free to attempt the like on Rupert's fleet, to right themselves otherwise, as occasion shall serve'.[17] The King obstinately refused to admit this. Towards the end of May, Blake took his ships down to the entrance of the harbour, out of the range of the castles and forts. His reason for this was his knowledge that Rupert had offered to leave, if he was allowed three days start. Possibly he hoped that his own withdrawal would lead the King to accept the Prince's offer, and that thereby he would be free to attack Rupert as he came out.[18]

By now the unsatisfactory nature of the proceedings made the Council of State grow restive. They began to consider the possibility of having to break off diplomatic relations with Portugal. At the same time the capture of English merchantmen in the Mediterranean by French ships made them view their relations with France as very critical. They acted upon the assumption that a breach with Portugal was almost inevitable, by sending Popham to reinforce Blake. He left Plymouth on 15 May in the *Resolution* of sixty-eight guns, with the *Andrew* of forty-two, the *Phoenix* of thirty-six, the *Satisfaction* of twenty-eight, with the merchantmen *Great Lewis, Hercules, Merchant* and *America*.[19]

On 21 May, the outward bound Brazil fleet sailed from Lisbon. Blake at once seized the opportunity to demonstrate to the King the power of his fleet. At the mouth of the Tagus he stopped the English vessels, chartered by the King, and added them to his fleet.[20] These were the *John and Mary, Agreement, Samaritan, Success, Mayflower, Reason, Hannibal, Sapphire* and *Prosperous.* This his instructions empowered him to do, but, as he had no authority to interfere with the Portuguese, he allowed them to proceed.[21]

This reminder of Blake's naval power was reinforced, on 26 May, by the arrival of Popham's squadron. Next morning Blake boarded him, and Popham showed him their new instructions.[22]

The Generals were empowered to attack Rupert anywhere: if the Portuguese refused to permit this, their ships were to be captured; and they were also authorised to seize French men-of-war and merchantmen.[23] They sent for Vane to come to them, and, at the same time, they sent to the King to demand Rupert's ships undertaking that, if this were done, they would release the English Brazil vessels. The King then sent for Vane, and told him that he considered the demand unreasonable. Whereupon Vane disguised himself and escaped aboard the fleet. He got away only just in time, for orders were sent out to all towns and villages to arrest him. All Englishmen in Lisbon, known to be well-affected to the Commonwealth were thrown into prison.[24] When Vane saw the new instructions he wisely decided not to return.

On 5 June, a Council of War on board the *Resolution* at which both Blake and Popham were present, decided to send Captain Legend next day to the King. He was to demand Rupert's ships. In case of refusal the King was to be warned that they would do 'what we could to right ourselves by force'. His answer must be given by the 10th. On the 7th the *Brazil* came in with supplies from Plymouth. Next day, as a small vessel slipped past them in shallow water into Lisbon the *Phoenix*, *Expedition* and *Providence* were ordered to lie off the Rock of Lisbon to stop any more such vessels. No reply came from the King on the 10th, so next day a Council of War was called and, at 8 a.m., Legend brought the King's answer, which was interpreted as 'delusory, or at least dilatory'.

On the 13th Vane was sent home in the *Constant Warwick*, to report on their proceedings.[25] On the same day every frigate was sent out to seize all the fishing vessels they met. Of these sixteen were taken, with the nets, fish and men. Two escaped, leaving behind all their nets.[26] The die had been cast, and hostilities had begun with Portugal. Next day, Badiley with the *Entrance*, *George*, *Leopard*, *Adventure*, *Assurance*, *Merchant*, *Tenth Whelp* and the ketch were sent off to Cadiz to bring back water and beverage,* and to look out for some Frenchmen said to be hovering there. This move was essential, as it was now obvious, with hostilities begun, that neither water nor supplies could be obtained from Lisbon. Fortunately it was axiomatic that emnity with Portugal

---

* Cheap wine which mixed with water from the casks, would disguise the taste enough to make it drinkable.

meant friendship with Spain. Badiley's squadron had to be strong, should the Frenchmen have the intention of joining Rupert. But it left the Generals with a much weakened fleet: the *Resolution*, *Andrew*, *Satisfaction*, *Phoenix*, *Tiger*, *Providence*, *Signet* and the four armed merchantmen, and the nine Brazil vessels. Nevertheless the blockade was rigidly continued.

In reply the King ordered thirteen ships to be got ready to act in Rupert's support. They were commanded by a very old man, Varejo, and their armament varied from twenty-four to forty guns. A Swedish ship that came out from Lisbon warned the Generals of these preparations. A few vessels managed to elude the blockade, and to slip into Lisbon, probably because they drew a shallow draught and could use the shallows, where the great English ships could not follow them. On the 28th another Swedish ship gave a further warning of the great preparations the King was making both by land and sea, adding that he had imprisoned all Englishmen who would not serve Rupert.[27]

On 22 July, Mr Rolles, of the Brazil Company, came aboard with a strange offer. The company would buy Rupert's ships for their own use. He undertook not to use them against the Commonwealth or to restore them to the Royalists. Rupert and Maurice were to have the liberty to go where they would. The Brazil ships, with all that belonged to them, were to be handed back, so that they could proceed on their journey. Popham commented that Rolles acted 'rather like a Portuguese than an Englishman'. This take-over bid, apparently without any compensation, was rejected out of hand.[28]

The Generals now faced a serious position. The Cadiz squadron had not returned and the shortage of drink was acute. So the *Tiger*, *Providence* and *Signet* had to be sent to Bayonne, to procure what they could on 5 July.[29] The *Assurance*, however, on the 16th, came in with more cheering news. Three Frenchmen had been found at anchor off Lagos. The *Adventure* had engaged one, which, after a stubborn resistance, was taken in a sinking condition, but the other two escaped. She also added that Badiley's ships would rejoin very shortly.[30]

On 21 July some Portuguese ships, with some of Rupert's, were seen coming down into Oeiras Bay. Next day they were joined by others, and now twenty-two vessels lay there. This clearly indicated that Rupert intended to make his way out. As the *Tiger*, on the 3rd, had rejoined from Vigo, the Generals had ten ships, and nine Brazil vessels with which to meet the allied fleet. The *Assurance* and the *Hercules* were away, probably on the look out for Badiley's expected squadron.[31]

Rupert's plan was that the Portuguese were to get in between his ships and Blake's. Then at night they were to show extra lights, so as to lure the Generals in shore, while Rupert with his lights extinguished, was to take the opportunity to escape.[32] On the 26th, between nine and ten in the morning, Rupert 'with much noise' came forth. With him were twenty-six ships, eighteen Caravels and ten or twelve fireships. The wind was at E.S.E. The Generals weighed 'and stood off with them, they keeping the wind of us'. Then 'having got a reasonable berth from the shore, we hauled our foresails to the mast'.[33] According to Captain Harris of the *Bonaventure*, the Generals' plan was 'to have got between them and their harbour, and so have forced them to sea'. The allied fleet was preceded by a large French ship of forty guns, flying a white flag at the main top. Four fireships attended her. Astern of her was Rupert, in the *Reformation*, about a mile behind. He likewise flew his colours. After him came two more Admirals.[34] With the *Resolution* were only the *Phoenix*, whose duty it was to 'put off fireships' and the *Mayflower*. The rest of the ships, according to Harris, had been unable to come up. The wind now changed to the south and the Generals 'filled our sails, tacked and got the wind' but the enemy also tacked.[35] The Portuguese Admiral's 'anchor-fluke had such a good hold that we were fair up with the enemy before he set sail'.[36] Both fleets were now standing out to sea in the direction of Cape Espichel.* According to Popham, shots passed 'between us and the Frenchman but we could never get within shot of Rupert, do what we could'.[37] Against this the Royalist account says that Rupert lost his fore-top mast.[38] Popham says that at this point the fireships tried to make an attack: 'Rupert and the Frenchman bearing up still as we neared them, thereby to get us to leeward by following them, that the fireships might the better do their work upon us, but the *Phoenix* put them off'. The Generals' joint account says, 'we bore away large upon the Frenchman, being betwixt us and the *Reformation* – but as fast as we bore upon him, he bore away large towards the harbour, and Rupert likewise (his mizzen always

* Cape Spartel

hauled up)'.[39] The Royalist account says when they found they could not weather Cape Espichel they tacked and stood north, till they came in six fathom water, near the Chachopa.[40] The Generals followed the foe till they came into ten fathoms of water, near the South Chachopa. As night was drawing on, and there being a leeward shore and tide, 'and being in the indraught of the harbour' they were advised to stand off to sea, while the enemy anchored between the two castles.

Next morning, as soon as it was light, the Generals stood in again, only to see the enemy under sail for Cascais Road, where they anchored under the castles. There was a very slight east wind, which made any attack hopeless, and the Generals could only keep the foe in sight. That night the *Assurance*, which had rejoined them, was sent in 'to alarm the enemy in the dark, thereby to keep Prince Rupert in apprehension that he might not steal way, and to give notice if he weighed.'[41]

By the first light of dawn next day, the foe were under sail, and the Generals stood in with them. But the enemy got as close to the shore as they could. If the Generals tacked, so did the foe. Blake and Popham therefore 'hauled off a backstays, and so lay from 10 a.m. to 5 p.m. in the afternoon'. With a slight south wind they allowed the enemy to get to windward, in the vain hope that they would attack.[42] Suddenly the enemy tacked, and at the same moment the top-mast men in the *Resolution* sighted some nine ships off at sea, coming towards them. Who they were they could not discover. At once the Generals stood out to sea. They might be Badiley's squadron, in which case they must be prevented from falling in unexpectedly with the enemy at night. On the other hand, if they should be the French, the Generals must interpose their fleet between them and Rupert, to prevent their uniting. Next morning, to their infinite relief and delight, the squadron proved to be Badiley's.[43] As they had but four days drink left in the fleet, 'we relieved our ships with a little liquor'. Then, sending their fast-sailing frigates ahead, they made for the shore. Through the haze they sighted the enemy at anchor in Cascais Bay. With their additional strength they had hopes of success, but an easterly wind prevented any action, and the foe also ran from them, in towards the Bar. They lay 'short that night, having resolved the next morning by the break of day, if possible to fall in among them, but when we sought them they were all gone in, to the great grief of our hearts'.[44] They had to console themselves with the fact that 'the King of Portugal himself was at Cascais to see the fight'. The failure of the allied fleet must have been a severe blow to him. For it had retired up the Tagus out of reach.[45]

On 14 August the *Constant Warwick* returned with a letter from the Council of State, dated 14 July. In it they complained that a richly laden Carrack had been allowed to get into Lisbon. Then they observed that it was increasingly difficult to keep out so many ships, or to supply them. So they suggested that the Generals should consult together as to how many ships were necessary to carry on operations and, after they had selected them, to send the rest home. In a somewhat contradictory manner they also suggested that, as they had heard that 120 Brazil ships were at the Azores, ships should be sent to intercept them by the Generals.[46]

To this the Generals replied, on the 15th. A rich carrack, from the East Indies, had come in. But, as she was to windward, and had run in close to shore, and under the cover of the forts, she could not be taken. Moreover they had no authority to seize her. As to the interception of the Brazil ships, a Council of War had unanimously decided that this was impossible, as the separation of the fleet would lead to 'many inconveniences'. So short were they of drink that they were 'in no capacity for such a service'. However, as the Brazil ships they had stopped were unfit to stay out any longer, they were sending them home. To the council's letter of the thirteenth bidding them seize on any Portuguese they could and keep them prisoners on board the ships so that English captives seized ashore could either be exchanged or released, they replied they had sent a captain ashore for this purpose but all in vain.[47]

In his letter to Sir Henry Vane, dated 14 August, Popham had filled in some details that are lacking from the joint dispatch. He revealed that Badiley had brought back six weeks water and beverage, of which a third had leaked away. In another letter he reported that the *Constant Warwick*, lying off the Rock of Lisbon, had fallen in with a rich East Indiaman on 19 August. After five hours fight she sank her. A greater part of her crew were rescued, but 200 were either killed or drowned, while the captain and twelve men got ashore. Some £100,000 worth of plate, with other goods of value went down with her.[48]

In accordance with the council's instructions, it was agreed that Popham, with the *Resolution, Andrew, Entrance, Satisfaction, Great Lewis, Tiger, America* and *Signet,* should go to Cadiz to get water and supplies, and then sail for England. On 3 September Popham sailed.[49] This left Blake with the *George,* his new flagship, *Leopard, Bonaventure, Phoenix, Expedition, Constant Warwick, John, Hercules* and *Merchant.* He intended to stay out 'a month or longer'. Only four days after Popham had left him, 7 September, Blake was cruising off the Rock of Lisbon in foggy weather. Suddenly at eleven o'clock in the morning, he caught a fleeting glimpse of Rupert and the allied fleet at sea. But not until four in the afternoon did he sight them again. This time he found himself, with only the *Phoenix* and *Expedition* in company, close to thirty-six sail of the enemy. The rest of his ships were lost in the murk. The enemy were to leeward, with Rupert in the *Reformation,* well to windward of his allies, so that he and Blake were standing towards one another on opposite tacks.[50] According to Gibson, Blake's Master pointed out that it was very doubtful if they could weather the Prince. 'Can you stem (ram) him?' asked Blake. 'Yes' was the answer, 'but then we shall hazard both ships'. 'I'll run that hazard' replied Blake, 'rather than bear up for the enemy'.[51] Rupert, confronted by three ships had to give way. As he passed, Blake and his consorts gave him broadsides, which brought down his fore-top-mast 'whereupon he bore up into the midst of his fleet'. The Royalist account has transferred this incident to the earlier engagement, but this is the correct one. Now once again the fog came down, and hid the contestants from one another. Blake therefore stood off to collect his ships, while Rupert and his allies returned to Lisbon.[52]

A week later, in the early morning of 14 September, the home-bound Portuguese Brazil fleet, of twenty-three sail, was sighted. With a strong wind at N.E. Blake made straight for them, and endeavoured to engage. But their Admiral, of thirty-two guns, was 'too nimble' for him and got away to Setubal, with his main-mast shot away, and with three or four foot of water in his hold. Blake then engaged the Rear-Admiral, of thirty-four guns. After a three hours fierce fight, on a rough and rolling sea, so that it was impossible for Blake to run out his lower tier of guns, the Portuguese ship surrendered. So close were the two ships together that, as they parted, the *George* received 'a crack in her bows'. The *Assurance,* under his brother, Benjamin, had boarded and burnt the Vice-Admiral, of thirty-four guns, but he had rescued most of her crew. Six other ships were captured, with 4,000 chests of sugar and 400 prisoners. Of the rest, nine got into the Tagus, so that five were unaccounted for, though possibly they may have been captured by Popham's ships on their way to England.[53]

Since neither water nor supplies could now be obtained from Lisbon, Blake was forced to sail for Cadiz, with his 'torn and lame prizes'. Here he arrived about 22 September. He was received with 'much honour' by the Admiral of Spain, as he entered the Road. For the Spanish King, Philip the Fourth, had good reason for this reception. On 29 May, English Royalists had murdered Anthony Ascham, the Commonwealth Envoy at Madrid. The King had no desire to add England to the number of his foes, France and Portugal. Especially as his fleet was concentrating at Palermo, in an attempt to recover the territories seized by the French in Tuscany. He seized the opportunity by allowing Blake to use his port. As three of his prizes were unfit for sea, Blake transferred their lading into other ships. Of the eleven Brazil sugar ships, the *Shepherd*, *Antonio*, *Lady Remedia* and *Mary* were sent home under Badiley, who also took with him the *George*, *Assurance*, *Hercules* and *Merchant*. He sailed on 14 October.[54]

Two days later, 16 October, the *Hopewell* came in with letters from the Council of State. What they contained is unknown, but they were probably orders to intensify reprisals against the French. These had already been given to Popham four months before. It is more likely that the council, impatient that Rupert's fleet was still neither secured nor destroyed, had realised that the attacks on Portuguese mercantile commerce would make the King eager to speed his going, had ordered Blake to lie in wait for him. So Blake, having got his four frigates cleaned, at once put to sea, taking with him his new flagship, the *Phoenix*, with the *Elizabeth*, *Expedition* and the *John*.[55]

He had left the Tagus open, but he may well have reasoned that, as Ireland had now been reduced and Scotland paralysed by Cromwell's victory at Dunbar, the Royalist reaction was ended. Now there was nowhere for Rupert to return to in English waters. He was therefore no longer a naval danger, but rather a mere buccaneer. 'A vagabond German' as Vane had termed him. Blake's removal to Cadiz would give the Portuguese King a chance to rid himself of an embarrassing guest, indeed an expensive one for

Portuguese shipping. Once Rupert became a wanderer upon the High Seas, there would be a final opportunity to deal with him.

If Blake reasoned thus, he was fully justified. For, though he did not know it, Rupert had sailed from Lisbon on 12 October. With him went the *Reformation, Swallow, Black Prince, Second Charles, Henry*, and *Mary*. The *Convertine* had been sold. The King, 'having no more use for our ships' had victualled and supplied them. Rupert decided to make for the Mediterranean 'poverty and despair being our companions, and revenge our guide'. He probably counted on reaping a rich harvest of prizes and on making a French port for his base, from which to operate. He stood out to sea for thirty-six hours, and so unwittingly avoided Badiley's returning squadron.[56]

Meanwhile Blake, spreading out the *John, Expedition* and *Elizabeth* to look for the enemy, had on 20 October met some four or five leagues off the Straits' mouth, the *Jules* a French ship of thirty-six guns, commanded by de la Lande, 'who after some dispute yielded upon quarter'. She was about to join Rupert, and had met the *Second Charles* at Sallee. Both made for the Straits, but the *Second Charles* took to her heels and fled. According to Gibson, when de la Lande obeyed Blake's summons to surrender, he realised that the *Jules* was more powerful and claimed he was deceived. Blake sent him back to fight it out, but his crew refused duty, and he had to yield. This sounds most improbable, and well may be added to another legend of the Blake saga.

Blake wisely resisted the temptation to chase the *Second Charles*. He knew Rupert's approximate strength, while the *Jules* incident indicated that the French might be sending him more aid. To have gone on with four small frigates was to risk being overcome, while his two powerful units lay idle at Cadiz. So he returned there, and hoisted his flag in the *Leopard*, and picked up the *Bonaventure*, the *Constant Warwick* and the *Hopewell*.[57] On the 28th he got information that Rupert, with his whole fleet, had been at Malaga two days before. At once he set sail, leaving behind the *Jules* as he could not man her. On the 30th he reached Malaga. Here he learned that Rupert was 'towards Alicante' after burning and sinking five or six English merchantmen at Veles Malaga. As Saltonstall, of the *John*, wrote, 'we stayed not two hours but went after him.' Blissfully unconscious that Blake was hot upon their heels the Royalists were strung out between Capes De Gata and Palos,

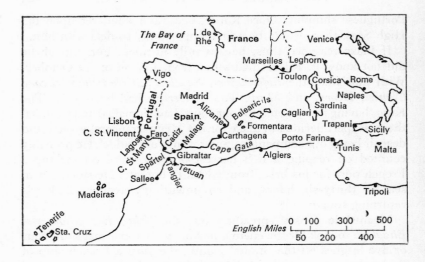

The Mediterranean

in separate groups, out of touch with each other.[58] On 1 November a French ship of seventeen guns, bound for St Malo was taken, and next day another of twenty guns was captured between the two capes. Rupert and Maurice had deserted their ships to chase a merchantman towards the African coast. On 3 November Blake rounded Cape Palos and fell in with the *Roebuck* and took her 'without many blows, except among themselves'. Next day, with his sails stretched to the utmost Blake, in the evening, sighted five more ships: the *Second Charles*, the *Black Prince*, the *Mary* and two prizes. Four frigates chased them into Carthagena Bay. The *Black Prince* was overhauled by the *John*, and she ran ashore three leagues east of Carthagena and there fired and blew herself up. On the 5th the rest put into Carthagena. Blake sent to the governor, who came aboard to persuade Blake not to fall upon them until order came from the King. While Blake was considering 'which way to effect our purpose with most speed and safety' a sudden gale forced the Royalists ashore, where they were all bilged, 'not a mast standing'.[59] Two days later Blake wrote to the King saying that he 'did forbear out of respect to your Majesty's authority, though with much indignation against those wicked men – but what I was not then permitted to do, Divine Providence did in a great measure accomplish shortly after –. The ships might have been most saved had I been permitted to come nearer them'. He requested that the artillery, cables, anchors and other furniture should be handed back to him.[60] Then, after leaving the *John* and the two French prizes off Carthagena, to await the King's answer, Blake sailed for Formentura.[61] On the *Henry*, one of the wrecked ships, a paper was found directing the Royalist ships to rendezvous there. Blake reached there on the 12th, but no ships were to be found, though the two Princes had been there on 4 November. Ignorant of the loss of his ships, Rupert had obligingly left orders for them, dated the 5th, in a box fastened to a staff flying a white flag, telling them to follow him to Cagliari in Sardinia.[62]

Though the new rendezvous was so conspicuous, the new clue puzzled Blake. For Rupert had also ordered that any prizes were to be taken to a place, whose name was erased and unreadable. If he was not there, the captains were to send to him for orders. If the wind was northerly they would find him at Cagliari.[63] Blake therefore sailed for Majorca, 'conceiving that this might be the place meant in the paper'. But Rupert was not there, nor was there any news of him. Blake concluded therefore that Rupert had 'in all probability, according to the winds, got either Villa Franca or Toulon'. As his provisions were running low, a Council of War decided to abandon the chase and return. So, on 23 November, Blake sailed for Alicante, and anchored there next day. Here he took in beverage and supplies, and then went on to Carthagena on 3 December. Here he got the King's reply to his letter, 'which being to my judgement not fully satisfactory', he sent him another note, asking that the artillery and other things might be handed over.[64] Either here or at Alicante, as R. C. Anderson thinks, he got the council's letter of 2 November, bidding him hand over to Penn, who was to succeed him, and to return with the rest of the fleet. For the council, although they knew of Rupert's escape from Lisbon, were ignorant of Blake's chase and destruction of his ships.[65]

By 11 December he was at Malaga, and on the 13th back at Cadiz. On the 21st he gave the council a report of his actions.[66] He had done his work magnificently. Rupert's fleet was, for all practical purposes, destroyed. Blake had achieved this because he possessed the faculty of divining his enemy's intentions. Experience had shown him that Rupert's real purpose was, not to take refuge in port, but to raid at sea. Though he had carried out the blockade with infinite patience, he had realised that it was impossible to seize or destroy Rupert's fleet in harbour. He believed that, since the capture of the Brazil fleet, the Portuguese King would be only too anxious to rid himself of Rupert. By going to Cadiz he boldly left the sea open for Rupert to escape. He reasoned that Popham's returning fleet would deter him from going north into the Channel. His objective therefore must be the Mediterranean. So he spread out his ships at the Straits' mouth to wait for him, especially as he knew the Spanish King had ordered his ports not to entertain Rupert's ships.

But great as this achievement was, even greater was his maintenance of the morale and confidence in his fleet. Only a superb leader, who had won the trust of his men, could have kept this alive in the monotony and weariness of a blockade. As Saltonstall wrote to the Secretary of the Admiralty Committee, 'the Lord had proved us exceedingly, since we have had but little of the arm of the flesh amongst us – I mean, Sir, since our great and powerful fleet of so many ships were reduced to a small squadron of ten ships under the command of General Blake, for since then we have taken the Brazil fleet, and after that our squadron being now but three ships and four frigates, we have taken three French ships, and destroyed and taken all Rupert's ships, seven in number, only two now remaining: thus God hath owned us in the midst of our implacable enemies, so that the terror of God is amongst them – the Spaniards are now exceeding kind unto us, and the King of Spain hath made large expressions to our general how acceptable our service hath been unto him since our coming into the Straits.'[67]

This was emphasised by the fact that, on the day this was written, 2 November, the Spanish King was sending Ambassadors to England to apologise for Ascham's murder, to promise punishment for the two murderers, and to allow the English fleet to shelter in Spanish ports. For Spain had recovered her possessions in Tuscany, though Mazarin had countered this by making peace with the Fronde, thus closing the sore left open by Spain. The destruction of Rupert's fleet had prevented the danger that it might join the French naval forces in the Mediterranean. It was imperative for Spain to keep on good terms with the English fleet that had now revealed its power in that sea.

Sir Julian Corbett has suggested that the council had lost their confidence in Blake by ordering him home, after handing over to Penn. Yet this seems most unlikely. Popham, who had arrived home on 24 October, had been with him quite recently,[68] so that he knew, at first hand the condition of Blake and his fleet, which had been at sea continually for eight months, and that after seven months off Kinsale. They had endured stress of weather, privation from bad victuals, lack of drink, to say nothing of conflict with the enemy. Popham probably had urged the need for fresh ships to be sent out, and that Blake should come home for a well-earned rest.

On 12 December the council got the welcome and unexpected news, written on 30 October from Malaga, that Blake was in full pursuit of Rupert's fleet, 'as far as Providence shall direct'. This was reported next day to Parliament. At once the council wrote to Blake saying they had heard of 'his very good service done against Rupert' and bidding him to continue abroad 'for so long as you find will be for the public service'. Penn, who had not yet sailed, was ordered to go to the Azores to intercept the home-bound Brazil fleet.[69] But not until 20 December, did he sail from Falmouth, so that he did not reach Spain until the middle of February.[70]

On the same day that the council wrote to Blake the French Envoy, who was endeavouring to treat unofficially, was ordered to leave England; the Portuguese Envoy was refused a hearing: and the Spanish Ambassador solemnly recognised the Commonwealth. As Vane wrote to Cromwell, 'the seven ships left with Colonel Blake are very likely to be the total ruin of Rupert's fleet, and a great terror to the French. This hath made the Spaniard solemnly to acknowledge us'. Such was the effect of Blake and his ships.[71]

On 10 February, 1651, Blake reached England. He was greeted by the news that Parliament had already approved his proceedings. And on the 23rd he related to the Commons 'the wonderful appearance of the powerful hand of God with him in his service at sea'. In their turn they voted him their grateful thanks, together with a grant of £1,000 for his 'great and faithful service'.[72]

CHAPTER 8

Amphibious Operations: I Scilly

*

THERE was to be no respite for Blake yet. On 10 March, 1651, he was appointed to command the fleet that was to guard the Irish Sea and to reduce the Isle of Man. It was composed of the flagship, *Phoenix, Providence, Tenth Whelp, Fox, Mayflower, Truelove, Hind, Convertine, Little President, Constant Warwick, Convert* and the *Hoy* galliot, while the *Portsmouth, Swiftsure, Concord, Fellowship* and *Hector* were detailed for special duty on the Irish coast.[1]

However, after his long absence abroad Blake snatched a brief visit to Somerset, and most probably, Bridgwater. For on 24 March he went to Taunton, where, 'for his faithful service to the Commonwealth by Land and Sea, he was entertained with much love and affection by the inhabitants of the town and also by the officers and soldiers of the Army.' The memory of the siege was still a vivid one and the county was proud of the sea career, which had opened with the destruction of Rupert's fleet.[2]

Sir George Ayscue had returned to Plymouth from Irish waters. He was to go to the Barbados to secure the islands for the Parliament. On his way he was first to reduce the Isles of Scilly. His squadron was made up of the *Rainbow* and six other ships.[3]

But a new and unexpected peril threatened both Parliament and the Scillies. From Weymouth, on 28 March, 1651, came a report that Martin Tromp, Admiral of Holland, had arrived in the bay to join the rest of his fleet, some eighteen sail, who had gone on to the Scillies. It was said that he had orders to require satisfaction from the Royalists there for the injuries they had done to Dutch shipping.[4] Such news aroused the Council of State to instant action. Already jealous of the Dutch, they suspected a design to seize the islands, which in Dutch hands, would be more dangerous to them than in Royalist possession. English trade at the mouth of the Channel would be at the mercy of Holland. On 1 April Blake was ordered to join Ayscue and to take command of the fleet. They were to sail for Scilly, and to demand from Tromp, what his orders and purpose were. Should they be prejudicial to the interests of the Commonwealth and were Tromp to persist in them, Blake was 'to use the best ways and means to enforce them'. At the same time he was to make clear that such action was not intended to defend the Royalists in the wrongs they had done to the Dutch or 'to hinder them from righting themselves upon them so that they act nothing contrary to the prejudice of the Commonwealth; but shall be ready to give them all assistance therein, and expect the like from them'.[5]

Instructions were also sent to the English Ambassadors to represent to the States-General that the Commonwealth regarded Tromp's coming 'without discovering his clear intentions therein, pretending it is to compel satisfaction for injuries done, without the limitation of the means, whether by possessing himself of those islands, or otherwise', as 'disagreeable to the amity and friendship between the two States and to the common laws and customs of nations'. Further they also pointed out that 'Your Lordships have not given any intimation of what is intended by so great a fleet approaching so near in such suspicious manner'. This remonstrance was presented to them on 10 April.[6]

Captain Hatsell, a Navy Commissioner, had been so prompt in collecting both men, and in pressing boats at Plymouth, that Blake was able to embark nine companies of foot under the command of Colonel Clarke, numbering some 900 to 1,000 men 'many of whom were but newly levied'. So on 12 April, at 8 p.m., the two Admirals sailed with some fourteen to twenty-two ships, according to various estimates.[7]

Tromp had arrived off the islands on 30 March. His orders were to secure the return of captured ships, with their crews and goods. In case of refusal he was to seize the ships belonging to the Scillies and to carry them off. On 11 April the States-General had assured Parliament that no orders had been given, either to seize the islands, or to do anything detrimental to the Commonwealth. After Tromp had sent an Envoy ashore, a strong wind forced his three ships out to sea.[8] On 1 April he was back again, and twelve Dutch prisoners were returned to him, but no ships. On the 2nd. he renewed his demand and twenty-two more captives were returned, but still no ships. The prisoners, in fact, told him that the governor had no intention of giving up the vessels. So, in the evening, Tromp went close in shore and signalled for his Envoy to come aboard. This he did, though 'the rabble in the Scillies treated him very roughly'.[9] This may have given rise to the English report that the governor had shown him the gallows and 'then kicked him'.[10] As the Envoy brought the governor's reply, Tromp saw that he had no intention of handing over the ships. According to one account the 'slighting of himself and his embassy so distasted Van Tromp' that he is said to have declared war on Sir John Grenville, the governor, and to have offered to assist in the reduction of Scilly and to give full assurance for yielding it up.[11] He then lay between Scillies and the Lizard, where he was joined by five more ships.[12]

On the same day, the 13th, before Blake arrived, Henry Leslie, Bishop of Down and an ardent Royalist, landed on St Mary's. He just managed to avoid being caught by the Dutch and the English fleets; for he records that on the 15th in the morning two great fleets came against the islands. One, an English fleet of twenty-two ships, besides many shallops and long-boats, carrying 2,000 men: the other, a Dutch fleet of thirteen vessels.[13] This would seem to indicate that Blake found Tromp lying before the islands, and delivered to him the council's ultimatum and that, thereupon, Tromp offered to assist him.[14] Already off Portugal and Spain Blake had proved himself notably tactful and diplomatic in dealing with a delicate situation. Though he made it plain that the council would brook no interference with, nor the possession of, the Scillies, he must have softened the blow to Tromp's sense of national honour. This he did by reference to that part of his instructions which bade him help the Dutch to get lawful satisfaction for their wrongs, and to expect the like from them. Thus it may well be that the famous letter of Tromp to Blake, on 2 June, 1652, in which he asked Blake to return a missing ship 'for friendship's sake' (as if they had previously met) may well refer to this incident. So that it does not necessarily support the story that Blake, in his youth, had lived at Schiedam and there had met Tromp. There is, moreover, no written evidence that Blake and Tromp ever met. Yet the bishop's letter is evidence that Blake had invited Tromp to join him in a joint demonstration, before the Dutch Admiral sailed home and left him to deal with his own affairs.[15]

The problem that lay before Blake and Ayscue was a double one. Before St Mary's could be attacked, with its strong castle and open roadstead wherein Grenville's chief strength lay, it was necessary to secure two things. First a land base for the troops; and secondly a sheltered road in which, at least, the victuallers could ride. And this had to be done at once, for, even if troops could be landed, storms might drive the ships out to sea again. Both Admirals recognised that the capture of Tresco was the key to the islands, together with the Isle of Bryhar, which would give them the possession of the sheltered harbour of New Grimsby. As Ayscue wrote, 'the two Islands command the road, as well as St Mary's, and the gaining of those Islands would render St Mary's useless to the enemy: besides it would be a speedy means to force St Mary's Island to submission'. Elsewhere, he added, 'the men-of-war belonging to these piratical rocks, will be like mice that run from a falling house, and must be forced to seek a new rendezvous: neither can St Mary's subsist without them'.[16]

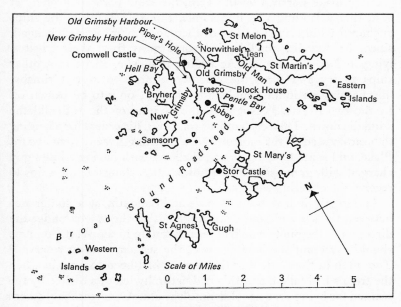

The Isles of Scilly

New Grimsby, however, was protected by two of the foe's best frigates, the *St Michael* of thirty-two guns, afterwards the *Tresco*, and the *Peter* of sixteen guns, afterwards the *Bryhar*. Also, according to Leslie 'by other helps so that they could not enter'. A military landing therefore was first necessary upon Tresco, on the side remote from New Grimsby, somewhere in the direction of Old Grimsby harbour. Of which Leslie wrote, 'where it was scarce known any great ship ever ventured to come in, they gained it, being of so great a breadth that it could not be defended'.[17]

Fortunately it is possible to gain a vivid picture of the opening phase of the operations, from the fact that afterwards a desperate quarrel arose between the soldiers and the seamen as to 'who did the work'. Partisans on both sides rushed eagerly into print. The soldiers' cause was championed by Joseph Lereck, a truly militant individual, whose object was to demolish 'the many and scandalous reports touching that service'.[18] The tradition of the silent service was more modestly, but no less scripturally, by an anonymous 'Special Hand'.[19]

After Blake's arrival on the 13th, the wind blew so strongly at east, that a landing was impossible, though several of the ships anchored within musket-shot of the enemy. Fire was exchanged, since the Royalists had landed some guns from their frigates, lying in New Grimsby.[19] According to Leslie, Blake sent other ships to try and force the narrow entrance to New Grimsby, 'discharging an infinite multitude of shot', only to be beaten off by the two frigates.[20] Not until the evening of the 16th did the wind die down. Then each officer was given his orders for a landing to be attempted on the morrow. Next morning Ayscue went aboard Blake, and some forty boats and shallops, each having a brass gun charged with grape-shot in the bows, came alongside the ships to receive the cheering soldiers.[21]

Apparently it had been agreed, at Plymouth, at a conference between the sea and land commanders, that the troops under the direction of the pilots who had been taken up in the West Country, should carry out the landing, with the seamen held in reserve.[22] Too often in the Civil War the seamen had been thrown in when the troops had failed, and this had naturally led to a dislike by the seamen for being used as soldiers. Blake and Ayscue probably were averse to the use of their men, since they would need every man they had in such stormy and dangerous waters. In addition, Ayscue had his voyage to the Barbados to consider. Blake remembered, too, how at Lyme, seamen had been landed to hold the line. This, though necessary, had impeded the use of the ships. At Lyme he had commanded the troops: here his position was reversed. The division of command in amphibious operations was a delicate one so, with his experience at Lyme in mind, he wisely left the landing to Colonel Clarke's charge. The colonel may have insisted rightly that he must have a free hand in this matter. Blake recognised his own function in the covering power of his guns and in the transport of the troops.

At 6 a.m. Colonel Bawden in the leading boat put off for St Helens to try and gain a landing on Tresco. The force was divided into two: one to land on a stony bay by the fort within Old Grimsby harbour and the other in a more sandy bay to the west.[23] The attack was covered by the ships, who fired 600 shots,[24] but the boats, tightly crammed with men 'who soon became tired with the unaccustomed effort of rowing and sea-sick with the roughness of the water', became wearied. Soon the boats became separated and divided by the rocks, while the swiftness of the tide drove the boats east towards the entrance of Old Grimsby harbour. The 'fearful pilots, in addition, directed their course in this direction being afraid of the rocks'.[25] To add to the trouble the boats now came under fire. Three companies were landed on Northworthiel, which the pilots declared was Tresco. Bawden himself landed and forced the pilot to declare that it was possible, at low water, to cross to Tresco, which was half a musket-shot off. Bawden then discovered that his boat was so fast aground that she could not be got off. Neither account mentions any covering fire from the ships, though Leslie indicates it, while one account says the fleet fired over 400 shots.[26]

Meanwhile Colonel Clarke, with the second party, came up to try and aid the first. He decided to attempt his own objective and rowed towards it. His pilots took the leading boats along a craggy and inaccessible coast, where it was impossible to land. Here the enemy had assembled their musketeers and opened fire from the shelter of the rocks. Some reply was made, but the men were so tightly crammed together that they could not even use their weapons. In addition most of them were so sea-sick that they could not fire. As the boats drew nearer, they were greeted with small, great and case-shot. Many of the boats, under such a fusillade, turned their helm and rowed backwards and aside.

Another party, however, did manage to land 'where the enemy's greatest strength lay' and for the moment, forced the foe to run. But Colonel Wogan, in command there, forced them back again.

Shot in the foot, he nevertheless succeeded in repelling the attack in a fierce struggle and forced the landing party to withdraw and to row off. Colonel Clarke, standing boldly up in his boat in the thickest of the fight, vainly tried to rally his boats, commanding and threatening them to follow him. Lereck relates that Captain Smith, a sea officer, was ordered on pain of death to return. But he merely rowed away. It was clear that the attack had failed and that the only thing that could be done was to withdraw. Clarke therefore rowed after his fleeing boats and took command of them. Three companies were already on Northworthiel and the rest were landed on Tean, to the east.[27]

Yet only six men had been killed despite the fact that Bawden's Ensign and the Pikes had their boat shot through and through, while another boat had lost all its oars, save two. Leslie declares that one shallop was sunk.[28] The men, young, raw and inexperienced, had lost all heart. There was little water and even that became foul and undrinkable, while provisions were scarce, as the ships were forced to ride at a distance owing to the rocks and stormy weather. The 'raw constitution' of the soldiers made the cold night 'irksome and comfortless'. Next morning the elated enemies opened fire on them. Small and great shot fell among the tents and damaged them, without doing any further harm. Clarke, a resolute and able officer, now surveyed Tresco and selected a spot suitable for another landing. He sent Captains Hatsell and Smith to acquaint Blake with the situation and to ask him for boats and reliable rowers.

Some commanders might have been tempted to abandon the project, or to postpone it until the troops had recovered their morale. Not so Blake: he never allowed a victorious enemy time to settle down and make good their success. Nor was he the man to abandon a good plan because it had miscarried owing to unforeseen circumstances. Clarke and Wogan had rallied their men by their resolute courage and efforts. He instantly sent provisions to Northworthiel and made the decision to make a surprise attack again the same night. But as supreme commander, he realised that he had made the mistake of allowing Clarke to proceed without a proper complement of seamen to manage the boats. Lyme had taught him that new soldiers or sailors in action for the first time needed to be stiffened by experienced men. He had made an error of judgment. The fresh landing would need leading by resolute men, who had both seen service and who would be immune to sea-sickness. He therefore sent 200 seamen, under Captain Morris, a passenger for the Barbados, with boats and rowers. Speed was essential if New Grimsby Road was to be secured, since at any moment storms might drive the fleet out to sea.

On Tean the raw troops, apprehensive of the sea and of the conditions which had prevented them from using their arms and fearful of being sunk in their boats, were in a state of mutiny. In true Puritan spirit the officers withdrew and held a prayer meeting. They rose from their knees confirmed in their resolution to fight again. On their return to their thankful surprise, they found in their men 'an alteration even unto admiration (wonder), declaring their readiness for a second attempt'. This may have coincided with the arrival of provisions and of Morris's seamen. Yet it was plain they had regained their morale. So, after Clarke's reconnaissance of Tresco, it was decided not to trust to the pilots, but to rely upon the seamen's guidance.[29]

Eighty men were left on Northworthiel 'to alarm and amuse the enemy', while fires were lighted on Tean in the darkness, 'as if we had continued there, the smoke whereof was blown towards the enemy, which somewhat obscured our passage'. This was surely a Blake touch, who had recalled how the enemy at Lyme had launched an attack under cover of a thick mist. Half-way over the enemy glimpsed them, and at once opened the fire with their guns. Morris, who had kept the boats well together, and the seamen were the first to land, and held their ground valiantly until the troops joined them. According to Lereck some of these were driven back into the water by the enemy, who resisted stoutly. Several soldiers waded ashore waist deep, with their bandoliers in their mouths. A fierce charge took place 'even to the club musket'.[30] Leslie says 'they overpowered our men with multitudes and strength of their pikes, having the help of 200 seamen, both to lead them on and to drive on their rear'.[31] In an hour the Royalists were routed. In the darkness Grenville, the governor, managed to reach his boats, hidden among the creeks, and to regain St Mary's though forty men were drowned in the mad rush to get aboard and away. By the next morning the whole island was in Clarke's hands, with twenty-five cannon and the two frigates, the *Michael* and the *Peter*, together with New Grimsby harbour and Bryhar, the island beyond. The Royalists lost a captain and four men killed, while 167 prisoners were taken. The rest had fled: 'none had escaped had we been acquainted with the place'.[32]

Blake at once brought his victuallers and some men-of-war into New Grimsby and sent off a dispatch, by a passing Dutch vessel, to the Speaker. In it he announced the capture of the islands, though he mentioned that 'as yet he had no communication with the shore'. Only four men had been killed.[33] Ayscue also wrote: 'the gaining of these two islands will render St Mary's useless to the enemy, for we now have the road, as well as they, and enjoy a harbour which they have not; so that I perceive they will be forced to a submission'.[34]

Blake's swift and bold decision to turn defeat into victory was rapidly justified, for next day a violent storm arose and drove several of his vessels from their anchors, with the loss of many boats. Had not the victuallers been in harbour, they would have been lost, as they had no ground tackle with which to ride.[35] Two days later, Grenville sent a trumpeter with a list of prisoners, which he proposed should be exchanged. He was instantly sent back again. Five days later, on the 25th, Blake sent in a summons to surrender.[36] But the Royalists resolved instead to die to a man. Leslie advised acceptance, 'that they might preserve their lives to do his Majesty service in another place'. He was called a coward for his pains.[37] But by the 27th the Royalists had weakened and Grenville sent a representative to ask to treat. This was granted though, as Leslie caustically observed, 'upon very high terms'. Hostages were exchanged and were lodged respectively aboard the *Guinea* and in the castle. On 2 May the Commissioners met on Sampson Island, only to break off negotiations next day. 'Their demands' wrote a Parliamentarian, 'being dishonourable for us to grant'.[38]

Blake however did not slacken his efforts. Two houses were built to store the provisions, and a platform was erected on a point looking towards St Mary's, upon which a whole and two demi-culverins were mounted. Some hundred persons assembled to see the first shot fired. Unexpectedly the whole culverin burst, probably from overcharging. The gunner was killed and also Ensign Jeffries, while eight others were wounded. Blake, Ayscue and others standing by narrowly escaped. Nothing daunted, Blake mounted a fresh gun the next day and sent his ships in to bombard St Mary's from the sea.[39] Pack, in the *Amity*, chased a vessel, which was trying to run the blockade, to France. After a chase

of twenty leagues Pack caught her and took her into Falmouth.[40]
On 10 May the Council of State wrote to thank Blake for his
care and diligence. But they also warned him of 'a design to
destroy our ships by fire, in a secret manner conveyed'. They
therefore bade him look to his gunners and mates and 'to allow
no stranger in the powder room upon any pretence whatsoever'.
They went on to express their fear that relief and supplies might
be thrown into Scilly and they urged him, with all the force at his
disposal, to effect the reduction of St Mary's and not to dismiss his
own or Ayscue's fleet until this was done.[41]

Meanwhile, on the 9th, one of his captured seamen slipped over
the side of the ship in which he was detained, secured her boat
and got back to Tresco. He reported that the enemy were 'not
above 600 men' and probably also spoke of the dejection that was
spreading among them. Next day a tremendous storm broke which
forced the warships out to sea. It blew down the soldiers' tents,
and drove ashore as total wrecks the enemy's two best frigates,
'which rode under the Hugh Hill, near their shore, to prevent our
boats coming to land there'.[42] The last two obstacles to a landing
on St Mary's had gone though blockhouses and forts, joined
together by breastworks, still remained. The garrison, however,
was too scanty to be able to hold them with any chance of success.

Blake, calculating upon the effect produced by the loss of the
two frigates, saw that he could gain his ends more speedily and
cheaply by negotiation than by force. He therefore sent in another
offer to treat. His personal experience, in four sieges, made him
realise that St Mary's Castle could only be taken by a prolonged
siege, or by a costly storm. Of the surrender of Dunster, he had
written, 'probably it might have been obtained upon other terms,
if the price of time and blood had not prevailed above other
arguments'. Leslie had observed, 'they were afraid to venture upon
this place without more forces,which they had sent for, and thought
it better to gain the place upon treaty, than to expect the coming
of their forces, and to venture the hazard of a battle'.[43]

Grenville accepted the offer and eventually it was agreed that
the Irish should be sent to Ireland and the English to Scotland,
while the bishop was to return to his Fatherless-in-God Diocese
in Down. Here he complained that he would be in more danger
from the Scots than from the Parliamentarians. He asked therefore
that he might live in a parliamentary garrison for his own safety,

'where I am sure my soul shall be more vexed than ever Lot's was in Sodom'.[44] The islands and castle, with fifty barrels of powder and match, two-thirds of the shot and all the ordnance, together with all shipping, were to be surrendered on 1 June. Sir John Grenville was to be paid £1,000 for the guns left behind; while an indemnity was granted to all for acts past: and estates were to be free from sequestration. All officers and men were allowed to carry away their personal goods without molestation or seizure.[45]

The reduction took place none too soon: 'for they would probably have made themselves too strong for us – for they depended upon 900 more men to have strengthened the garrison this summer and to have made up their fleet to eighteen sail'.[46] Owing to foul weather the garrison was unable to march out until 3 June, when they were permitted to do so with full honours of war. Leslie considered the terms to be very generous and they were taken to Parliament by Colonels Axtell, Sadler and Le Hunt, who had been imprisoned in a cellar in the castle.[47]

A sequel should be recorded. On 14 June, 'we had that night (at Plymouth) a great quarrel between the seamen and soldiers, much harm had likely to have ensued, only it was timely prevented; there were many bloody pates, and one or two dangerously wounded, but none slain; the soldiers with the butt ends of muskets and swords, and the seamen with oars and poles; after a few broken pates the quarrel was taken up and all made friends.' Someone, it may well be supposed, had incautiously asked the fatal question, 'who did the work'. On the 28th Blake came in to Plymouth, after the Irish had been landed at Kinsale.[48]

On 2 June Tromp had again arrived off the Scillies. He sent Captain Evertsen aboard Blake, who was lying off the North Island with seven ships. Blake informed him of the surrender, with the bitter news that 'the pirates are to retain all their ships and prizes and goods, which they have captured from the Parliament and other nations, and they were to be removed to whatever place they desired'. It was a direct snub to the Dutch, though it seems to have been misunderstood. For all the shipping was surrendered to Blake and the soldiers sent to such places as they desired. Tromp wrote in his diary, 'when I learned that information and perceived that there was nothing more to be done, I went off on a cruise round the Channel Islands'. Ayscue was at last free to sail for the Barbados, which he did on the 27th.[49]

In less than two months Blake had subdued the islands and had made the western seas safe for the Commonwealth shipping. It was a great achievement, for it was wrought at the cost of seven men killed and without the loss of a single warship from a fleet which had to operate off a dangerous coast, with narrow channels and treacherous reefs, amid sudden storms and changing weather. He had instantly picked out the key to the position, and his was the brain that planned the operation. He had nevertheless conferred with Clarke and had wisely and tactfully left to him the control of the military operations. When, through no fault of Clarke's, his raw and inexperienced troops had failed him, Blake refused to be deterred. At Clarke's request he had instantly given him the support of 200 experienced seamen, with which to lead the attack. This was in accord with his established tactic of never giving the enemy the time or opportunity to consolidate his position. Instead he instantly sprang upon him a surprise attack in the silence and dark of the night. With the command of the sea he had established a rigorous blockade. Then, choosing the psychological moment, he completed by negotiation what he had begun by force. Though he could be bold enough when occasion called for it, he never threw away the lives of his men unnecessarily, and it was this quality that led them to serve him so faithfully. As he is reported to have said to Myngs, 'he loved not a foolhardy captain'. So at Scilly he showed a deep sense of the value of a fleet in being. He had shown Tromp that he would brook no interference in Commonwealth matters. To a beaten foe he displayed his usual generosity. Thus he anticipated the maxim of another great Englishman: 'in defeat defiance, in victory magnanimity'. Never did his 'passive courage', as Pepys called it, more signally exhibit itself than in these amphibious operations off the Isles of Scilly.

But now a new danger threatened the Commonwealth. Charles the Second, who had landed in Scotland, found his position at Stirling outflanked by Cromwell's march through Fife. So, suddenly in July he broke up his camp and marched south. On 6 August he crossed the border on the wild career that was to end at Worcester. In alarm orders poured forth from the Council of State. Among them were those for Blake at Plymouth. On the 19th they sent him a commission to command all the forces in Cornwall, Devon, Somerset and Dorset in the absence of Major-General Desborough, who had been sent off to deal with the invader.[50] However, this never took effect. For, on the 22nd, it was speedily followed by another. The council wrote 'General Popham, having lately died, you must forthwith go to sea in person to keep those affairs in good order, and to prevent any impression that may be made on the seaman by mis-representation of affairs'. They also charged him 'to take care to prevent any supplies being sent from foreign parts to the King of Scotland: it will be convenient for your better managing that affair to come unto the Downs as soon as you can settle matters upon those coasts'.[51]

Before he sailed for the Downs, in the *Victory*, with the *Phoenix* and *Swan* in company, he called attention, on 27 August, to 'divers poor mariners' who had been pressed in western ports, and discharged at Plymouth. As they lived far from London, Edward Pattison with other Plymouth citizens had, out of their charity, paid their tickets which were promises to pay at a future date. But they had been unable to get repayment and had been without their money for some time and now began to fear they would lose it altogether. Blake certified the correctness of their payments and asked that it should be refunded, and 'thereby Mr Pattison be not put to unnecessary attendance'.[52] It was by this attention to petty detail that Blake won the trust of his seamen and of the ordinary public as well. On 3 September, he arrived in the Downs. On the same day Prince Charles was defeated at Worcester and the last hopes of the Royalists in England were shattered.[53]

CHAPTER 9

Amphibious Operations: II Jersey

*

WITH the Scilly Isles now in their hands, the Council of State now determined to complete its task by securing the last Royalist strongholds, those in the Channel Islands. From here a host of privateers had preyed upon English shipping during the Civil War and up to this very moment. Though the islanders were largely for the Parliament, they were held in check by three powerful Castles: castle Cornet in Guernsey, and two in Jersey, Elizabeth Castle held by Sir George Carteret and Mont Orgueil Castle, held by Philip Carteret. Practically speaking a stalemate existed. For the inhabitants could not storm the castles, nor could the garrisons leave the shelter of their walls. In Guernsey Major Harrison commanded a small parliamentary force, while in Jersey Carteret had some small support from the islanders.

On 20 September, 1651, orders were sent to Colonel Heane to 'prepare for an expedition thither'.[1] With a vivid recollection of Blake's brilliant operations against Scilly, the council also wrote to him on the same date. 'We have given instructions to Colonel Heane for reducing the Isle of Jersey, and for the better effecting, we desire you, with such ships as you shall think fit, to set sail for that place and there give your best advice and assistance for its reduction.'[2]

Blake selected the *Happy Entrance* of thirty-eight guns, under Captain Coppin, for his flagship, with the *Phoenix* (thirty-eight), Captain Wadsworth the *Elizabeth* (thirty-six), Captain Reeves, the *Pearl* (twenty-four), Captain Cuttance, the *Laurel* (thirty-six), a new frigate, Captain Taylor, the *Tresco* (twenty-four), Captain William Blake, the *Eagle* (fourteen), Captain Dover, the *John* (twenty-eight), Captain Bennett, the *Tenth Whelp* (sixteen), Captain Gething, the *Hart* (ten), Captain Collins, the *Paragon* (thirty-four), Captain Badiley, the *Nightingale* (twenty-four), Captain Reynolds, the *Hunter* (twenty-two), and a battery ship. With the transports the fleet consisted of some eighty vessels.[3]

Heane was in Bridport assembling his troops. They consisted of his own regiment, six companies of Sir Hardres Waller's foot, with two troops of horse, commanded by Captains West and Margerum; in all some 2,200 men.[4] On 17 October they embarked and sailed from the Nothe, at Weymouth, at 4 p.m. Some five leagues out a violent storm from the N.E. blew with such force as to cause considerable damage. The fleet was forced to return to Weymouth as the open boats could not live upon such a sea. On the 19th in the morning it sailed again, and at midnight anchored under the shelter of Sark. Early next day the fleet made for Jersey and at noon it anchored in St Ouen's Bay, but it was still too rough for the small boats to be hoisted out.[5] The bay had always been favoured by invaders for, between L'Etac and Corbiere Point, large vessels could ride in safety from the easterly gales though it was also very much exposed to westerly ones.

Sir Philip Carteret, Sir George's brother, looking out of the windows of his Manor at St Ouen, saw, to his surprise and dismay, the arrival of the fleet. Instantly he sent a messenger to warn his brother at St Elizabeth's Castle, who had the bells of twelve parishes ring the alarm. So vigorously in one case that a bell was actually broken. Sir George promptly assembled 300 horse and dragoons, 2,000 militia men and six small field pieces and brought them down to the bay.[6] The sea still continued too rough for a landing to be attempted, and at night Sir George tried to persuade some Flemish sailors to take fireships among the enemy fleet, for he was no novice in naval warfare. But they refused to take the risk. Early next morning Blake sent a double shallop from his flagship, with a letter from Heane to the islanders, inviting them to surrender and so avoid pointless bloodshed.[7] When the quick-witted Sir George saw the shallop approach, he guessed her mission so he ordered guns to be trained upon her and fired several shots and forced her to return. He knew 'that the greater part of his men desired nothing more than to surrender without a fight'. This nearly led to a mutiny, for his men, even the most loyal of them, protested that at the very least the mission might have been given a hearing.[8]

With the return of the shallop Blake, seeing that offers of peace were useless, ordered some frigates to hoist sail and to get close to the shore and to begin firing. Carteret's men, who never imagined that ships of that size would venture within musket-shot of the

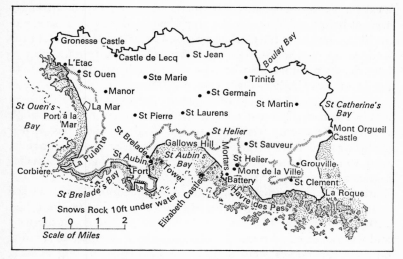

Sketch map of Jersey in 1651

beach, were so terrified that they showed signs of breaking. Carteret wisely withdrew them to the shelter of the sand dunes. As the terrified islanders cowered behind the sandhills he, with some of his officers, remained contemptuously in the open, in order to give them confidence, while the tall ships belched fire and the smoke slowly drifted away to leeward. Then, as they became accustomed to the thunder of the guns, the islanders shamed by Carteret's courage began to return and to fire muskets at the ships. Mouth valiant they abused the Parliament men as 'traitors, rebels and murderers of their King'. For four hours the bombardment continued, in which 500 cannon shots were fired, which killed seven or eight men and wounded a few others. The reply was made from the forts along the bay and from the muskets and field pieces, but with little effect. However a shot was registered on the *Eagle*, which pierced her side and fell into her hold, without doing any further damage.[9]

As the rough weather still held, Blake decided to sail round to St Brelade's Bay to find out if the conditions there were more favourable for his purpose. As Carteret saw the ships move off, he felt bound to follow, as he dared not risk a landing with only the local forces to oppose it. So he marched his own men there. He arrived before the fleet, for the ships had to sail well out to sea to avoid the danger of the Corbiere rocks. Carteret therefore had time to draw up bodies of troops upon the beach, and to hold the two batteries in readiness. So he was able to welcome the ships with fire from these bodies. Blake now put into service the manoeuvre he had used at Lyme. He sent part of his ships eastwards to St Aubin's and St Clement's Bays, while the other returned to St Ouen's. The enemy were thus forced to divide their troops. Sir Philip was ordered by Carteret to send back to St Ouen's 300 men, who were to disguise their weakness by splitting into smaller bodies so as to appear more numerous.[10]

Blake and Heane now reconnoitred the position. They observed a line of works, running from one end of the bay to the other, with two batteries. The bay afforded good anchorage on the west and was sheltered all round by high ground. But time was running out, for the horses were suffering from being so long aboard, while their forage was getting very low. As Kempton Hilliard, a soldier aboard the ships, wrote 'all this while the wind continued so high that we could not tell what to do, seeing apparent ruin to us all if the wind ceased not. About six at night we considered that though the weather was not seasonable, and sixteen sail of our fleet left at Guernsey, our horse provisions was quite spent, so that they must be lost if we either lay still or returned; and we, being willing to do the work we were sent about, resolved to throw ourselves upon the Lord, and tomorrow to endeavour to do it'. However in the evening the wind dropped 'and within an hour after we had a calm sea and quiet weather'.[11] So at 3 a.m. next day, a council was held on the flagship at which it was decided to make a landing at St Ouen's Bay 'as being the most convenient place to land in'. Rising from their knees, in true Puritan fashion, they began at 5 a.m. to boat their men. Blake gave orders that the boats and vessels that carried the horse and foot were to be manned out of his own ships, as the hired vessels' masters refused 'the risk of damaging their craft by beaching them ashore'.[12] With a vivid remembrance of Scilly, he put men of naval experience in charge of the flotilla: Coppin, Reeves, Taylor, Blake, Cuttance and Gething, with Dover leading the forlorn hope.[13] Then they set sail for St Ouen's Bay.[14]

From a Royalist pen we have another picture of Carteret.

Through the clear night he watched the movements of the ships from the low tide rocks in the bay and estimated their forces to be about 4,000 men. As day broke he reviewed his little army and, to his dismay, found it diminished. He said nothing for fear of spreading alarm among the faithful. Leaving the dragoons and musketeers to aid the local militia at St Brelade's, he marched back to St Ouen's with the rest.[15] Blake had left some of his ships at St Brelade's. These now sailed close in shore and opened a bombardment. As a letter from the *Happy Entrance* reported: 'when we weighed from Brelades Bay, the General, to amuse and distract the enemy and keep them in alarm, left part of the fleet there and by their guns and shooting in their boats did so alarm them that the Pastor of a village in that bay with his flock and the forces ran away to Elizabeth Castle'.[16]

By the time Blake had got round to St Ouen's Bay, the tide had begun to ebb and there was nothing for it but to wait for the next. He was cheered, however, by finding that, in his absence, Major Harrison with 200 soldiers had arrived from Guernsey in sixteen ships which had run there for shelter after being scattered by a storm.[17]

As he waited for the tide Blake distracted the enemy by sailing to L'Etac, as if he was about to land there. His flagship led the fleet, with the frigates, shallops and other vessels and boats following in battle array. Carteret's weary troops had to plod after him on the sandy shore, their spirits being further damped by a steady fine rain.[18] To their discomfort the fleet now put about and sailed back across the bay. The miserable islanders, who had been under arms for 48 hours, had again to trudge after the ships. 'The *Elizabeth*, *Phoenix*, battery ship and *Eagle* began to play upon the forts with their great guns and so continued near two hours continually pelting insomuch that they did execution both on horse and foot and prevented them getting into bodies'. Apparently the casualties were only one horse and two men.

Blake's manoeuvres, however, had been dictated by other reasons than those of merely wearying the foe: for when the fleet arrived in St Ouen's Bay the tide had turned and the men were forced to lie in open boats, 'in much danger, without bread or beer, until the next tide'.[19] 'In this predicament General Blake and his officers were exceeding active and careful, showing much valour in the business'.[20]

Carteret too had problems. The wearied and disheartened militia again began to show signs of flight and he had to rally them at the sword's point. At this, three or four levelled their muskets at him, 'which he pretended not to notice, and did so much with threats and entreaties that he got them into order to receive the foe'. When night fell, the foot, drawn up in position, lay down to rest while the horse went to pasture a quarter of a league away. Dark clouds obscured the sky and the sea 'began to moan as it usually does on that coast before a storm' while a solitary figure paced ceaselessly up and down the edge of the shore, the tireless and faithful Carteret, observing every movement of the enemy. At 11 p.m. the tide being at half-ebb, he noticed a large ship hauling on her cable as if to run aground. Rousing his little force and having sent for the cavalry, he asked the fishermen if such a ship, at that state of the tide, could be beached in such a place. Every man answered that it was impossible, 'but they had not finished speaking when two cannon-shot, passing over their heads, showed them plainly to the contrary'. As the horse had not yet come up, Carteret went to look for them. When he met them two thirds had taken to flight 'and the officers told him he might as well do the same, unless he would throw away his life in sheer lightness of heart, adding that they were nevertheless ready to obey him'. Carteret answered, 'very well then, in God's name let us go to meet them, that it may not be said that they had us without a fight'. And he led them to the beach to within a pistol-shot of the enemy.[21]

Meanwhile the boats had hoisted sail, cut their cables 'for expedition's sake' and run ashore. They grounded in from three to seven feet of water, and the forlorn hope, led by Captain Dover, leapt overboard some waist and some neck deep in water and waded ashore.[22] The Royalist account says they had 'in front of their shallops great bridges which gave passage to ten men abreast' so that they were able to land 1,200 men.[23] Carteret acted promptly. He ordered Colonel Bovil to charge with the horse, while he drew up the foot. Bovil flung himself at the head of the boats and even up to the muzzles of the muskets and so impetuous was his charge that the enemy were forced back into the water. Dover and his lieutenant were wounded, and four men were slain and sixteen wounded.[24] Coppin, Reeves, Taylor, Blake, Cuttance and Gething also 'did very gallantly in this service'.[25] For half an hour a fierce conflict raged and had the horse supported the foot with a sabre charge, thus giving them time to reload, the result might have been different. Only the St Ouen militia remained and that only because of the presence of Carteret. They fired a volley and the horse were about to charge again, when Bovil was struck down by a bullet. This sudden loss so bewildered them that all that Carteret could get them to do was to carry off his body.[26] Heane had by this time disembarked more men, and with three volleys forced the islanders to run. Carteret accordingly could only retreat, leaving behind his guns, since the wagoners had fled, with the exception of two, one of which was saved by man handling. He made his way to St Brelades, where he found the Parliamentarians had merely given an alarm. So he moved on to St Aubins, where he took boat to its tower, bidding the governor hold out and promising to send him supplies by water from Elizabeth Castle, to which he retired.[27]

Heane, after he had driven away the enemy, drew his men up on the sands seizing twelve guns and some colours, while the horses were swum ashore. He then advanced about a mile inland, and encamped upon some hilly ground until 5 a.m. Finding no enemy to oppose him, he marched round the shore to St Brelade's Bay, where he drew up on a nearby hill. To get rations for his tired and hungry men he then marched down to the bay itself, where he secured twelve abandoned guns. Resuming his march he came, at 3 p.m. in the afternoon, to a hill from which Elizabeth Castle and St Aubin's Tower, lying in the sea beneath it, were both visible. The tower greeted him with several great shot and Heane at once sent in a summons to be answered in two hours. Here he learned that Carteret and his men had retreated to Elizabeth and Mont Orgueil Castles. The tower had by now capitulated on the condition that its garrison could withdraw to Elizabeth castle. This was granted, and that night they left by water. In the tower twelve guns were taken and, what was more important, a safe harbour was secured in which ships could lie; the value of which became apparent next day when exceedingly stormy weather broke.[28] All Blake's ships got in safely, but unluckily the *Tresco*, commanded by William Blake, the general's cousin, anchored too near the guns of Elizabeth Castle. In trying to shift her position, she struck one of the sunken rocks and foundered with 300 hands.[29] Chevalier's

Journal records however that a dozen of her crew had taken her boat and gone pillaging, when she foundered.[30]

On Sunday, 26 October, Blake sent a dispatch to the Speaker. 'It hath pleased God, that after much conflicting with seas and winds and other difficulties, and a short dispute with the enemy: about 11 at night on Wednesday last, our forces landed on the south (he meant west) side of the island in a bay called Portala Mar, with good resolution and success. The enemy, after a hot charge with their horse flying before them, forsaking divers small works and forts; the next day our men took by surrender the tower of St Aubin with fourteen guns in it, which affordeth refuge and safety for our victualling ships and others. Carteret is gone to Elizabeth Castle which is blocked up by a party. The rest of our men are now about the fort of Mont Orgueil, our ships riding before it. We have not above four or five men lost as far as I can hear: some barques and other vessels are still in that bay aground, and have received some damage since the landing. It hath been such weather, as I could not have intercourse with the shore, so that I cannot give your Honour a perfect narrative'.[31]

Heane, without any delay, had marched on to St Helier with his regiment and West's horse. His purpose was to contain Elizabeth Castle, 'which is within a musket and a half shot of this town upon an island in the sea'. The castle was thought to be impregnable, as it was surrounded by sunken rocks, which prevented any frigate from approaching near it, while it was too far from land for any ordinary artillery to make any impression upon its massive walls. On the 24th he summoned Carteret to surrender, to which was returned but 'a scurrilous reply'. Leaving Major Ebzery with Waller's six companies of foot, three companies from Guernsey and Margerum's horse to watch Carteret, Heane, with his own regiment and West's cavalry, moved on to Mont Orgueil. Here he encamped in a rabbit warren and, on the 25th, summoned the governor, Sir Philip, to surrender. He offered generous terms with a warning that if any of his men were killed, there would be severe reprisals and he required 'a speedy answer before I am put to the trouble of bringing up my train of artillery and mortar pieces hither'. Carteret asked to consult his brother at Elizabeth Castle. Heane refused and Carteret threatened to starve the prisoners in the castle. But as an English master gunner and another

officer, backed by the garrison, threatened to hand over Sir Philip
if he did not capitulate, he accepted the favourable terms offered.
Carteret was allowed to retain his estates and to take away two
horses and to carry away some of his goods. An Act of Oblivion
for past offences was granted to all, and some sixty men who
wished to go to Elizabeth Castle were allowed to do so, while others
who wished to go overseas, were given free passage. In the castle
were found forty-two guns, 1,000 arms, much ammunition and
two months' provision for seventy men.[32]

Well might the triumphant Hilliard reflect, 'Truly I cannot but
wonder to see how the Lord doth strike these people with fear and
terror that they should so suddenly deliver up such a stronghold;
it is seated very high upon a round rock and many vaults cut in it
out of the firm rock, that in my judgement tis neither stormable nor
to be injured by mortar pieces'. He ended in true soldier fashion,
'my true love to you and my dear sister; I am well, only a little
lousy'.[33]

By giving such generous terms, Heane had set himself free to
tackle Elizabeth Castle, a much harder nut to crack. Sir George
had divided the garrison into three companies, which mounted
guard in turns. As he knew the besiegers possessed scaling ladders,
everyone had to be under arms at night, when the tide was out,
to watch for an attack from the land.[34] Heane, however, had no
intention of throwing away the lives of his men in a costly attempt
to storm. So, on 29 October, he erected batteries of guns, some
of which he had brought from Mont Orgueil, consisting of six
thirty-six pounders, on the town hill. But they only succeeded in
knocking down some turf parapets. So, four days later, three more
batteries, one of four and the other two of two guns, were mounted
on the same spot. With great difficulty three great mortars, one of
which weighed 450 lbs., were hoisted out of the ships and dragged
to the south end of the town hill. Breastworks nine feet high were
built around them, and Thomas Wright, a skilful engineer, took
charge of them.[35] A night sortie, made by fifteen horsemen from
the castle, brought back an inhabitant, who spoke of 'two cannons
as large as barrels'. There was much speculation as to what they
could be, but seven or eight days later their reality was proved by
'a huge bomb which fell in the midst of the castle, confirming the
belief that they were mortars of an extraordinary size, the bomb
being actually thirty inches in diameter'.[36] This was probably

R.B.–I

exaggerated, but records exist of payment made for some of sixteen and eighteen inches.[37]

The first bomb burst on the ground without doing any damage, but the third had a disastrous effect. It fell on the church, which had a large store of provisions beneath it, and set fire to twelve barrels of powder, threw down five or six houses and buried forty men beneath the ruins. This unexpected disaster filled the garrison with consternation and Sir George tried to reassure them by telling them it was not the bomb, but the powder that caused the explosion. Some men in the outer defences, however, threw down their arms and deserted to the enemy, telling them of the terror in the garrison. Heane at once sent in another summons, which Carteret answered by opening fire upon his camp. Yet more desertions followed, including the master mason, who knew the defences intimately. One man was caught and hanged but this proved no deterrent 'the fear of the bombs being greater than that of the rope'. Envoys, who had been sent to the King, who had safely escaped to France, returned with the news that he could give no hope of relief and instead gave Carteret full permission to surrender if he was obliged to do so.[38]

Heane, having learned of the tremendous effect of the bombs, continued to fire over as many as he could. One landed on six corn heaps and burned them all: others passed over the castle, which led to Lady Carteret and the women being evacuated to St Malo.[39] The powder had to be buried in various spots to preserve it safely. Blake, too, had ordered a strict blockade to prevent small vessels from slipping in from France. For this purpose the small French island of Chose, between Jersey and Normandy, was seized. Frigates, too, lay off Noir Mount, Les Pas and in St Aubin's Road, with the result that every blockade runner was captured.[40]

Misfortune now overtook Heane. Mr Wright, in his enthusiasm, overcharged the mortars with the result 'that the middle of them have broken their carriages, and the biggest is in a manner unusable'. Heane at once sent to London for another and, in order to conceal the mishap, sent in a summons on 3 December.[41] All Carteret's officers begged him to accede, on the grounds that hardly any provisions were left and that there was little likelihood of any help being sent to them. Realising that the position was hopeless, he gave way. On the 5th he wrote to Heane: 'although the consideration of any damage we are likely to receive by your Grenados, an advantage which you may imagine to have hitherto gained upon us, be too weak an argument to incline me to harbour your desire, yet I conceive it not amiss to hear what you have to propose unto me'. Commissioners were agreed upon. A delightful passage in the Royalist account records: 'All the officers and soldiers had orders to be under arms on the arrival of the Commissioners and to talk to each other as though they were not greatly concerned about the success of the treaty; but the bearer of this order explained it so ill, that instead of this, as soon as the men appeared, the whole garrison gave a shout as though of joy, which made them think that however good a face the governor put on it, he must be in difficulties; and this was the cause, as they afterwards admitted, that they did not give us good terms as they would otherwise have done'.[42] Heane must have reflected grimly upon Carteret's letter, as he now drew up twelve Articles of Surrender. Elizabeth Castle, with all it contained, with vessels, shallops and boats, was to be delivered up on 12 December, at noon. Sir George was to go to St Malo with his goods, money and plate. He and his men were free to go either to France or Virginia, and the English to England, if they did not take up arms again. Heane was to give them passes and transport. Prisoners on both sides were to be freed, while Heane would care for the sick. The garrison were to march out with full honours of war, though they were to hand over their arms afterwards. The private soldiers were allowed to retain their swords, and the officers their horses, swords, armour and pistols. In the castle were fifty-three guns, 450 muskets, with powder, match and shot, while eight vessels were in the harbours. Everyone was indemnified against past offences.[43]

Blake had very properly left the completion of the capture to Heane and his troops. He turned his attention to Guernsey. Parliament controlled the island, with the exception of Castle Cornet, which was in the charge of Colonel Burgess. Blake arrived off the island early in November, for a letter from Weymouth, dated the 12th, says that a ship had come in whose master had anchored off Guernsey, where he found Blake in treaty with the governor. As the master did not go on shore, he did not know the issue. However he saw the General's boat go freely into the pier, and boats likewise passing between the castle and the ships under flags of truce. On Saturday morning last (the 9th) as he was a little way from Guernsey, going to England, he saw many guns fired both from the town and the Castle, which he thought must mean some agreement for the surrender of the island. But Blake and Burgess could not agree on terms, though they were in treaty for some time. 'The enemy were so high in their propositions' that Blake broke off negotiations. He refused to risk either his men or his ships in an attempt to take the place, for as supplies from Jersey were now cut off, the fall of the castle was merely a matter of time. So he put the affair into the hands of Colonel Bingham, Lt-Governor of Guernsey, and sailed for England where he arrived on the 21st.[44]

On the same day that Elizabeth Castle was evacuated, Burgess surrendered and on 19 December the garrison marched out with full honours of war, with drums beating, colours flying, bullet in mouth and match lighted at both ends,* and then laid down their arms on the pier at St Peter Port. The terms were honourable as well they might be, for the place had held out for nearly nine years. All were allowed to keep their swords and granted an indemnity, with rations for twenty days, with transport to England, France or Jersey, as each man selected. No property was to be sequestrated. Great quantities of guns, arms, ammunition and stores were left in the fortress.[45]

On 19 November, Parliament sent letters of thanks, approving the Articles of Surrender for Mont Orgueil, to Blake, Heane and their officers and men. Blake was also made a member of the Ordnance Committee, of the Admiralty Committee, of another for looking into the complaints, made by the Duke of Tuscany, against the Levant Company; and of a committee for the disposing of Scottish prisoners. And finally, as if in happy token that he had fought his last fight against his own countrymen, his name was added to the Committee for Foreign Affairs, on 8 January. From henceforth Parliamentarians and Royalists alike were to be proud to acclaim him as a fellow Englishman.[46] Yet Blake was no honorary member: for he attended the council and various committees fourteen times in December, thirteen in January, eleven in February and six in March.[47]

In the Jersey operations the guiding hand of Blake can be recognised. Once again he had selected a landing place remote from the enemy's chief strength; once again the tide and weather had prevented a landing. By a brilliant stroke Blake had again

* In honourable recognition that the soldiers had fought gallantly.

turned a setback into an advantage. By repeating Warwick's manoeuvre at Lyme, he had forced Carteret to keep his men constantly upon the move. He had recognised the mistake, made at Scilly, of sending soldiers to land without any experienced officers and seamen to direct the boats. Though the tide had failed him, at night, by the skilful direction of the seamen, the soldiers were set ashore and the exhausted enemy eventually driven back. Then in a series of rapid advances, in which the defences collapsed like a pack of cards, Heane had contained the castles by land and Blake by sea. Though he worked in the closest collaboration with Heane, he had properly left to him the direction of the military operations. Both men had resolutely refused to throw away the lives of their men in costly and useless storming of the massively built castles. Instead they had relied upon blockade by sea and land, and by the shattering power of the mortars. Then, seizing the psychological moment, they completed by negotiation what they had begun by force. Once again they had met mishap by defiance, and victory with magnanimity.

There was still to be no rest for Blake. His committees called for much of his time and so too did naval matters. Some twenty letters, addressed to the Navy Commissioners, are concerned with administration and with personnel. They reveal his care with detail and justice, both to officers and men, by which he was quietly and effectively to promote the efficiency and well-being of the navy. On 4 March he was ordered to take command of the fleet, for another ten months. Six days later he was asked to go to Deptford, Woolwich and Chatham, to hasten out the Summer Fleet, 'for which there is extraordinary occasion'.[48] The activities of the Dutch had aroused the suspicions of the Council of State: so much so that when he took command in the Downs at the end of March, Cromwell and Dennis Bond, a member of the Admiralty Committee, were sent to confer with him. His finest hour had sounded.

CHAPTER 10

The Approach of War with the Dutch

*

As the Commonwealth was now firmly established, their thoughts turned towards an alliance with Holland. After the death of William the Second of Orange, the Dutch had formed themselves into a republic, stoutly Protestant and the foremost commercial power in Europe. Walter Strickland, a man of first-hand acquaintance with Holland, summed the idea up: 'let us make them one nation'.[1] United the two peoples would have the monopoly of the world trade in their hands.

He and Oliver St John, the Lord Chief Justice, were sent as Ambassadors Extraordinary to the Hague. On their arrival on 17 March, 1651, a mob, incited by Royalist *émigrés*, shouted abuse and even broke their windows.[2] It was not a happy start to negotiations. The Dutch Commissioners were startled by the English demand for 'a more strict and intimate alliance and Union' with its terms undefined.[3] The Ambassadors demanded, too, that the property of the House of Orange should be confiscated and the exiles expelled.[4]

But the Dutch had just won their independence from Spain, led by the House of Orange. To be absorbed into the more powerful State of England, which would make them a mere satellite, was unthinkable. They refused to have the will of the Ambassadors forced upon them and negotiations were broken off and on 20 June the Ambassadors returned to England.[5] They bent their minds towards persuading their countrymen to aim at securing the carrying trade of Europe, at the expense of the Dutch.

They were rewarded by the passing of the Navigation Act on 20 August, 1651. It decreed that no goods should be imported into England except in English ships, or in the ships of the country which produced the goods imported.[6] It struck directly at the vast Dutch carrying trade. In alarm the Dutch, on 15 December, 1651, sent over three envoys, headed by the aged Pauw. Their instructions were to get the Act repealed. They were to establish the doctrine that the flag covered the goods, except in the case of contraband: that any nation had the right to carry any goods any-where with out interference. This obviously raised the question of the right of search.[7]

Yet English insistence on Sovereignty of the Seas, and dipping of the flag in token of it in the present temper of English and Dutch seamen, was likely to bring about trouble.

It arose from the anger and dislike of Englishmen for a pros-perous neighbour, whose maritime trade was so much greater than their own. In the Civil War the Dutch had seized the chance to fasten upon, and make their own, the carrying trade of Europe:[8] to say nothing of the arms the Orange party had sent over to the Royalists.[9] Strickland and St John had done their work only too well in inflaming the minds of their countrymen against the Dutch.

The Dutch now decided to fit out 150 ships.[10] This was taken as evidence that they were determined to make good their position by force, rather than by argument. Though their Ambassadors declared that the vessels were intended to maintain free navigation, and that they had not the least intention of doing the slightest harm to neutral States, especially England, the Council of State saw in their action, a challenge. The Dutch meant to enforce their claims by offensive means. More so, when such a fleet could deny to the English the right to capture and search Dutch ships suspected of having French goods aboard.

They accepted the supposed challenge. On 11 March, 1652, Blake was ordered to assemble his ships in the Downs. He was bidden to go to Deptford, Woolwich and Chatham 'to examine the cause of the backwardness of the fleet; to let them know whose fault it was and to remove negligent officers, and to place honest men in their room'.[11] On the 25th Cromwell and Dennis Bond, of the Admiralty Committee, were sent to Chatham to see how things stood, and to hasten out the ships there. Then they were to confer with Blake, as to what instructions were 'fit and necessary to be given to the Commander-in-Chief of the fleet'. Orders poured forth to the Victuallers, the Commissioners of the Navy, the Admiralty Committee and to the officers of the various ports.[12]

Nor were the Dutch behind in their preparations. Tromp was appointed to command. Instructions were submitted to him by the States General and, at his suggestion, he was directed to free Dutch merchantmen from 'visits and search and to engage, and if possible, to capture all foreign ships attempting to visit or search Dutch ships'.[13] With both sides in a state of nervous tension, the slightest spark might trigger off a conflict.

In England the control of naval affairs was in the hands of a committee of the Council of State, known as the Admiralty Committee, with Sir Henry Vane the Younger as its chairman, and Robert Coytmor as its Secretary. Under this body was the Committee of the Navy and Customs. It took no practical part in the administration, which it was requested to leave to the Navy Commissioners, and in 1654 it was dissolved.[14]

As Oppenheim wrote: 'the brunt of administrative work and of responsibility fell on the Navy Commissioners who – laboured with an attention to the minutest details of their daily duties, with a personal eagerness to ensure perfection, and a broad sense of their ethical relation towards the seamen and workers, of whom they were at once the employers and protectors, with a success the Admiralty never attained before, and has never equalled since.'[15]

The Admirals and captains at sea were ordered to address the Commissioners directly on all administrative details. Matters of the highest importance were to be left to the Admiralty Committee to deal with which, however, after having decided upon a course of action, often deferred to the wisdom of the Navy Commissioners, if they disagreed.[16]

The actual command of the fleet was entrusted to the Generals-at-Sea, who were now free from the interference of local authorities. This had been one of the handicaps of the Admirals and Captains in the Civil War. The new system provided for the subordination of one naval authority to another.

Oppenheim wrote thus about the seamen: 'For the first time they found themselves well-treated, comparatively punctually paid, properly clothed, well fed, cared for when sick or wounded and promised advantages in the shape of prize money, never previously allowed'.[17] This was certainly not the case in the Civil War. Warwick had to ask for money and mutiny was threatened by the men who did not get their pay. Pay was often deferred; in lieu of it tickets, or promises to pay, were substituted for cash. No person in his senses would accept such cheques post-dated to infinity. The victuals were often bad and clothes were lacking. These things were probably at the bottom of the seamen's revolt to the Prince of Wales in 1648. The fact was that Parliament were desperately short of money, and this fact continued right through the seventeenth century. Save for this handicap the new system, for the moment, worked well.

At the end of May, 1652, the Dutch had 118 ships ready for sea.[18] Against these Blake had ninety-nine ships ready in January, 1652. Six more were in the Straits under Penn: another eight were with Sir George Ayscue at the Barbados: two had gone to Virginia; another three, under Appelton, were convoying vessels to the Mediterranean, and four more, under Badiley, were on the same duty, while Thorrowgood was taking two ships to the Straits. This made an addition of twenty-nine ships. In answer to the Dutch order to set out 150 vessels, merchantmen were ordered to be hired.[19]

England's naval finance was a heavy burden as the estimates for 1652 amounted to £829,490, the previous revenue assigned to it being only £376,000.[20] But Parliament was supreme: it could borrow money, and assign revenue, as it pleased. Unlike the States-General it was not liable to the obstructions of seven different Boards of Admiralty. The lack of a central control and administration was to prove a fatal disadvantage to the Dutch, as they stood on the brink of a naval war. They were to enter upon it with an overwhelming handicap.[21]

Yet they possessed a navy with a long tradition of victory, backed by a numerous mercantile marine, and a tough sea-going population. Their ships were commanded by numerous captains of great experience, led by the greatest Admiral of his age, Tromp. Though his flagship, the *Brederode*,[22] was of 800 tons and fifty-six guns, the English had twenty ships of greater tonnage, and more heavily gunned, while the Dutch merchantmen, though far more numerous, were smaller than their English counterparts, with the exception of their great East Indiamen, mounting fifty guns apiece. Most of their ships suffered from another great disadvantage. As they had to work in shallow waters, they were much more lightly built than the English. Yet they were supremely confident, for they reckoned but little of Blake, that soldier seaman who, as yet, had never fought a great fleet in open combat upon an open sea. What chance did he stand against the long tried seamen, with years of sea experience and skill, exulting in the tradition of constant victory?

But Blake, too, was quietly confident. His officers and seamen had been forged by Warwick to a fine temper. And Blake had restored to them the morale, which they had lost by the folly of the Independents in introducing their politics into the fleet. So fine now was that morale, that he could feel it respond to the magic of his touch. He stood calmly upon the threshold of his greatest opportunity. Little could the Dutch dream that his fleet would wrest from them the supremacy of the Seas.

CHAPTER 11

The War with the Dutch breaks out

*

BLAKE lay ready in the Downs, while Tromp was cruising with
forty sail between Nieuport and the mouth of the Meuse, ready
to protect Dutch merchantmen from search or capture. He told
his captains 'to keep their guns and firearms ready, and if they
shall meet with any foreign ship of war they are to make everything
ready, and, with all the haste allowed by wind and weather, to
join themselves to the rest of our ships and there remain in a good
posture; observing well the signal of war for fighting, either
defensively or offensively, with the object of freeing the ships of
this country from search or visit'. These rights, especially of ships
suspected of carrying foreign goods, particularly French ones, the
English were equally determined to exercise.[1]

It might well be expected that, if war was to break out, it would
obviously be upon this issue. Yet, as so often happens, it was
precipitated for an entirely different reason.[2] On 12 May, 1652,
Captain Anthony Young, in the *President,* was off the Start on his
way to take command of the Western Guard at Plymouth. With
him were Captain Reynolds of the *Nightingale* of twenty-six guns,
and Captain Chapman of the merchantman *Recovery.* A fleet of
ships was sighted, which Young took to be Sir George Ayscue's
ships returning from their conquest of the Barbados. As it drew
near it proved to be a Dutch fleet of seven merchantmen, from
the Straits, escorted by three men-of-war. It was headed by their
Admiral, with the Rear and Vice-Admirals following. As the
Admiral came under Young's lee, he still kept up his flag. Young
at once sent his boat to notify him that he had orders to enforce
the striking of the Dutch flag, in token of the English Sovereignty
of the Seas. Whereupon the Admiral took it in and saluted Young
with three guns. Young fired a similar salute in return. The Vice-
Admiral, contrary to the rules of navigation in the narrow seas,
came up to windward. He saluted with thirteen guns without,
however, striking his flag. As he passed Young called to him to do

so, but without result. Young then followed him and sent his boat aboard him to bid him strike. The Vice-Admiral refused to do so, telling Young to come and take it down himself. Young's retort was a broadside to which the Vice-Admiral also replied. Several more broadsides were exchanged. Reynolds now came up, and after firing six guns at the Rear-Admiral, fired part of a broadside at the Vice-Admiral who, at that moment, had changed his mind and was taking in his flag. The Rear-Admiral did not fire but still kept up his flag, saying he dared not take it in as long as his Vice-Admiral kept his own up. Nevertheless he then took his flag in. Young then sent to the Admiral to demand that either the Vice-Admiral, or his ship, should be taken into port, to make good the damage he had done. He answered that the flag had been taken in, but that he personally was bound to prevent his Vice-Admiral, or his ship, being taken. Young next consulted his two captains and they decided not to proceed further in the affair. Young's ship was damaged in her hull, and two men had been killed and four wounded. The Dutch Admiral sent him word to explain that he had orders that, if he struck, he would lose his head: 'but at length he struck, which makes me conceive he had had enough of it'.[3] Another account says, 'having banged them handsomely, they began to fawn like spaniels and so in conclusion we parted friends'.[4]

Meanwhile, on 9 May, Blake with his Rear-Admiral, Nehemiah Bourne, had weighed from the Downs and put to sea with some twenty ships, for Rye. Besides the *James* of forty-eight guns, he had the *Victory* of forty-two, the *Garland* of thirty-four, the *Speaker* of fifty, the *Ruby* of forty, the *Sapphire* of thirty-eight, the *Worcester* of forty-eight, the *Portsmouth* of thirty-eight, the *Martin* of thirty-six, the *Mermaid* of twenty-two,[5] the *Rueben* merchant-man and an unknown merchantman, making thirteen in all. With Bourne in the *Andrew* of sixty, were the *Triumph* of sixty-eight, the *Fairfax* of sixty-two, the *Entrance* of forty-six, the *Centurion* of forty, the *Adventure* of forty, the *Assurance* of forty, the *Greyhound* of fourteen, and the *Seven Brothers* of twenty-six. On the way to Rye Bourne put back into the Downs.[6]*

Tromp was cruising off the Weilings and Ostend, with some fifty sail, until 14 May. Then, with a strong wind at N. he found himself close to the Flemish Sands and he decided to anchor off Dunkirk. Here, with a N.E. wind and a rough sea, he remained

* see also Appendix 2

for four days. Three captains came aboard him to report that they had lost their cables and anchors. So Tromp decided to cross over, so as to lie under the lee of the English coast. He explained to all his captains his reasons for so doing. He was evidently anxious to obtain their approval for what might be interpreted as a dubious action.[7] About 1 p.m. he sent two frigates to Bourne to explain to him that his orders were to cruise off the Dutch coast, but that bad weather had forced him to seek shelter off the English coast. The frigates were met by the *Greyhound*, and taken to Bourne. They gave him Tromp's message, and added that they were sent to prevent 'any thought, misapprehensions or alarms by land or sea'.[8] Tromp would have come personally, but he was anxious to avoid any differences with regard to striking his flag. Bourne replied that 'neither more nor less would be expected from them, but what they knew to be the ancient right of this nation'. He bade them tell Tromp that his message was civil and that Blake was to the westward and was hourly expected; and that the reality of his message might be manifested 'by their speedy drawing off from this place with their fleet'. The two frigates then departed and Bourne sent off a ketch post-haste with the news to Blake. All that night Bourne lay ready, with his anchors apeak, and with two frigates, apart one from the other, watching the enemy, with orders to signal, by day or night, if Tromp moved towards Blake or elsewhere.[9]

Tromp, however, drifted off westward and at 7 p.m. anchored off Dover. Late that night Blake got Bourne's message and instantly sent him an order to join him, as wind and weather would permit. Next day, the 19th, the weather was fair with an east wind, and at 10 a.m. Bourne received Blake's orders. By noon he was under sail.[10] Tromp, meanwhile, took the opportunity to exercise his raw crews in musketry and in the firing of the guns. It was a foolish action, for it naturally angered the governor of Dover Castle, who fired some shots at Tromp to remind him to strike his flag.[11] But Tromp defiantly kept it up. At 2 p.m., after he had finished refitting, Tromp stood over towards the French coast.[12] About 3 p.m. Bourne was off the entrance to the Downs, keeping to windward until Blake should come up. Blake himself was struggling against the wind, some miles short of Dover, while Tromp, on the port tack, was standing for Calais. Suddenly Tromp sighted a vessel working up from the westward, with a weft at her

masthead, indicating that she brought important news. It was
Captain Van Zaan come post-haste with the news of the encounter
off the Start.[13] He had left seven rich merchantmen off the
Fairlight on the previous evening, which he feared were in danger
of capture by Blake's ships at Rye. Indeed he told Tromp that the
frigates had come to visit them, and he feared that they had been
already captured, and he begged for Tromp's aid. Full of anger
Tromp, as his instructions had bade him prevent this very thing,
set sail to take the ships under his protection.[14] But unfortunately
Zaan's information was incorrect. Blake, finding that the ships
came from Genoa and Leghorn and were therefore unlikely to
have French goods aboard, had left them unmolested.[15] Tromp's
anger was understandable. He had kept away from Bourne to
avoid any trouble about striking his flag and had returned towards
Calais to avoid an encounter with Blake. He was not the man to
risk opening a quarrel by way of bravado. But now he swept down
to the rescue of his ships. Nevertheless he took in all his sails,
with the exception of his top-sails, and even these he lowered 'to
the middle of the mast', in partial acknowledgment of England's
claim to the Sovereignty of the Seas.[16] His object was to cut off
Bourne from Blake.

Blake was still laboriously beating his way up to join Bourne
when a small vessel came out from Dover with forty volunteers
aboard. He met them at the gangway and gave each man a glass of
old Malaga, poured out for them by Richard Gibson, who had
missed the boat to take him to his ship, the *Assurance*, in the
Downs. Lieutenant Adams, who had served with Blake at Taunton,
had instead made him at home in the flagship.[17]

When Blake was within three leagues of the Dutch, he saw them
weigh and stand off eastward. He supposed 'their intention was to
leave us to avoid the dispute of the flag'. It was now about 2 p.m.
and he was amazed to see that 'about two hours after they altered
their course and bore directly with us, Van Tromp the headmost:
whereupon we lay by and put ourselves into a fighting posture,
judging they had a resolution to engage'. He was the more
mystified, as he had not interfered with the Dutch merchantmen,
but had left them alone.[18] Though he had only thirteen ships to
Tromp's forty or so, he was not the man to decline what seemed
to be Tromp's unprovoked challenge. Both fleets were strung out
in a rough line, which was the feature of that day.[19]

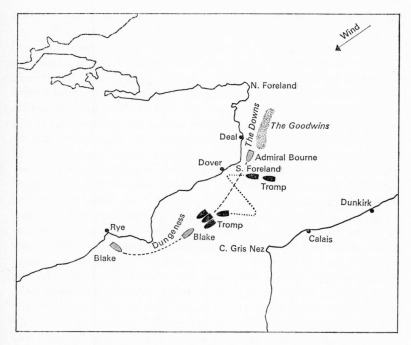

Blake and Tromp's Operations in the Straits of Dover,
19 May, 1652

As the fleets approached each other about 4 p.m. Blake now ordered his ships to put about and steer south towards their own coast. His ships that were originally astern were now ahead of him. His flagship was thus nearest the enemy and to Tromp evading the Dutch van. Blake observed Tromp's sails half lowered in salute. To this half defiant action, he replied with a single shot from the after gun on the stern side, as a signal to Tromp to strike his flag.[20] Tromp, however, held on and Blake fired another shot. What happened next is almost impossible to discover, so confused are the accounts on both sides.[21] Apparently Tromp had a man aloft at the halliards, but assuredly did not strike his flag and in all probability never intended to do so.[22] The English claim that Blake fired another shot, to which Tromp replied with a broadside. A report from Dover, of 20 May, probably is nearest the truth by

saying that Blake fired three or four shots, and that Tromp replied
with a broadside, to which Blake answered with another.[23]

Both fleets were on the starboard tack,* with Blake ahead, and
Tromp to windward. Both flagships engaged fiercely, with the rest
of the fleets gradually joining in as they came up. Meanwhile
Bourne had 'calculated the time and tide, so that we might most
opportunely make conjunction of our forces'. He came into action
about half past four, taking the Dutch ships in their rear. 'They did
their utmost to decline us and avoid our coming near, which we
endeavoured by all means; but their Admiral, leading the van,
they made all sail after him and so left the rest of their fleet to us,
which we endeavoured to sever from the rest, and accordingly did
in part break the body; and some of us, who were the nearest, fell
upon the sternmost who, I suppose, found it hot work'. Bourne
'divided them into two or three parts, wherein they shuffled themselves into clusters, but by reason many of our ships sailed very
heavy, by reason they are foul, we could not fully attain our desire
upon them'. As no definite signal code existed, Tromp was unable
to detach any of his ships to deal with Bourne. After a stout fight
the *St Laurens* of thirty guns was captured, while Lawson in the
Fairfax, took the *St Maria*. Her mainmast had been shot down and
as she was so full of water in the hold that she was in danger of
sinking, she had to be abandoned. Her crew were taken off and
made prisoners.[24]

Night put an end to the fight, and Tromp drifted off westwards,
with a light burning in every ship, so that he could collect his
scattered vessels. Next day he found, in mid-channel, the *St Maria*.
He then continued cruising to and fro to meet the merchantmen
coming from the Straits, while Blake returned to the Downs.[25]

He and Bourne had fought a brilliant action against odds of two
to one. Blake, by accepting battle, and by standing away southwards towards the English coast, had kept the majority of Tromp's
fleet out of action for a considerable time. Though the *James* had
received over seventy shots in her hull and masts, her sails and
rigging, 'without number', she had held on. Blake had six men
killed and thirty-five wounded, after four hours' desperate fight.
Bourne, by his well-timed attack upon the Dutch rear, had split
the enemy fleet in two, in which it had lost two ships.[26]

* Starboard i.e. the wind coming on the right side of the ship: Port
tack i.e. wind coming on the left side of the ship.

The news of this apparently unprovoked attack upon Blake aroused fury in London. So much so that the Council of State, fearing that many people 'being thereby highly incensed'[27] might attack the Dutch Ambassadors, ordered four files of musketeers, and twenty horse, to guard the Embassy in Chelsea. Orders, too, were sent out to secure two Dutch men-of-war, lying in the Thames and to take away their sails and rudders until further orders.[28]

On 21 May, Parliament sent a letter of thanks and approval for his action to Blake. Cromwell and Bond were sent to Dover to enquire into the action.[29] Captain William Brandley gave evidence as to the details, that the two fleets 'had engaged a little east of Sandgate Castle'.[30] A prisoner, Captain Tuynemans, of the *St Laurens*, said that when he met the *St Andrew* and two other English ships, near Calais, some four weeks before, he had four other Dutch ships with him. Tromp had asked him if he had struck his top-sails. When he replied that he had done so, Tromp answered 'Were you not as strong as they were, and being so, why were you so afraid?' In further evidence, Tuynemans said he had told his lieutenant that when Tromp blamed him, he had added that he had married a young wife and that he was afraid, and hastened home. The lieutenant now admitted that Blake had made a shot, without ball, at their Admiral's flag and that, after two shots more, Tromp did not strike his flag, but instead made a shot at Blake, following it with a broadside. The Court of Enquiry held that Blake had been fully justified.[31]

Penn was now appointed Vice-Admiral, and Bourne Rear.[32] The council wrote to let Blake know that they were taking every care to supply him with ammunition and victuals, and that they would hasten out to him all the ships in the Thames. They also determined to strengthen the fleet as they thought fit.[33]

Meanwhile, on 23 May, Blake was astonished to get a letter from Tromp. Tromp wrote that on their meeting, 'my intention was to greet you but, seeing that I was attacked, and not knowing your intention, as I was not spoken to by any of you, either before or at that time, yet by no means suspecting that we were other than friends and good allies (after Commodore Bourne had shown me by his answer to those persons sent to him by me to communicate to him my order and my upright intentions), I was forced, as a man of honour, to defend myself.' He then went on to beg 'for friendship's sake' to return to him the *St Laurens*. He ended by assuring himself that the good alliance and union between the two Governments, their common religion and friendship would prevent Blake from refusing his request.[34] The phrase 'for friendship's sake' has given rise to much conjecture. It has been held either to confirm the Schiedam story, or to refer to the meeting of the two Admirals off Scilly. From the context it seems more probable that Tromp referred to the good relations of the two countries, which he hoped Blake, by the return of his ship, was willing to continue, despite the recent fight.

The Dutch Ambassadors were not so optimistic as Tromp. On the contrary they were appalled by the situation. They feared the dread consequences it might bring to the negotiations. So, on 24 May, they wrote to the Council of State. They spoke of 'an unhappy and unexpected mischance; of the horrible report that hath amazed us that there should have been a fight between the fleet of the Commonwealth, and that of the United Provinces; and that ours should have been the cause of this unfortunate business by beginning the fight, and that it having been entered on with the greatest fierceness, so that the report that we had broken the Treaty, and had engaged in open war, was spread'. They declared, 'that the fact, as it is reported, has been committed without the knowledge, and against the will of, the United Provinces and of their Ambassadors'. On the contrary they had hoped that the Treaty might be agreed upon and that 'that excellent matter may be finished in a very few hours'. They ended by asking for a copy of the relation of the things that had happened that they might, by the council's permission, forward it to their Government, that all things here 'may remain whole and untouched, that the business of the concluding of the Treaty may, by no means, be put off but, in order that such unfortunate mischances may be avoided and everlasting peace may be established between both nations'.[35]

On the next day they wrote to Tromp. After reciting the English account of the action, they told him that they had heard that Blake was about to pursue him without delay, 'to avenge this untimely injury – which the whole Government here considers has been inflicted upon them'. This had given rise to 'general dissatisfaction and uneasiness – and hath created the strong prejudice now very apparent against us, and against all dealings hitherto had with us'. As, however, Tromp's account differed so greatly from that of the English, yet it appeared to them 'a most unexpected and unfortunate occurrence; this the more so since they had in accordance with the reiterated commands of the Dutch Government – so far arranged matters here with the Government, that we were confident – of bringing our negotiations before long to a satisfactory conclusion'. Nor they could not conceal from Tromp that warlike preparations were being made, as though an open future had taken place, as though with the fore-knowledge, and by the orders, of the Dutch Government. They ended by begging Tromp 'to avoid all further disputes and causes of reproach'. They again asked him to send them his account 'with his reasons for acting – in order that we may, if possible, have better means of allaying the strong feelings at present entertained, and of convincing those who are prejudiced against us'. They could hardly have expressed their disapproval of Tromp's action more sharply.[36]

In England, preparations went forward briskly to have everything in readiness for a war that now seemed inevitable. Twenty ships were ordered to go to the Downs.[37] Ports in Shetland and Orkney were to be inspected, so that they could be trusted to defend the harbours.[38] Forty additional vessels were to be added to the fleet; and the Vice-Admirals of Norfolk, Suffolk, Kent, Sussex and Hampshire were bidden to impress all seamen from 15 to 50 years of age to man the fleet. Each man was to get a shilling a mile from the place of impressment to Deptford.[39]

Nor was discipline neglected. Captains Thorrowgood and Gibbs were reported by Blake, 'concerning their miscarriages' in the late engagement.[40] Thorrowgood's officers and men interceded for him and he seems to have been dealt with leniently: Gibbs was dismissed from the command of the *Garland*.[41] Blake, however, replaced Thorrowgood by giving Young command of the *Worcester*, while Graves took over Young's ship, the *President*.[42] On the other hand the good services of the Dover volunteers were rewarded out of the tenth of the money for captured prizes.[43]

Blake himself was naturally very busy. On the 29th he wrote to the Mayor of Sandwich to ask him to 'stay all pilots, experienced on the coasts of Flanders' until he sent for them. He requested that quarters should be provided for Colonel Ingoldsby's regiment, which was coming to garrison Deal. Search, too, was to be made for certain seamen, who had deserted, and who were hiding in the town, and who must be detained. No mariners must be allowed to pass, unless they had Blake's written permission.[44]

On the 30th, Blake replied to Tromp's letter, asking for the return of the captured ships. He expressed 'astonishment' at the letter: 'wherein, though representing yourself as a person of honour, you introduce many gross mis-statements; and this just after having fought with the fleet of the Parliament – instead of employing the customary forms of respect, which the occasion demanded, and which you yourself have hitherto employed, and having thought fit to commit an act of hostility (which you yourself style a falling out with the Republic) without receiving the slightest provocation from her servants, who are assailed by you at a time when your Government, and their Ambassadors, were engaged in negotiations with Parliament – and seeing we have taken some of your ships, you have thought well to demand the same of us again, as though your former proceedings had been nothing but a salute (as you assert), and, failing this, to follow up your former insults by your present letter: to which the only answer that I can return is that I presume Parliament will keenly resent this great insult, and the spilling of the blood of their unoffending subjects, and that you will find in the undersigned one ever ready to carry out their commands.'[45]

On the same day the council forwarded to Blake a letter from the Mayor of Weymouth, reporting that sixty sail of Dutchmen were making for the Downs. Blake was to seize them and to send them into port untouched.[46] Apparently Blake took some of them and, on 2 June, he was ordered to send 'the Dutch ships, taken by him, into the Thames'. The seamen were to be sent back to Holland, probably to avoid the expense of feeding them, though the officers and commanders were to be held back.[47]

On 3 June, the Dutch Ambassadors wrote to the council in great concern. Their Government were trying to find a remedy 'to mitigate that raw and bloody wound, so that the cause of all further evil may be taken away, and that there might be a better hope of our Treaty'. They begged the council 'to suffer nothing to be done out of much heat'. They concluded by desiring 'again and again, so much the more because we understand that the ships of our Lords and of our Shippers, some by force and some by fighting, both on the broad sea, as in the ports of this Commonwealth, are taken by your men and kept'.[48] On the 5th, Parliament replied. They had showed friendship towards the United Provinces, but 'do find themselves much surprised at the unsuitable returns that have been made thereunto, and especially at the acts of hostility committed in the very roads of England, upon the fleet of this Commonwealth'. Then they drew attention to the 'extraordinary preparations of 150 sail without any visible occasion, but what doth now appear a just ground of jealousy in your own judgments when your Lordships pretend to excuse it, and the instructions themselves given by your said superiors to their commanders at sea'. This led them to believe that the Dutch Government 'have an intention by force to usurp the known rights of England in the Seas, to destroy the fleets that are their walls and bulwarks, and thereby expose this Commonwealth to invasion at their pleasure'. They intended, therefore, to seek reparations with security that their wrongs should not be repeated. They still desired that 'all differences to be composed' but they added ominously that such efforts must be 'less dilatory and more effectual' than those hitherto employed.[49]

In a desperate attempt to prevent a rupture, the Dutch, on 20 June, sent over the aged pensionary, Pauw, to try and rescue what he could from a calamitous situation. But he was told bluntly that nothing could be done, until his Government agreed to pay full compensation for all injuries inflicted by their subjects.[50] On the day after Pauw was sent over, Tromp replied to the Ambassadors. He now introduced a new version of his story which was, somewhat curiously, supported by the officers of his ship.[51]

He declared that, after Blake had twice fired at him, he had his boat, which was being towed behind him, 'hauled up and ordered to be manned, with a view of sending my captain on board to salute him from me, and to ascertain his intentions, but before half the crew had got into the boat, the Admiral (Blake) sent a shot on board us, that carried one man's arm off, and wounded several others with the splinters'. He then answered Blake with a shot, 'aiming a long way this side of his ship, hoping he would wait for us to come up, but instead of this he got to windward of us, and turned his broadside towards us – with the obvious intention of sinking us: our men were surprised and the crew of the boat climbed back again into the ship, whilst the man, who was aloft striking the flag, came down on deck; whereupon we turned and gave them a broadside, though before this we had no intention of firing a single hostile shot until we were so hotly attacked and

forced to defend ourselves.' Even the Ambassadors could hardly
swallow this unlikely tale.[52]

Somewhere before 10 June, Taylor of the *Laurel* and Peacock
of the *Tiger*, fell in with two Hollanders on the coast of Flanders.
The Dutchmen refused to strike their top-sails.[53] After 'a short
dispute' one of the Dutchmen was boarded, and her officers and
crew were captured, though the ship was so badly damaged that
she sank shortly afterwards. The other avoided capture by running
herself upon the sands.[54] Peacock was commended by the council
for his 'worthy deportment' but, on the other hand, not so Taylor
whose behaviour, it seems 'was very unbecoming his duty and the
great trust committed to him'. The council told Blake that they
did not 'doubt but you will take care he shall receive according to
his demerit, to the terror of others, upon the like occasion'. He
was probably only reprimanded for not capturing the second
vessel, as he was continued as captain of the *Laurel*. Blake may
have taken into account the fact that, though he had failed, at
least he had gone into action.[55]

On 10 June, Colonel Thompson was sent to Blake by the Council
with secret instructions 'suitable to the present juncture of affairs'.[56]
At the same time they ordered the fleet to be victualled until 1
October. Blake, however, on the 9th, had written to Penn to say
that 'in view of the many businesses that at present lie upon my
hands' he could not deal with the victualling, which he consigned
to Penn's care.[57]

It was a wise decision, as his conference with Thompson,
concerning the Instructions, showed. For the Council had decided
that the best way to seek reparations from the Dutch, was for
Blake to seize and secure all the Dutch East India fleet, now
homeward bound, and to send all the ships he could capture into
English ports. He was also to 'interrupt and disturb' the Dutch
fishing fleet, off England and Scotland, and to seize and secure
the fishing busses. Then he was to do the same with the Dutch
Baltic trade and, at the same time, to preserve and protect the
Eastland trade of the Commonwealth. Finally he was authorised
'by force to take and surprise, or otherwise to burn, sink or destroy
all ships that should withstand or resist him, and to order his
commanders to do the same'. It was a bold plan, aimed at the
Dutch economy, by attacking them at their weakest point, their
vital lines of communication.[58]

Blake sent similar orders to Penn, commanding the Western Guard,[59] while Sir George Ayscue, with the returned Barbados squadron, was ordered to sail from Plymouth to the Downs. Here he would be able to intercept such Dutch merchantmen as came through the Straits of Dover.[60] The plan was probably based upon the knowledge that Tromp had only managed to collect some fifty sail, and that his retreat, after the last engagement, amounted to a confession of weakness. This division of the English fleet appeared to be without much risk to their strength.

So the council continued to work with energy, dealing with every kind of detail. They directed Blake to send warships to clear the western regions of the pirates that infested them. Trinity House was to treat with the owners of armed ships in the Thames, which were unemployed, for their use with the navy.[61] The Navy Commissioners were to take up thirty merchantmen for the same purpose, and also to provide fireships. These they were to man with commanders, boatswains, gunners, pursers, carpenters and cooks, who were to be sent to the Downs.[62] Thompson was to enquire how many ships, in the Downs, were State vessels, and how many were hired merchantmen: how many men were on each ship and to order the captains to complete what they lack: to look into the state of the victuals and, if any were defective, he was to note it. Gunners, boatswains and carpenters were to present their indentures for all stores, and what they lacked, so that every ship might be serviceable until Michaelmas: trusty captains (and no owners of shipping) were to survey the stores of the merchantmen, and to enquire if the ships, fitted as men-of-war, were in accordance with their contracts.[63]

The seizure of Dutch shipping went gaily on. In the Barbados, Ayscue had gleaned up a number, to the intense fury of the Dutch. And, on 11 June, Blake reported that eleven Dutch ships, laden with salt, had been sent into Dover.[64] The council bade him to make sure that no embezzlement had taken place, and they directed the customs authorities to remove their sails and rudders, and to spike their decks and to keep them in the Thames. To ease the burden upon Blake, they were to take charge of any captured ships. The order to send home the captured seamen was rescinded, and they were now to be held captive on their own ships. This was obviously directed at hamstringing Tromp, by depriving him of mariners to man his vessels.[65]

In order to protect English shipping, all ships in the Baltic were to rendezvous at Elsinore, and to keep together the better to defend themselves, until a convoy was sent to them.[66] Ships bound for Newfoundland, detained in the Downs, however, were now allowed to proceed. They had been kept back owing to a rumour that Prince Rupert's fleet had a design to go thither.[67]

The constant seizure of Dutch shipping naturally aroused an outburst of fury in Holland against their authorities, who allowed such injuries to go unredressed. The Government realised that any further cringing before the arrogance of England might bring about a revolution in favour of the House of Orange.[68] So they ordered Pauw, on 30 June, to present a final demand for redress. But this only served to stiffen the council's attitude. For, next day, they wrote to Blake to say 'we perceive the fleet very suddenly will be in a condition to put to sea, in order to the execution of the instructions you have received'. They added the *Sovereign*, *James*, *Resolution* and *Vanguard* to the thirty merchantmen that were to join the fleet.[69]

On 21 June Ayscue, with eleven ships, arrived in the Downs. He saluted Blake with all his guns, and the whole fleet returned it. This so alarmed the country folk, that they came flocking to the seaside, thinking that a naval action was taking place. Ayscue boarded Blake, and dined with him and all his captains.[70] They must have discussed the instructions. In view of what happened later, they have often been blamed for the division of the fleet. But the responsibility lay, not with them, but with the council. They had to obey orders. So, on the 26th, Blake sailed north, leaving Ayscue in the Downs.[71]

A new and urgent problem now faced the council. Hemp from Riga, which was essential for rigging the ships, had previously been brought in by Dutch vessels. But now no Dutch ship, naturally, would undertake the task. However, being commercially minded, the Dutch proposed to carry out their contract by employing Dantzig vessels, which, however, was prohibited by the Navigation Act. So it was argued that the Dantzig vessels were Polish, and that hemp was a Polish product, and so thereby was exempt from the Act. This ingenious solution was agreed upon. The council got their hemp and the Dutch saved their contracts.[72]

On 29 June, the Dutch Ambassadors announced that they had received orders to return home. Next day they were received in audience to take their leave and, after a ceremonious farewell, they departed. As they left, one of them uttered his foreboding. 'The English' he said, 'are about to attack a mountain of gold: we are about to attack a mountain of iron'.[73] On the same day the council sent Blake an account of the meeting. According to this, the Dutch had demanded that an enquiry into the action off Dover should be referred to Commissioners, to be appointed by both sides, supposing Parliament to have been incorrectly informed as to matters of fact. In the interim there was to be a cessation of hostilities, and a continuance of the negotiations for a Treaty. The council considered this 'dilatory and impracticable' as it would 'needlessly draw into question things that stood clear in proof, on purpose to delude the States in point of their just satisfaction'. In view of this the council asked Blake to keep in close touch with them, as they had heard nothing from him since he had sailed. They particularly wished to know 'your resolution as to Tromp's fleet – to deliver this Commonwealth from the danger thereof'.[74]

With war declared on 8 July, the Dutch were in a vulnerable position. Holland depended upon her huge commerce, without which her people must starve. First then, she must protect her trade. For her ships would have to run the gauntlet up the Channel until they could reach the shoals off Flanders, and the safety of Flushing. Otherwise they must make the long and dangerous voyage round Scotland. Even so they ran the risk of being cut off by an enemy fleet before they could reach the shelter of the Texel. Though Tromp and his Admirals were to prove themselves as superb commanders who came from a warlike race, they were to be fatally handicapped by the sluggishness and rivalry of their several naval boards, so that their fleets had to put to sea unprovided with the barest essentials. Besides they had to convoy huge fleets of merchantmen. This put them in the position of shepherds, trying to protect their flocks from the continual attacks of wolves. They had not even David's advantages, for he was unencumbered when he met Goliath. A further drawback was the fact that they had not fought a fleet action since the time when Tromp had trapped Oquendo in the Downs in 1639, and wrested the mastery of the seas from the Spaniards.

The English, on the other hand, possessed officers and seamen, many of whom had gained their naval experience by almost continual service in the Civil War. They were proud to serve under a commander, whose sole aim was 'the service of this Commonwealth': the genius of whose leadership they could recognise and whose care for, and whose trust in them, was evident to the humblest mariner. Now they were about to fight in their own home waters, which was to give them an enormous geographical advantage. For the prevailing wind was westerly, which would prevent the enemy from attacking their harbours and, as the Dutch commanders were pinned down to the obvious trade routes, their movements could be reckoned to a certainty. From Cornwall to Dover, and along the east coast, their harbours could furnish the English with supplies, and with ports to which they could, if necessary, withdraw. Thus the enemy's long line of communication lay at their mercy, for the Dutch merchantmen must either pass through the Channel, or else take the long route round Scotland. For once the English could master the lines of communication, the Dutch must be mastered too. Blake's ships were more stoutly built and were larger than the Dutch vessels, and also more powerfully gunned. But, as yet, the English had not met an enemy in battle upon the open sea, for the action off Dover could not be classed as such. Now they were to meet men born to the sea, and veterans in seamanship. For both sides it was to be a struggle for existence, for the mastery of the ocean, a struggle which would be fought to the death.

CHAPTER 12

Blake's Northern Voyage

*

ON the same day, 26 June, that Blake sailed north in the *Resolution*, (the *James* had been too badly mauled to be fit for sea) the States-General wrote to Tromp. He was to attack the English fleet, whether united or separated, without any distinction of place, and to do all imaginable damage to it. He was to capture or destroy all other English men-of-war, wherever they could be caught with all merchantmen, but they were not to be plundered, nor their crews mishandled nor injured.[1]

Blake himself was off Sunderland on 29 June. He had sent a frigate into the port, with some Dutch officers and seamen he had just taken. He was resolved to lose no time in seeking out the Dutch East India fleet, which he hoped to capture. On 1 July he sent orders to Penn, when he came among the Dutch fishing fleet, to deal first with the men-of-war guarding it, and only after them with the herring busses.[2]

Next day Tromp sent the States-General important news. That morning one of his scouts had taken a small Dover vessel off the North Foreland. From her skipper it was learned that Blake had sailed for the north, and that only Ayscue's Barbados squadron, with a few prizes, lay in the Downs. Tromp therefore proposed to sail after Blake with his whole force of eighty-three vessels and nine fireships. He added the warning that the latter 'cannot well stand the sea, and are but ill-provided with rigging and sails'. He was then at Scheveningen.[3]

On the same day Ayscue had learned of thirty or forty Dutch merchantmen coming from Portedos in Portugal. They were escorted by four warships and were near the Narrows, between Dover and Calais. With nine sail he put out to meet them. At dawn next morning his leading ships came up with them. They offered practically no resistance. Twenty-six ran themselves ashore on the Calais sands, while Ayscue took five, burnt three and recovered two from the sands. The French did their best to defend the stranded vessels, after the Dutch had got ashore and abandoned them. They took the opportunity, as Ayscue observed, to plunder them and to carry away their goods in carts. Eight ships got away, chased by Captains Wright, Pack and Jordan, who only managed to overtake one, 'a rich ship which very strongly defended herself against Wright, who behaved himself very gallantly'.[4]

Meanwhile Pauw, returning to Holland, fell unexpectedly in with Tromp's fleet, probably about 2 July. He at once boarded him to give him information as to the whereabouts of the English fleet, information which must have been invaluable to the Dutch Admiral.[5] Pauw then resumed his voyage home for, on 5 July, after consideration, he wrote to Tromp to suggest he might well attack Ayscue's ships in the Downs, especially as the north wind had prevented Tromp from following Blake.[6] Tromp replied that De With had just joined him with eight ships, and that a Council of War had decided to attack Ayscue. Tromp himself must surely have thought of repeating his exploit of 1639, when he had trapped Oquendo at that very spot. He would himself, with Evertsen and all the fireships, enter the Downs from the north and attack the English, while De With and Floriszoon blockaded them from the south.[7]

All unconscious of the danger threatening Ayscue, the council ordered Cromwell, on 2 July, to send 300 soldiers to Tilbury, to embark for the Downs, with another 300 to follow. Twenty-four merchantmen with some fireships were to hasten to Ayscue on the 6th.[8] Their commander, Captain Harrison, was told that if, on arrival, he found that Ayscue had sailed westwards he was to follow him.[9] General Fleetwood was ordered to appoint competent officers to go with the soldiers to see the men aboard, and to end 'such disorders as happened among the soldiers, who were last sent aboard and to prevent them being practised by those who are now going aboard'.[10] Ayscue himself had been given leave on the 5th to go ashore 'to take physic for the recovery of his health, provided he left an able person fit to command the fleet'. So unaware was the council of any cause for alarm.[11]

They received a hasty shock. For, on the 8th, Ayscue's scouts at the North Sands Head, the northern extremity of the Downs, came in post-haste to report they had sighted sixty sail of Dutchmen approaching.[12] Ever since the 5th, Tromp had been endeavouring to get to the Downs, but he had been hindered by calms on the

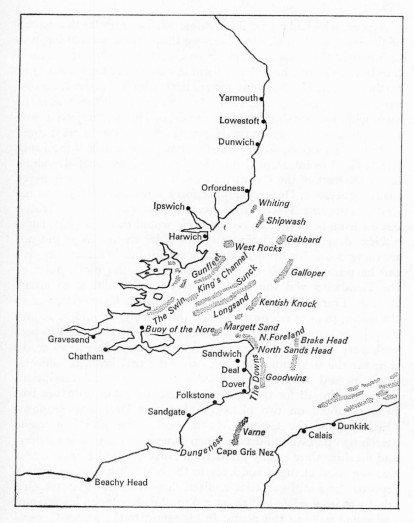

The Thames Estuary

6th and 7th. On the evening of the 8th, just as he had sighted his prey, a wind from the N.W. and N.N.W. forced him to anchor for the night. Out of the sixteen fireships, nine had separated from him for fear of sinking, so that he had seven left, of which three were liable to sink at any moment.[13]

Ayscue, who had rejoined his ships, was lying under the shelter of the guns of Deal Castle. Guessing that Tromp's intention was to intercept the vessels coming from the Hope before he attacked him in the Downs, he ordered them to stay where they were until further orders. He then sent 200 soldiers, who had arrived, aboard various ships to help man them. On the 10 July Tromp came in view with 102 warships and ten fireships. His first objective was the capture of the ships at the Hope, which he believed must come to Ayscue's support, so he posted seventy-two vessels at the Long Sands Head to intercept them. He himself with twenty-five ships lay at the back of the Goodwins so that he could watch any move made by Ayscue. He sent another forty ships three leagues to his south to prevent Ayscue from escaping that way. He had Ayscue cut off from help or from escape.[14] He would deal with him later.

Next day, Tromp, finding that the ships in the Hope did not move, now divided his fleet into two squadrons. With seventy-five sail he posted himself between Brake Head, the north point of the Goodwins and the North Foreland in readiness to attack Ayscue. Thirty-five ships lay at the back of the Goodwins, and to the south, so as to fall on Ayscue, if the fireships should force him to quit his station in either direction. But, as the ebb tide was past with very little wind, Tromp had to anchor a league away, to wait for the next tide.[15] Ayscue 'knowing that both his officers, mariners and soldiers were filled with courage and resolution, prepared himself for their reception'. Six pieces of ordnance had been mounted on two platforms, between Deal and Sandown Castles, while the County Militia, both horse and foot, came marching up. Two hundred seamen came in to offer their services, and fireships were hastily prepared at Dover.[16] But before the next tide the wind changed suddenly to the S.W., 'turning' as Tromp reported 'to a stiff gale'. He realised that an attack against such a wind was impossible and so, at 5 p.m., he abandoned his attempt and sailed away to the north. In his report to the States-General he spoke of how 'exceedingly disquieted we are about the manner of taking in victuals'. This was nearly impossible to do 'with great ships in open seas' and in bad weather hopeless to attempt. Nor was it possible to appoint a rendezvous while, if the victuallers sought him at random, they would run the risk of meeting the English fleet. He had 11,000 men aboard, so that he might have to disembark the soldiers in Norway, with the added risk of his crews deserting him. He had only three weeks provisions, which would be consumed in a voyage from the Shetlands to the Texel, which he would be forced to make unless supplies were sent to him before reaching the Shetlands.[17]

Meanwhile, on the 11th, the council wrote to Blake to warn him of Ayscue's plight, though they did not suggest his return.[18] On the 14th day they acknowledged his letter from Sunderland, and informed him that Tromp was now sailing north.[19] Blake never allowed himself to be deflected from his main objective by a minor operation. It was clearly too late to go to Ayscue's rescue: moreover the danger was over. Instead he pursued his instructions, the capture of the Dutch East Indiamen, for this would deal Holland's mercantile trade a severe blow. So when, on the 12th, he fell in with the Dutch fishing fleet off the Orkneys, he sent six frigates ahead, who at once engaged the guard of twelve warships. The Dutch Vice-Admiral opened fire on them, and Captain Taylor replied with a broadside, in which the other five frigates joined. For three hours there was 'a hot dispute'. Taylor captured three men-of-war, and made a fourth strike, while Mildmay secured another.[20] Soon the whole twelve were made prisoners. Three, being badly shattered, sank; six others Blake added to his fleet, and sent the other three to Inverness for Deane's use. While the fight was going on, 600 busses seized the chance to fly.[21]

From Dutch sources came the Schiedam story, referred to earlier. What probably lies behind it is the fact that some busses were captured and that Blake had no wish to be encumbered, either with these small vessels, or with a multitude of prisoners. As a merciful man he regarded the fishermen as non-combatants and so let them go home.[22] Hundreds of Dutch officers and men had been dispersed at random among the English ships, while seamen had been sent to man their captured vessels. So, on the 15th, Blake ordered Penn to make a reckoning of both, so that they might be equally distributed, and no ship was unduly burdened, either by want of seamen, or by too numerous prisoners.[23]

But now Tromp was hot upon Blake's trail, which he picked up from some merchantmen of Ipswich and Newcastle. He aroused much resentment by taking all the fit men and pressing them for service in his own fleet.[24] By 20 July he was off the Forth and from here he wrote another querulous letter to the States-General. His ships were foul and short of equipment, while his men were known to be disaffected, since they could not get their usual allowance of eight pints of beer daily. Scurvy, too, had broken out. Unless he was supplied with three weeks' provisions, it would be impossible for him to keep the sea.[25] As the wind was at N.N.E. and N.N.W. he was not able to sail northwards. Instead he was cruising between Newcastle and the Farne Islands. However, by the 23rd he had reached Fraserburgh where he took an English trader. He told the master that he intended to fight, but that he was in no hurry to do so, as he was expecting a reinforcement of sixty ships.[26]

Blake was now to the north of the Shetlands, scouring the seas for the East Indiamen. He was aware nevertheless that Tromp was on his heels and he was anxious to bring him to battle. Next day, the 24th, Tromp sighted five ships to the N. or N.E., and at once gave chase. They scattered and Tromp had to give up the pursuit in case his ships got separated. As the weather was 'misty, dirty and thick', course was laid for Fair Isle, which was reached at 5 p.m. Next morning, Tromp sent in two ships to try and get news of Blake's whereabouts. At 4 p.m. in the afternoon they returned with information that the English were either near or in the roadstead of Shetland, as they had seen three vessels to the N.N.E., and another six to the W.N.W., which they thought must be on the outlook for the East Indiamen. By 5 p.m. Fair Isle lay S.W. and S.W. by S. some two miles off. Tromp laid his course E. and E. by N. 'with a strengthening wind, hard rain and thick weather'. By 7 p.m. the rain slackened and the Dutch found themselves close to the Shetlands with several of their ships to leeward, close to the shore which, without great danger, they could not weather. Accordingly the whole fleet went S.W. by S. so as to clear the land.[27] Then, as night came on, the wind shifted to the south, 'with an extraordinary tempest, and by degrees got round to the west, so that by 11 p.m., it was at S.W. and we could but sail N.W. and N.W. to N. so that it was impossible to clear the land, and it blew so hard that it was impossible to tack. It ripped up the sails, or actually blew them into shreds, so that before the end of the night they had been quite blown away from those ships that had no good sails'.[28]

Another Dutch account gives a graphic picture. It describes the wind as 'making such a din that it was terrible to hear it: but what was far more awful was to see the boiling sea foaming and dashing up to the height of a house upon the rocky cliffs of Shetland.

Generals-at-Sea.
Popham (top),
artist unknown;
Deane by
R. Walker

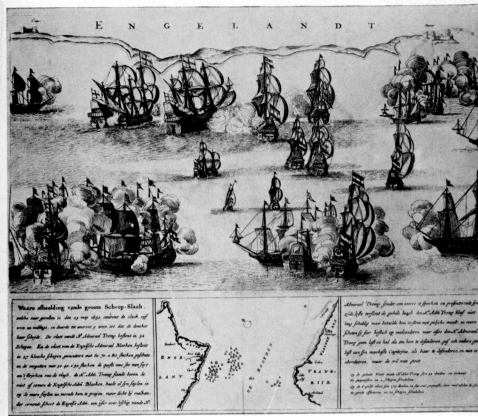

Blake defeats Tromp off Dover, 19th May, 1652

Everyone thus seeing his graveyard before his eyes, did his best to save life and ship by keeping off the danger, whilst many of the Dutch ships had these rocks to leeward, they all, except four or five (amongst which were some fireships which, though destined to perish by fire, were now consumed by another element), were preserved, though many ships appeared rather to sink than to drive through the great troughs of the sea, which boiled as if they would swallow up each ship. In the morning were seen two ships, almost uninjured, lying between the rocks, upon which they had been driven, and the hulls of three others, and the corpses of their crews being dashed about'. The furious elements, as if in malicious humour, hurled the East Indiamen, the *Lastdrager*, the *Salamander* and the *Coning David*, into the midst of Tromp's storm-tossed ships.[29]

Next day, the 27th, Tromp could only muster thirty-nine vessels, mostly damaged. Others had found refuge in Galloway, and in the bays to the west and south-west of Shetland, and some even as far as Norway. Of the ninety-two ships, fifty-two men-of-war, six fireships, a supply vessel and two galliots were missing. In the hopes of picking them up, Tromp cruised for two days between Fair Isle and the Shetlands. How many ships were sunk or wrecked he did not know. Some of his captains told him that they had seen a number of ships to windward, which might be his: but they had also seen many wrecks on the lee shore. It was therefore decided, on the 30th, to make for home.[30] By 10 August, Tromp reached Holland with forty sail, while another fifty-one followed and got into the Texel early in September.[31] Tromp is reported to have come in, leaving a galliot and a frigate to pick up the stragglers, 'very melancholy, without shooting a gun or wearing a flag'.[32] The fickle mob laid the blame upon Tromp, who then resigned his commission, which the States-General accepted, seizing the chance to rid themselves of a supporter of the House of Orange. In his stead De With and De Ruyter were appointed to command the Dutch fleet.

Blake had escaped the full fury of the storm by lying in Brassa Sound. According to a Dutch report he sighted Tromp but did not seek to fight him, but turned aside as some of his ships, injured by the gale, were fit rather for careening than for an engagement.[33] Many of them had been scattered and the greater part of their supplies spoiled, as they had been brought them by small vessels

from Scotland.[34] Though the elements had scattered Tromp's
ships, they had also deprived Blake of his objective, the capture of
the East Indiamen. Scouts were sent out to look for Tromp, only
to report that he was nowhere to be found, and that the seas were
clear. Whereupon Blake sailed south. By 2 August he was off
Newcastle and next day off Scarborough.[35] Here he summoned
Penn and his captains to consult what they should do. If there
was more foul weather, and the fleet got separated, the rendezvous
was to be off Southwold if the wind was northerly, and if southerly,
off the Spurn. The watchword was characteristic of Blake: 'Patience,
Hope'.[36] As he still anticipated meeting Tromp, he sent his swifter
vessels to cruise between the Meuse and the Wielings, to discover
if anything was afoot. As nothing was observed, the fleet concentrated at Yarmouth. Here frigates were sent out to drive off Dutch
privateers, who had taken advantage of Blake's absence to be
active.[37]

A week after Tromp had failed to trap Ayscue, the council
ordered him to sail west. His squadron had been raised to thirty-
eight ships and his instructions were to secure English trade from
the southward, especially all ships from the Indies, the Straits,
Guinea, Spain and Portugal.[38] If necessary he was to ply off Land's
End and the Scillies, and even further. He was to seize all Dutch
vessels and, with the exception of those that had a licence from
the council, or which were small fishing vessels, all French ships,
men-of-war and merchantmen. All that should resist him he was
authorised to take, surprise, burn, sink or destroy.[39]

Simultaneously like orders had been given to De Ruyter. He
hoisted his flag in the *Neptune*, and joined his squadron of twenty-
two ships and six fireships at Ostend on 30 July. A fleet of sixty
merchantmen was gathering at the Texel, which he was to escort
down the Channel.[40] When he learned that Ayscue had sailed
west, he decided not to wait for his convoy and put to sea on 1
August.[41] Next day he fell in with some English barges, who told
him Ayscue was in mid-channel, near the Isle of Wight, with
forty-two ships.[42] Ruyter thereupon posted himself near Cape
Gris Nez, to await his convoy. In the interval he cruised along the
coast of Sussex, appearing off Brighton on the 14th, and so alarmed
the inhabitants that they fired the warning beacons.[43] This also
alarmed the council and they requested Blake to leave Yarmouth
for the Channel, where he would find either the Dutch or Ayscue.[44]

But Ruyter had been joined by his convoy and ten warships.
He sailed down the Channel.[45] Ayscue had reached Plymouth at
the end of July and escorted home five English East Indiamen on
the 30th.[46] He then put to sea again and returned with five prizes.[47]
On 15 August he learned of Ruyter's approach and put over to the
French coast to look for him.[48] On the 16th both fleets sighted
each other and a battle took place between Plymouth and the Isle
of Batz, lying just off the coast of Normandy at its north-west
extremity. Though both sides claimed the victory, honours lay
with Ruyter who was able to continue his voyage, while Ayscue
returned to Plymouth. His ships were badly damaged in their
masts, sails, rigging and hulls. Pack, Ayscue's Rear-Admiral, lost
a leg and fifteen men were killed and sixty wounded.[49] An English

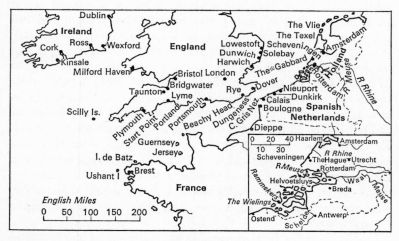

The English Channel

account put Ruyter's strength between fifty-five to sixty warships,
with twenty-five to thirty merchantmen, so that Ayscue may have
thought that Ruyter was considerably stronger than he really
was; since the merchantmen were large and well-armed ships, this
mistake would have been a natural one.[50] Ruyter sent on the convoy
with two warships and decided to attack Ayscue in Plymouth. Off
the Start the wind shifted to S.S.E., blowing hard, and Ruyter,
who had no wish to risk his vessels on a lee shore, abandoned his

attempt.[51] So he cruised off the Lizard, looking out for Dutch home-bound ships.[52] On the 29th he learned from a Lubeck ship that Blake was sailing west with seventy-two ships, and that he had been seen off Beachy Head on 20 August. He summoned all his captains and ordered them to be on the look out and sailed S.W. By the 31st he was fourteen miles off the French coast. 'This' he wrote, 'we did to avoid General Blake, with his fleet, and so continued till 1 September.'[53]

His decision to retire was correct, for on 22 August, Blake was even further to the west of the Isle of Wight, unaware that Ayscue had been defeated, and hastening to reinforce him. But reports now reached London that Tromp was bringing out a great fleet from the Meuse and Scheveningen. The report was incorrect: De With, now in supreme command, had superseded Tromp, and many of his ships were not ready to bring on a general action immediately. This of course the English Government did not know, and so they ordered Blake back towards the Dutch coast.[54] He was ordered to send six frigates to reinforce Ayscue. He had taken several Dutch ships. One, coming from Mata, in the Bay of Alicante, had fought with the *Dragon* for three hours, while another was driven ashore near Dieppe. A third, from the West Indies, was captured. Her skipper said that eight weeks before he had left Prince Rupert, with six ships, in St Christopher's Sound. Two more from Cape de Verde were also taken. This rich little haul was sent into Dover and to the Thames. A Lubeck vessel from Lisbon came in with Colonel Chester aboard. He had commanded the *Swallow*, one of Rupert's ships, and was detained by Blake. This report was dated 26 August, and Blake was now plying in the Narrows.[55]

On the same day Blake ordered Penn to take under his command eleven frigates, and to ply between Dungeness and the French coast for three days, and to surprise and destroy all ships coming from any place 'not in amity with this Commonwealth'. This move was to secure English trade from interference. Penn was not to go further west than Dungeness, so that Blake would know where to find him.[56]

Two days later Blake, who was now off Dover, informed Penn that the commander of the Spanish ships before Dunkirk had told him that a Dutch fleet of sixty sail was ready to come out of the Vlack, a shoal of the Meuse, for an unknown destination. He was sending Captain Moulton to him to bring back his squadron to him. The name of the informant was to be kept secret 'lest upon discovery he should receive damage'. However it was not until 11 September that De With made his appearance off the English coast. Much was to happen in the interval.[57]

For the French had been assisting the Dutch in their operations against Badiley's squadron in the Mediterranean.[58] In the Council of State the pro-Spanish party was now in the ascendent. War with the Dutch meant war with France. So, on 12 August the council asked Cardenas, the Spanish Ambassador, to draft a commercial Treaty with Spain. On 2 September he laid his proposals before them. As their reply must take time, he pressed upon them a further step. He had learned of the preparation of a French squadron at Calais, which was about to go to the relief of Dunkirk, now besieged by a Spanish army. Three days before the squadron sailed he secured an order from the Council of State for Blake to attack it.[59] The French squadron was commanded by Du Menillet in the *Triton*, with the *Shepherd*, *Gift of God*, *Duchess*, *Crescent*, *Hunter*, *St Louis* and the *Fort*, with six fireships.[60]

Such a step had already been urged by Charles Longland, the English Agent at Leghorn. On 1 May he had suggested an attack on a French squadron, arming for the relief of Barcelona, commanded by La Ferrière 'a famous thief that has done much mischief, and now intends the like ruin to any of our ships'. The Levant Company had also complained, as early as 1649, of the injuries done to them by the 'French fleet within the Straits'.[61] The proposed English action was therefore not without some justification.

On 27 August the Council of State ordered Blake to seize Du Menillet's squadron.[62] Blake immediately called a Council of War: 'upon advice whereof it was resolved to weigh anchor, and waylay them'. Though no dispatch of Blake's seems to exist, it is possible to reconstruct the action from various sources. Led by the *Sovereign*, a swift sailer, with Blake in the *Resolution*, and a fleet estimated at anything from twenty to fifty-four vessels, sail was set for Calais at 3 p.m. About 5 p.m. Du Menillet, who was at anchor, as he saw Blake approach, hoisted his colours, thinking that his squadron had been mistaken for the Dutch. But Blake bore up with his pennants flying and his trumpets sounding, in the pomp and circumstance of England's war.[63] There was no mistaking his intention. Du Menillet at once weighed his anchor and made for Flushing. He sent twelve Dieppe shallops, with supplies aboard, ahead of him and followed with his men-of-war, to give them time and space to escape. The English fleet greeted the enemy with 200 shots, doing great execution. A second broadside sank a French frigate, battered five more and, with key shot, cut off their mainmasts. All that the unfortunate Du Menillet could do was to retreat. He had strict orders not to intervene in the differences between the English and the Dutch, nor to commit any action tending to such, but instead to retreat rather than to fight. About 9 p.m. as darkness began to fall on the evening of 4 September, he found himself surrounded. The *Gift of God*, a ship belonging to the Knights of Malta, was boarded and taken and soon the *Triton, Shepherd, Duchess, Crescent, St Louis* and an unnamed Calais frigate were captured. Three fireships were also taken. Blake ordered the *Sovereign* and some frigates to chase the shallops, which were making for the sands of Dunkirk, where the more heavily built English ships could not follow them.[64] Then he sent back to Dover for men to be sent him to man the captured vessels. At midnight the chase was abandoned, 'for the pursuit had gone as far as we durst', and danger lay in the possible running on to the Dunkirk sands.[65] Blake then returned to the Downs. The *Sovereign*, which had the French King's Standard and pennants aboard, triumphantly fired a salute with all her guns, which caused the nervous inhabitants ashore to circulate a rumour that there had been a great fight with the Dutch.[66]

The French lost 300 men killed, and 500 wounded, while 1200 soldiers had been captured and landed at Dover. Du Menillet and his officers and men were consigned to the care of the mayor. They cost two shillings a day for their lodging and another shilling for their food. In entering the harbour two or three of their ships received damage beyond repair. Guns, powder, cables, ropes, munitions and provisions were seized, with the belongings of the officers and men. Reporting this Du Menillet begged for letters of credit, repayable when he returned to France.[67] He sent this letter by Captain Roche, of the *Crescent*, who disguised himself and escaped in an English packet boat, bound for France. Probably he thought that this was the last place where anyone would look for him. He was correct, for the Governor of Dover was ordered, though in vain, to find and arrest him.[68] One of the captured ships

turned out to be the *Hunter* and not the *Shepherd* which had, in
the darkness and smoke, eluded the English and escaped to Havre
with two fireships.[69] The Dieppe shallops seem to have escaped.

Thus seven ships were captured and three fireships. In the
captain of one of these Blake recognised one who had previously
served under him. When he heard that the ship did not belong to
the French King, but had been chartered, he at once restored it
to him again. Blake never forgot faithful service even in a foe. To
such he was always generous.[70]

On the 9th Du Menillet, in his report, wrote that after being
surrounded he had demanded to speak to Blake, 'but it was
impossible to reason with these people'. He had been treated as an
enemy, and not until 7 September, had he seen Blake. He had
shown him his orders, and had asserted that his action was a
matter for the King of France alone. To which Blake replied that
he would inform Parliament, and that Du Menillet would have an
answer in a few days.[71]

On 13 September, Admiral Vendôme sent Blake a protest
against the capture of the French ships. As war had not been
declared he could not believe that this had been done by the order
of the Commonwealth. He quoted Du Menillet's orders and asked
that the ships should be restored, signing himself 'Yours affection-
ately'. Not until 12 December did the Council of State reply.
They were perfectly prepared to maintain friendly relations with
France, as with other nations, but they reminded him of the wrongs
done to English shipping in the Mediterranean, including those
done by the King's own warships for some time past. As soon as
restitution and satisfaction was obtained for these wrongs and
injuries, the council would comply with Vendôme's request. As
answer there came none, the ships remained in English hands.[72]

On 14 September the council arranged for a passage to Dieppe
for the French seamen, though Du Menillet and his captains were
still detained. The council anticipated Jorrocks's maxim, 'con-
found all presents what eats'. It was not mercy that restrained the
noble rage of the council, but chill penury, for each man cost
them daily sixpence to feed. Before they sailed, however, a strict
examination was made to ensure that no cavaliers or any of
Rupert's men from the Mediterranean were among them.[73]

As a result of Blake's action in preventing relief, Dunkirk had
to surrender to the Spaniards on 6 September. Its fall had revealed

to Cromwell its vulnerability to naval power. Its possession, if it could be secured, would give England a bridgehead for placing an army on the Continent. More important still, it would form a great commercial centre, with its waterways extending eastwards, so that trade could be carried into Central Europe without any dependence upon the Dutch. The idea was to simmer in Oliver's mind for future use.

Blake's action in sailing north to intercept the Dutch East Indiamen had compelled Tromp to dance to a tune he had not called. By the irony of fate the storm had deprived Blake of his prey and given them safe to Tromp, though at the same time it had scattered the Dutch fleet in utter confusion. It had also prevented either opponent from engaging the other. Though De Ruyter had defeated Ayscue, De With was unable as yet to get to sea, and Blake used the respite to teach the French a sharp lesson: that English ships could not be captured with impunity. France, Spain and Portugal had learned that England's naval power was something with which to be reckoned. The Dutch, too, knew that they stood on the brink of a further, fiercer struggle.

CHAPTER 13

Blake, De With and De Ruyter

*

ON 6 September, 1652, Blake sailed from Dover, down Channel picking up Penn off Dungeness,[1] and arrived at Plymouth on the 8th. Here he sent in for Ayscue to come out and join him.[2] At a Council of War next day, it was decided to look for De Ruyter, as a fisherman had reported on 30 August that he was off the Scillies, and had asked him why Ayscue had not put out to sea.[3] The opportunity to deal with De Ruyter before De With had come out of harbour was too good to miss.

The Dutchman had endured a rough buffeting amid the islands, and had complained that it was 'very vexacious to cruise with such insolent officers, when the smallest boat act individually and independently'.[4] On the 13th he sailed for Ushant, probably to look out for returning merchantmen.[5] Meanwhile Blake had divided his ships into three squadrons, his own, Penn and Ayscue. On the evening of the 9th, they sailed westward towards the Hollander, 'or where they should discover them to be'.[6] But Ruyter was nowhere to be found. Blake thereupon concluded that he must be in the Channel, so he turned back, headed south to clear Bolt Head and by the 14th he anchored in Torbay. On the same day Penn had hove to to collect his scattered ships due to rough weather. Next morning at 9 a.m. he was off Bolt Head, uncertain as to where Blake was. At 10 a.m. Mildmay in the *Nonsuch* came up and told him that Blake was near shore to leeward.[7]

By now Ruyter was aware that large English forces were planning to crush him and he determined he must make for home. He made a clever and daring move. With the wind at N.N.W. he was, on the 15th, eight miles south of the Start, sailing north. He was thus in English waters, where he believed the enemy would not look for him. At noon he sighted Penn to the E.N.E., slightly ahead.[8] At the same moment Penn sighted two Dutch ships 'four miles in the wind of us', and shots were exchanged. His topmastmen now reported a fleet five miles to windward. Though he had only twenty-five ships, and so was numerically inferior, Penn decided to fight, and a Council of War confirmed his decision. He was unwilling to call the council, 'lest any dirty mouth should say I called for council whether I should fight or no'. But he had to prevent his captains from bearing up to join Blake in Torbay and to let them know, of which most of them were ignorant, that it was the Dutch fleet they saw to leeward. A ship was sent back to Blake to tell him of the decision, and the *President* and *Foresight* were sent off to watch the Dutch and to report, while Penn gathered up his squadron.[9] At 3 p.m. the two scouts returned and reported the enemy strength between thirty-five and forty sail. Then, just before 4 p.m., the Dutch stood away four or five miles to windward of Penn. For Ruyter was a well balanced man. He knew that the English main force must be near at hand, and he was not to be tempted by a possible temporary advantage to engage. His duty was to keep his ships intact and to join De With. Suddenly the Dutch were lost to sight in a thick mist, just as Penn was four leagues south of the Start.[10] All through the thick and dirty night, with a wind blowing hard from the west, Ruyter pressed on and made Guernsey next day, despite all Penn's efforts to locate him.

At dawn next morning, the 16th, Penn was reinforced by seven ships, sent by Blake.[11] The *Assurance*, sent by Penn to look for Ruyter came in and reported she had been in a fight at midnight, but had to break off action. She saw several lights to the south, steering away east, and was convinced they were Dutch 'who made use of the darkness of the first part of the night to pass by us'.[12] This was true, for on the 18th Ruyter made Dieppe, where he got orders from De With to join him, which he did at Nieuport on the 22nd.[13]

As there was no sign of Ruyter, Penn decided to join Blake whom he met coming out of Torbay. The fleet then sailed east, spreading out their ships between the coasts of England and France, 'almost as if a bridge had been made over the Channel, the ships within gunshot of each other'. But it was too late; no enemy was to be found and, on the 22nd, the fleet anchored in the Downs. Frigates were sent out as far as Dunkirk to gain news of the Dutch.[14] On the 24th Blake asked the council for victuals, and reported that Captain Warren, of the *Merlin*, was in custody for murdering one of his crew.[15] He was executed, but his wages were paid to his widow for her own and her children's relief.[16]

Something certainly had gone wrong. Ayscue had sat supinely in Plymouth and could give Blake no idea as to the whereabouts of Ruyter. Blake, with his principle of never dividing his fleet, had concentrated upon the sea round Scilly. But in the rough and thick weather he seems to have got separated from Penn, whose squadron was scattered. Blake, therefore, posted himself at Torbay, in the hope of catching Ruyter if he came up Channel or if he was already there. But Penn had lost touch with him and by the time he sighted Ruyter, south of him and in his rear, he was still collecting his squadron. By the time he had learned where Blake was it was too late for them to join forces, and in the thick mist Ruyter got away. It was not until next day that Blake spread out his ships to look for Ruyter as he moved up Channel. He did not forget the lesson; at Portland he spread out his fleet to meet Tromp. But opportunity to crush Ruyter had been missed.[17]

Already in June the Dutch trade was at a standstill, and the States-General was anxious for De With to get into action. In September, three Amsterdam firms had gone bankrupt. Seamen had mutinied and order was only restored after two mutineers had been hanged.[18] De With complained of defects in his ships, due to the lack of a central organisation. Though he was a man of sterling courage, he had a fiery temper which he vented in strong language, that made him unpopular. But by the 11th he appeared off South Sands Head, of which the council warned Blake[19] but it was not until the 22nd that Blake had assembled his fleet in the Downs. De With had sent out four frigates, on the 15th, which had chased a pink into Sandwich, and next day had forced ashore the *Swan*, between Folkestone and Dover. The *Ruby* and *Briar* eluded him, after an exchange of shots, and got into Dover. De With came close in shore to fire broadsides at the stranded ships, only to be driven off by the guns of Sandgate. By the 18th he was at the back of the Goodwins.[20]

De With had now sixty-four ships, so, on sighting Blake in the Downs on the 25th, with, as he thought sixty-eight vessels* he called a Council of War. At this Ruyter considered that the strength of the English, better armed and manned, made it unwise to risk the fleet by giving battle. But De With, in the first flush of supreme command, was anxious to distinguish himself. He ignored Ruyter's advice and decided upon action. He hoped to trap Blake,

* see Appendix 2

as Tromp had trapped Oquendo in 1639. He ordered Ruyter's squadron to lead, followed by his own, with De Wilde held in reserve. With this intention he anchored off the North Foreland.[21]

In the evening, however, a S.S.W. gale made the attempt impossible. Not until the night of the 27th did the storm moderate, and it was too late to catch Blake at anchor. Ruyter's squadron had been scattered, and five ships had either been blown off, or had made off, so that the fleet was reduced to fifty-nine.[22] In frustration De With withdrew to the Kentish Knock, fifteen miles N.E. of the North Foreland. It was an adroit move. With the wind blowing from the S.W. there was no danger of running on the shoals, while the enemy, desirous of keeping the wind, might well do so. They would, he calculated, be forced to attack instead from leeward.

Blake was far too clever to be trapped in the Downs. He took advantage of the S.W. wind to slip out. Before he sailed he sent to the council to say he would do or die. 'I engage about seventy Dutch men-of-war, which lay by the Goodwin Sands, and this may possibly be the last before I seal my faithful service with my best blood'; a uniquely flamboyant message for him.[23] About noon on the 28th the Dutch were sighted six leagues east of the North Foreland.[24]

As De With sighted Blake bearing down on him he collected his scattered vessels and left the *Princess Louyse*, and made for the *Brederode*, Tromp's old flagship, to hoist his flag on her. But her crew refused to let him come aboard. Instead he had to go to the *Prins Willem*, 'the worst sailer in the fleet'. He found a captain of seventy years, the officers drunk, a sick crew and many men who did not know even how to handle the guns. So he had to take over all these offices. By now Blake was within two gunshots of him to windward. As De With was now in the centre of his fleet, he hoisted sail to come to close quarters with Blake.[25]

Mildmay, in the *Nonsuch*, had sailed well ahead until he was within gunshot of the enemy. Blake, with only Bourne in company, was two leagues ahead of the rest of his fleet. Accordingly he lay to till the rest of his ships could come up, for the storm had kept them far astern.[26] About 3 p.m. Penn, in the *James*, came up with his squadron and sent to Blake to beg him to allow him to attack. Blake came alongside and called Penn aboard. He told him that 'as soon as more ships came up, they would all bear in among the enemy'. Penn then went ahead of Blake 'to give room for my squadron to lie between him and us'.[27] Blake wisely kept out of range, though De With fired three guns 'at General Blake to beg him to come on'. At this Blake gave orders that no shots were to be fired until the fleet was within range of the enemy.[28] His plan of attack was a bold one, which anticipated that of Nelson at Aboukir Bay. He would keep the wind by thrusting in between the Kentish Knock and the Dutch. Between 3 and 4 p.m. the rest of Blake's ships had arrived.[29]

S. R. Gardiner has said, 'Blake was no Nelson, and he had none of the innovating tactical skill which had enabled Cromwell to convert a mere success into a crushing victory. He was, however, a bold and inspiring leader, who might be trusted to fight to the last, and to do everything compatible with the somewhat primitive tactics of the day'.[30] This is a little unfair. Tactics at that time were conceived on a military basis. The ship represented either an infantry or cavalry unit, firing to its front, or advancing on the foe at 'push of pike', or riding into its ranks with the sword. The ship therefore charged into the body of the enemy and, if possible, boarded him with the cutlass. It was not fully recognised that the ship was no longer a regiment, but a mobile artillery unit, which did not fire to its front, but at right angles to its line of advance. The conception of 'line ahead' had not yet been evolved. Instead the squadrons advanced upon the enemy in line abreast. The first object was to gain the wind, in order that the fireships could be launched upon the foe. The ships could thus bear down on the enemy, and thrust through their fleet, attacking individual vessels on their vulnerable side, the bow or the quarter. By dispersing the attack among individual ships the advantage was thrown away. This could have been gained if the whole fleet, or even a large part of it, could have concentrated its fire, as it passed through, on a single portion of the enemy. Moreover ships, approaching in line abreast, exposed themselves to a raking fire, which would sweep them from bow to stern, without being able to bring their broadsides into action. Once the attack was over, the enemy were free, with the advantage of the wind, to attack in the same fashion.

Blake surprised the Dutch by appearing on their weather quarter, and by delaying his attack till he was ready. In so doing he displayed his natural genius for handling a fleet. At 4 p.m. Penn, in the *James*, led the onslaught. Blake in the *Resolution* followed, with the *Sovereign*, the *Dreadnought* of her day, as she was so large and strong that she could withstand any amount of battering. But at the very start of the attack the *James*, with the *Resolution* and the *Sovereign*, which Penn says was 'without us', grounded on the Kentish Knock in less than three fathoms. Blake's comment was that it was fortunate 'that fair weather and smooth water' saved many of the great ships from 'perishing without a stroke from the enemy'. When Penn grounded, Blake observed it and kept outside him, hoping to avoid danger. Bourne was still coming up in the rear, so that at this point Blake was S.S.W. of the Dutch, who now tacked to meet him.[31]

Blake appears to have been the first to get free by tacking to the south. He then led his squadron north to meet the Dutch, closely followed by the *Sovereign*, which had also got free. About 5 p.m., they sailed through the Dutch, both vessels exchanging many broadsides with the enemy. The *Sovereign* is said to have had as many as twenty Dutch frigates about her, but her size made their attacks of no avail.[32]

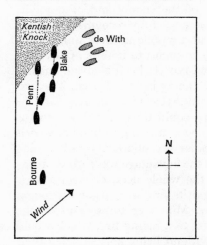 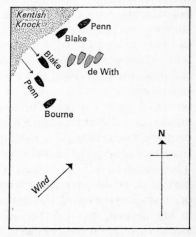

The Battle of the Kentish Knock, 28 September, 1652
(The figures represent groups of ships, not single vessels)

Penn had more difficulty in getting free of the Knock, and was forced to tack to the south. This luckily turned out to his advantage. 'For as the Dutch fleet cleared themselves of our General, he standing to the northward and they to the south, we fell pat to receive them, and so stayed by them till night caused our separation'.[33] To add to the Dutch confusion Bourne's squadron had now come up and, as Blake wrote, 'the dispute was very hot for a short time, continuing till it was dark night'.[34] At 7 p.m. Mildmay saw three great Dutch ships: a dismasted Rear-Admiral: another of thirty guns without her mainmast: and another of thirty guns, which had her in tow. Mildmay came within musket-shot and fired a few shots into her and she cast off the tow rope. When Mildmay boarded her with thirty men, she surrendered. He then chased the ship which had her in tow, sent thirty men aboard her and captured her. Though several Dutch ships were near, they made no attempt to go to her aid. The Dutch Rear-Admiral was also taken. By this time Mildmay had lost sight of his own fleet, and was driven to leeward of the enemy fleet, which was a mile off. One Dutch ship he left to sink after taking out her crew, and then he set sail to join his own fleet, some four leagues off.[35]

Badiley, probably the brother of Richard, now in the Mediterranean, charged 'exceedingly gallantly'. The Dutch were so close to him, charging against him 'that one might have flung biscuits out of his frigate into the Dutch ships'. His sails were so torn that he could neither sail to nor fro, and was in great danger of losing his ship. He had 100 shot in his hull, with sixty of his men dead. Six enemy ships surrounded him, but the *Speaker*, *Diamond* and *Greyhound* came up and rescued him. Jordan, in the *Pelican*, who was close to him, did very gallantly also, though his ship and the *Guinea* were badly shattered.[36]

De With had undergone even more difficulties. Among his crew were a number of 'unskilled men'.[37] He described his experiences: 'we were within gunshot of General Blake and we began to exchange fire, and both fired heavily, being nearest the enemy we stood the first onset of their greatest force, nor were we idle meanwhile, so that from about 3 o'clock in the afternoon, we saw nothing but smoke, fire and the English, until the sun went down'.[38] His rigging, spars and foretopsails were shot away, so that his ships lay damaged and unmanageable, unable to put about on either bow. De Ruyter, too, was very severely damaged. The other vessels, most of them astern, kept firing but, though De With lay helpless, they did not go to his aid. The more advanced ones, 'who might well have come nearer the enemy, even fired at them many times

over and through our ship. When dark fell in the evening and the
enemy, who were to windward of us, left us, it was quite apparent
that several of our ships had dropped off to leeward without orders,
when they perfectly well might have remained further to windward'. De With had to let his ship drift, sailless. He then returned
to the *Princess Louyse*.[39] His only comfort was that he had been
able to fire his guns more rapidly as he was using parchment
cartridges. This enabled his cannon to carry more than half as
far than before. But he also commented that 'we found the guns
on their smallest frigates carry further than our heaviest cannon:
and the English, I am sure, fired smarter and quicker than did
many of ours'.[40]

That night both fleets lay in sight of one another, repairing
their ships. Blake had lights upon his poop and maintop, while
the Dutch lights could be 'seen plain a short distance to leeward
of us, which made us believe they wished to engage us the next
morning'.[41] Next day De With called all his captains aboard to
tell them that some of them had not done their duty, as they had
kept to leeward and, instead of firing on the enemy, had damaged
one another. He urged them to do better.[42]

At daybreak Blake sighted the Dutch two leagues N.E. of him.
There was little wind, and he bore up with them with all the speed
he could. 'They seeming a while to stay for us till afternoon'. The
wind then shifted to the north, and the Dutch stood away eastwards for their own coast. Blake followed 'as much as we possibly
could'. As the Dutch now had the wind, many shots were exchanged
'between some of our headmost ships and their stern fleet, but
nothing could engage them'. As it now grew dark Blake tacked to
collect his fleet, so as to gain the weather gage. Then being 'half
Channel over' he was advised by his captains and pilots 'to lie
close upon that tack till 10 of the clock, so that we might have
length enough to spend that night, presuming likewise that they
would tack before the morning, which would have again brought us
together if the wind had stood'.[43] But that night there was but
little wind, and that westerly. Penn says, 'our General perceiving
that their spirits declined, by their making no great haste in their
way towards us, commanded our frigates to ply so near them as
they could, and keep firing at them, while the rest of us did our
best to get near them. About 3 a.m. some of our frigates got within
shot, and much powder and shot was spent on both sides, it

Sir William Penn, a portrait painted after the Restoration by Lely

The Battle of the Kentish Knock, an engraving by J. Pass published in November 1799

continuing till night, but I think to little purpose. At which time, three in the afternoon, the Dutch set their mainsails – to get away from us – towards their own shore'.[44] Mildmay adds that the great ships could not get up with the enemy, except 'the *Sovereign* and some others got within shot, and plied many shot, and for that they kept their great East India ships in the rear-guard, we could not get up any competent strength to break them, for they did their utmost to get from us. So many thousands of great shot passed from one to another, till it was so dark that we could not know our own ships. So we drew off to our Admiral, who straight put up his lights upon the poop and mainmast: but the Hollanders showed none, but most poorly and sneakingly stole away'.[45]

De With's story is somewhat different. At noon, when the wind shifted, he stood towards the English, so as to get to windward of them. But the wind dropped so that 'our ships were badly damaged'. He saw 'sundry ships were following us very slowly, more than usually so, and therefore we fired several shots at them'. It was very evident that his captains had paid no heed 'to my faithful appeal that very morning'.[46] At 3 p.m. he called Ruyter and Evertsen aboard him. Twenty captains had deserted during the night before, but De With was still anxious to renew the attack, and even steered towards the English.[47] He was neither followed nor obeyed by some of his ships. Both his commanders advised him not to risk the fleet further. Ruyter 'who was never deficient in courage, telling him that a fleet commander sometimes does better service by giving way and retreating than by fighting'. They urged him in fact to keep his fleet 'in being'. They gave their reasons. The ships were scattered a mile apart from one another: because of the calm it would be 5 p.m. before the first ship, and evening before the last, could reach the enemy fleet: the English had eighty-four ships to the Dutch forty-nine: three severely damaged ships had gone off in the night, while thirteen others had vanished, how, no one knew: further the English had fireships, while they had none.[48]

The arguments convinced De With and he took stock of the situation. With so little wind it was inadvisable to attack, as that would give the enemy the opportunity 'of laying their fireships aboard us'. At night his injured ships might be cut off and captured. The fleet must be kept together, though he observed that 'several ships were strongly inclined to sail a good way ahead of us away

from the enemy'. He commented they 'seem in every way to try
and show the white feather, indeed brandish it so, that we are
put to shame before the world'. Towards evening the fastest
English ships attacked to the W.N.W., with the Dutch steering
N.E. Blake's frigates fired several rounds at De With's rearmost
ships, 'among which we were ourselves, and we fired on them in
reply'.[49]

Nevertheless at a council next day, the 30th, De With again
proposed to beat to windward and await the foe. All the captains
strongly objected; their men were sick with scurvy and the English
were much too strong for them.[50] 'Never in my life' burst out
De With in a fury, 'have I seen such cowardice among sea-
captains as these have shown'.[51] But there was nothing he could
do but to retreat to Goree, where he arrived on 3 October.[52]

The same day, with the wind at S.W., Blake wrote that 'from
the topmasthead we discovered their fleet, and stood after them.
Many of our frigates ahead of us, some so far that they saw the
West Gabbard'. Penn was of the opinion that the Dutch hoped to
entice them on to the sands, where the great ships might have
foundered. Blake, however, 'perceiving that they fled from us as
fast as they could, and bent their course for Goree, it growing less
wind, I sent for the Vice and Rear-Admirals, and also the greater
part of the Captains'. They consulted 'what was fittest to be done'.
As the merchantmen were practically out of victuals, and as there
was nothing to supply them with, it was agreed to return home.
On 2 October the fleet anchored in Margate Road.[53]

Blake had won his first battle upon the open sea. It was not to
be his most important one. He had wisely waited for his ships
to come before he attacked. Then after getting free from the
Knock he had retrieved what might have been a disaster by attacking the Dutch van as it came to meet him. Thus he gave Penn,
when he got free, the opportunity to 'receive them pat'. Bourne,
too, was now in time to attack the head of De With's ships as
they cleared Penn. He had displayed his natural genius for handling
a fleet. Yet only one Dutch ship was sunk, and two captured.
The Dutch had been defeated but not destroyed. On the other
hand it was only thanks to De Ruyter and Evertsen that prevented
De With from making a suicidal new attack, and so preserved the
Dutch fleet 'in being'. The battle had demonstrated that the
English ships, heavier and more stoutly built, were more than a

match for the lighter Dutch vessels. The heavier, more accurate, and speedier firing of Blake's guns, had outranged those of the enemy and had done much to lower the already low morale of the Hollanders. Blake had instilled into his fleet the discipline, resolution and pride in themselves, that had raised the morale of his men to the highest pitch.

De With had, however, brought home a shattered fleet. The number of dead was unknown, but 2,000 wounded men were landed.[54] The crews had to be kept on board to prevent them from deserting. The Boards of Admiralty had to order seamen to go aboard, while the ringleaders of the mutineers had to be punished. The soldiers aboard were growing sullen and needed to be relieved.[55]

A Commission of seven members, one from each Province, was set up at Helvoetsluys to enquire into the defeat. The result was accusation and counter-accusation. Each man excused himself by laying the blame 'upon this and that and the other misfortune, and upon the English being too strong for them'.[56] De With was made the scapegoat, and paid the penalty by being dismissed. Yet the Government was largely to blame. The seamen had resented the replacement of Tromp, the ablest, most beloved and trusted Admiral, by De With. He was impetuous, headstrong, with a bitter tongue and he had neither the leadership, nor the inspiration, to gain the affection of the seamen. On the contrary they strongly disliked him. From the first he was fatally handicapped, because he was the victim of his own defects. Before the battle he had boasted, 'I shall bring the fleet merrily to the enemy, the Devil may bring it off'. A current jest added that he 'had saved the Devil the trouble, having brought it off himself'.[57]

The repercussions of Blake's victory were immediate. The Dutch dared not stir out of their ports, and the small English frigates reaped a rich harvest. On 15 October, Captain Peacock, in the *Tiger*, put into Yarmouth with a small squadron. He had taken twenty prizes, including a warship the *Morgenstar*, which he had boarded after an hour's fight, only losing his bowsprit and not a single man.[58] Captain Ball, too, had returned from the Sound, bringing with him the crews of twenty English merchantmen, who had been interned by the Danes. Unfortunately for him, on 30 September, a severe storm struck his squadron and his ship, the *Antelope*, was driven ashore and lost.[59]

Blake, on 3 October, asked the Council for a considerable supply of victuals, that he 'might answer all opportunities that may present'. He warned them that it was 'likely that the Dutch will make all the power they can, by the first easterly wind to force their way through the sea with their convoys to several parts, the welfare whereof is their subsistence'.[60] The warning was soon to be justified.

CHAPTER 14

With Tromp's Recall a Dutch Victory

*

THOUGH Blake had been victorious, he had no delusions about the Dutch. He knew well the defeat would not deter the enemy. He was right, for the Dutch had not the least thought of making peace. Rather, they considered that English success as merely local and temporary: and they attributed their defeat to De With's unfitness for command, and to the misconduct of his captains. So it was not surprising that there was a general call for Tromp to command the fleet again. This was supported by the King of Denmark, and the States-General bowed to the blast, and reinstated Tromp. He accepted the decision though he confessed 'that fighting the enemy, and venturing my life, gives me not the least trouble, but all my trouble arises from this, that after I have contributed all that is in me to the service of the country, I may be molested on my return home with subtle questions, which never happened to me in my life till now after my last voyage: so that when I am at sea, I shall have not only to study to damage the enemy, but also to take trouble to do nothing, however serviceable I may judge it to be, which is capable of being otherwise interpreted by ill-disposed and hostile persons.' He made it clear that, when he returned, he hoped he might be 'set free from the annoyance of the investigations of accounts, examinations etc., it being unheard of that a commander-in-chief of a whole force should have to answer all kinds of subtle question, why he did not rather do this, and why he rather did that'.[1]

De With, De Ruyter, Evertsen and Floriszoon were reappointed as his Vice-Admirals, but De With declined upon the ground of ill-health: but in reality on account of fatigue, chagrin and anger. The others accepted without hesitation, and De Ruyter was given De With's squadron.[2]

Tromp was ordered to take a large convoy to the Island of Rhé. He himself was to remain in the Channel, but to send part of his fleet on to Rhé to bring back the homebound merchantmen, who were to collect there. The States-General expected him to sail about 22 October. He at once objected that this division of the fleet would be fraught with danger. For he would need his full strength to meet the English, either to blockade or to pursue them. In such a case, was he to leave the merchantmen to be a prey to the fast sailing frigates of the foe, or was he to stay by them? His objections were accepted. He was now to take the whole fleet to Rhé, and then to careen and overhaul his ships there. But on his way he was instructed to do as much damage as possible to the foe.[3]

The task of preparation was extremely difficult. Most of the ships were so foul that their sailing capacity was much reduced, so that they would be an easy prey to the fast sailing frigates. But there were also other and more pressing problems, the chief of which was the want of seamen. This was due to various causes. One was their complaint that, after serving, they could get no pay and they declared that two seamen had been hanged for demanding it. When at sea they asserted that they were badly fed, sometimes on bread and water only. Even if they did get paid on return, half of it was retained, so as to force them to serve again in order to get it.[4] Small wonder was it that they preferred to serve on merchantmen, where they ran little risk of losing their lives in action. In spite of soldiers being put on board to prevent desertion, the seamen still got away. Only thirty seamen had come aboard and, as there was a likelihood of mutiny among those already there, Tromp was ordered to give them a month's pay with a month in advance, to such old seamen who would take it. But none appeared to claim it, and that very night a whole crew deserted. On 12 November, it was reported that Ruyter's crew had mutinied at Rotterdam, and had gone to Amsterdam to demand their pay from the States-General.[5] Two days later, Tromp reported that Commodore De Wilde had come to him to say that most of his oldest and best seamen were running outside the dyke, towards Amsterdam, declaring that they would not go to sea unless they also got the higher wages that were being paid to the newly enrolled men. This incredible piece of administrative stupidity was promptly dealt with by Tromp. He brought the seamen back by promising them the increased rates of pay. He also asked for a Fiscal or State Prosecutor, and a Provost Marshal, to deal with men who had deserted, and to keep proper order among the crews ashore. This provision would also enable him to hold Courts Martial on officers and men, who failed in their duty, especially as in the case of De With's captains.[6] For it had not been possible to deal with these persons, owing to the bitter rivalry of the provincial and maritime jurisdictions. So, with vigour and, above all, with common sense, Tromp straightened out the muddle and disorganisation into which the Dutch naval administration had fallen. His great qualities enabled him to solve difficulties that seemed, at first sight, to be insuperable. So it was that, amazingly, on 21 November, he had overcome all hindrances and had put to sea. He had collected eighty-eight ships, five fireships and eight smaller vessels. He divided the fleet into four squadrons under the command of De Ruyter, Evertsen, Floriszoon and himself.[7]

Blake, who was lying in the Downs, must have been delighted to learn that, on 28 September, the Council of State had ordered thirty new frigates to be built, at the instigation of Sir Henry Vane.[8] This indicated to him that Parliament had resolved to carry on the war with vigour. But this, however, was tempered by the action of the Danish King, alarmed at the growth of England's naval supremacy, in detaining in the Sound twenty merchantmen, laden with supplies for building and fitting shipping. For this was the convoy that Captain Ball had been sent to bring home. The council instantly sent Richard Bradshaw to the King to demand their return, together with the guns and furniture of the *Antelope*, which had been seized when she ran ashore. Bradshaw was authorised, upon their release, to promise that all Danish ships, with their lading, detained in English ports, would be sent home. This the King refused, in the hope of hampering the outfitting of English shipping. Instead, at the end of the war, his policy recoiled upon his own head. For the supplies needed were obtained from other sources, and he had to pay damages for what he had done. However, for the moment, Ball was allowed to bring home the crews of the detained vessels.[9]

In England the war was becoming unpopular, especially with the army, which was strongly hostile to a conflict with a Protestant nation. There was a false belief that, as the Dutch appeared to have confined themselves to their harbours, they would shortly open negotiations for peace. So, early in November, it was proposed to send Ambassadors to the Hague to ascertain the views of the Government as to the terms of peace. The election for the

fifth Council of State, on 24 November, revealed a victory for
the Peace Party. Cromwell headed the poll, and the War Party
was largely excluded. Blake himself, regarded, in S. R. Gardiner's
words, 'as the incarnation of the war spirit' was shut out.[10]

For the war had turned out very differently from what had been
expected. No crushing blow had been inflicted upon the Dutch.
The cost of the new frigates was £300,000 while the annual bill
for the fleet was £985,000. To meet this the revenue set aside was
£415,000, so that the total deficit was £870,000, with the Baltic
trade paralysed.[11] Nor did the Dutch prizes captured avail to
redress the balance. Moreover, when English vessels were taken,
the loss had to be borne by individual owners, while the benefit
from the Dutch prizes accrued to the State. Hired merchantmen
had to be added to the fleet, which, as Penn pointed out, was
dangerous, since the masters, often part owners as well, were
naturally more concerned with the safety of their vessels in fighting,
than with public advantage. Instead he suggested that they should
be commanded by a State captain, but his advice was ignored.[12]

In supreme confidence in their power to defeat the Dutch,
resulting from their victory over Tromp, De With and De Ruyter,
the council ordered the dismantling of the coast defences between
Deal and Sandwich. They allotted Blake only forty-two ships, less
than a third of those at their disposal; a report from the officers of
the *Garland*, after its capture in the subsequent battle, showed
that, besides Blake's fleet, ten ships were cruising about Ushant,
eighteen had sailed for the West Indies, twenty-six were preparing
to go to the Mediterranean, thirteen were lying at Portsmouth
and another fourteen were in the Thames, while twenty under
Penn were set aside for the escort of colliers from Newcastle to
London.[13]

Blake had not been idle for, on 30 October in company with
the *Nonsuch* off Cape La Hogue, he had met and taken four
Hamburg vessels to the Downs.[14] On the same day Captain
Willoughby wrote gloomily to the Navy Commissioners from
Portsmouth. He was 'beside himself with worry', for the seamen
were 'clamourous for their money, and will not go to sea unless
they are paid'.[15] As the council did not anticipate much naval
activity during the winter, this report did not unduly perturb them.
They even sought to reduce the number of ships in commission.
On 11 November, they told Blake that they would replace the

twenty ships, going to the Mediterranean under Peacock, by others taken from the Winter Guard. But this was easier to promise than to effect. So stringent was the financial situation that, for some time, it had been impossible to pay the seamen their wages. On the 24th, the Navy Commissioners informed the council that, because of this fact, the crews of the *Fleece*, the *Maidenhead* and the *Resolution*, had mutinied, declaring that they would not serve without pay. Robert Locksmith and Thomas Backworth had been arrested, and the crews ordered back to their ships in the Thames. This they had refused to obey. It was impossible to procure victuals, since the victualler had not been paid since May, and refused to supply goods on credit. The Commissioners ended upon an ominous note, which was to have full effect in the near future: men could not be got to serve on the prizes now fitting out in the Thames.[16]

Disconcerting news was reported from Holland by English newspapers, on 22 October. 100 or 120 ships were preparing there, of which twenty were fireships. Tromp and Evertsen, with seventy vessels formed the vanguard, while De Ruyter was to follow with fifty more. They were to escort 200 merchantmen southwards. They were only delayed by the lack of men.[17] On the 29th it was reported from Rotterdam that 150 ships were also preparing, and that the States-General had bidden Tromp to hasten out the fleet.[18] From Amsterdam, on 19 November, it was stated that Tromp had seventy-eight warships and 300 merchantmen.[19] Yet despite these rumours that Tromp was about to sail, the council showed little anxiety, and did not strengthen Blake's fleet. They were to receive a rude shock; and that at the very moment when it was proposed to send Ambassadors to Holland to discuss the possibilities of making peace.[20]

For, on 21 November, Tromp had put to sea with over 300 men-of-war and merchantmen. On the evening of the 22nd he was joined by Ruyter and Evertsen, with ten warships, some fireships and merchantmen, which brought the total to 450 vessels. On the evening of the 23rd he was off Dunkirk, and with a N.E. wind he set his course for Dover.[21]

On the same day Blake reported to the council that the *Sapphire*, which had been sent out to scout, had taken a small Dutch hoy, and then had chased a frigate, of twenty-four guns, which was with her, but had lost her in the darkness. The hoy was taken into the Downs, where the skipper told Blake that Tromp was at Goree, while other ships were in the Wielings and at the Texel. It was probable, wrote Blake, 'that they were preparing to go to sea, and sent out this scout on purpose to discover our station, motion and strength'. It seems more likely that the hoy was purposely sent out with false information, so as to deceive Blake.[22]

Hardly had he sent off this dispatch, than he followed it with another. This was alarming. In the afternoon, from his top-mast, eighty sail had been sighted off the North Foreland, and supposed to be the Dutch fleet. In the evening he got news from Margate, that 400 sail had been observed from the steeple there. At once a Council of War was summoned, at which it was decided that, as the wind was at S.W. by S. and likely to blow and to rain, the fleet should ride moored that night, and that another council should meet at dawn to consult further.[23]

But, to everyone's surprise the next day, the Dutch had vanished from sight. Then the *Katherine* came into the Downs with the news that she had sighted 300 sail of the Dutch. Blake at once sent her off to ply off the South Foreland, with three frigates, to watch them. Obviously he thought that they must have sailed down the Channel. But the four ships remained there, until the 27th, without sighting any of the enemy.[24]

The explanation of the Dutch disappearance was a simple one. Bad weather had decided Tromp to retire, and on the 25th, he was off Ostend, where he was probably sighted by the *Katherine*. Many of the merchantmen had gone back to the Weilings, without informing Tromp. More vessels begged to be allowed to put into Goree, by reason of the wind. Then a storm sprang up, which caused much damage. At night ships fouled one another, and bowsprits and beakheads were broken off. So, on the 26th, it was resolved to await a fair wind. 'I could wish' wrote Tromp, 'to be so fortunate as to have only one of two duties, to seek out the enemy, or to give convoy'. He had sent out six ships to discover the English fleet. Four returned to report that they had seen four ships and two merchantmen, off Margate. But, as the weather was so thick and gloomy, it had been impossible to observe the situation in the Downs.[25]

On the same day, Blake informed the council that he intended to put to sea. This they approved, and sent orders that the

Speaker, Hercules, Sapphire and *Ruby* should join him from Portsmouth. As the council knew that Tromp was at sea, this was an incredibly foolish order. To send out these ships, without warning them of their danger, was to send them to probable destruction, unless Blake, with his inferior numbers, could secure a victory.[26]

But before Blake had put out, Tromp had intervened. He had collected his ships between Calais and Dover at 4 a.m. on the 29th. The merchantmen he left behind, with some men-of-war and fireships to guard them. At daybreak he sighted Blake, lying in the Downs, from the back of the Goodwins, with the wind at W.S.W. and W.N.W. He must have hoped that he could trap Blake, as he had done with Oquendo. At 11 a.m., with a slack tide, both fleets made sail. Tromp estimated Blake's fleet at fifty-two ships, of which forty-two were 'middle-sized'.[27]* Gilson, of the *Speaker*, managed to slip in with two prizes bound from Cadiz to Amsterdam, richly laden. This bold act 'much incensed the Dutch'.[28] On Tromp's appearance, Blake instantly called a council of officers. Then, 'after great consultations and prayers', it was resolved to fight. Prayers were then said on every ship, and Blake set sail. He sent three scouts ahead, who encountered five Dutchmen, who declined engagement and so they rejoined the fleet.[29]

The wind now shifted from S.W. to N.W., which prevented any possibility of coming to grips. About 5 p.m. Blake 'anchored close under the high land west of Dover',[30] as Tromp noted. The Dutchmen did the same 'about two leagues to leeward of us'[31] according to Blake. All night it blew a gale, so that in the morning Tromp found that some of his vessels and fireships were missing.[32]

Next morning the wind was N.N.W. and according to Blake, less than before. With a rising tide Tromp weighed 'taking all pains to get at them'.[33] With trumpets sounding, and drums beating, Blake did the same. It was, however, ominous that twenty ships remained where they were, aloof from the rest. As Blake's seamen cheered wildly, there came answering cheers from the Dutch.[34] The English Admiral stood west, with two objects in view; first to keep clear of the Rip-Raps, now known as the Varne, on which, if he charged through Tromp's fleet, he was in danger of running. Secondly, by sailing west, he would give the Portsmouth ships an opportunity to join with him. The Dutch were

* see also Appendix 2

now 'sailing fair by us', and Blake held firmly on to the weather gage, which Tromp unsuccessfully attempted to wrest from him.[35] Following Tromp in the van, came Ruyter in the centre, with Evertsen leading the rear-squadron. Blake estimated the Dutch at ninety-five ships, with three Admirals and two Vice and Rear-Admirals, 'almost all great ships'.[36]

At 1 p.m. some of Tromp's fastest ships began to open fire. But not until both fleets were off Dungeness, did Tromp turn in to charge Blake, in a desperate attempt to seize the weather gage from him.[37] As far as it is possible to ascertain, both fleets were approaching each other on an oblique course. Blake foiled Tromp's purpose by passing under his bow, both ships exchanging broadsides as they passed. As a result Tromp crashed into the *Garland*, of forty-four guns, under Captain Robert Batten, which was coming up, close on Blake's lee quarter. So violent was the impact that the bowsprit and the beakhead of the *Brederode* were broken off close to the stem. Walter Hoxton, in the merchantman, *Bonaventure* of thirty-six guns, instantly laid himself alongside Tromp on the port quarter.[38] Batten's and Hoxton's crews boarded Tromp's ship in a desperate attempt to capture her. Pike and cutlass, axe and musket clashed as Tromp's crew fought doggedly to keep their ship. Evertsen, seeing his Admiral's plight, cleverly manoeuvred his ships alongside the *Bonaventure*, and the four ships lay locked together, unable to use their guns, for fear of harming their friends.[39] Now the situation was reversed. For Evertsen's men swarmed aboard the *Bonaventure*, whose crew rushed back to defend their own ship. Tromp's men, relieved from pressure, poured likewise on to the decks of the *Garland*. Two more Dutch Admirals came up, and also engaged the *Garland*. Overwhelmed by numbers, in a last struggle to free himself, Batten blew up his decks, killing himself and flinging the enemy boarders into the air. About 4 p.m. after Batten was killed, as the darkness closed in on the short December day, the *Garland* surrendered. Of her crew of 200, sixty officers and men had been killed, and many wounded, while 100 were made prisoners. Tromp took possession of her, placing a crew of sixty men aboard. Hoxton, too, had 'cleared his decks many times, fighting as a private man' until he also was overwhelmed and killed, in a fresh onslaught by Evertsen's crew. With his death the *Bonaventure* yielded.[40] Both Tromp and Evertsen 'were miserably torn'. As Tromp admitted, his ship had not a whole spar in her, and was very leaky, and with hardly a shroud that had not to be spliced.[41] 'During the fight' wrote Tromp, 'a part of our ships (which might have come up) were busy about Blake in fighting his remaining ships, which retreated back to Dover for the Downs'.[42]

Lane, in the *Victory* of forty-six guns, was at the same time beset by the enemy. The *Vanguard* of forty-six guns, under Mildmay, with some other ships, came up to her assistance. Almost immediately they had twenty Dutch vessels around them, among them two flagships. But though they were very much battered in their sails, yards, rigging and hulls, they got off well.[43]

Blake had conducted himself 'admirably, both by exhortation and example, and by the feats of his own sailors and by the hull of his ship'.[44] Only late in the action had he notice of the sore plight of the *Garland* and the *Bonaventure*. Instantly he gave the order to bear up to them, 'but immediately our fore-mast was shot away, our main-mast being shot before, and our rigging much torn, so that we could not work our ship to go to their relief: and by occasion thereof, and night coming on, we saved ourselves, who were then left almost alone'.[45] He had lost only six men killed, with ten wounded. From his own observation he explained these figures by the fact that the Dutch fired too high, so that the shot passed through the sails and rigging, and not through the hull.[46] Indeed such shots as did find the hull did little damage, owing to the stout build of the English ships. His own ships, on the contrary, made the hull their target, so much so that Ruyter, in his struggle with Blake, was forced to withdraw his ship to the shelter of his own squadron.[47] According to another account, Blake was twice boarded,[48] which seems most unlikely, since Blake himself says nothing of it. If it had happened, he must have lost more men, 'having only the *Vanguard* and *Sapphire* standing close to him: yet he got off well out of the crowd of enemies, and so did the rest, save only the two that were taken'.[49]

At night Blake, and his ships, retreated to Dover. Next morning 'the weather growing thick and fearing a S.W. wind we stood away for the Downs, where (by God's Providence) we now are'.[50] Tromp had anchored off Dungeness, where he listened, until 9 p.m., to the firing of his ships at the English. Then, in the darkness, he saw a Dutch ship on fire, which suddenly blew up. This the English also witnessed. Her captain and part of her

crew were drowned, but the rest were rescued. All through the
night the Dutch were engaged in stopping their leaks, securing
their masts, and repairing their tackle. So fierce had been the
fight.[51]

On 1 December, Blake wrote to the council. He warned them
to be prepared for bad news. After a brief account of the battle,
he reported 'that there was much baseness of spirit, not among the
merchantmen only, but many of the State's ships'. He asked for
a commission to be sent down to enquire into the conduct of
several captains, and he complained of errors and defects, and
especially of the discouragements by the want of seamen. The
trouble, he believed, was due to the large number of privateers
in the Thames, in which the seamen preferred to serve. Then,
in severe dejection at his defeat, he asked the council to give him
his discharge 'from this employment, so far too great for me,
especially since your Honours have added two such able gentlemen
for the undertaking of that charge, so that I may spend the
remainder of my days in private retirement and prayers for a
blessing upon you and the Nation'. This was written in no sar-
castic or resentful spirit, as the 'two able gentlemen' Deane and
Monck, had been appointed Generals of the Fleet on 26 November. This Blake must have known before he sailed, and to which
he had raised no objection. As his own commission was about to
expire, the council affirmed their belief in his qualities, by
appointing him to serve for another year. 'Which' replied Blake,
'I shall endeavour to put into execution with all the power and
faithfulness I can, until it shall please your Honours to receive
it back again, which I trust may be very speedily'. Then the true
Blake flashes out for a moment, as he asks the council to order
the frigates at Portsmouth, and in the west, to secure themselves,
'until the enemy be drawn off, or this fleet reinforced, especially
by recruits of seamen to fight again'.[52]

Unfortunately his warning came too late. For, on the same day
that he wrote, the *Hercules*, *Portsmouth* and *Ruby* sailed from
Portsmouth to join Blake. On their way they met two Dutch men-
of-war, each of forty guns. After an hour's engagement, in which
many broadsides were exchanged, one of the Dutchmen had her
main-mast shot by the board, the other her main-yard and fore-
yard, so that it was hoped to 'carry them'. At this point the *Ruby*'s
masts were shot down and fell overboard. The *Portsmouth* took

her in tow, and got her safely back to Portsmouth. The *Hercules*, now left alone, was forced to run herself ashore, where eighty of her men scrambled to the land. But, with a favourable wind, the Dutch got her off and captured her.[53]

Tromp now took the opportunity to land raiding parties in Sussex and Kent. The first party got away safely, after seizing some cattle and sheep, but Colonel Rich got between the foraging party in Kent and the sea, and captured them all, some sixty men.[54] On 1 December, Tromp weighed at 1 a.m. 'intending to seek out the English in Dover or the Downs, but, as the wind shifted north, he had to anchor S.E. of Dover. Next day, owing to a contrary wind, his heavy ships could not get up to him, so that he arrived off the Downs with only a small fleet. On the 3rd there was a strong gale, with a wind at E.N.E. Tromp weighed with the flood tide and, with difficulty, reached Boulogne. Here he anchored so that his dispersed vessels could join him.[55]

On 2 December the council wrote to Blake to thank him 'for his good deportment in the late engagement'.[56] Blake replied next day to say that he proposed to move the fleet to Long Sands Head, as he dared not expose the fleet 'to the attempts of so potent and experienced an enemy by continuing in this Road'.[57] On the 5th the council suggested to him that, instead of going into Lee Road, Harwich might be a better place, but they left it to him, after holding a Council of War, to do what was thought fit. They also warned the northern ships not to sail to the Downs. By this time they had summoned Deane and Monck to report to them.[58] On the 7th Blake once more wrote asking for reinforcements for the fleet, for the loss of seamen was extraordinary. He urged that money should be found for their payment, as they refused to serve free. He pointed out that the Dutch paid their men prize money, and forty shillings a month, whereas his own men got no prize money, due to the method of sharing prizes, and only eighteen shillings a month.[59]

With Blake lying at the mouth of the Thames, Tromp and his captains debated whether it might be possible to attack him there, but, as there were no experienced pilots aboard, it was decided to abandon the idea. Instead Tromp resolved to sail for Ushant with his convoy, there to pick up a second large mass of merchantmen, and take them both to Rhé.[60] He had an agent at Calais, De Clarges, who got information from 'a good friend who came over from England'. The agent reported that thirty-four great ships were preparing in the Thames, but that they were hampered by the lack of seamen. 'It was', he added, 'both difficult and dangerous to obtain intelligence in England'.[61]

Meanwhile, on 14 December, a council of officers, under the chairmanship of Blake, had decided that a fleet of sixty ships should be got ready, all State vessels, forty carrying thirty-six guns, and none with under twenty-six guns. If merchantmen had to be employed, they must not number a fifth of the whole fleet. They must carry twenty-eight guns each. Six well-fitted fireships, able to keep the sea, must be provided and the whole fleet must be completed with able seamen. With such a force 'we shall, with all cheerfulness, go forth and engage the enemy'. Should, however, the Council of State insist upon a smaller number, 'we shall in obedience to their commands, be ready to commit ourselves unto Divine Providence', which looks as if they preferred to obey the commandment not to tempt the Lord their God.[62]

The blame for the defeat has often been laid upon Blake, because of his resolution to fight. But there was no other course left open to him. To decline action would have been to suffer the fate of Oquendo. Nor can he be blamed for fighting with such an inferior number of ships. He believed he had a sufficient force, though he could not anticipate that twenty ships would keep out of action. His ships were more strongly built, with a heavier gun power. His chief complaint was the lack of men, who naturally preferred to serve on the privateers, which gave them better pay, and more safety. This was no fault of his, but of the Council of State, who could not find the money for their wages. More unjustly still, he has been blamed for the division of the fleet. The same charge was to be brought in 1666, against Rupert and Monck. But in both cases the decision and therefore the responsibility rested upon the shoulders of the Government itself, as the ultimate authority. Moreover the council had told Blake that twenty ships would be taken from him to go to the Mediterranean, and that they would replace them with ships from the Thames and from Portsmouth. This they failed to do, and instead actually detached five more ships to convoy the colliers.

There remains the more difficult question of intelligence. The English newspapers had shown clearly that Tromp was preparing to sail. It was plainly one of the duties of the council to get information, and to pass it on to their Admiral. This is borne out in a letter that passed between them and Blake in which such a newspaper report is alluded to. Blake has also been blamed for bad scouting. Yet the information he required could only come from Holland itself. The weather at this time of year was often thick and foggy, as Tromp himself had found. The *Sapphire* had been entrusted with the duty of scouting, but Tromp had cleverly availed himself of this fact, by sending out a hoy, with false news, and allowing herself to be captured. This had led Blake to believe that Tromp's ships were still scattered in the ports of Holland and Zeeland. Blake probably expected Tromp to sail down the Channel, and so posted himself in the Downs in readiness to deal with him, should he do so. Here Blake can fairly be criticised.

The real reason for the defeat lay in the undermanning of the ships. This fact later on emerged at the trial of Benjamin Blake, Robert's brother, who commanded the *Triumph*. With him stood accused Saltonstall of the *Lion*, Chapman of the *Entrance*, Taylor of the *Laurel*, and Young of the *Worcester*.[63] They had not enough men to work the ships. Though all five were sent for trial, ultimately they were leniently dealt with; Taylor and Young being given command of merchant ships.[64] Saltonstall was later on set free, upon giving a personal bond with two sureties, to appear if called upon.[65] He died in command of the *Golden Cock*, at the battle of the Texel in 1653.[66] Benjamin Blake, Robert's brother, was discharged from his command, and was not 'to be employed nor go forth in the service'. Francis Harvey, Blake's secretary was 'not to be employed in the service of the fleet'.[67] Blake's action, in reporting his brother for neglect of duty, showed both captains and seamen that he would maintain discipline at all costs, and that any failure of duty would be severely dealt with.

The merchantmen, too, whose owners did not wish to risk the loss of their vessels, when they did not have sufficient men to work them, could hardly be blamed. Nor was it the fact that the seamen objected to fighting, for they fought most valiantly when occasion required it. Rather they naturally demanded their full pay, and not a mere part of what was owing to them. They had wives and families to support, and they preferred to serve, where pay was certain and greater. But the State had little or no money to supply the Navy Commissioners. It was abundantly clear that naval administration needed an overhaul, if Blake and his men, competent and able as they were, could meet the foe with any prospect of success. Blake's first victory over Tromp had lulled the Council of State into over confidence. They had divided and reduced the fleet, owing to their false belief that the Dutch were only too ready to make peace. Now they were face to face with the fact that Tromp controlled the Channel.

CHAPTER 15

Blake and Vane Reorganise the Navy

*

THANKS to the researches of Doctor V. A. Rowe, in her able study of Sir Henry Vane the Younger, much new and valuable light has been thrown upon the administration of the Admiralty Commission. He was the Treasurer of the Navy, and had made himself an expert on naval finance and on foreign affairs. He had already, on 26 September, 1652, persuaded the Council of State to build thirty new frigates. Just before the battle of the Kentish Knock he had gone down to Dover, early in October, to confer with Blake about the council's dispositions for the fleet. He thus met Blake for the first time, and both men must have impressed each other by their strong personalities and their devotion to the navy. The value of this personal contact had deeply influenced Vane. On 2 December, 1652, Vane's name headed the twelve members of the parliamentary sub-committee of the navy. But already he was anxious to reorganise the Admiralty. He wished to purge it from the 'amateurs who strolled in' to its meetings[1]. Tromp's victory at Dungeness gave him his opportunity. Parliament, after digesting the miserable news, decided to appoint a small committee, with full power and authority responsible only to Parliament, to organise the provision of ships for the navy and for the necessary supplies. The Bill was rushed through in one day, 10 December. The committee was to be composed of four M.P.s two of whom were not to be members of the Council of State, with Blake, Monck and Deane, who had been recalled for naval service, and two non-M.P.s. Vane had at last a small, expert committee, with freedom of action, an instrument for the work it had to do.[2]

Already on 4 December, 1652, the three Commissioners appointed to enquire into the defeat, had reached Deal.[3] Here they were joined by Blake. After dealing with the cases of the reported captains, they sent in their observations. They pointed out that the thirty prizes, lying in the Thames, would make better men-of-war than the merchantmen. But they had been neglected, whereas if they had been fitted out at once, the cost would not have been four times as great as under the present system. The cause of the defeat was due to the fact that many ships were so grossly undermanned that it was impossible to work them. Mariners were not coming forward because those who had served for twenty years, drew no more pay than 'an ordinary seaman, prest from the Thames, that never saw the sea before'. Only a national wages policy could remedy this.[4]

By Vane's efforts on 10 December, Parliament had raised the tax assessment from £90,000 a month to £120,000. Previously this had been paid to the army. Now it was ordered that enough soldiers should be disbanded so that the army must subsist on £80,000, leaving £40,000 for the needs of the navy.[5] The pay of able seamen was raised from 19/- a month to 24/-, a shilling being deducted for the benefit of the Chatham Chest, which looked after sick mariners. The ordinary seamen got 19/3, the gromet* 14/3 and a boy 9/6. Officers and men, who had served six months and upward, now got a bonus of a month's wages, apparently in lieu of prize money. In future the crews were to get all the plunder above deck, with 10/- per ton, and £6.13.0 per gun for every ship captured, while for every warship sunk or destroyed they were to have 10/- a gun only. Presumably the new wages were made equal to the pay offered by the privateers.[6]

Nor were the sick and wounded overlooked. Half the beds in the English hospitals were reserved for the navy. Sick and wounded men, on their discharge were to have their tickets and conduct money paid. The port authorities were to provide accommodation, at the State's expense, for the relief of such men sent ashore. A tenth of the prize money set aside for the Lord High Admiral (there being now, like Mrs Harris, 'no sich person') was to be used for the sick and wounded, and for the relief of widows, children and helpless parents, of all men slain in the service.[7] Medals and other rewards for officers and men 'found to have done any eminent or extraordinary service,' were to be awarded. Under this heading came Captain Coppin of the *Speaker*, who had lost a leg,[8] while Rachel Hoxton, Hoxton's widow, was also to benefit. Some principal grievances had been adjusted.[9]

Above all, discipline had to be dealt with. The Laws and

*A class between ordinary seamen and boys.

Ordinances of the Sea were prepared by Whitelocke, Bradshaw and Sidney. Though they were only appointed on the 18th, the articles were read to the council on the 21st and passed on the 25th. There were thirty-nine of them, which surely must have had a sinister connotation for the Puritans. Blake had complained that he had no jurisdiction to punish faint-hearted captains. Now he was given the right to hold Courts Martial. It was laid down that in time of fight every captain was to see that all was in its proper posture. He, and every officer, in their own persons, were to hearten and encourage the seamen, and not to behave faintly, or to yield to the enemy, or to cry for quarter, upon pain of death. He was to observe his superior's commands, both for attack and defence. No member of the crew was to withdraw, or not to come into the fight and engage, but to do his utmost to take, kill and endamage the enemy, and to relieve and assist all other ships. Cowardice or disaffection would be liable to death, or to such punishment as a Council of War should decide. Failure to chase the enemy, beaten or flying, was punishable by death or otherwise. Any person suspected as a spy, bringing seducing letters from the enemy, or joining with them, was to be sentenced to death. No officer was to receive money from the vessel he was convoying. Religious services were to be held, particularly on Sundays and profaneness and irreligiousness avoided. Cursing, drunkenness and uncleanness were to be punished by a Council of War. Nothing was to be embezzled, and captains must keep a full complement of 'able and healthful seamen, and not to be pestered with idlers and boys'. Blake's authority had been made supreme.[10]

From the first, as Dr Rowe has pointed out, the tone of the new Admiralty Commissioners' letters was very different from the formal ones sent by the old sub-committee of the Council of State. For, on 17 December, 1652, five of the new Commissioners wrote to Blake setting forth their plans. 'We are preparing inducements and encouragements to seamen to cheerfully engage in their service. We are also taking care how victuals may be provided for the next year's service – seeing the fleet well officered that is now in preparation – we think it requisite to have a meeting and conference with yourself, and to that end do (God willing) resolve to make repair down to you, either on ship board or some convenient place ashore'. The last sentence struck the key note of Vane's policy: co-operation rather than formal orders. Blake wil-

lingly agreed and on the 27th the Commissioners wrote to say
how glad they were of his approval 'of consulting with you personally' and that they desired 'in this, as in all particulars that
concern the service, to have frequent and mutual correspondence
with you in all freedom for the good of the service'.[11]

As there was a possibility that a Dutch fleet might be in the
Narrow, or at the back of the Goodwins, orders were given,
probably at Blake's suggestion, on the 17th, to the lighthouse
keepers. They were to light their lamps dimly till 8 or 9 o'clock
and then to alter them as agreed. This order was to be kept secret.
If the wind was easterly, they were to alter them at the North
and South Forelands and at Dungeness. This was to be continued
until they had contrary orders from the council or from the
Generals.[12]

Reports now came in reflecting the beneficial effects of the rise
in pay. On the 29th the Mayor of Dover wrote that 'the seamen
liked well of them',[13] while from Poole it was reported that the
imprest men repaired to Portsmouth 'with more readiness than
usual'.[14] Monck saw to it that the increase of pay for carpenters,
which had been overlooked, had been adjusted.[15] On 4 January
news came from Dover that Blake's fleet 'is in very good equipage'
and would put out shortly, 'while a great number of men are come
in for service'.[16]

But there was still trouble among the seamen at Portsmouth.
Commissioner Thomas Thorrowgood reported that the crew of
the *Worcester* demanded their pay if the ship was to sail. He had
offered them six months' pay and two more when they joined
Blake.[17] Instead the crew mutinied. On the 27th the *Pearl*'s crew,
who had been at sea for 18 months, refused to stir without pay,
'and indeed they want necessaries for their comfortable living at
sea'. The *President*, after 13 months at sea, merely asked for 'some
encouragement'. As for the mutineers he would try to quell them
and to arrest the ringleaders.[18] The merchantmen, *Bonaventure*
and *Crescent*, in port for twelve months were daily being deserted
by their crews, who, by a council's order, were not allowed to
go ashore without a special leave from the Generals. In fact the
Bonaventure's crew, after the captain had paid them five months'
wages, out of the nine owing to them, had promptly run away.
Their ship was at once discharged from the service. On the other
hand the *Anthony Bonaventure*'s crew, in respect of their 'stout

and honourable defence against the enemy were paid; and those, who were carried to Holland' got six weeks' pay above their wages in consideration for their losses.[19] 'The truth is' he wrote, 'that ships are fearful to go out without a fair wind for, if they were put to leeward, they would fall into the hands of the Dutch'.[20] Nor was this all for, on 12 January, he wrote that twenty-eight men, who had received half a crown for their travel money, had not appeared, save for one man. 'The State is intolerably abused in this particular'. He had given tickets to the *Pearl*'s crew, who badly needed money. To others, who were mutinous and ready to raise a disturbance, he proposed to give wages. Among them was Thomas Miller who, if he appeared, was not to have his ticket paid. For Thomas had broken the windows of the Pay Office, and then threatened to pull it down. His captain, Cuttance, reported him 'to be active in raising disturbance'. Such were the problems at Portsmouth.[21]

On 30 December Captain Houlding of the *Ruby*, with Dornford of the *Portsmouth*, were ordered to sail westward from Portsmouth to look out for Dutch ships. On 5 January they fell in with a Dutch warship of forty-six guns, and fought her for four hours. A high sea and a strong wind prevented them from using their lower tier of guns, which the Dutchman could do. They kept him company all night, hoping that a fair wind next morning would enable them 'to conclude the work'. Between Portland and the Isle of Wight the weather forced them to leave the enemy for fear they might be forced to leeward. Houlding lost six men wounded, with damage to his hull, rigging and sails, while Dornford had a man killed and nine wounded. Houlding asked to have a forecastle fitted, which would make his ship 'a third better for service'. Blake did not intend that the Dutch should cruise in the Channel unchallenged.[22]

At last on 4 January, 1653, Vane with other Commissioners were able to leave London to confer with Blake. They met him at Chatham, after sending back their coaches to bring back £12,000 from the Navy Treasurer. They found the seamen 'in some distemper, calling for their pay, being many months due to them'. They kept back two months' pay, as they feared if the sailors had been paid in full, they would have promptly gone home. The rest they disbursed on shipboard, and then only after the ships had been put into condition. Behind the seamen's demand they suspected there lay a Royalist agitation to get the seamen, after being paid, to leave the service.[23] This was confirmed by the Generals, in a letter dated the 10th, saying that the council had approved their action with regard to the seamen, which they owed 'very much unto your candid representation', which referred to Vane and his fellows. They reported that 'one of the principal incendiaries, which blew the trumpet of sedition, is gone to London'. They hoped, if he could be apprehended, to make him an example, and they gave information, in shorthand, as to where he might be found. 'The mariners at present are hushed, and we hope the plot of that distemper (if any were) is hushed'. They had been unable to move owing to a low tide, but they hoped the *Vanguard* and *Triumph* would join them shortly with other vessels. Men were badly needed, who should be hastened down to the fleet at Gravesend.[24]

Before returning to London on the 8th Blake, Monck and Vane must have discussed the question of their priorities. It was clear that the most urgent need was to get the fleet ready for sea so as to meet Tromp on his return voyage from Rhé. All else must be sacrificed to this end.

On the 12th Nehemiah Bourne, who had been recalled from sea service to become a Commissioner at Harwich, where his practical experience of the fleet's requirements would be invaluable,[25] arrived at Chatham with Richard Hutchinson, the Treasurer of the Navy. With them they brought £25,000. They boarded the *Triumph* to confer with Blake.[26] Here the Admiralty Commissioners forwarded them a letter from John Poortmans at Gravesend. He complained that there were only three commanders aboard their ships and very few other officers. 'The service must needs suffer when men go and come as they please and do what they list, and none of authority to control them'. The *London*'s crew had refused to serve any longer, and had taken their chests ashore 'despite of all the officers'. This could have been prevented if their wages had been paid. He had taken the names of the ringleaders. The bosun of the *Sussex* was a Cavalier and a profane man, and the bosun of the *Kentish*, a late revolter, but recently come into the service. Philip Marshall, captain of the *John and Elizabeth*, had been commander of the *Marmaduke* under Rupert. Her crew, however, had brought him as a prisoner, with his ship, into Plymouth. He ended by reporting that he was going to

Chatham to confer with the Generals and the Navy Commissioners.[27]

The Admiralty Committee had been busy for, on the 14th, they laid down that each General was to be paid £3 per day; Vice-Admirals £2 and Rear-Admirals £1. The fleet was to be divided into three squadrons, Red, Blue and White. The first Admiral's ensign was to be Red, the second Blue and the third, White. Each Vice-Admiral was to wear the usual flag in his fore top, with a pennant under his flag and an ensign of either Red, Blue and White, while the Rear-Admirals wore the usual flag in their mizen tops, with pennants and ensigns of their respective colours.[28] On the 15th they warned Blake that they had news from Holland that Tromp was bringing back the Dutch merchant fleet, and that it was important to have the fleet speedily at sea to meet him.[29]

On the 19th, Bourne from aboard the *Vanguard*, reported that he had paid off thirteen ships and others as they came in, probably much to their astonishment. He had visited various ships to discuss matters with their crews, who welcomed him as their old Vice-Admiral. He commented, for the generality 'I find them in a hopeful constitution and spirit of temper', but not all: 'for some few of them expecting a complete paying off, at the first a few were a little distempered, but are since better satisfied, and the most ingenuous among them are sensible that the rudeness of some among them hath justly merited and occasioned the abatement and stop upon their pay for the present, which may be a good caution for the future'.

He then turned to the problem of the merchantmen. They were, he noted, 'cordially affected to the present cause in hand'. But they insisted upon their difficulties. First, that the greatest part of their estates had been ventured in their ships, and they asked, in case their vessels were lost in fight, that they might have some assurance of encouragement. Secondly, as they had either contracted with the Navy Commissioners for their ships, or had them pressed for service, that, as the State had raised the wages on their own ships, that they too might have this allowance paid by the State, as their officers and men expected. He then drew attention to the obstruction caused by the want of iron-bound cask, of which about 200 were needed. As these had to be stowed in the lower tier, the taking in of provisions had to wait. Bourne's report enabled Blake and Vane to solve the cause of the recent defection of the merchantmen, which lay in undermanning and under-paying.[30]

Blake and Monck, on 16 January, wrote to the Navy Commissioners asking for men to man the great ships, and complaining that the beer still arrived in wood-bound cask. They reported that it was agreed that first rate ships were to have at least 400 men, second rates 300, third rates 200, fourth rates 140, fifth rates eighty and sixth rates forty. They hoped to be at sea (if men and victuals were sent) 'with a considerable strength'. As they had been asked for their opinion as to taking soldiers aboard, 'we hold it at this time of year to be very unseasonable – and of little advantage – as they were not able to brook this winter weather'. They reported that the *Merlin*, riding off Faversham, had detained four vessels from Ostend, Nieuport and Dunkirk, which pretended they had come for oysters, but were probably being used to get intelligence, and so they still held them.[31]

On the 20th Bourne was sent back to report on the state of the fleet. Blake complained again that iron-bound cask came in very slowly, and that no victuallers had yet appeared. Frigates, which were lying at Gravesend to bring down seamen, had none of them arrived. He begged Vane to write to the Navy Commissioners 'to quicken them herein, the want of men and victual being like to be the greatest obstruction', and he begged that the rest of the ships should be hastened down to him.[32]

On the 23rd Blake and Monck held a Council of War at Queenborough. They sent the Navy Commissioners the depositions taken by Willoughby concerning the mutiny on the *Worcester*. As they sat a letter was brought them, dated the 21st, from the Navy Commissioners, concerning soldiers to be sent to them. For the Council of State had discussed what they should do with the supernumerary soldiers disbanded from the regiments in Scotland. They had the inspiration of sending them to the fleet in view of the great want of men, 'for the speedy manning out of the ships'. The Admiralty Committee was to write to the Generals as to the proportion of these men. To this proposal the Council of War was unanimously opposed, for the reasons given on the 16th. If the Council meant that these men should form part of the ship's company and not to be mere supernumeraries, they were in error, which was based upon the supposition that they already had their proportion of seamen aboard, whereas they actually were far short of mariners. Once soldiers were aboard they found 'an aptness, in many above, to believe that all was well'. Due to this assumption 'to our great grief in the last engagement with the Dutch the greatest part of our fleet (especially the merchant ships) were in a great measure nearly disabled of that service which was expected from them'. They were not averse to soldiers, 'which can hardly be imagined from us, who have had such experience of them ashore'. They were willing to receive Cromwell's men, if they were officered and if they would form part of the ship's company, accustomed to sea labour and duty. From this previously soldiers had been exempt, indeed 'many of them incapable as being young striplings'. What they did object to was raw undisciplined men, a fault from which Cromwell's men would be free.[33]

They followed this by saying they had forgotten, when they wrote that Captain Marshall said to be in command of the *John and Elizabeth*, was now in the service. They did not know if this was true, but they asked for 'a speedy scrutiny of the commanders of ships in the Thames' as there was great cause to suspect that 'our old enemies are again at work among us'.[34] In another letter they complained about the merchant ships, which they hoped 'had been long settled by Bourne'. Few had come to them, and they did not know either their burden, or if they were fully manned. This must be dealt with. As to a hospital for the sick and wounded, Sandwich would be 'the most commodious as men could be landed there in all weathers, whereas at Deal this was only possible in fair weather.' Lastly they wanted to know 'what encouragement was intended for such as shall undertake the charge of fireships'.[35]

On 24 January Deane attended a meeting of the Admiralty Committee. Several English prisoners, freed from Holland, were at Ostend in a state of starvation. They were brought to Portsmouth at the cost of a shilling a man. Here they were put aboard the State's ships. It was like a miraculous answer to the Generals' prayer for seamen, but what the wretched prisoners thought is not recorded.[36]

On the 26th Vane and the Commissioners returned to Chatham to confer with Blake. New clerks of the cheque were appointed, and were ordered to take up their posts by the next night. Urgent letters were sent to the Treasury asking for money. The lighthouse keepers, now that the fleet was about to put to sea, were to restore their lights to their former stations.[37] On the 28th the Navy

Commissioners were ordered, since not more than a fourth part of dry provisions had reached the fleet, 'to quicken the victuallers therein' and to find out 'when the remainder may be expected, that the fleet be not retarded'. Cask for fresh water 'must be expedited' and also seamen. If the frigates were not at Gravesend, the mariners must be sent down to merchantmen, while masts and provisions must be sent to Portsmouth 'without more delay'.[38]

On 3 February, they boarded the *Triumph* at Queenborough to aid Blake in getting to sea with all haste. On their return to Chatham, at midnight, they wrote to Blake to inform him that 1,000 soldiers from Cromwell's and Ingoldsby's regiments were about to join him. With regard to the proportion of sailors to soldiers they answered that, 'we ordered your desires to be put into execution'. They ended by warning him that Tromp intended to convoy his merchantmen before the English fleet could leave port, and they impressed upon him the urgency of getting to sea. On the 6th they returned to London.[39] All through these months they worked incessantly, day and night, pouring out letters, finding suitable officers, enquiring why ships assigned to the fleet had not arrived, ordering ammunition to be sent from Hull: sending the General news of Tromp's whereabouts and arranging means by which to keep in touch with them.[40] How cordial were the new relations with the Admiralty Commissioners is revealed by the act that Blake now signed his letters to them as 'your affectionate friend'[41] in place of 'your obedient servant' when he wrote to the Navy Commissioners.[42] On 29 January the council had acceded to the desire of the three Generals to go to sea by ordering them each to do so.[43]

The effects of Tromp's recent victory were still being felt. The price of coal in London had risen sharply. It was hoped that the arrival of colliers from Newcastle would bring this down to twenty-four shillings a ton in the summer and to thirty shillings in the winter. The price at Newcastle was low, but the high cost was due 'through the danger of the sea' for Dutch privateers were taking ships and barques going to and from Newcastle.[44] But Blake and Vane would not yield to popular clamour. They held firmly to their priorities. They refused to divert ships northwards. Everything must be subordinated to the need to defeat Tromp. It was Blake's great virtue that, with two exceptions, he never lost sight of his true objective.

By 8 February the Generals had moved to the Swin to collect the fleet. They complained that 'neither ships or men do yet appear here – the whole stress of our business lies now upon their coming down to us' so that they would be able to sail for the other Channel.[45] Next day they wrote more severely: 'many ships were in great want of men, who must be hastened to them' and more were badly needed. 'You cannot but be sensible of our condition that if the ships be behind and men not hastened, we may be put either to lose the first opportunity of wind and weather to get into the other Channel, or else be forced to go before we are in such a capacity as you could wish, for the action and service which probably may be expected.' Next day they appointed Penn as Vice-Admiral, in the *Speaker*, to take command of twenty-two warships and nine merchantmen.[46] Hence the reason for the incessant labours of Vane and his fellows during this month.

Peter Pett went to inspect the fleet spending two nights 'on the hard deck of a dirty sprat boat' but was compensated by the sight of 'so gallant a fleet, being upwards of fifty sail, and truly I think well manned'.[47] On the 10th he returned with a letter from the Generals, reporting that they had divided the fleet into three squadrons, though they could make but fourteen ships to each one. They were still short of over 500 seamen, and had heard nothing of the mariners and watermen, said to be coming out of the Thames. Nevertheless they had determined to sail with the first opportunity.[48]

At 9 a.m. on the 12th they arrived off Dover, and at once embarked the soldiers waiting there. To add to their troubles no more than sixty men had come from the Thames, and no ships whatever. Nothing had been heard of the powder that was to be shipped for the vessels at Portsmouth, or of the ships laden with masts and provisions for that place. As the Admiralty Commissioners had raised the question of how to keep in touch with them, they had no opinions to offer, but said they would try to send into any place as they had opportunity. If the Commissioners would send messengers aboard them 'or allow us pay for any we shall take, (as you do to them of the Council of State)' then, where there was no settled stage for post, they would send one of the messengers express. Their lieutenant had just informed them there were a few imprest men come aboard 'that have never been to sea, and are very boys, by which means you are deceived, when you think they send us seamen, and the service cannot but suffer if there be not greater care taken'. These men had been impressed by the masters of the Watermen's Hall.[49] It may be suspected that the press gangs either were bribed by the able seamen to let them off, or that they feared violence from them.

On the same day, the 12th, Blake and Deane wrote to the Speaker. With fifty ships, great and small, and with a favourable wind they would 'hasten westward to wait for the return of the Dutch fleet. We dare not in this great business to promise anything for or to ourselves, because it is God alone who giveth courage and conduct – only we desire Parliament to believe we are very deeply sensible of the extraordinary importance of the present service in hand, the high expectations raised about it, and the obligation of the great trust reposed in us. . . . The consideration whereof had much driven us out of ourselves . . . to a more entire dependence upon the Lord in faith and humility; and if it please Him to continue us in such a frame and temper of spirit, we doubt not but He will more abundantly be good unto us and our Nation, the interest and seal of which is more dear to us than all worldly respects'.[50] Such was the determination with which they consecrated themselves to the great issue with which they would shortly be faced. Already the reorganisation had made the fleet and its commanders confident of being able to meet Tromp on equal terms. For they knew that behind them Vane was straining every possible effort to provide them with everything that they needed. To this great end he would sacrifice all else.

CHAPTER 16

Portland: the Balaclava of the Sea

*

ON 6 January, 1653, Tromp arrived at St Martins, in the island of Rhé, opposite La Rochelle. Before starting out, he had foolishly not replenished either his provisions or his ammunition. He had left Commodore Balck, with twelve ships at the mouth of the Channel, both to annoy the foe and to tell home-bound vessels where to find him. He warned the Dutch merchants that he would sail home at the end of the month, and then set to work to clean and repair his fleet, which had suffered stormy weather on the voyage. The merchants asked him to delay his return until the middle of February, but he replied that the convoy must be ready at the appointed time.[1] Such were the orders given to him, and moreover his provisions were running short. Above all it had been reported to him that the English would soon have 100 sail ready, so that he must be home before they could put to sea. On 30 January he left. To convoy 150 merchantmen, he had seventy-five men-of-war, one fireship, four small provision vessels and a store ship. Five warships were left behind to protect the merchantmen that were not ready yet to sail. He may have had some misgivings, for the discipline of some of his captains, on the previous voyage, had been bad.[2]

Rumours of his progress were vague. From Plymouth the *Dorset*, an Isle of Wight privateer, related that on 7 February, she had sighted 300 Dutchmen between Ushant and the Isle of Basse. A N.W. wind had so scattered them that 200 were in one body and the rest in parties of twenty, ten and five, all turning to windward. On the 9th, a strong wind forced them either to lie to, or to bear up before the wind. The *Dorset* was driven into Mounts Bay, but the skipper did not think that the Dutch could be to the eastward, but rather were 'close aboard the French coast'. The *Marmaduke*, from Ireland, reported too, that she had lain at Scilly on the 15th, 'while the Dutch fleet passed by'.[3] The log of the *Monnikendam* bears this out. for it shows that on the 14th the

Dutch were sixteen miles N.N.E. of the Scillies. Next day, in the evening, they were four miles south of Land's End. Next day with a N.W. wind, they were four miles S.S.W. of the Lizard. In the evening the Start was sighted four miles to the N.E.[4]

Tromp had thus sailed round the Scillies. It may have been Ruyter's suggestion that he should repeat the latter's manoeuvre of 1652. It will be recalled that after being sighted off the Scillies, Ruyter had sailed back to Ushant, doubled back to the English coast, and then sailed up it, on the assumption that this would be the last place where the English would expect to find him.

Be that as it may, Tromp adopted the same course. It had much to commend it. With the wind at N.W. he had the weather gage, which would enable him to slip up the Channel. Should he meet the foe, he would have room for manoeuvre, as the enemy would be to leeward. The very size of his fleet would blanket the English ports, and so prevent the ships from coming out. He had sent off de Wilde, with six ships, towards the land to try and gain some knowledge of the whereabouts of the English fleet.[5] Having collected his convoy on the 17th he sailed on without anchoring under the shelter of Portland. Next day, before dawn shots were suddenly heard in the rear of the fleet. A pink had come in posthaste, with letters from the States-General to Tromp. She reported that, on the previous day, she had been chased by the English fleet, some sixty strong. The news was instantly taken to Tromp.[6] Portland was three miles to the N.W. and, looking to leeward, Tromp saw a fleet of seventy sail. They were the English fleet, some two leagues distant.[7] He had been taken by surprise.

His keen eye detected that the enemy's fleet was separated. One squadron was leading, with a group of five ships astern. This group had a larger one a good way astern of it, while a fourth squadron was very far astern and to leeward of the others.[8] Here was the chance of a lifetime; to destroy a fleet in detail. Moreover, it was in full accord with his orders. He could not count upon the wind holding to take him up the Channel for, if it shifted, the advantage might pass to the English.[9] He instantly decided to fight. He put his convoy to windward and bore down on the foe. Ruyter was on his port side, though a good deal to his rear, while Evertsen was on his starboard.[10] As he knew, from experience, that the English ships were larger and more stoutly built than his own, and that their guns could outrange the Dutch ones, he decided that his tactics should be to try and neutralise this by closing with them. Then, by firing at their masts and rigging, to cripple them and, if possible, to board and capture them.

Blake had left orders at Dover that the ships from the Thames should join him at the Isle of Wight.[11] He and Deane were together in the *Triumph*, the flag ship of the Red squadron. Lawson, in the *Fairfax*, was his Vice-Admiral, with Howett, in the *Laurel*, as his Rear-Admiral. Penn, in the *Speaker*, commanded the Blue squadron with Lane, in the *Victory*, as Vice-Admiral and John Bourne, in the *Assistance*, as Rear-Admiral. Monck commanded the White squadron in the *Vanguard*, with Peacock, in the *Rainbow*, as Vice-Admiral and Martin, in the *Diamond*, as Rear-Admiral.[12] Penn's squadron included the *Convertine, Kentish, Advice, Dragon, Ruby, Assurance, Success, Gift, Waterhound, Nightingale, Sampson, Plover, Paradox, Speaker's Prize* and *Merlin*, with the merchantmen *Richard and Martha, Reformation, Ann and Joyce, Charles, Giles, Providence, Chase, Thomas and William, Elizabeth and Anne*.[13] It is, however, impossible to discover how many of these actually took part in the subsequent battle. Blake's squadron, according to a not very reliable source, was made up of the *Adventure, Discovery, Foresight, Nonsuch, Tiger, Angel, Pelican, Lion, Providence, Satisfaction, Roebuck, Old Warwick, Ruth, Nicodemus, Amity, President, Cygnet* and *Happy Entrance*.[14] Of the White squadron only the flagships are recorded.*

Blake sent out his scouts, while a squadron, probably Penn's, was sent ahead to try and discover the foe.[15] Blake himself sailed from Beachy Head on the 15th, with the wind at N.W. That day and the next, the fleet plied between Beachy Head and the Seine. Some Ostend and Hamburg vessels, coming up Channel, informed Blake that the Dutch were thirty or forty leagues to the westward. On the 10th the weather became so foggy that it was impossible to see more than a musket-shot from one ship to another. It was feared that part, or even the whole, of the Dutch fleet might have passed them.[16] A letter from the *Waterhound*, however, declared that 'as we ordered the matter, we could hardly have missed them, for we stretched the Channel over, as far as the Isle of Alderney, and were close aboard Cape La Hogue.'[17] This would seem to answer S. R. Gardiner's strictures on Blake for the inadequate measures he took to find the foe. He instanced particularly that

* see also Appendix 2

he should have sent forward some fast-sailing vessels to act as
scouts.[18] Nor should it be forgotten that both Blake and Penn
had sailed these western waters, looking for Ruyter in the previous
year. Both of them must have recalled, especially Blake, who never
forgot a lesson, how Ruyter, after hiding in the Scillies, had gone
back to Ushant, and then doubled back to the English coast.
And how, by the aid of fog and stormy weather, he had eluded
them and had joined De With. They were determined that this
should not be repeated. Their mistake had been to look for Ruyter
in the widest part of the Channel, between Ushant and the Scillies,
which gave the Dutchman room in which to manoeuvre. Now,
they waited for Tromp in the narrower part of the Channel,
between Cape La Hogue and Portland, some fifteen leagues across.

On the 17th the Generals were off the Isle of Wight, where they
sent in for 150 tons of water.[19] Here, too, they were joined by
ships from Portsmouth and Plymouth, as Drue Sparrow, their
secretary wrote, 'ships came dropping in'.[20] In the afternoon they
stood over to the Casquets, where a Spanish vessel told them that
Tromp was twenty leagues to the westward. Accordingly they
laid themselves between that place and Portland. On the 18th, in
the morning, 'being some five leagues distant from the English
shore' they sighted the Dutch fleet. Behind it lay the grim mass
of Portland, looming up out of the cold February weather.

They estimated the Dutch at eighty men-of-war, and some 200
merchantmen. They were 'a league and a half to windward of the
weathermost of our ships, and of most of the fleet two and three
leagues'.[21] The English probably amounted to between sixty and
seventy ships. Each squadron presumably was composed of some
twenty vessels, without counting the armed merchantmen.[22] Much
discussion has taken place as to the position of these squadrons.
Whether Penn and Lawson were ahead of Blake and Deane, or
whether Lawson was astern of them. The clue lies with Floriszoon,
of the *Monnikendam*, who wrote that he 'ran across in front of
our Admiral, at the English Vice-Admiral (Lawson)'.[23] As Tromp
was bearing down on Blake, with Penn well ahead of him, it seems
clear that Lawson, Blake's Vice-Admiral, was referred to, since
he was astern of the *Triumph*, especially as Evertsen was on Tromp's
starboard.

Blake now found himself in a precarious position, as he was to
leeward of the Dutch. He says that some twenty to twenty-five

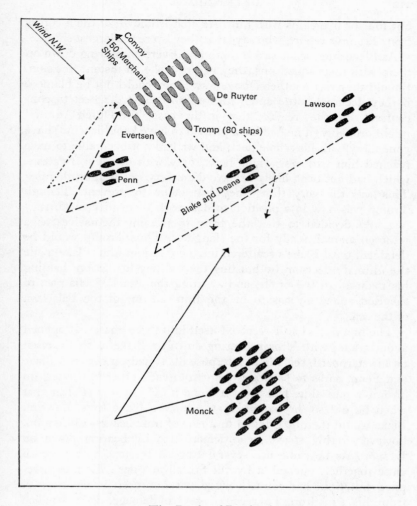

Wind N.W.

Convoy
150 Merchant
Ships

De Ruyter

Lawson

Evertsen

Tromp (80 ships)

Penn

Blake and Deane

Monck

The Battle of Portland

of his ships were nearest to the foe.[24] According to Penn and Gibson, Penn's squadron was well ahead of Blake, with Lawson about a mile on the 'starboard quarter, and as much astern of the General'. Monck was a considerable distance to the south, well to the leeward of Blake, and well to his rear.[25] Blake himself had but four or five ships with him. All that is known of them comes from Tromp's report, who says that they 'were the largest ships'.[26]

As Blake and Deane saw Tromp and Evertsen bearing down on them with their squadrons, they had to make an instant decision. Should they risk another Dungeness? They could not be blamed, if they declined battle and withdrew to enable the fleet to concentrate. But they realised that, in this case, 'the Dutch Admiral might probably (if he had been pleased to have kept his wind) have gone away with his whole fleet, and we had not been able to have reached him with our whole body, only with our few frigates – which had not been likely to have done very much upon them'.[27] This was the very thing they had come to prevent. Though Tromp was now in a position to deal with them piecemeal, they instantly decided to bait the trap; to present themselves as a tethered animal, ready for the slaughter. Thus Tromp would be detained, until Blake's scattered units could join him. Blake made the ultimate decision by hoisting the red flag for action, hauling his mainsail to the brails, and awaiting the attack.[28] His part of the Red squadron was to be the thin red line of the Balaclava of the sea.

The first day's battle resolved itself into three phases. It opened about 9 a.m. with Tromp bearing down on Blake, with Evertsen on his starboard, seeking to interpose his squadron between Blake and Penn, so as to separate them from each other.[29] Ruyter, on Tromp's port side, had not yet come up,[30] but it was clear that when he did so, he would try to separate Blake from Lawson. Blake would then be gripped in a pair of nutcrackers. Floriszoon, however, rashly strove to anticipate this by bearing down on Lawson. As he came up, several English frigates, that were all close together, opened 'a fearful fire all at once'. Floriszoon replied, but, as he had run to leeward, without receiving any support from his squadron, he received severe damage. Five English ships followed him and shot so effectually that nothing was left standing, and his ship was totally disabled.[31]

Despite the claim of the author of the *Life of Tromp*, that the Dutchman poured several broadsides into Blake, Tromp himself wrote 'we have seen in this engagement that divers of our captains were not so staunch as they ought to be: they did not second myself and their other honest comrades as the English did, for I observed that in attacking Blake, that before I could get at him, I had such

Monck. Another of the Flag-men series painted by Lely

The Battle of Portland from a print published in Augsburg in 1658. The portraits of Tromp, bottom left, and of Blake, bottom right, are presumably imaginary a welcome from three or four of his ships, that everything on board us was on fire, and Blake still unhurt.'[32] Some thirty Dutch ships were now in action, and the *Triumph* was surrounded by seven of them.[33] Yet the English discipline was amazing: as the Dutch owned 'they always shot at our round timbers and never shot in a hurry'.[34] The Dutch, on the contrary, followed their usual custom of firing at the rigging and sails. The *Triumph*, however, 'was so tight in her hull that she never so much as pumped for it'.[35] Soon Blake's small group was lost to sight in the rolling smoke that enveloped it from the cannonade that poured from the Dutch guns, broken only by the flashes of fire from the cannon of both sides as they blazed at each other.

Meanwhile Penn, directly he saw the Dutch attack developing, hauled to the wind and thus was able to open fire on Evertsen, who was now on his starboard bow. But the Dutchman refused to be diverted from his course, and strove still to interpose his squadron between Blake and Penn.[36] Penn realised instantly the danger that Blake might be overwhelmed, and so he tacked to the northward, so as to break through the rear of Evertsen's squadron. Lawson's problem was very different. If he hauled on the wind, as Penn had done, he saw that Ruyter could bear down on him and bar his way to Blake. So, with great skill, he bore away to the south, with the wind abeam, and rounded the smoke of the *mêlée* that hid Blake, and then tacked north to follow Penn's path and crash into the heart of the battle.[37]

The second phase of the fight now began. It was about 10 a.m. when Penn came into action, just about the same time as Ruyter had come up to join Tromp.[38] Lawson came in shortly after. His advent brought the number of English ships to about thirty, 'and even then not half our number'.[39] By this time the sea was a mass of floating planks and torn sails, and broken spars. As Evertsen wrote, 'the two squadrons reduced one another to a condition of helplessness'.[40] Yet the flag of England still flew steadfast above the *Triumph*, as the thin red line yet held out. Upon her quarter-deck stood Blake and Deane, resolute and collected, with calm courage inspiring their men. Her stout hull was undamaged, but the more slightly-built Dutchmen had suffered severely. Their ship had lost 100 men out of a crew of 350; Drue Sparrow, Deane's son-in-law, and Blake's secretary, had been killed; a bar of iron had shot away part of Deane's coat and breeches, wounding Blake in the thigh, a little above the knee.[41] 'He would scarce go down to have it dressed, nor was he out of his place all the time of service'.[42] As they came in, Penn and Lawson were hotly received, and could do little to relieve the pressure on Blake. Bourne was badly wounded in the head, and his flagship, the *Assistance*, had lost her main-mast, but she managed to escape the enemies' clutches and to limp back into Portsmouth. The *Oak* had her mast maimed, her guns dismounted and she was taken with other ships. The *Advice* was surrounded by five Dutchmen, who boarded her and seized her forecastle.[43] Had all Tromp's ships joined in the fight, the situation would have been even more serious for Blake, for the struggle was now in complete confusion. Each ship, or group of ships, on either side, were seeking out any foe they could, as chance offered. It seemed more than probable that the English ships would be overwhelmed by sheer weight of numbers and that, as so many vessels had been captured, the day would be lost. Ruyter had engaged the *Prosperous*, a merchantman, of forty-four guns 'which fired most terribly at him, and put in such perplexity that he thought the best way to shelter himself from her fury, would be resolutely to board her'. This his seamen did, only to be so hotly received that they were forced to retire. Ruyter angrily drove them back, and in a fierce attack they swarmed over the ship, and secured her.[44] It seemed that it would be only a matter of moments before more of the English ships would be lost.

At this desperately critical moment Monck, who had been anxiously and frantically battling his way from the rear, against an adverse wind, came into action, about midday. Most writers have stated that he did not arrive until 4 p.m., basing this upon the Generals' dispatch, that 'those that were weathermost had a sharp conflict of it the whole day till about 4 of the clock in the afternoon, by which time a considerable number of our ships and frigates had got so far ahead, that by tacking they could weather the greatest part of the Dutch'. But further on in the dispatch they wrote, 'the leeward part of our ships – being engaged within two hours as soon as we'.[45] This can only refer to Monck's squadron, and this time is confirmed by a letter from the *Eagle*, which goes on, 'by the assistance of General Monck, with the *Vanguard* and others, before three of the clock on Friday, we had taken, sunk and fired fifteen sail'.[46]

So opened the third phase. Monck, with some twenty ships led by the *Vanguard*, burst into Ruyter's rear.[47] Soon he was in the thick of the battle as the death of his captain, Mildmay, with some thirty of his crew slain and wounded, shows.[48] His fresh and undamaged ships began slowly to swing the balance in favour of the English. Five of Monck's vessels now surrounded Ruyter,[49] who was forced to recall his men from aboard the *Prosperous*, which was also being attacked by Vesey's crew in the *Merlin*.[50] Evertsen, seeing Ruyter's plight, came up with Captains Balck and Ness, together with other ships, to his aid and drove the English off.[51] Ness had already been attacked by Lane, Vice-Admiral of the Blue, in the *Victory*, who bore down on him from windward. Peacock, Vice-Admiral of the White, came up on his leeward side. As they passed both ships exchanged broadsides.[52] One by one the captured ships were attacked, and the Dutch were driven out, and the vessels repossessed. Another English ship came up to the beleaguered *Advice*, drove off three of her assailants, and set her free.[53] All the four ships now grappled together. First the Englishman, then Swers, then the *Advice*, next Poort. After a severe fight Poort's vessel was sunk, and he was wounded. As his ship went down, he could be seen, waving his hanger in defiance. Then Swers's ship was sunk and he was made a prisoner.[54] De Munnick's ship, which had lost her main-mast, was captured and burnt, while Captain Wigglema's powder exploded, and his ship blew up.[55] The *Ostrich*, a huge East Indiaman, of 1200 tons and forty-four guns, was heavily battered by the *Lion*, and eventually surrendered to the *Pelican*. Most of her crew were found to be dead, while the ship was in danger of sinking, so Stoakes abandoned her and let her drift[56]. Ness, by this time had run out of cartridges, and had to withdraw from the fight, while Ruyter, apparently, was again attacked by some seven ships.[57]

Blake, knowing now that he had the battle well in hand, sent off seven or eight fast sailing frigates to bear down on the Dutch merchantmen, which Tromp had left in his rear, before he began the battle. But directly Tromp saw their danger, he broke off the fight about 4 p.m. in order to drive off this threat to his convoy, fearing that all the merchantmen would 'be cut to pieces, fired and sunk, unless we protected them'.

Tromp now summoned Ruyter and Evertsen aboard: first to admonish Floriszoon 'who, with some others, had shot very much

at random': next to consult what to do. Should they attack again
and let the convoy drift? For they were not strong enough to set
aside a sufficient guard for it, nor did they know what reserves
the English might have in the Straits of the Channel. Or should
they abandon fighting, and protect the convoy by letting the
merchantmen sail ahead of them? This latter course was agreed
upon, with the provision that no useless shots were to be fired, as
their ammunition even now was beginning to run low. Then,
after sending De Wilde to take in tow the drifting *Ostrich*, the
fleet and convoy were collected together. With a light breeze from
the N.W., sail was set up the Channel, only to find out, in the
evening, that the wind had dropped to a dead calm.[58]

Blake had only lost the *Sampson*, which had been so badly
damaged that her captain had taken out his crew, and let her sink.
All night the crews were busily repairing their damages, mostly
to their sails and rigging, spars and masts. Men were transferred
from the less serviceable and seaworthy vessels, to those that
were more powerful.[59] The wounded from the *Triumph* and the
Worcester, which had stood magnificently beside Blake, were
sent into Weymouth.[60] The *Oak*, *Assistance*, *Advice*, *Prosperous*
and *Providence* all limped next day into Portsmouth, while the
Merlin brought in the drifting *Ostrich*, which De Wilde had
abandoned.[61] This done, Blake followed the lights of the Dutch
fleet up the Channel, 'as near as we could conveniently without
mixing'.[62]

Like Waterloo, it had been 'the nearest run thing'. Tromp's
bold attempt to destroy Blake's fleet in detail had failed. The
thin red line had held. Blake's confidence in the strength of his
ships, the superior weight of their gunfire, with the cool and
collected way with which his men had served them, 'never shooting
in a hurry', with the high morale of all ranks, had been justified,
even in the critical moments of the first and second phases of
the conflict. He had been magnificently supported by all ranks,
eager to wipe out the shame and dishonour of Dungeness. His
flag officers had shown initiative when they had to act upon their
own, while Monck had led his fresh ships straight into the thick
of the fight. By so doing he had turned seeming defeat into definite
victory. Blake had boldly accepted overwhelming odds, which he
had calculated to a nicety, supremely confident that he could hold

the foe, until the Blue and the White squadrons could get up to him.

It was very different with Tromp, splendid seaman that he was. In his first attack, some of his captains had hung back. Ruyter had taken an hour to come into action, while Floriszoon, by his rash attack on Lawson, had only succeeded in immobilising himself, while other ships had fired wildly at random. Even when Ruyter's attack seemed to have achieved victory, Blake's little group, the soul and spirit of the English fleet, refused to be overcome. The battered Dutch ships were in no condition to withstand Monck's fresh vessels, hard though they fought. Tromp now had no reserve with which to meet a fresh attack. His outlook was grim. Some of his captains had even deserted him, and the morale of his crews was low, and ebbing fast. His ammunition was already running out and he had lost five ships. Only his courage never failed him; but he would need all his skill and seamanship if he was to get his convoy safely home.

Next day, Saturday, Blake sighted the Dutch early in the morning, a good distance ahead to leeward. Progress was slow, as there was only a slight west wind. Tromp had formed his fleet into a crescent, with himself at its apex, and the merchantmen in front of him.[63] He summoned his captains together to exhort them to do their duty, according to the oath that they had taken, and to obey their commanders, under whom they served.[64] Ruyter says that 'a number of them behaved very badly'.[65] Floriszoon, too, says that 'they had little support'. He reminded Captain Theuniszoon that he must stay with him, as he had been ordered. To which the captain insolently replied that he took little account of that. Floriszoon snapped back, that if he got home, he would take 'care to deal with such rascals'.[66]

Tromp was now some three or four leagues south of St Catherine's Point, in the Isle of Wight.[67] About 10 a.m. he was heavily attacked by five or six frigates, which were sailing on either side of his fleet, in order to cut off any ship they could. Six times their attacks were beaten off. De Wilde reported that he had been compelled to cast off the tow rope from the *Ostrich*, as the crew were drunk and would do nothing to help him. As a result she was taken and carried into Portsmouth.[68]

Not until noon were any others of Blake's ships able to get into action and his main body did not do so until 2 p.m., when he 'drew very near the enemy, and had warm work until night parted us'.[69] In the afternoon Ruyter was so badly damaged that Tromp ordered Captain Duijm to take him in tow.[70] Van Ness, who had kept just ahead of Tromp, was ordered to sail up to the merchant-men to tell them to sail N.N.E., a course which would take them directly to Calais. Their present course was S.E., which would take them straight to the French coast, to which they urgently hoped to escape. Van Ness did so, exhorting them to crowd on more sail, which they stubbornly refused to do, even though he had set their course, sailing ahead of them.[71]

The frigates had now developed a new and successful tactic. With the Dutch to leeward, they sailed on ahead, keeping out of range, to windward of the larboard side. Then they set their star-board tacks, and stood right into the foe, and boarded the first vessels they met.[72] Thus two stout frigates 'cut off and boarded Le Sage's ship' and took her, Le Sage being killed. Van Seelst's vessel was also taken and burnt.[73] As a result twelve merchantmen were captured, but others, with two men-of-war, escaped, and got away to Dieppe.[74] To add to Tromp's worries, several ships came up to him to report that they had run out of powder and ball. As there was still a quantity left in the store ship, Tromp ordered that any ship, firing an eight-pound ball, should be supplied from her.[75] Small wonder, for the guns of Tromp's ships had been snapping and snarling, like busy sheep dogs, at the wolves that were threatening their flock.

With his lights showing, Tromp sailed on up the Channel, his ships repairing without taking in sail. Blake followed him, with the wind at N.W. 'a fine little gale' as he gladly described it. He had taken, or destroyed, some five ships and he observed that the convoy was now six leagues east of Dungeness, strung out all along the Channel.[76]

Next morning the weather was dirty and cold, with the wind still at N.W.[77] Blake was now about a mile in the rear of the Dutch, 'with five great ships and all the frigates of strength', though many others could not get up. About 9 a.m. he came up with the foe, and attacked them with vigour.[78] Tromp calculated, before the fight had lasted two hours that half his ships would have exhausted their powder and ball. Indeed, for this reason, several of them had taken to flight. He fired shots after them to recall them. On their return he asked them if they were going to fly like knaves. To which they answered they had no ammunition left. So he ordered them to remain a little distance off, in the centre of the fleet, and he would protect both them and the merchantmen. Now he had only twenty-five to thirty ships that still had powder and ball.[79]

Seeing 'their men-of-war somewhat weakened' Blake sent his smaller frigates and ships of less force to get up amongst the convoy. This 'put their whole body to a very great trouble, that many of them and their men-of-war began to break off from their main body, and towards the evening we pressed so hard upon them, that they turned their merchantmen out of their fleet upon us (as is conceived) for a bait'.[80] The merchantmen now threw overboard hundreds of hogheads of wine, in order to lighten their vessels, so that they could get away the faster. These came floating by past the *Waterhound*, much to her regret. She had just seen that Graves, of the *President*, had lost all his masts by the board, somewhat mysteriously, as it was not the result of enemy action.[81] Meanwhile Van Ness again had sailed up to the merchantmen, to urge them to crowd on all sail, and speed forward. Once again they refused, intent on getting to the French coast somehow. Tromp then sent his Fiscal, or Treasurer, with the same urgent order, but still they refused to go forward. Some of the English frigates now got amongst them, and they fell into utter disorder. Part threw themselves blindly among the frigates, while others fell foul of one another, and knocked themselves to pieces, while their warships, without any ammunition, were powerless to protect them.[82]

Blake, who thought this was a bait to delay his ships, gave instant orders that no ships that could get up to their men-of-war, should meddle with any of the merchantmen, but leave them to the rear ships to deal with.[83] Van Ness complained 'the merchantmen closed up, some with the ships of war and some with one another athwart them, so that they lay all together'.[84] The Commissioner for Prize Goods at Dover reported 'the Dutch made a running fight, who making such great sail, left their merchantmen astern of them, who began to straggle in a confused manner, some falling in amongst the thickest of our fleet which, in regard of the pursuit of the Hollanders, were forced to sink and fire the rest'.[85] Penn's nimble frigates 'gleaned up several warships and merchantmen above forty'. Martin, in the *Diamond*, and Graves of the *President*, despite the loss of his masts, each took a ship.

Lawson, with seven ships was also busy;[86] he boarded and took a warship of thirty-eight guns, and carried her into Dover. But he had suffered severely in the action, losing 100 men, either killed or wounded, while the *Fairfax* was also badly shattered.[87]

Tromp, still fighting desperately, was making for Calais, with Cape Grisnez under his lee. With the wind at N.W. and Blake to windward, his position appeared hopeless. He had ordered De Wilde to take in tow Floriszoon, who had received several shots under the water line, and all his repairs shot to bits,[88] while Balck's ship was so unmanageable that he was forced to put into Dieppe.[89] At this point Blake estimated Tromp's numbers at thirty-five warships and 100 merchantmen.[90]

Tromp saw that Blake was remaining out of range, and was collecting his ships. Then he saw him hoist the signal for attack. Tromp struck his top-sails and awaited the expected onslaught. Evertsen, with the ships around Tromp, was completely without ammunition. Suddenly, to Tromp's astonishment and relief, the English veered off. Had he had to fight another hour he calculated his fleet would have exhausted all their powder and ball, and must have fallen into Blake's hands, 'when our fleet would have been utterly cut to pieces'. Some twelve or fourteen English frigates, however, followed Tromp until nightfall keeping up a continuous fire, so as to cut off any ship they could. Evertsen and other ships took the opportunity to come up to Tromp, clamouring for ammunition, which he doled out to them.[91]

Tromp's hopeless situation was naturally unknown to Blake. Had the light lasted some two or three hours longer, he wrote, he could have interposed his fleet between the Dutch and their home. 'So that they must have been forced to have made their way through us with their men-of-war, which were at this time not above thirty-five, as we could count, the rest being destroyed or dispersed; the merchantmen also must have been necessitated to have run ashore, or fallen into our hands, which, as we conceive, the Dutch Admiral being sensible of it, just as it was dark, bore directly in upon the shore, where it is supposed he anchored, the tide of ebb being come, which was a leewardly tide.'[92] 'So near that we durst not follow them, it being nigh a lee shore, and most of the great ships had their masts, yards and sails in such a condition as they were ready to fall down every hour, we thought it best to come to an anchor, the tide being leewardly, and the Dutch fleet between

DWARD Ist:
l of Sandwich

Mountagu by Lely

Sir Richard Stayner from a mezzotint by C. Turner

the French shore and us at anchor.'[93] Blake had not forgotten the occasion when, with Penn, he had gone aground on the Kentish Knock, in that former battle. Deane agreed with him, as their joint dispatch to the Council of State, written on the 22nd from near the Isle of Wight, shows. Nevertheless they also consulted with their pilots, who had expert knowledge of these waters, as to whether Tromp could weather Cape Grisnez. They replied that, with the wind as it was, this would be impossible. Nor could the English fleet in the condition it was in, weather it either. Even if the fleet had been in a much better state, it would have been with extreme hazard as it was night.[93]

It has been said that a Duncan, or a Hawke, would have seized such an opportunity. But, though Blake was always ready to accept risks, he always calculated risks carefully. Moreover these Admirals had won their victories after a single day's battle, whereas Blake had to make his decision at the end of three days continual fighting. To preserve his fleet for another day's conflict, was surely a right one. He had taken five more men-of-war and fifty merchantmen already, and he hoped to secure the whole of Tromp's fleet.

But both Blake and Deane, to say nothing of the pilots, had reckoned without Tromp's superb seamanship. For, as soon as it was dark, he hung out his lights and, with shortened sail, so as to keep his ships together, he set out to weather Cape Grisnez, four miles to the N.E. He could see the lights of Blake's ships to windward. After midnight they were no longer visible. Next morning he had reached Calais. Not an English ship was in sight, and he rightly assumed that they had gone back to the Isle of Wight. He could count seventy-six vessels, great and small, though the merchantmen were very scattered and some had even sailed ahead. He asked that supplies should be sent to him as soon as possible, for he had neither ammunition nor provisions left. There were many dead and wounded men, while some of his ships were so badly damaged that he feared that they might not make port. On the 23rd he summoned his captains aboard, as the States-General had ordered him to blockade the Thames. But, with the fleet in so damaged a condition, it was resolved that it was only possible to return to their own ports.[94] He had lost upwards of 4,000 killed and wounded, including many of his best captains, while 1,500 officers and men were prisoners.[95] An English newspaper gives a gruesome account: 'all the men-of-war who are taken are much dyed with blood, their masts and tacks being moiled with brains, hair, pieces of skull'. It ended in true Puritan piety: 'dreadful sights though glorious, as being a signal token of the Lord's goodness to this Nation'.[96]

'This night being very dark and blowing hard, the Dutch got away from us, so that in the morning we could not discover one ship more than our own, which were between forty and fifty, the rest being scattered and as many prizes as made up sixty in all'. So the three Generals wrote to the Speaker, on the 27th. All that night and day were spent in repairing the ships' masts and sails. After which the fleet returned to the English coast, to avoid staying upon a lee shore. By the 23rd the fleet came into St Helens Road, where the disabled vessels were sent into Stokes Bay.[97] On the 25th Deane wrote to the Admiralty Commissioners to report that he had sent out ten ships, under Captain Dornford, of the *Portsmouth*, to ply westwards, as far as the Start, while Hill, of the *Sapphire*, with another ten, were to ply between Fairlight and Boulogne, to pick up any stragglers they might meet. He ended his report by saying that Blake had gone ashore 'somewhat feverish'. Here Blake developed 'a great cold, which puts him into some distress'.[98] He just managed to struggle aboard the *Triumph* to sign the dispatch on the 27th, though his signature was in a very shaky hand, testifying to the severity of his wound, which had been increased by his chill.[99]

The losses of the English amounted to 1,200 killed and wounded, mostly upon the first day of the battle. Compared with the Dutch losses, it was a light price to pay for one of Blake's greatest victories.[100]

The success of the victory was marred by a report from Willoughby at Portsmouth. On the 22nd, the workmen had refused to work on the repairs to the ships because they were in arrears of wages and did not know when they could be paid.[101] The poor wretches can hardly be blamed, for that lay upon the shoulders of the Government. A really disgraceful case was reported from Dover, on the 24th, by Bourne. Cables and hawsers had been stolen and sold from prizes, that had been brought in. The men who manned the prizes, some ten to fifteen seamen, had sold all the goods between decks before they came in and then had sold the rest for half their value, under the very noses of the prize officers, thus 'wronging the generality of seamen'.[102] A very different complaint came from Coytmor, the Secretary of the Admiralty Committee. He pointed out that there were 2,000 seamen on the ships bound for Newfoundland. These were a sheer loss to the navy, and he was afraid that many, who were aboard the States' ships would run away to join them.[103]

There yet remains the legend of Tromp's broom. Most Englishmen know nothing of the splendour of Portland, save this story. The legend had been immortalised in their minds by a popular ballad. As it has not the slightest foundation, the belief is likely to be everlasting. Ironically enough it is partly based upon a report from the *Nonsuch* frigate, at Portsmouth, written on 28 February, two days after the victory off Portland. 'Their gallant Mr Tromp, when he was in France (we understand), wore a flag of broom and, being demanded what he meant by it, replied that he was going to sweep the narrow seas of all Englishmen. And, indeed, at our first encounter he, having the weather gage, came on so furiously as though he intended to swallow all up'. Another pamphlet 'New Brooms Sweep Clean' says: 'Van Tromp is now pleased to declare against those who have purchased themselves fame – as evidently appears by his setting forth a flag, or standard of broom and, being demanded what he meant by it, replied that he was once more going to sweep the Narrow Sea of all Englishmen.'[104] No other newspaper mentions the affair. There is no mention of the usual story of a broom hoisted after the battle off Dungeness. The broom is said to have been hoisted in France, that is, at a later date, when Tromp was at Rhé, waiting for the return convoy. It is most unlikely that a writer, on a frigate at Portsmouth, could have known anything happening near the mouth of the Garonne. Moreover the two authorities quoted know nothing of any broom hoisted during the three days battle. After the battle had been won, there was every temptation for an English scribbler to invent such a story, exposing Tromp as a braggart who failed to carry out his boast, or even to invent a letter from Portsmouth to conceal his own mendacity. Those who have read Tromp's modest dispatches will be the last to credit him with a boastful display. S. R. Gardiner has given the *coup de grâce* to the legend. But nothing can destroy the popular ballad[105] which belongs with Alfred and the cakes.

CHAPTER 17

From a Sick Bed to the Gabbard

*

'WE have many men wounded and divers both of honesty and worth slain. The condition of the widows and orphans of the one, as also the languishing estate of the other, we do humbly present to your consideration, and most earnestly desire that you will be pleased to take effectual course for the relief and supply of them, as may be answerable to the great trust God hath reposed in you – and as may encourage others – to hazard their lives and limbs in the future – for the rights and liberties, which God and nature hath afforded us.' Such was the plea for their men and their dependents, with which the Generals closed their dispatch, announcing their victory.[1] The Navy Commissioners responded by granting wounded men a gratuity, not exceeding £10, or pensions of £6.13.4 a year, while widows and orphans and impotent parents got a gratuity not exceeding £2.10.0.[2] Nor were individuals behindhand. For Elizabeth Alkin, better known as 'Parliament Joan', requested to be sent to Dover to nurse the sick and wounded.[3] The Commissioners asked the civic authorities in the seaport towns to provide hospitals, to which they would send physicians and surgeons.[4]

Dr Whistler, the foremost physician of his day, was sent to Portsmouth to supervise the medical arrangements. He found an appalling state of affairs there. The sick were scattered in private or requisitioned houses, difficult of access, badly ventilated and lighted, and unprovided with water. Besides Portsmouth, Fareham, Gosport, Dover, Deal and Sandwich were crowded. So he advised that the recovered or slightly wounded men should be sent back to their ships, where the salt meat would do them less harm than strong drink. The more serious cases should be sent to London, in wagons in the charge of surgeons and nurses.

But his chief anxiety was over Blake. On 16 March, 1653, he reported that he 'mends but slowly, which detains me here, awaiting an opportunity of his desired firmer recovery, as also to see the new sick men provided for, as to all accommodations for their recovery'.[5] Doctors Bates and Prideaux had also, on 6 March, been specially sent down by night coach to report on Blake's progress.[6] On the 21st, Whistler wrote again. 'General Blake, I hope, mends but I am checked from too presumptuous prognostics by that maxim, *de senibus non temere sperandum*'. He also complained that the sick and wounded men had had to be long exposed in the open air before quarters could be found for them. Even when they were housed, long intervals elapsed before notice of their removal was given to the doctors, who were insufficient in numbers to visit them frequently. He proposed, therefore, to see if a hospital could be built in the ruins of Porchester Castle, where the air and water were healthier, and where the sick men could be landed with ease.[7]

Nevertheless alarming rumours circulated concerning Blake's health. The chief one came from Royalist sources. 'It is believed Blake will never be able to go to sea again, for one of his hamstrings is broken, and he hath a continual rheum that falls into his eyes, which almost blinds him'.[8] Perhaps the wish was father to the thought. But the sick man must have been greatly cheered when he heard that the Council of State had replied to his brother, Benjamin's, petition with the answer that 'they had no charge of crime against him'. This was, of course, the charge of neglect of duty at Dungeness, alleged against him.[9]

But there was to be little rest for the invalid. The Navy Commissioners had consulted with him, and his colleagues, as to the building of forecastles in the frigates, for the better defence of the crews, probably as a result of the last battle. It was agreed to commend this to the Admiralty Commissioners.[10] Blake also managed to struggle aboard the *Triumph*, to help in the drawing up of instructions 'for the better ordering of the fleet in fighting'. These probably originated in the alert and adaptable mind of Monck. He had led an army in the field, which neither of his colleagues had done. At Portland, as he strove to join Blake and Deane, he had the opportunity, as the clouds which enveloped them cleared away for the moment, to see what was happening. He observed that in the confused fighting, in which all direction seemed to have been lost, each ship or group of ships, fought with the nearest enemy, though Blake's thin red line was the focal point of the battle.

Monck had grasped the fact that the ship was a mobile artillery unit, whose power lay not to its front, but in its broadside, A new naval tactic was needed if this latent power was to be used to its fullest. Deane, as an artillery expert, also realised this while Blake with his alert and adaptable mind would be anxious to work out some new mode of attack.

The new instructions laid down that, when a General was seen to engage, or when he hoisted a red flag at his maintop mizen 'then each squadron shall take the best advantage they can to engage with the enemy next unto them, and in order thereunto all ships of every squadron shall endeavour to keep in a line with their chief'. If the chief was lamed, or disabled, 'then every ship of the said squadron, shall endeavour to get into a line with the Admiral, or he that commands in chief next to him and nearest the enemy'. To keep in a line did not mean what was later on called 'Line ahead' but on a line of bearing parallel to the line of the enemy.[11]

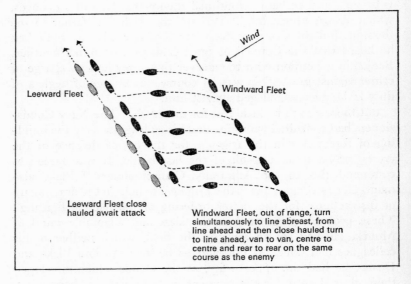

Leeward Fleet

Windward Fleet

Wind

Leeward Fleet close hauled await attack

Windward Fleet, out of range, turn simultaneously to line abreast, from line ahead and then close hauled turn to line ahead, van to van, centre to centre and rear to rear on the same course as the enemy

Line of Bearing Diagram

Another new direction laid down that, if the Admiral has the wind of the enemy, and other ships are to windward of him, upon a blue flag being hoisted at the mizen, every such ship then is to bear up into his wake, or grain, upon the pain of the severest punishment. If the Admiral was to leeward of the foe, and the ships to leeward of him, upon such a signal 'none that are to leeward are to bear up, or to keep his, or their, luff* to gain the wake or grain'.[12]† These instructions were the fruit of the lessons learnt at Dungeness and Portland. Fireships, too, were to endeavour to keep the wind, and to remain near the great ships, so as to be ready for any signal.[13]

The new sailing instructions directed that, in sailing, or tacking, everyone was to keep good order, and neither to strive for the wind, nor for a place, one of another, whereby prejudice or damage might come to any ship or ships. Signals were provided for use both by day or night, or in foggy weather. This was done by the firing of various numbers of guns, the display of lights upon the poop, or in the shrouds, and by the beating of drums, and the sounding of trumpets. Anyone wishing to speak with the General was to spread a flag from the head of his top-mast down to the shrouds, lowering his topsail and firing a gun. If a ship met another in the night, after separation, 'the better to know one another, he that hails shall ask what ship is that? He that is hailed shall answer "Commonwealth" and the ship that haileth shall reply "Flourish".' As the service of this Commonwealth was Blake's guiding star, these passwords can be attributed to him.[14]

The difficulty of manning the ships still continued. About 8 March it was reported, 'we have so fleeced this river (Thames) that there is not one able man to be found'. Men were seized from the merchantmen coming into port, and only a number sufficient to work the vessels into harbour were left aboard.[15] The Council of State had tried to solve the problem by stopping the granting of commissions to privateers.[16] Monck and Deane suggested, on the 25th, that there should be a form of continuous service for the seamen, but this obvious solution was not adopted.[17] The need for mariners was emphasised, by a warning from the council that De With had sailed for the north, probably with the intention of intercepting the colliers about to sail from Newcastle. They asked the Generals to send Penn with all available ships to the Swin. There he was to join Lawson 'to attend the motion of the Dutch'. The Mayor of Newcastle, and Peter Mootham, of the *Bear*, who

---

* To bring the ship's head nearer the wind.
† To follow the water of the ship ahead.

was in charge of the colliers, were also warned not to venture forth till the coast was clear.[18]

In their reply the Generals, on the 30th, wrote that they had already sent off Penn 'with nimble vessels and frigates' to Dover. Here he was to take in powder, and to leave eight frigates to ply between the North Foreland and Calais, and to seize any Dutch or French ships they should meet. The letters ended by the Generals complaining that they were continually being pestered in the streets by seamen, asking for their tickets to be paid, as they had no money, and had lost their clothes in the last battle. Even their tickets being 'little pieces of paper' were apt to be lost.[19]

On the 31st Jeremiah Tolhurst wrote from Newcastle. Four hundred colliers were about to sail, with 5,000 seamen aboard. He warned the authorities that, when the vessels got to Harwich, or Lee, their captains would send the crews to Ipswich and other places, to avoid them being pressed. On their return the captains picked them up again on the ships. Press masters should be sent into Essex to prevent this evasion.[20]

A still more important question worried the Generals. For the council were toying with the idea of sending a fleet into the Mediterranean. They tactfully suggested to the council, probably after consultation with Blake ashore, that this needed serious consideration. They supposed Badiley's squadron, which had been there, was about to come home. But, if this was not so, they thought it advisable to recall him until a 'more fit opportunity to manage the affair there be offered'. In this case ten ships could ply at the mouth of the Channel, between Ushant and Scilly, and another fifteen should lie off the Blaskets, and the north and north-east of Ireland. The summer trade of the Dutch and their home-bound East Indiamen, could thus be dealt with, which would do them more harm near home than 'by sending a fleet so far off, and upon less hazard'. They urged strongly that '. . . uniting your forces will be better than by . . . separating, though upon never so plausible a pretence to the contrary'.[21] The division of the fleet had already been partly responsible for Dungeness. To deal successfully with Tromp would need all their resources. Next day, 5 April, they returned to the problem of getting men, for they had heard that 1,000 seamen had gone from Dartmouth to Newfoundland. Unless men could be got, it would be impossible to get out the fleet. The seamen were still at their doors, begging for their tickets to be paid. They had seen a letter from the Treasurer of the Navy, ordering the Portsmouth Commissioners not to cash any tickets. The Generals spoke their mind forcefully. 'It is neither reason, nor conscience, to compel men to go, who must perish for want of clothes, having formerly lost them in the service, nor yet when their families are ready to starve' by reason that money was due to them from the State.[22]

Nor were the Dutch in any happier a condition. The States-General, after consultation with Tromp, had realised that merchant-men could not go, either in or out, while the English were so strong at sea. Until a fleet could encounter the enemy and either beat them, or drive them into their harbours, they were helpless.[23] But already, on 24 March, De With was complaining that his ships lacked equipment. What was worse, when he went on board De Wilde's ship, to take it over as his flagship, the crew refused to receive him, so that he had to surround her with three men-of-war.[24] Two days later he wrote to say that he feared the mutiny might spread to other ships. He added that he had been personally insulted on six separate occasions.[25] However, on the 29th, he was able to report that the mutineers had been shipped on two fishing boats, and sent to Amsterdam. He had expected to find fifty ships ready for him, but there were only fourteen, and there was not a first-rate vessel among them, much to his anger.[26] Nevertheless, on the 31 March, he put to sea with eighteen ships and two galliots. He intended to intercept the colliers from Newcastle; on 4 April he sighted them, when he was between Flamborough Head and Scarborough.[27] At De With's threat to the colliers, Mootham ordered them to put into Scarborough, where the small vessels anchored under the pier, and the others under the shelter of the castle and her guns. Their captains however were 'very refractory' and would not stay in safety, but stole away by night, with the object of being the first to sell their coal in London, while the price was still high.[28] On the 8th, at 8 a.m., De With stood in and fired broadsides, which were returned. For two hours the cannon-ade continued. De With then put to sea, and held a Council of War. This decided that, owing to the narrowness of the channels, the danger of the shoals and rocks and of the strong wind, not to make another attack, especially as De With's guns were only six pounders. So he returned to the Schoonvelt to complain that

unless some first-rate vessels and some reinforcements were not
at once sent to him, 'our country will suffer'.[29]

Meanwhile Penn had reached Sole Bay on 9 April, where orders
came to him to sail to Scarborough to escort the colliers. He
brought them into Lee Road on the 14th[30] where Nehemiah Bourne
started to impress men out of them. This action provoked such
anger that he had to fire fifty shots to stop their ships from
escaping him. He brought them to anchor by this means, and 'dug'
out the unfortunate men.[31] Penn then sailed to join the Generals
in the Downs. While he was there seven Swedish ships came in,
on the 25th, with cargoes of masts, tar, pitch and lead, badly
needed by the naval authorities. Sailing on, he met the Generals,
on the 29th, off the Isle of Wight.[32]

A dramatic event now intervened. A Bill for a Free Parliament
was before the Commons, but the Rump were determined to
perpetuate their own power. Weekly they delayed matters. Cromwell therefore decided upon a *coup d'état*. On 20 April he entered
the House with a company of musketeers. Vane rose and protested.
Cromwell burst out with the words, 'the Lord deliver me from
Sir Henry Vane' and turned the Members out into the street and
locked the door. With his officers he was assured of army support.
As Vane could not carry on his work under the authority of the
army, he retired to the country. But his work endured.[33] On the
22nd Deane and Monck, keen Cromwellians, cleverly avoiding
any suspicion of a desire to draw the navy into the political
current, circulated among their captains a declaration for them
to sign. They skilfully announced that they had found it laid
upon their spirits that they were called and entrusted by the
nation 'for the defence of the same against the enemies at sea'
and that they were 'resolved in the strength of God unanimously
to prosecute the same, according to the trust placed in them'.[34]

Neither Blake, nor his nephew, Robert, signed the document.
The nephew, for the simple reason that his ship, the *Hampshire*,
was not at Portsmouth, but was refitting in the Thames.[35] Blake,
too, was a Cromwellian, but he was ashore sick and speed was
essential for the Declaration. Nevertheless rumour soon got busy.
A Royalist reportedly declared 'Blake is outed of his command,
and is come to town, highly discontented: he is much for the
Parliament'.[36] But Cromwell was no fool, and he was not likely to

have risked unrest in the navy at such a time by depriving himself of the services of his great Admiral. Blake, too, was a realist. He had served the Commonwealth as a *de facto* authority, and he probably accepted the new regime as a *de jure* one also. Experience in command had taught him the necessity for strong authority. But experience had also warned him of the danger to the navy of the intrusion of politics. The revolt of the fleet in 1648 had split the fleet in two, and had threatened the Parliament with the possible loss of all that it had gained by its victories. Since then, on several occasions, he had had to deal with the infiltration of politics, by Royalists' agents in his ships. He seems to have taken the attitude, expressed probably by Mountagu, but attributed to himself, that it was not for the seamen to mind State affairs, but to obey orders. Dr Gardiner, on the contrary, took the view that 'Blake was known to be highly dissatisfied, but was incapacitated by his wound from taking an active part in affairs, and that, before the end of April when he travelled up to London, he was still suffering and was in no sense able to throw his influence on the side he favoured'.[37] Like the converse view, this is only surmise. At any rate he was at work in Whitehall on 12 May, which would indicate that he had accepted the new order, and was willing to serve under it.[38]

Meanwhile the situation in Holland was growing serious. In Amsterdam 3,000 houses were empty, grass was growing in the streets and unemployment was rife. The hopes, raised by Cromwell's assumption of power, were dashed when the negotiations for peace, discussed in the previous month, were broken off. The terms insisted upon were too high for the Dutch, who still hoped for a naval victory, which would free them from the strangle-hold on her maritime trade routes.[39]

Tromp in a letter to the States-General, of 18 April, asked that the fleet should be united into one body. He needed twenty-four fully equipped fireships, with powder and ammunition and, above all, men. His plan was to attack, if an opportunity offered, so as to cover the home-bound trade, or else to cruise 'about between home and the Dogger Bank, in the Channel along which the expected ships must sail'. This would allow the vessels, bound for Norway and 'those bound for the west round England' to get protection.[40] On the 25th he complained that De With was off the Meuse with 'forty weak and crazy ships'. Eversten and

Floriszoon could not sail, because the refitting he had asked for had been neglected.[41]

But, like the great patriot that he was, Tromp made the best of a bad job, and with Ruyter, sailed from the Meuse to the Texel. Here, on 4 May, De With joined them and also a convoy of 200 vessels, outward bound.[42] Tromp's fleet consisted of eighty men-of-war, five fireships and five small vessels, with which he made for the coast of Norway.[43] On the 8th the fireship *Hammeken*, as he had prophesied, sprang a leak and sank, though her crew were saved.[44] By the 10th he had reached the north of Shetland, where his west-bound convoy, on the 11th, left him and he sailed back to Norway. He then cruised between the Dogger Bank and the Texel. On the 17th a Gothenburg ship came in, which had left the Texel on the 14th, to report that on the 10th the English fleet of eighty ships, had been off the Texel.[45] In the afternoon four merchantmen, of Anteunisz's convoy, told Tromp that they had left Anteunisz off Bergen on the 15th. However on the 19th he came into the Vlie with his convoy of 100 vessels. Tromp gave their captains strict orders to stay with him, so that he could take them safely into the Meuse. But, at dusk, several unarmed ships slipped away 'wantonly exposing both ships and cargo'. On the 20th, Floriszoon, with sixteen warships, joined Tromp and they sailed on to the Meuse to pick up Evertsen. As Tromp had now 'a goodly number' he proposed to attack the foe, 'the sooner the better'. He had now ninety-two men-of-war, five fireships and six small vessels.[46]

Deane and Monck, with Penn, reached Dover on 2 May. Off Calais some outward-bound Hamburgers told them that Tromp had been south of the Texel on 30 April. A Council of War was held at which it was decided to seek out, and attack, the enemy.[47] So, next day, the fleet stood over to Holland. On 4 May they chased and captured forty fishing boats. The crews were set free, on the condition that they would not serve against the Commonwealth. Off Camperdown, on the 5th, some small vessels were captured, from whom it was learnt that Tromp had sailed from the Texel at 5 p.m. the day before.[48] Since they had missed Tromp by so narrow a margin, it was decided to go after him, and on the 10th they were off Aberdeen[49] and on the 12th they reached the Orkneys. As there was no sign of Tromp, they moved on to the Shetlands on the 13th. But still there was no sign of him, for

The United Provinces in the XVIIth Century

his return to Norway had taken him out of the path of the English fleet. After watering at Brassa Sound, they sailed E.S.E. on the 18th, to look for Tromp at the Riff, the entrance to the Kattegat in Denmark. On the 22nd they changed course and by the 24th they were off the Scheldt, and next day off the Vlie. Here a Council of War decided to lie before the Texel, so as to prevent twenty ships there from coming out to join Tromp who, they supposed to be about the Wielings or Goeree. On the 27th the flag officers resolved that they must cross over to Yarmouth to pick up twenty-six ships lying there, and to leave scouts off the Texel and the Meuse, to observe the foe.[50]

But where was Tromp? On the 22nd he had left the Meuse and next day he decided to attack the foe, either by occupying the Thames, or in the Downs, where he supposed them to be. 'I have speculated very carefully on the position in the Downs and in my opinion, with a favourable wind, tide and weather, it would be perfectly easy to destroy the enemy lying there, with a smaller force than we have now, because they would run towards the land, and get aground under the castles; and then we could readily send the fireships alongside and set them on fire'.[51] Possibly he had heard of Badiley's return from the Mediterranean and hoped to catch him there. Unfortunately Badiley was at Chatham, where Pett was trying to force his men to go aboard the frigates, about to set forth. He found them instead the 'most disorderly men I have ever had to deal with'.[52] Bourne, too, reported that 'they are enraged that they are sent after this manner'. He had to assure them that, as soon as the crisis was over, they would be free to go aboard their own ships.[53] But surely sympathy is due to these men, who after long and arduous service, hardly expected at their homecoming to be sent immediately out in strange ships, without being granted any shore leave.

On reaching the North Foreland, Tromp decided to lie outside it so as to avoid discovery. Ruyter and Floriszoon were to remain without the Goodwins, so as to be able to tack into the Downs from the south with twenty-five ships and two fireships. Tromp, De With and Evertsen, with sixty-five warships and three fireships would then enter from the north. It was the old Tromp technique. At 2 p.m. on the 25th, he went in only to find, instead of the fleet he had expected, two small merchantmen lying under the castles with whom he exchanged fire. Then, as no foe was to be found, he passed on at 3 p.m. to Dover, where his other squadron joined him. He anchored and sent in five light frigates which captured three small merchantmen and forced the *Drake* frigate to run herself aground. Many broadsides were poured into the town, and much ammunition was expended. At 6 p.m. he weighed and anchored off Calais.[54] The *Drake* was then refloated and lay under the castle to make repairs.[55]

On 29 May Tromp, who was now at Walcheren in the Netherlands, was astonished to learn from a Flushing privateer, that she had been fired upon on the evening of the 24th, off the Vlie, by the English fleet while a fishing boat brought news, on the morning of the same day, of the English fleet off the Flemish coast steering west. From Amsterdam Tromp learned that the enemy numbered from 100 to 120 ships. He immediately told his captains to be ready to fight, and steered west to look for them.[56]

Meanwhile the Generals, who were now off Dunwich, got news from a ketch that Tromp had been sighted on 30 May, off the Long Sands Head.[57] Immediately they sent back orders that all ships between that place and the Ness* were to join them, that night if possible. They were probably unaware that Blake, though still a sick man, was in the Thames, supervising the getting of the ships there to sea. He had even got them into the middle of the Gunfleet.[58] At long last the two opponents, who ironically enough had been looking for each other in opposite directions, were about to meet.

On 1 June, at 6 a.m. the Generals left Sole Bay.[59] They had with them 105 ships with 3,817 guns and 16,269 men.[60] The Red squadron under the Generals, in the *Resolution*, were in the centre. Penn, with the White, in the *James*, was on their starboard. Lawson, in the *George*, commanding the Blue, was on their port side. Scouts had been pushed ahead to watch for the foe and the fleet anchored in the Shipwash. About noon the frigates let fall their top-gallant sails (the new instructions had come into force) and Lawson passed the signal on to the Generals to let them know the foe had been sighted. The whole fleet weighed and made for the enemy, who were some four leagues distant to leeward. At 4 p.m. the Blue squadron halted in order to let the Generals, and the many ships astern of them, come up.[61] Then, as the leeward tide set in, with the weather 'proving hazy and dark, we lost sight of the enemy and stopped upon the tide, expecting the coming out of those ships with Admiral Blake'.[62] The fleet was now 'about two miles distant within the south head of the Gable', roughly forty miles east of Harwich and about N.E. by E. of the North Foreland, from which the Dutch were lying two leagues N.E.[63]

An order was sent back to tell the ships not to stir below the Gunfleet until further directions. Blake who was in charge of them, wrote giving the Generals his station which was in the middle of the Gunfleet. In his opinion it was 'not safe nor rational' to stir

* Orfordness

below the Gunfleet. He asked for 'further intelligence touching our fleet, that I may resolve accordingly, being desirous to put in for my share for the service of the Commonwealth in this present juncture – such as the infirmities of my body will bear, which I find increases upon me'. Just as he had finished writing on the evening of 2 June, orders came from the Generals for all ships to come out and join them. Ill as he was, Blake's old fighting spirit was aroused. That very same afternoon, in the *Essex*, he led out thirteen ships.[64]

Deane and Monck had apparently resolved to put into execution the new fighting instructions. As experienced artillery officers, they realised the great superiority of their gun power over the Dutch. Their ships, too, were much more stoutly built. To utilise this advantage to the utmost, they determined that, instead of closing with the enemy, they would keep him at a distance, by long range fire. So they ordered that no ship was to be boarded until she had been shattered and rendered helpless.[65] As the seamen knew that £10 per gun, of any ship sunk or destroyed, would be theirs, they were assured that they would not lose prize money, which would ensure that the order was obeyed.[66]

Deane and Monck had 105 ships in three squadrons. The Generals leading in the Red, followed by Penn in the White and Lawson in the Blue.[67] Against these Tromp had 104 vessels. Yet he was full of confidence believing that his tactical skill would more than outweigh his material disadvantages.[68]

The battle began on 2 June. The English were 'about two miles distant without the south end of the Gable' while Tromp was four leagues N.E. of the North Foreland.[69] With the Generals in the centre, with Penn on their starboard and Lawson on their port side, the Generals stood towards the enemy. As the wind was slight only at eleven o'clock did any long range exchange of shots begin, which battered the Dutch ships badly. This was 'so great a terror to most of the State's ships, as few of them durst bear up or abide it.'[70]

About 3 p.m. Lawson, with some of the Blue squadron, driven either by the current, or impelled by his own rashness, closed with De Ruyter. At once Tromp hurried to his aid. As he did so the wind shifted to the east, and for the moment gave him the weather gage. He attempted to interpose his squadron between Lawson and Monck, who had been to starboard, and now was to leeward. Tromp drove into the gap and closed with Lawson. Fortunately Monck was not too far to leeward and in the *Resolution* led the Red to Lawson's aid.[71] Even so, Lawson had to endure the brunt of the struggle,[72] and seven of his vessels were badly damaged.[73] Monck, too, is said to have been attacked by sixteen ships.[74]

At this moment calamity overtook the English. Deane was slain by a chain shot, and fell at Monck's side, drenching him with blood. Monck threw his cloak over the mangled body, and quietly ordered it should be taken below to a cabin, in case the news should discourage the crew. Now he was in sole command.[75]

Gradually Penn with the White came up, and Monck's counter-attack, as he regained the wind, forced Tromp to leeward. As dusk fell the Dutch were in full retreat. They were swept past Blankenberge, wildly striving to reach the Wielings. Instead they were driven along their coast towards the Meuse.[76] Their captains through carelessness or lack of experience became disorganised, as Monck's long range fire still battered them.[77] In the pursuit, disabled vessels were captured and at night both fleets were near Dunkirk.[78]

Monck had not lost a single ship and it seemed as if the new tactic had been successful. But on the 3rd, at sunrise, a council of flag officers was called. Here it was resolved, 'by reason divers the Blue squadron had showed too much timorously the day before' that 'all flags should sail abreast, having our General in the centre – to pass through and scatter the enemy's fleet'. Monck asked all officers 'to wipe out the past and do their best in the present'. He would 'pursue the enemy as far as the shoals would permit'.[79] It was clear that the new fighting instructions had neither been understood, nor obeyed, by some of the captains. Wisely the old method was adopted for the present.

The same morning Tromp, too, held a council. Most of the ships were very short of ammunition, owing to the reckless expenditure at Dover. It would be impossible to fight for long. Tromp, therefore, would make 'one more sharp attack and then we shall be forced to retire'. So it was decided to fight on the defensive, which must have increased the already low morale.[80]

At midday action recommenced. After hours of manoeuvring in vain, Tromp had to withdraw towards the Flemish coast. He was still fighting hard, with Monck in hot chase, when suddenly a fresh English squadron appeared on his port bow, led by Blake's nephew, Robert, in the *Hampshire*, who burst through the enemy line and brought to the wildly cheering crews the news that Blake himself had come.[81]

The rout became complete and Tromp could not stem it. Only by the bravery of De Ruyter, De With and Eversten, was the *Brederode* saved from capture. All night long the retreat continued, with the Dutch making for the safety of the sandbanks along their coasts, with the English hot behind them. But Tromp's knowledge of his home waters and the shallower draught of his vessels saved his fleet from utter destruction. When darkness fell Blake and Monck were off Ostend, and the disordered Dutch gained the Wielings, but only seventy-four of them.[82]

The Dutch lost six ships sunk, two blown up and two fired and eleven made prize. Their losses were put at 800 killed, including two Vice-Admirals and two Rear-Admirals, while between 1,300 and 1,400 were prisoners. The English had twelve ships disabled, with 126 killed and 236 wounded.[83]

John Bourne of the *Resolution* had hoped for 'one hour more to have ended the war'.[84] The Generals, reporting the news to Cromwell, took the same view. 'We should have destroyed most of them, but it grew dark and, being off Ostend among the Sands, we durst not be too bold, especially with the great ships'. So at 10 p.m. they anchored, leaving scouts.[85]

Next morning the scouts suddenly let fall their top-gallant sails, as a signal that the enemy had been sighted between Ostend and Blankenberge. A mighty cheer went up from the seamen at the prospect of engaging again. After a Council of War, the Generals stood in towards the enemy, only, as it fell calm, to anchor again,[86] so that Tromp, with his lighter ships, was able to enter the Wielings. Here 'the water was too shoal' so that the English were unable to follow him.[87] In the letter to Cromwell, Blake characteristically accorded Monck the honour of signing before him, thus giving him the full credit for the victory. They wrote that they were about to pursue the foe, 'so far as with safety we might, and then to range along the coast as far as the Texel, the better to improve the victory'.[88] On the same day, 4 June, they asked the Navy Commissioners for powder and shot, masts and rigging, hammocks, wood and candles. They were sending back thirteen prizes, with twelve disabled vessels of their own, which they asked to be returned as soon as they were repaired. The *Resolution* needed fresh sails, as the old ones had been shot away.[89] With the ships went Stayner, in the *Foresight*, carrying Deane's body to Woolwich, from whence it was taken to Greenwich to lie in state[90] and then on to Westminster for a State funeral and interment in the Abbey. Here Popham already lay. In four years' time the body of Blake was to join them.

The victory seemed to the pious John Poortmans, the Admiralty Commissioner on board the *Resolution*, as a sign that 'the time of Anti-Christ's glory was now expired'.[91] Perhaps he was a little over-optimistic. The outspoken De With burst out to the States-General 'Why should I keep silence any longer? I am before my Sovereigns: I am free to speak, and I must say that the English are at present Masters both of us and of the Seas'.[92] He had summed up the effects of the battle of the Gabbard.

CHAPTER 18

Victory Over the Dutch

*

ON 17 June, 1653, a ship sailed up the Thames under a white flag. She carried Beverninck, who was to be followed by Nieuport, and others, who were to try and arrange peace terms. So great had been the shock to the Dutch authorities of Tromp's defeat.[1] Rumour in London spoke of 5,000 or 6,000 veteran troops being prepared for a landing in Holland.[2] Clarges, at Calais, reported that twenty-three large and small vessels were in the Thames laden with provisions, thousands of spades, axes and other tools for this purpose.[3] But there is no mention of such a scheme in the letters of Blake or Monck. Blake's personal experience of amphibious operations at Scilly and the Channel Islands had made him well aware of the dangers and difficulties of such an expedition. To carry out such in Holland would have been much more hazardous. The landing of forces among the shoals against troops ready to receive them would involve many risks. Even if a landing could be made, the troops would be completely dependent upon the fleet for supplies, and storms might well force the ships far out to sea. Colonel Goff, Nehemiah Bourne and Captain Hatsell visited the Generals on 12 June and they may well have discussed the idea with them.[4] If so it is probable that Blake advised against it. Nor was it likely, now that the Dutch Envoys had again arrived, that Cromwell would have done anything to interfere with the negotiations. Nevertheless, rumour took wings and flew to Holland. Here hasty preparations were made to fortify the Texel, while many inhabitants of the Vlie fled from their houses with their goods.[5]

After refitting off the Meuse, the Generals sailed for the Texel and the Vlie on the evening of 6 June.[6] As they had only sixteen rounds per gun left, they asked for 7,000 barrels of powder, with shot in proportion, to be sent to them, with top-masts and fishes to replace those the ships had lost. Their immediate task was to prevent the Dutch ships from coming out to join Tromp in the Wielings, and also to hinder the mercantile and fishing trade of

Holland. They gave warning that, as soon as the enemy was ready, they supposed 'he will endeavour to attempt somewhat upon our own coast'. His target probably would be Dover, and they hoped the Navy Commissioners would take steps to prevent this. This indicated that they did not intend that such a move would divert them from their main task of blockade.[7]

Blake's previous experience of blockade off Lisbon was to stand him in good stead. Though he was now much nearer to England, his fleet was a much larger one. One of the main tasks, therefore, would be that of administration; Yarmouth, Harwich and Hull were selected as the bases for supply. They were fortunate in having Nehemiah Bourne at Harwich, for he stood shoulder-high above his fellows, Taylor at Chatham and Kendall at Deptford. Monck was to speak of him as having fitted out twenty-two ships in half the time taken at other yards.[8] The Generals' correspondence, therefore, dealt largely with supply. They needed wood and candles, paper and canvas for cartridges, twine and old junk for oakum, hammocks and provision made for the sick.[9] Supply ships were to collect in the Swin, from whence they were to proceed to the fleet with a 'competent strength' to protect them.[10] This careful organisation provided for that freedom of movement essential for the fleet, without the necessity of diminishing it by the need to guard the supply vessels from attack. They asked that the names and lading of the victuallers and the water ships sent out to them should be supplied to them beforehand. Thus, when they arrived they should go aboard the Admiral to report where they came from, with their lading, under the victualler's own hand, so that they could get their discharge. This would prevent them from staying in the fleet without the Generals' knowledge and also from going away without the Generals' order.[11]

Blockade is ever a wearying business, whose tedium is only occasionally broken by moments of action. Here it was no exception. On 19 June, the frigates plying before the Vlie, sighted eleven incoming ships, some from the West Indies 'being ships of force', and fought with them for some time. The Dutch vessels then took to flight, and five escaped, but one was sunk and another burnt. In the encounter Captain Vesey of the *Merlin* was killed. The Generals commended the plight of his 'poor widow, with a great charge of children' to the Admiralty Commissioners. On the 22nd frigates north of the Vlie met thirty sail, which 'being of no force', tried to escape. Eleven were taken, and the rest scattered and got into port. It was a valuable capture, for two of the ships were Swedes, laden with 360 guns, twelve to sixteen pounders which, as the Generals observed 'will be as seasonable for us as for them, had they escaped'. It is probable that other captures took place, which are not recorded, for no Dutch ship could enter or leave without risk.[12]

But this was not done without cost. On 20 June, after reporting the captures, the Generals spoke of 'blowing weather' which had forced them far out to sea. In the storm the *Ruby* lost her foremast and bowsprit.[13] On the 28th they reported that cables and anchors had been 'lost in this wild road, by reason of blowing weather'. But more crippling than the storms was the increasing sickness of both officers and men, which led them to ask for four surgeons, as some were sick and two had died. It was largely upon this account that, on the 30th, they decided to cross over to England with their main body, 'to get some refreshment for our seamen, which fall sick every day very fast'. They left behind 'a considerable number of our cleanest and best sailers, to ply it before the Vlie, or to the northward.' Accordingly they sailed, but blowing weather 'drove them to leeward as far as Flamborough Head, with men still falling sick, eighty alone on the flagship.[14] Whistler, who had been sent down from London, reported that the air and water at Harwich was bad and he proposed that the sick should be sent to Ipswich, where the fresh water would help to cure the 'sea-scurvy'.[15]

On 5 July the fleet anchored in Sole Bay. Here Monck reported that Blake had been unable to sign their dispatch, as he had gone ashore sick.[16] But next day he managed to struggle aboard the *Resolution* and sign, with Monck. They spoke of continual complaints of the badness of the victuals and especially of the beer.[17] This probably reflects the unpaid bills of the victuallers.

A Royalist source says that '1,500 sick men were put ashore with a high fever (some call it the plague) raging among them. Blake is likewise so ill on shore that we fear his life: some report him dead, and that Colonel Pride must be successor'.[18] Blackborne, secretary to the Navy Commissioners, and Captain Limbery, on the evening of the 6th, visited him ashore. They found him in a very 'weak condition, full of pain both in his head and left side, which has put him into a fever, besides the anguish he endured by the gravel in his kidneys, insomuch that he takes no rest night and day, but continues groaning very sadly. This place affords no accommodation at all for one in his condition, there being no physician to be had hereabouts, nor any to attend him with applications necessary. Mr Halstock, his surgeon, is for the present with him but expects to be called on board every hour'. They suggested that Whistler should be sent to him, and that he should be moved to a proper place.[19] Monck, on the 8th, described him as very weak, and his condition dubious and uncertain, though sometimes he gave hope of amendment. There could be no question of his going to sea for some little time.[20] On the 11 July, Monck went to sea only seven days after his return, which speaks volumes for the excellent administration of Nehemiah Bourne.[21]

On the victualling side there were still serious deficiencies; beer, bread and butter were so bad that the crews refused to do their fair share of repairs when the ships were in dock.[22] The heavy sickness led to a lack of seamen, and the recovered often deserted, which led to a heavy press on the Thames.[23] The mayors of the East Anglian towns were ordered to arrest all the runaways they could discover.[24] George Kendall, at Deptford, declared that the reason lay in the withholding of their wages, which caused distress to their families, for the violent pressing left the seamen's dependants without support, while the bad food served to them at sea led to their death, so that the families were left without a breadwinner. He begged that this should be remedied.[25] At Harwich, on 12 July, Bourne reported a mutiny caused by 'drunken, debauched seamen', so that he had to use soldiers to drive them aboard their ships. He arrested the ringleaders, and sent them to the Generals to be dealt with, and put a restraint on the alehouses.[26] 'Parliament Joan', too, pleaded that the £5.5.0 she had been given was exhausted, so that she had to spend £15.0.0 of her own to help the sick, and, even so, was in debt for her own food.[27] Had it not been for the kindness and care of the country folk, and the Bailiffs of Yarmouth, affairs would have been much worse.[28] The lack of money was the root cause of all these troubles.

Tromp had been hard at work. He asked for warships, fireships, ammunition, beer and water so that he could be ready to sail. He had dealt severely with the disobedient captains.[29] On 17 June he had seventy-seven vessels ready. His plan was to unite himself with the ships lying at the Vlie and Texel.[30] But so tight was the blockade that orders were sent to the East Indiamen to sail round Scotland to Norway and the Sound, to lie there 'until the Seas be open'.[31] Some 300 or 400 vessels, bound for the Baltic, were detained so long in the Vlie, that they had almost consumed their provisions.[32] So cleverly had the frigates, left by the Generals, done their work, that they had given the impression that they were far more numerous than they actually were.[33] Indeed it was not until 14 July that Tromp learned that the English fleet had left the Dutch coast, and by that time Monck was back again.[34] Tromp never knew what an opportunity he had missed. Poortmans observed 'the enemy hath hardly a peep hole, for our small vessels and frigates keep so near into the shore that their galliots for intelligence can hardly pass us'.[35]

Meanwhile Monck, on 23 July, reported that contrary winds and blowing weather had forced him to anchor near the Texel. Owing to sickness he still needed men, and he asked for soldiers to take their place, who should bring their own clothes with them to avoid the sickness, and that he needed water and beer.[36] How effective the blockade was is shown by a letter from the Hague, of 22 July. 'Our trade is nearly gone and our banks . . . cannot hold out long, our East India actions fall to nothing . . . and the want of money extreme much . . . there is nothing to raise money on'.[37] To the suggestion of the States-General that Tromp should send out ships to draw the English fleet away from the Dutch coast, he replied that his advice was to keep the fleet together and not divide it.[38] On 24 July, as if he had a presentiment of his own death, he asked that a deputy might be sent to him in case he fell sick or was shot. For if the fleet should be deprived of its commanding officer, they could judge 'of the harmony that would reign among the officers next in command'. He had heard from the envoys in London, that the English had 150 ships and he complained bitterly that 'fine ships half completed were lying useless all over the country.'[39]

As the battle about to begin lies outside our scope, it can be briefly summarised. On 29 July Tromp managed to draw Monck from his station, so that next day he was able to effect a junction with De Witt, who came out of the Texel.[40] Next day one of the bloodiest battles of the war took place. In the course of the fighting, Tromp fell, pierced in the breast by a musket shot fired reputedly from the *Tulip*, of the Blue squadron. He was taken below to a cabin, where his chief officers stood round his death bed. To them he addressed his last words: 'I have finished my course, have good courage.' Thus England's most formidable antagonist was spared the humiliation of seeing his fleet in full flight. It was a disaster for the Dutch.[41] But it was a success for the new English tactic. Cubitt refused to allow his men to board and loot a disabled ship: all must be subordinate to the destruction of the enemy fleet.[42] The Dutch lost, according to Cubitt, fourteen ships, but Penn puts it at thirty. They were either burnt, sunk or captured, while 3,000 or 4,000 of their men were killed, wounded or made prisoner.[43] The English lost the *Oak* and the *Hunter*, with 500 men killed or wounded. Great satisfaction was afforded by the recapture of the *Garland* and the *Bonaventure*[44] lost in 1652, at Dungeness, even though they were so badly damaged that they had to be burnt and sunk. Blake especially, on his sick bed, must have rejoiced.

At a Council of War, on 1 August, Monck decided to return to Sole Bay, as 'it was not fit to be bold on that shore, not knowing how the wind may take us, many of our ships being much disabled.'[45] He bent his efforts to repairing his ships and in getting provisions. His expenditure of ammunition had been enormous and he asked for 1,000 barrels of powder and eighty tons of shot, with masts, sails and rigging, to be sent him.[46] Thus he was able, on the 29th, to send out forty-five ships, under Lawson, to join the eight vessels off the coast of Holland, which were on the watch for home-bound traders.[47]

Meanwhile Blake's health had varied. On 15 July, as we have seen, his life was feared for and Colonel Pride was rumoured to be his successor[48] but by the 22nd, he had recovered. According to a Royalist report, he 'will instantly for sea again, the *Portsmouth* frigate attends him for that purpose; this puts out Monck's nose, who gaped after the absolute command, and a commission to that effect was intended for him: he hath Penn for his great adviser'.[49] Another attempt had been made to stir up trouble in the fleet, but this was unsuccessful. The same source reported on the 29th that Blake was still unfit for duty, though he was shortly expected in London. This time Ayscue was named as successor.[50] He was very popular with the seamen but, as Cromwell was suspicious of him, he was unlikely to be appointed.

The real state of Monck's relations with Blake is shown on

4 August, when Monck wrote that Blake had desired him to recommend Captain Adams, who had served under him at Taunton, for the command of one of the new frigates. Monck also reminded the Admiralty Commissioners that Mrs Vesey, whom both he and Blake had put forward for compensation for the loss of her husband, had not yet received it. This caused her and her six children much affliction.[51] Blake had obviously received much benefit from a visit to Bath, where he had been taking the waters to relieve his gravel and kidney troubles, for on 5 September, he was able to write from Portsmouth to ask for a new mast for the *Essex*, adding that he hoped soon to be in Whitehall.[52] By October he was there, dealing with naval matters.[53] He found time, however, to take his seat in Parliament on 10 October, when he received, through the Speaker, the thanks of the House 'for his great and faithful service'.[54] On 8 August Parliament had ordered that two gold chains, valued at £300 each, should be given to Blake and Monck, with two to the value of £100 each, to Penn and Lawson. Four other flag officers got chains to the value of £40 each. Four gold medals were also awarded to Blake, Monck, Penn and Lawson. They were made by Thomas Simon and showed an anchor, from the stock of which three crosses were suspended: St George for England, St Andrew for Scotland and the Harp for Ireland. On the reverse was a naval battle, with many ships sinking in the foreground. A further 161 gold medals, of which seventy-nine were small ones, were also distributed probably to officers.[55]

In the interim, on 29 August, Monck had sailed from Alde-burgh Bay with eighteen ships. Two days later he had met Lawson, and together they stood for the Texel. A frigate had brought them news that De With had sailed on the 30th for Norway. A meeting of the flag officers decided to go back with the great ships, leaving behind some frigates to scout on the coast.[56] It may be wondered why they did not sail north with their sixty ships, to search for De With. It would seem that their vessels were in no condition to remain long at sea, or to face the dangers of the equinoctial gales in the North Sea. But the news was wrong, for not until 1 September did De With leave the Texel. He escorted 340 outward-bound vessels with forty-three men-of-war. He was also to bring home the merchantmen which were sheltering in the ports of Norway. Had Monck known the truth he might have taken the risk, and gone after De With, so as to secure such a rich prize. But the opportunity was missed.[57]

Trouble now broke out among the English seamen. They had been promised that no ship's company should be sent ashore without receiving their pay, but this was avoided by keeping the ships at sea indefinitely. The result was that their families were destitute. On 9 October, 200 of the *Unicorn's* men 'in a mutinous way' told Pett at Chatham, that they would not go aboard or do duty until they got their pay. Their example was followed by the crews of the *Laurel* and *Kentish*. Pett promised them money if they would fit the ships and go to the Hope. But instead they made their way to London, and Pett begged for a troop of horse to aid him.[58] At Harwich Nehemiah Bourne met the crews of the *Assurance* and the *Mermaid* in the streets, on the 21st, who demanded money and clothes. 'In fair persuasive language' he promised them that he would make speedy provision for them, if they would go aboard. Instead they took to the fields, destroying all the gates and stiles.[59] More serious trouble broke out on the same day, when 400 men from the ships in the Thames marched to Whitehall. Cromwell and Monck met them, and Monck struck the ringleader with his sword and, by the strength of his character and his resolution persuaded them to retire. But next day they returned. This time they found the streets blocked by a regiment of foot and four troops of horse. Angrily they pushed in among the foot, seizing their muskets out of their hands, while one man even pointed one at Cromwell himself. A cavalry charge routed them. One man was flogged and another was hanged.[60]

Next day an additional Article of War laid down that mutiny would be severely punished. But promises were made that measures would be taken to secure the payment of wages and prize money.[61] This was still easier to promise than to perform. Bourne dealt with his mutineers by paying the *Mermaid's* men last, and that not until they were about to sail, while the *Assurance's* crew only sailed after four of their ringleaders had been imprisoned in Landguard Fort. Here they remained 'seeming very sorrowful' while Bourne took stern measures to 'banish strong waters'.[62] Oppenheim's claim that the seamen were 'comparatively punctually paid, properly clothed, well fed . . . and promised advantages in the shape of prize money never previously allowed' hardly seems to accord with these facts. The officials cannot be blamed. They knew that the root of the trouble lay in the postponement of payment till the crews were dismissed the service. Of this grievance the Government had said nothing. They were at their wits' end for money.[63]

On 2 December, Blake and Monck had their commissions renewed, while at Monck's suggestion, Penn had been made a General-at-Sea, together with Desborough, and all four were added to the Admiralty and Navy Commissioners.[64] Desborough did not go to sea, since he had been appointed for his administrative ability. Instead he worked from Whitehall. On the 17th the Generals issued an Order dealing with the danger of fire on the ships. Candles were only to be used in lanterns; tobacco was not to be smoked between decks, or in the holds, or in cabins; no strong drink was to be sold aboard, under the penalty of the most severe censure and punishment.[65]

On 5 January Blake and Desborough, on the latter's only voyage, sailed from London to Gravesend to arrange for the departure of the Dutch Envoys for Holland, after the peace negotiations had again broken down.[66]

Blake, Monck and Penn were in St Helens Road, on 17 January, where Monck left the fleet to take up the pacification of Scotland at Cromwell's request.[67] Not until 1666 did he again see naval service, when he was once more appointed a General-at-Sea. Blake and Penn got to work to get the *Sovereign* out to sea. How essential this was was due to the news, sent by the Admiralty Commissioners, on 28 February, that the Dutch intended to be at sea by 1 March, with 120 ships.[68] This did not perturb the Generals, who did not even recall the vessels plying off Land's End. For they had heard that Beach, a former Royalist captain, in the *Sorlings*, previously the *Royal James*, of twenty-four guns, was thereabouts. On 4 March news came that the Dutch 'intend to be suddenly at sea with a considerable body'. The Generals' calm was rewarded, on 10 March, with the news that Captain Potter of the *Constant Warwick* had captured Beach and brought him into Plymouth. Strangely enough Potter had previously taken Beach in the *Tresco* at the Scillies. When Beach had hailed him as to who he was, Potter answered: 'Your old friend Potter'. Beach replied with a curse and tried to escape, but all in vain.[69]

The Generals, in the *Swiftsure*, cruised in the Channel, taking three small vessels. They had six frigates plying between Ushant and the Seine to watch the Brest privateers, which had infested the trade route between the Welsh and Irish coasts, while the main English fleet was in the North Sea, dealing with the Dutch. A west wind made it too dangerous to lie before Brest itself.[70] On 12 April the Generals dealt with Roger Harvey, of the *Tiger*, who when drunk had stabbed and killed another seaman in a quarrel. He had fled ashore, only to find himself pressed into the *Triumph*, where he was recognised and captured. Blake asked for him to be sent to Harwich, where the murder had taken place, so that he might be dealt with by the Coroner's Inquest. He hoped that 'due care shall be taken to rid the fleet of this Achan' which probably meant that he should be hanged.[71]

Though the Generals were confident of their ability to deal with the Dutch fleet, should it come out, the enemy were in no condition to put out to sea. They were unable to man their ships, while their merchantmen waited for peace before they would venture forth. The Dutch finances, too, were in a deplorable state, so that the country stood on the brink of complete ruin.[72] It is not surprising that, on 5 April, they agreed to sign a Peace Treaty. The terms were severe. They must expel the adherents of the House of Orange: salute the English flag and so acknowledge her sovereignty of the seas. They were only to pass through the Straits of Dover by permission, and they were to restore the Island of Pularoon in the East Indies, and pay £3,615 to the heirs of those killed in the Amboyna Massacre of 1623, as compensation. Another sum of £170,000 was to be paid to the East India Company as compensation, with £97,163 damages to the English traders in the Baltic. However the proposal to unite the two nations was dropped.[73] In addition the Dutch had lost 1,500 ships, taken as prizes. Nor did Denmark, Holland's ally, escape, for she was made the subject of separate and equally stringent conditions.[73]

England was now the supreme naval power in Europe. Small wonder was it that Cromwell's mind turned to the idea of distant expansion. In Professor Lewis's words: 'what the war had done was to let us into the trade: it had not shut the Dutch out of it; and it had also introduced us to a principle of naval warfare, which was to become peculiarly our own – Seek out the enemy fleet and destroy it. We were already realising that this is the prime requisite for command of the Sea'.[74] Admiral Mahan puts his finger on the real reason for Blake's triumph. 'The natural

steadfastness and heroism of the Hollanders could not wholly
supply that professional pride and sense of military honour, which
it is the object of sound military institutions to encourage – the
annals of the Dutch sea fights gave instances of desperate enterprise
or endurance, certainly not excelled and perhaps never equalled
elsewhere; but they also exhibit instances of defection and misconduct which show the lack of the military spirit, due evidently
to the lack of professional pride and training.'[75]

The jealousy of the various Boards of Admiralty, to say nothing
of the Dutch Admirals themselves could not make for a united
fleet. The Dutch could not describe themselves as 'we happy
few, we band of brothers'. Portland, the Gabbard, and Tromp's last
battle, all display instances of each man for himself, and the
Devil take the hindermost. Though Tromp had insisted upon
concentration, and of making the enemy fleet his main objective,
he had also been obsessed with the Downs as a trap in which to
catch the English fleet, which led him to neglect his true objective.
He could conduct a retreat with amazing skill, and in seamanship
and navigation he stood supreme. But as a tactician and a strategist,
in Blake, Deane and Monck he met his equals, nay more, his
masters.

Blake had created a navy, not merely of ships, but of men.
And he had inspired it, with the slogan of 'the service of this
Commonwealth'. The spontaneous outburst of wild cheering that
greeted his thrust through the enemy line at the Gabbard, is a
reminder of the cry, 300 years later, of 'the Navy's here'. It was
'Blake's here', for Blake was the Navy incarnate. Behind the
cheering lay the respect and affection of his men, their trust and
belief in him as their commander, and their pride that, sick as
they knew him to be, he had come to share in their triumph.

This explains an apparent contradiction. The mutinies ashore,
the efforts to avoid the press-gangs, the desire to serve on the
merchantmen and privateers, which gave better pay and more
security, were not directed against Blake. They were the only
and natural means of expressing their indignation against the non-
payment of their well earned wages. The letters of the Admirals
to the authorities reveal how constantly they strove to get the
matter of wages, of bad provisions and drink, of the care for the
sick and wounded, of the support needed for the widows and their
children, put to rights. Nor did they overlook the cases of indi-

viduals however they humble might be. Once aboard, their men did their duty and in battle they fought like true Englishmen.

In his captains Blake tried to instil sound common sense, as the story of Myngs shows. Gibson says that in the *Elizabeth* of thirty-six guns, he took, off the Scillies in 1652, three Dutch warships. He proudly brought them to Blake with their colours flying at his stern. Blake gave him a cool reception. 'You believe you have done a fine act to take three Dutch ships singly, but what if they had carried you to Holland? What account could you then have given the State for the loss of their ship? I do not love a foolhardy captain, therefore temper your courage with discretion and undertake nothing hazardous if you can avoid it, so you may come to preferment'. This story may well be part of Blake's legend. Yet its survival shows how deep Blake's common sense in action had sunk.[76]

Blake was no longer included in the Council of State, nor upon the committee for Foreign Affairs. This was no slur cast upon him by Cromwell. As England was now the supreme naval power in Europe, the Protector had other and more important duties for Blake to do upon the High Seas. In his mind a new foreign policy was shaping itself, in which Blake's fleet was to be the spearhead.

CHAPTER 19

Return to the Mediterranean

*

CROMWELL was now aware that he held the balance of power between France and Spain. He was therefore determined to restore to England her former proud position in Europe.

Ready to his hand was a magnificent fleet of 160 ships. Secretly he began to muster his great armada. His intention was to divide it into two bodies. One, under Penn, was to sail to the West Indies, with an expeditionary force of troops, with secret instructions to attack and take the islands. The other, under Blake, was to go to the Mediterranean to restore English prestige. In so doing he would leave it uncertain, until the last moment, as to whether France or Spain was to be the real enemy. For such a fleet would be in a position to threaten both countries. With the secret locked securely in Cromwell's brain, the wildest rumours inevitably circulated as to the destination of the rapidly collecting ships. The only clue lay in the special sheathing of the vessels, which seemed to point to service abroad.[1] Salvetti, the London Envoy of Tuscany was seriously alarmed. He knew that Cromwell was in possession of letters, written by Van Galen, who had commanded the Dutch squadron that had defeated Badiley at Leghorn in 1653, in which he boasted of the favour the Duke of Tuscany had showed him at the expense of the English.[2] When he heard that Badiley, 'the author of all this mischief' was to sail with the fleet, he grew more anxious still. For it was hinted that part of the great fleet might visit Leghorn. But Salvetti could get no news of the fleet destination. So anxious was the Duke to know if, or no, Badiley would be with the fleet, that he wrote in cypher to the envoy.[2]

On 6 May, 1654, Blake dined with the Protector, together with the Lord Mayor and his Councillors.[3] It well may be that Cromwell took him aside and instructed him as to the destination of the fleet he was to command. Blake could be trusted to keep a secret, even from his captains. Blake, on 14 March, 1655, stated that his orders were 'to seize, surprise, sink and destroy all ships belonging to the Kingdom of Tunis that we shall meet; which as it doth not expressly forbid us to enter their ports to that end, so neither doth it expressly empower us, especially being compared with that part of the general instruction, concerning Turkish pirates, limiting us in such cases only to block up their harbours for some days'. He asked that the instruction might be made clear and explicit.[4] It is true that there were orders, misdated 22 July, 1656. S. R. Gardiner considered that the real date of these was 22 July, 1654.[5] But Sir Julian Corbett has pointed out that at that time Blake had no fleet under his command, and that the real date is 1655,[6] and that these instructions were the reply Cromwell sent to Blake's request for express authority to attack the Algerian ports, which the Admiral wrote on 14 March, 1655. Corbett may well be correct.

Longland, the able and astute English agent at Leghorn, had never ceased, from August 1653, to urge that a fleet should be sent into the Mediterranean to restore English prestige.[7] The French were making ever worse raids upon English shipping. Only an English squadron could prevent this. He added an additional proposal, attractive to Cromwell's eager ears, that such a fleet might maintain itself without expense to the State, by reprisals upon the rich Levant trade of France. His thinking was in line with that of Cromwell.[8]

At a secret meeting of the Council of State, on 5 June, 1654, it was decided that a fleet of fourteen ships should be prepared for the 'Western Design'. At the same time it was decreed that twenty-four ships should go to the Mediterranean.[9] On 26 June, the Venetian Ambassador in London reported 'the Generals have been in London, where they held very secret conference with the Protector, and then rejoined their ships as hurriedly as they left them'.[10] It would seem that Cromwell informed them of his decision, for Longland had learned that Mazarin, now in control of France, had determined to reconquer the two Sicilies. In Toulon, Guise was preparing a powerful expedition for this purpose, while Nieuchèse, with a squadron from Brest was to join him.[11] Longland forwarded an accurate list of Guise's fleet, which he requested should be given to Blake.[12]

On 26 July he reported that the Toulon ships dared not sail for fear of Blake. He made a daring suggestion. Genoa was the State least prepared for war. She had, he wrote, 'the best port in

Italy, and I wish it were in the hands of others that have more occasion for it'. But this daring proposal only arrived after Blake had sailed.[13]

On 5 August, Cromwell wrote to the Spanish King to ask for the hospitality of his ports for Blake's fleet. He had apparently thrown in his lot with Spain. On the 16th Blake hoisted his flag in the *George*, with Badiley as his Vice-Admiral, and Jordan as his Rear-Admiral. The fleet was composed as follows:

Rate		Guns	Men	Commanders
2	George	60	350	Robert Blake, Admiral
				John Stoakes, captain
2	*Andrew*	54	300	Richard Badiley
2	*Unicorn*	54	300	Joseph Jordan
3	*Langport*	50	260	Roger Cuttance
3	*Bridgwater*	50	260	Anthony Earning
3	*Worcester*	46	240	William Hill
3	*Plymouth*	50	260	Richard Stayner
4	*Hampshire*	34	160	Robert Blake
4	*Foresight*	36	160	Peter Mootham
4	*Kent*	40	170	Edward Witheridge
4	*Taunton*	36	160	Thomas Vallis
4	*Diamond*	36	160	John Harman
4	*Ruby*	36	160	Edmund Curtis
4	*Newcastle*	40	180	Nathaniel Cobham
4	*Amity*	30	120	Henry Pack
4	*Maidstone*	32	140	Thomas Adams
4	*Princess Marie*	34	150	John Lloyd
4	*Elias*	32	140	John Symons
5	*Mermaid*	24	90	James Abelson
5	*Pearl*	22	100	Ben Sacheverall
5	*Success*	24	60	William Kendal
5	*Sophia*	24	60	Robert Kirby
5	*Hector*	16	35	
5	*Dolphin*	16	45	John Smith
5	*Nonsuch* ketch	10	30	
5	*Hope* flyboat			
5	*Merlin*	14		George Crapnell.[14]

As Blake was held up by the non-arrival of his victualling ships, he took the opportunity to request the payment of his salary, which was at the rate of £3 per day, 'it being uncertain whether I may live to see you again'.[15] This would seem to indicate that his health was still troublesome. Indeed he never properly recovered from the effects of his wound. If the Government could not even pay its chief Admiral, let alone its seamen, the finances must have been in a desperate position. A few days later he complained of the 'unsafeness and hazards of this Road, which to us is worse than a prison'. He referred to Plymouth, where the fleet was assembling. He also thanked the Admiralty Commissioners for 'their favours to my brother', Benjamin, who had been given the command of a ship in Penn's fleet.[16] It was not until 8 October that the arrival of the victualling vessels allowed him at last to sail. With him went a Cornishman, John Weale, who had served in the Dutch War. He was recommended by his captain, Roger Alsop, to Colonel Desborough as one 'who had a more than ordinary desire to go with General Blake'. It would seem that, among the younger officers, there had grown up a hero-worship for their great leader. Fortunately Weale kept a diary, which is invaluable in filling up the gaps in Blake's missing dispatches.[17]

Mazarin's anxiety grew apace. He ordered Bordeaux, the new Envoy in London, to find out Blake's destination. For the leisurely Guise had only left Toulon on 7 October, while Nieuchèse was still at Brest. But the wretched Envoy could not get an audience.[18]

On 30 October, Blake anchored in Cadiz Road. He was saluted by many guns. As Weale wrote, 'the Spaniards know not what to think of us, whether or no we come for war'.[19]

The Dutch Admiral, De With, never wore his flag during Blake's stay.[20] The Governor invited Blake to enter the harbour, but he replied he was bound immediately for the Straits.[21] The English Chargé d'Affaires had informed Blake that, four days before, nine French men-of war had gone by, making for the Straits.[21] So, after handing the Governor Cromwell's letter, Blake, on 2 November, sailed for the Straits. He was out to chase Nieuchèse who, as he thought, was ahead of him. It was reported throughout Europe that Blake had said he was out to fight the Frenchman, if he could find him.[22]

On the 3rd Blake arrived at Gibraltar. Next day the *Dolphin* came in. Her Captain, Smith, related that on 25 October, when foul weather separated him from the fleet, he had fallen in with Nieuchèse's nine vessels and two fireships. He was taken aboard the flagship, and asked where Blake was. On hearing that he was at the Straits, the startled Admiral drank Blake's health and let Smith go. The encounter occurred between Cape St Vincent and Cadiz. Smith got to Cadiz on the 3rd, the day after Blake had sailed.[23] Nieuchèse put back into Lisbon.

With the news that Nieuchèse was at sea, Blake spread out his frigates to look for him, under Hill of the *Worcester*. Stayner, in the *Plymouth*, finding no sign of the Frenchman's ships, rashly assumed that he had done all that was required from him, and returned alone to Gibraltar to report the fact to Blake, without getting leave from Hill. Blake angrily ordered him to go out again.[24] The Dutch War had taught him the importance of scouting and so he would tolerate no slackness in his captains. On the 8th Hill was relieved by Cuttance of the *Langport*, with several frigates. They fell in with four Algerian warships, who handed over an Englishman, and other captives, whom they had compelled a Sallee warship to deliver up to them. Thus commented Weale, aboard *Amity*, 'we see plain that we are not only a terror to the French, but also the Turks seek to get into our favour'.[25] In the evening an English merchantman brought the news that the French were at Lisbon, cleaning their ships. This aroused keen hopes that they were about to come out and fight. On the 10th the frigates met De With with five sail. He saluted them with guns and small shot. This made so much noise that Blake, thinking they were in fight with the French, sent out ships to support them.[26] Wearily the days dragged on, watching for a foe who never came. Cuttance, who had been told by the Agent at Cadiz, that the French showed no sign of leaving, passed the news on to Blake. So on the 21st Blake decided to abandon his wait for Nieuchèse and sailed for Malaga, leaving some frigates behind, on 21 November.[27] On the 30th Blake sailed for Cagliari, in South Sardinia, to look for Guise. Here his frigates rejoined him with the news, brought by a London ship the *Levant*, that Guise was off Naples with twenty-two ships and galleys, on 5 November.[28] Actually he was at Castellamare nearby. 'Many gallants' noted Weale, 'went aboard the flagship and were too courteous, that the General compared them to an ape that hugged so much, that he many times killed'. This witticism went round the delighted fleet. Just as Blake was about to sail on the 9th, he was prevented by a visit from the Viceroy. However by the 11th he had reached Naples only to find that his prey had gone.[29] For Guise had failed to take Castellamare, and had returned to Toulon.

Writing to Thurloe on 18 December, Longland reported that eight French frigates, of Guise's fleet, had put into Leghorn. If Blake, he lamented, 'had not stayed at the Straits' mouth, but come direct for Italy, he had found all the French fleet in a pound, where he might have done what he would with them, but t'will all be for the best'.[30] In reality, by staying at Gibraltar, Blake had already won that victory. For in interposing himself between the two fleets, he had rendered them both powerless. He had demonstrated that though the Straits joined Spain and France by sea, they also separated them. Cromwell had understood the importance of Gibraltar. Mazarin's ambitious scheme was killed stone dead. Now all the Italian States believed Blake was coming to the aid of the Spaniard, for it was still rumoured that Penn's fleet would shortly join Blake.

Naples must have viewed the arrival of Blake with some apprehension. Had not the Grand Duke imprisoned two of Badiley's commanders in January 1653? So when Blake saluted the town with his guns, in great relief it replied all night with cannon and small shot. The Viceroy sent Blake £1,000 worth of sweetmeats and victuals. But the General did not tarry long. He might yet catch the eight French frigates, said to be at Leghorn. He made for that port, leaving three frigates behind to get intelligence.

On the 20th he arrived there. Leghorn was even more apprehensive than Naples, remembering the treatment it had meted out to Badiley after his defeat in 1653. So when Blake saluted the town, it, and the ships, answered time and time again. Blake turned his attention to discipline. Three seamen were whipped from ship to ship, for stealing money, striking a Commander and for drunkenness. The Grand Duke invited him to dine, no doubt to probe his intentions. Instead Blake sent Jordan, with some captains.[31] This was due to 'some distemper of my health' which had also prevented him from writing to the Admiralty Commissioners since 29 December.[32] As the Venetian Envoy at Florence wrote, 'the Duke is trying to keep Blake friendly, the more so because he seems to be a very touchy and particular old man, who treats his Captains with extreme severity'.[33]

From the Consul ashore Blake learned that Guise had decided to lay up his ships for the winter, and only to send out privateers.

'So that this occurrence' wrote Blake, 'will give no further stop
to our proceedings from Trapani'.[34] Here he was to be joined by
the ships he had left at Naples. The Florentine Envoy reported
that rumour spoke of Blake going to Barbary. He was right, for
that was the objective Blake had been sent to carry out. But even
the English merchants did not know this for certain, 'as Blake is a
deep sombre man of few words; owing to his advanced age he never
shows himself, even on his own ship, except when the sun shines,
and although invited, he would never go ashore to see the place
and gratify his countrymen'.[35]

Not until 15 January, 1655 was Blake able to sail, for two
captured French ships from Alexandria and Constantinople, 'both
infected places' forced his ships to be kept in quarantine for the
plague. There was not much wind and the weather was clear.
They were among the islands off the Tuscan coast 'a place of no
small danger, especially for a fleet: at night we were hauling up a
sail and, it proving calm, we drew upon a sudden so near Capraria,
that, if it had not pleased God to spring up a fresh gale in the very
nick, this ship would have been in hazard, almost inevitable, of
perishing there. The *Worcester* and *Langport* were in the same
danger – being nearer the shore than we, especially the *Langport*,
which was in much less than the ship's length of it, being a steep
and upright rocky place. The *Andrew* and some others were also
in no small danger: but it pleased God wonderfully and in great
mercy to bring us all off in safety without any loss, but of an
anchor and cable of the *Langport*'. But as the wind was blowing
hard with thick weather Blake was forced to bear up for Leghorn.
By the 18th he was back there. 'It pleased God' he wrote in his
simple fashion, 'to exercise us with a variety of wind, and with
divers mixed Providences, and strange dispensations, never to be
forgotten by us: especially in regard that He hath been pleased
likewise in them all to cause His compassion to prevail against His
threatenings, and His mercy to triumph over his judgment'.[36]

While he was pondering the meaning of this strange check,
news came to him of a concentration, at Tunis, of warships for
the service of the Sultan, about February the 12th.[37] Sir Julian
Corbett, with vivid insight, has conjured up the possible motives
which were stirring Blake. All Italy was ringing with the heroic
exploit and death of Mocenigo, the Venetian Admiral, who with
a few ships, had cut his way out of a great Turkish fleet off the

Dardanelles. He had dealt it such a blow that it was a month before it could go to sea again. But another Turkish fleet had been able to go to the relief of the army which, for ten years, had striven to wrest Crete from Venice. Both Badiley and Longland were at Blake's side to remind him that Venice, though hard pressed, had released English ships to go to Badiley's aid against the Dutch in 1653. Here was an opportunity to return this generous aid. For the Venetian plan was to divide their fleet in two; one division blockading the Dardanelles, while the other besieged Malvoisis, the Turkish advanced base in the Morea. If the Turkish army before Candia could get aid from Barbary, the Venetian task would be very complicated. If the combined Barbary fleet could be crushed by Blake, the ordering of the campaign lay with Venice. In Blake's mind the affair was plain: the finger of God was at work. Here lay the reason for the storm: that he might crush the infidel. So reads Sir Julian. His guess may well be correct.[38]

At Naples the Venetian Envoy observed that it seems that the Spanish Ministers are beginning 'to feel doubtful about the proceedings of General Blake, whose plans it is not easy to find out'. He would not even reveal them to his captains, but merely let them see Cromwell's letters with his seal, and not the contents. He only took them into his confidence to let them know the place of rendezvous, in case of being scattered by a storm.[39]

Stormy weather prevented Blake from sailing until 30 January. Then he lost no time and by the evening of 7 February, he reached Tunis.[40] 'On a great hill a watch tower flashed its light some eighteen times as the fleet came in' answering as Weale thought 'the number of our ships'.[41] But morning brought a great disappointment: there was no concentration. The information was false. After a Council of War, Blake sent ashore to the Dey, demanding the restitution of the *Princess*, which the Moors had seized, with an indemnity, and the release of all captives. Both sides met on the flagship and the Moors expressed their desire for an agreed peace for the future, but they flatly refused to give any satisfaction for past events.[42]

They could hardly be blamed. In 1646 Edmund Casson had concluded a Treaty with the Dey of Algiers which ensured in the future that no Englishman should be held in captivity. This may also have included Tunis. Agreement was ended by the operations of an unscrupulous rascal, named Mitchell. He had been chartered to carry a small body of Turkish troops to Smyrna. Instead he sold them to the Knights in Malta, who put them to work in the galleys. The English Consul at Tunis tried to ransom them, but the Knights would not let them go. The Dey retorted by ordering his vessels to bring in any Englishman they could. This was the state of affairs that Cromwell had determined to end. Neither he, nor Blake, seemed to have taken into account the natural and just irritation of the Dey. It was enough for them that Englishmen were held captive by the infidel, and therefore they must be set free.[43]

On 12 February, Hill of the *Worcester*, with the *Amity*, *Newcastle* and *Maidstone*, were sent north to Porto Farina.[44] Here they found nine of the Dey's ships at anchor. This fact probably had given rise to the report of a concentration. Hill sent his boats to take soundings. They were instantly fired upon, but the Turks' range was too short to reach them. The Moors were seen to be erecting new works, while horse and foot came down to the town. Their fire was continued, with the *Worcester* as their target. Nevertheless Hill kept up a constant patrol, and on the 27th both the castle and the works opened fire on his boats. They even tried to take the *Worcester*'s boat, but she escaped from them.[45]

On the 22nd Blake himself came in with the fleet.[46] He found the nine ships lying close in shore, lightened and unrigged, under the protection of the strong castle. Additional batteries were being thrown up, with an entrenched camp manned by thousands of Berber horse and foot. The castle and the ships flew blood-red flags, and the Admiral an ensign of white and green. The Moors on horseback and on foot swarmed along the shore, flourishing their naked scimitars in the brilliant sunlight, to show they would oppose any landing with their lives. Strangely enough they sent a boat, under a flag of truce, to invite the English agent, Browne, who was with Blake, to come ashore and take up his post. But he knew them too well to trust himself to them.[47]

A Council of War debated whether to sail in and destroy the ships. But this meant anchoring within half musket-shot of the castle. The harbour was too narrow in which to turn. It was decided too difficult to attempt. Moreover Blake had only three days drink left, and very little bread. Furthermore, on scanning his instructions he was puzzled as to whether he had authority to enter Turkish ports, or no. Writing to Thurloe he asked that these might be made 'more clear and explicit'.[48] It was agreed therefore to sail back to Cagliari. The *Plymouth, Kent, Newcastle, Mermaid, Taunton* and *Foresight,* were left behind to watch the port. On 22 February Blake sailed and arrived on the 26th, meaning to give them 'a more sudden and hotter visit'.[49]

At Cagliari they found the four frigates which had been sent to cruise round the Balearic Islands, when Blake left Naples. They had captured a French frigate called the *Fame,* and had driven ashore and sold to the Governor of Majorca another of thirty guns, called the *Percy,* a well-known English built ship.[50]

Blake ordered the *Hope* to stay and bake bread while the *Langport* and *Diamond* were to go to Majorca to get what supplies they could. Then they were to ply as far as Alicante, or Cape Paulos, and to return to Genoa. The *Maidstone* and *Hampshire* were to go to Genoa to careen, and get bread. Here the *Langport* was to bring on what bread had been obtained. The other three frigates were to resume cruising about the Balearic islands, keeping watch upon the French. The final rendezvous was to be Alcudia Bay, in Majorca, from where all would go to the coast of Provence to gain news of 'the state and motion of the French fleet'.[51]

On 4 March the *Nonsuch* came in from Leghorn with letters from the Admiralty Commissioners. Another was from Cromwell 'writ in his own hand'. Its contents are unknown, but as it was written a month after Penn had sailed for the West Indies, it may have warned Blake of the coming war with Spain.[52] Another was from Thurloe telling him of Cromwell's dissolution of Parliament. Blake's answer supports the belief that he could not have been opposed to the arbitrary events of nearly two years previously. 'I was not much surprised with the intelligence: the slow proceedings and awkward motion of that assembly giving great cause to suspect that it would come to some such period, and I cannot but exceedingly wonder that there should yet remain so strong a spirit of prejudice and animosity in the minds of men, who profess themselves most affectionate patriots, as to postpone the ways and means for the preservation of the Commonwealth'.[53]

On 6 March, a Day of Humiliation, with a prayer for God's blessing upon their proceedings, was held and on the 16th the fleet sailed for Tunis. By the 18th Blake was once more before the town. A French ship brought him a packet of letters, and next day a French ship, which had withdrawn into the Goletta, boldly came out and anchored in the midst of the English fleet. 'From which' wrote Weale, 'we conclude the packet to the General treated of a league with our neighbouring nation France'. It would seem that Blake had got orders to suspend operations against French commerce, though the letters' contents are unknown. Once again the Protector's demands were sent in to the Dey. Many boats now passed between the shore and the flagship.[54]

'We found them more wilful and untractable than before,' wrote Blake, 'adding to their obstinacy much insolence and contumely, denying us all commerce of civility, and hindering all others as much as they could from the same. These barbarous provocations did so far work upon our spirits, that we judged it necessary for the honour of the fleet, our nation, and religion, seeing they would not deal with us as friends, to make them feel us as enemies'. A Council of War resolved to fire the Moorish ships, but in order to lull into a state of security, it was agreed to draw off to Trapani. Here they arrived on 25 March, and stayed for a week, taking in water.[55] The Dey's taunt rang in Blake's ears: 'these are our castles of the Goletta, and the ships and castles of Porto Ferina; do what you can, do not think to fear us with the show of your fleet'. On 1 April the challenge was accepted, and Blake sailed for Tunis. By the afternoon of the 3rd he was again off the port.[56] The nine warships were still lying under the batteries, a pistol shot from the shore. All the coast was lined with musketeers and some sixty guns peered from the castle and the works. A Council of War of all the captains was called and, 'after we sought the Lord by prayer' it was unanimously agreed to attack and burn the ships on the next day.[57]

At dawn Cobham, in the *Newcastle*, led in the fourth-rate frigate *Kent*, *Foresight*, *Amity*, *Princess Maria*, *Pearl*, *Mermaid* and *Merlin*. Weale adds the *Ruby* and *Diamond*.[58] A light westerly breeze carried them into El Bahira and they anchored near the galleys. From their previous soundings, they knew the depth of the water.[59] Badiley in the *Andrew* and Stayner in the *Plymouth* went in next, followed by Blake in the *George*, with the *Worcester*, *Unicorn*, *Bridgwater* and *Success*. They anchored against the castle, within musket-shot and opened fire with their broadsides on the castle and forts.[60] The whole manoeuvre was performed with ease. 'The Lord' wrote Blake, 'being pleased to favour us with a gentle gale from off the sea, which cast all the smoke upon them,

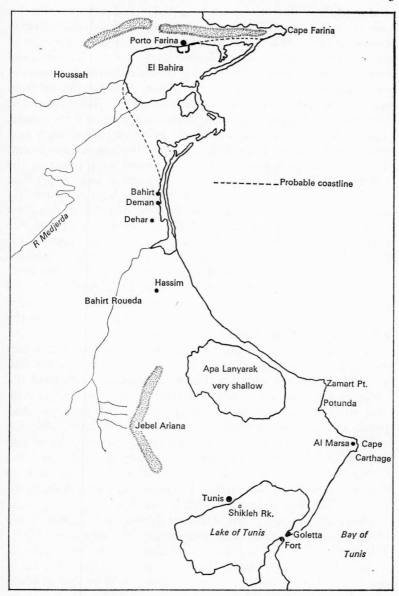

Tunis and Porto Farina

and made our work the more easy'.[61] He had not forgotten his use of smoke at the Scillies, and here it blinded the Moorish gunners. The action now became general, but Blake's weight of fire continued for four or five hours, soon silenced the castle and forts. Under the cover of the rolling clouds of smoke the 'boats of execution' commanded by Captain Jeffery Pierce,[62] put off from the frigates, and rowed for the dismantled galleys. As they emerged the panic-stricken crews jumped overboard and swam for the shore. The panic spread to the works and batteries, whose men took refuge in the castle. The galleys were speedily boarded and burnt. The flags of the Admiral and Vice-Admiral were burnt in the flames, but the boarders secured the others, as prized trophies, the *Amity* having got one.[63] By 8 a.m. all nine galleys were furiously alight, and an occasional shot from the fleet into the blazing mass checked any attempt to extinguish the flames. By 11 a.m. all was over, and the frigates started to warp out, as Blake hung out his flag of defiance. Badiley was the last to leave. Hardly a man was hit in the ships, but twenty-five were killed in the boats, and some forty were wounded, chiefly by small shot. All night long the galleys burned 'like so many bonfires', until nine the next morning.[64] By the irony of fate the *Princess*, 'about her began the controversy' as Weale wrote, was also burnt.[65]

It was a complete, an artistic triumph, planned with care and executed with precision. For the first time the guns of a fleet had overwhelmed shore batteries. Blake had correctly estimated the range of the Moorish guns and the inefficiency of the gunners. Well might Weale term it, 'a piece of service that hath not been paralleled in these parts of the world'. Blake himself, with his usual modesty and brevity, wrote characteristically, 'it is also remarkable by us that shortly after our getting forth, the wind and weather changed, and continued very stormy for many days, so that we could not have effected the business, had not the Lord afforded that nick of time in which it was done'.[66]

Blake, having given the Dey his lesson, now resumed his blockade of the Goletta. The unrepentant Dey sent him a letter. The burnt ships did not belong to him, but to the Sultan. It remained for Blake to right the Sultan for what he had done. If the Sultan was content with this, the Dey would be also. If Blake wished to negotiate, let him come ashore. But Blake was too wise to risk such a dangerous step.[67] There was nothing for it but to return to Cagliari, first sending the *Merchant's Delight*, which was lying in the Goletta, with a letter to Sir Thomas Bendish, the Ambassador at Constantinople, to warn him of the possible consequences to the Levant merchants living there.

Blake also wrote to Thurloe, hoping that the Protector would not be offended at his action, 'seeing it hath pleased God so signally to justify us therein'. But he expected 'to hear of many complaints and clamours of many interested men: I confess, that in contemplation thereof, and some seeming ambiguity in my instructions – I did awhile much hesitate myself and was balanced in my thoughts, until the barbarous carriage of those pirates did turn the scale'.[68] After replenishing his stores he sailed for Algiers, where he arrived on 28 April. On 1 May the *Langport* brought a dispatch, dated 12 March, from the Admiralty Commissioners, which she had probably picked up at Leghorn on her way from Genoa. It possibly directed Blake to proceed on his former orders to threaten Toulon and Marseilles. Next day the *Hampshire*, *Maidstone*, *Diamond* and possibly the *Taunton*, came in. With them came the *Seaventure* ketch from England, with a letter from Cromwell, dated 2 April. It informed Blake that three months' provisions were being sent to him. It contained also, more importantly, Secret Instructions, referring him to 'a former instruction touching the Plate Fleet coming from America'.[69]

These former instructions were contained in a letter, dated 19 March, 1655, which had not yet arrived. Blake's dispatch of 12 June, enables the point, which puzzled Gardiner and Corbett, to be cleared up. The question to them was, whether the 'secret instructions' could have reached Blake, when he was at Formentara, by 16 May. Blake's letter however shows that they reached him even earlier, on 2 May, while he was still at Algiers. He now knew that Spain, and not France, was to be his enemy. His fleet had enabled Cromwell to play his double game to the last possible moment, by forcing France into peace, and by lulling Spain into a false security.

The Dey of Algiers, mindful of Blake's action at Tunis, received him with professions of esteem, and at once agreed to renew Casson's Treaty, with an additional clause, added by Blake, which included the natives of Scotland and Ireland.[70] The Dey was fully aware that his fortress was an excellent target for Blake's guns. He therefore released all captives upon the payment of their market value. Some Dutch sailors took the opportunity to escape and swim out to the English ships, whose crews gave a dollar each to buy the freedom of their late foes. On his return Blake saw to it that those crews, from whose pay the Navy Commissioners had not deducted the promised sum, should be made to redeem their promise.[71] Then, after taking bread and beef aboard, and placing a new agent, as the former one had died, ashore, Blake sailed for Formentara, in the Balearic Islands. This was his appointed rendezvous for his former intention to range the coast of Provence. Here he arrived on 14 May, and began to take in wood. Next day the *Elias* came in from Naples with provisions, with the *Warwick* pinnace from Leghorn, with letters that had been sent overland. These were dated 19 March, and must have been the 'former instructions touching the Plate Fleet'. They confirmed Blake as to his orders. He was to make for Cadiz, and seize the home-coming Plate Fleet.

On 17 May he sailed, sending the *Amity* and the *Hector* to Alicante and Carthagena to secure some fifty guns and some anchors, belonging to Prince Rupert's wrecked ships. This work had obviously to be done before war was openly made against Spain. On the 24th Blake, 'being then a little short of Gibraltar' sent home a brief dispatch by a merchantman bound for London 'wherein I hinted only our proceedings so far, wanting time to acquaint you with our particular motions'. He probably wrote this from Malaga.[72] Here another legend was added to the Blake Saga.

The legend comes from Bishop Burnet. Some of Blake's seamen were ashore at Malaga. Meeting the procession of the Host, they jeered at the people for making obeisance. At the instigation of the priests, the crowd set on the seamen, badly handled them and sent them back to their ships. On their return they complained, and Blake sent a trumpeter to the Viceroy to demand the surrender of the ringleader of the priests. The Viceroy replied that he had no authority over the Church. Blake answered that if he was not sent within three hours, he would burn the town. The priest was sent, who justified himself by the behaviour of the seamen. Blake answered if he had complained to him they would have been severely punished, since he would not have established religion insulted anywhere. But he would have the world know that an Englishman could only be punished by an Englishman, and then he set the priest free. Cromwell, says the bishop, was so delighted that he read the letter in council, saying that he hoped he should make the name of an Englishman as great as ever that of a Roman had been.[73] Unfortunately Cromwell does not seem to have attended any of the five council meetings at the end of June, when the report reached him.[74] In none of his existing letters does Blake record the incident. On 28 November, 1654, Weale described how he had been filled with true Puritan indignation at seeing a statue of the Virgin carried in procession, which made the Friars look angrily at him.[75] Some time later on 28 July, 1655, Weale, ashore at Lisbon, met a Eucharist procession 'and we not kneeling were cursed and called devils'.[76] Weale says nothing of the priest, or of Blake's threat to burn the town. It is possible that the two incidents, greatly exaggerated, have been mixed together. Weale, a stout Puritan, would surely have recorded Blake's humiliation of the priest, and of the hearty approval of the fleet at their Admiral's action. Moreover the diplomatic situation was very delicate. Blake had no authority to burn the town, and he never exceeded his orders. Such an action would have instantly aroused Spanish hostility. In addition, two of his ships were engaged at Carthagena in shipping the guns, with the permission of Spanish authorities, that had been recovered from the wreck of Rupert's ships. The legend can be added to others. A Genoese source relates that Blake demanded from the Duke of Tuscany 150,000 scudi as damages for the maltreatment of English ships, and for prizes sold by Rupert in Tuscan ports. Ludlow retails the story of how Blake, at Civita Vecchia, extracted from the Pope 60,000 ducats for allowing Rupert to sell his prizes in Papal ports.[76] Men saw Blake as cast in heroic mould, who had humbled the Mediterranean potentates. They enshrined his exploits in legend. His saga expressed the deep impression his deeds left on the minds of simple men.

A small vessel, on 28 May, brought Blake the news that victuallers were waiting for him at Gibraltar, convoyed by the *Centurion* and *Dragon*. He sailed the same night, and took a good proportion on board. On the 28th, when the *Hector* and *Amity* had joined him, after getting the guns aboard, he sailed for Cadiz. He anchored in Rotta Road and started clearing the victuallers. This took three days as stormy winds caused a great sea, so that the victuallers had to be ballasted as they grew lighter as the supplies were taken out.[77] Though invited to use Cadiz harbour, wisely he did not do so. There it was reported that he had told the English merchants that his design was to capture the Plate Fleet if Penn missed it. In view of Blake's well-kept secrecy this is most unlikely, yet everyone in Cadiz had no doubt as to his real errand. The King himself ordered that incessant prayers were to be offered in every convent for the safety of the Plate Fleet.[78]

On 12 June, sending home the *Amity*, *Fame* and *Seaventure* with dispatches, his letter to the Protector said that the Plate Fleet was expected at Cadiz in about four weeks' time. He was therefore spreading out the fleet between Cape St Mary and Cape Spartel to watch for it. 'They of Cadiz are very distrustful of us'.[79]

On 4 July, off St Vincent, Blake got three letters, dated 21 May, 13 and 14 June. The June ones were from Cromwell, approving of his action at Porto Farina, with instructions that, in view of Penn's operations in the West Indies, Blake was to prevent Spain from sending any help thither. This was to be done by forcible action if necessary. Blake was to intercept them at sea, fight with, take, or otherwise to sink and fire them.[80] Blake replied that he would carefully carry out his orders. But he drew the Protector's attention to the condition of his fleet, especially of the *George*, the *Andrew* and the *Unicorn*, which were all foul, leaky and defective. In their places he asked for three frigates to be sent him.[81] The same day he told the Admiralty Committee that he had changed his station from Cape St Mary to Cape St Vincent, by the advice of a Council of War. He begged for carpenters' and boatswains' needs, as many of the ships were badly in need of repair. The turbulence of the weather had left very few ships with more sails than those they had at the yards. The three great ships should be replaced, and he desired them to take into consideration 'the insufficiency of the frigates that are not sheathed'. Above all he needed 300 tons of beer, which must be sent in iron-bound cask. Money must be sent him to buy beverage wine, as this had to be obtained upon credit.[82]

Two days later, 6 July, he drew attention to the families and relations of the seamen, and he asked the Committee to make out twenty tickets for each ship, which should be passed and paid as soon as they were presented, to relieve their sufferings. Though this reflects the financial stringency of the Commonwealth, who were apt to postpone the needs of the seamen, as they were too far off to cause any immediate trouble, it also reveals Blake's care

for the humblest of those who served him.[83] To Thurloe also he
stressed the sad condition of the fleet, the need for liquor and the
necessity to replace the great ships and the scarcity and rottenness
of the casks.[84]

Boldly he wrote direct once more to Cromwell at the same time.
He was sending home as the Protector had ordered, the *Pearl*
and *Mermaid*, but the rest appointed to return he was keeping
with him. He implored the Protector 'to lay his quickening
command upon the Commissioners of the Navy' to send him
supplies speedily, as he had information of great preparations in
Cadiz to send out a fleet to bring in the Plate Fleet, for which end
divers Holland and French ships have been taken up.[85]

On 6 August, Blake got news from Captain Smith of the
Richard and Martha, written on 4 July, that a combined fleet of
thirty-two vessels was to sail from Cadiz on 5 August. First, it
would go towards the Barbary coast, and then westwards, so as
to avoid Blake's fleet for five or six days, until their men had
recovered from seasickness.[86] Whereupon Blake stood over as far
as Marmora, north of Sallee, but no foe could be found. So they
returned towards Cadiz, sending two frigates ahead of him. On
the 12th these brought him news that the Spanish fleet had sailed
the day before, and were plying off Cape St Vincent.[87] With them
came the *Assurance*, with a letter from Cromwell, of 30 July,
acknowledging Blake's letters of the 4 and 6 July, and cancelling
the instructions of 13 June to send home part of the fleet. In
view of Blake's news of the naval preparations in Cadiz, it was
judged to be safer to keep the whole fleet with him. He was also
to retain the *Centurion*, the *Dragon* and the *Nantwich*, which had
been sent to Lisbon with the Envoy, Mr Maynard. Blake was
assured, with regard to the defects of the fleet, 'that nothing shall
be omitted, which can be done here for your supply and encouragement'. To this Thurloe added a postscript, in his own hand, of
the news of 'twenty ships coming across the Straits, and of thirty-
one ships, and eight fireships preparing in Cadiz.'[88]

With the news that the Spanish fleet was at sea, Blake made
after them. On the morning of the 15 August he sighted them to
the westward, near the Bay of Lagos, where he had hoped to water.
They were thirty-one sail in all. Blake at once called a Council of
War, for the Spaniards appeared to be bearing up to them, at
which it was resolved to attack them at the first opportunity. The

resolution was based on an 'eager desire to see some end of our
tedious expectation, and to prevent that accession of strength . . .
and also out of a despair of being able to keep the sea many days
longer for want of liquor.' They clearly believed that the Spaniards
were either waiting for the Plate Fleet, or else might be going to
bring it home. However, the Spaniards tacked and stood the other
way, keeping far off to windward. Early next morning Blake was
up with the enemy, but there was so little wind that nothing could
be done. Moreover as a great sea prevented his lower tier of guns
from being run out,[89] Blake personally went below decks to make
certain of the facts.[90] A thick fog also hampered him, and though
he stood on the other tack, he could not work up to the Spaniards.

Next day the Spaniards were 'so far to windward as we can
see them, and the weather so calm that we cannot come up with
them'. Blake sent some frigates ahead, to try and get the wind
and engage the enemy, but all to no purpose. In the evening the
Maidstone, in which Weale was now serving, took a Spaniard who
had fallen to leeward.[91] As the greater part of his fleet was now so
far astern, Blake decided to hold off from pursuit, and in the night
the Spanish fleet stood through his ships. 'These checks of
Providence did put us upon second thoughts' and a Council of
War was called. As at Leghorn, the finger of the Almighty again
seemed to have intervened. So the council scanned their instructions, as to this new and puzzling situation, only to find that there
appeared to be no authority to attack a fleet which was not bound
for the West Indies. It was therefore resolved to leave the Spaniards
alone, especially as it was thought that it 'was not the intention of
your Highness, that we should be the first breakers of the peace,
seeing that your Highness, having notice of the coming forth of
the Spanish fleet, did not give us any new direction at all touching
the same in your last order of 30 July'. The ships too were foul,
liquor was so short that some ships had only four days' supply.
Nevertheless Blake kept the Spaniards in sight until the 22nd, when
he was assured by one of their captains, possibly commanding
the ship taken by the *Maidstone*, that they had no order, or
intention, to begin the fight, and that they knew nothing of the
coming of the Plate Fleet.[92]

Blake now sailed to Lisbon, where he arrived on the 24th.
Here he expected to find the *Taunton* with Maynard on board.
Maynard had been sent there to discuss with the Portuguese

King the compensation due from him for the damage done by Rupert's ships to the English merchants. But the King refused to give an answer, and Maynard had left, two days before Blake came in. Blake sent out some frigates to look for the *Taunton*. On 30 August he reported his proceedings to Cromwell, as well as 'the sad and dark condition' he was in: 'our ships extreme foul, our men falling sick through want of drink, and eating their victuals boiled in sea water for two months'. Neither news nor supplies had come from the Navy Commissioners. 'We have no place nor friends, our recruits here slow and our mariners (which I most apprehend) apt to fall into discontents through their long keeping aboard'. He would not trouble the Protector 'with any complaints of myself, of the indisposition of my body, or troubles of mind, but rather in the firm purpose of my heart, with all faithfulness and sincerity to discharge the trust, while reposed in me'.[93]

Next day he was more cheerful. The *Taunton* had come in, and he sent Maynard home in the *Hampshire* to give Cromwell his account of the Portuguese negotiations.[94] By 7 September he had managed to get beverage for his ships, through the good offices of John Bushell and William Bird, Lisbon merchants.[95] As no victualling ships had come, and as his supplies had run so low, it was only possible for him to return home. A Council of War confirmed the decision. The *Nantwich* was sent to call off the frigates from Cape St Vincent, and the Governor of Lagos was bidden to tell the victuallers, when they should arrive, to return home.[96] About the end of September Blake sailed for England. On 3 October, thirty leagues off the Lizard, the *Hampshire* met him. Her captain boarded the flagship. Probably he brought Cromwell's kindly letter of 13 September. In it, though the Protector did not conceal the fact that an attack upon the Spaniards would have been in accordance with his instructions, or that it would be desirable still to carry out such, he left it to Blake to make a personal decision. For he had no certain knowledge of the strength of the enemy fleet, nor of the condition of Blake's ships. Blake, he wrote, 'must handle the reins as you shall find your opportunity, and the ability of the fleet to be'. If it was necessary he was to come home. The delay of supplies was due, he explained, to a storm which had driven the victuallers into Plymouth, after leaving Portsmouth. They had, however, express orders to sail with the first opportunity.[97]

On 6 October Badiley arrived in the Downs, followed next day by Blake, sick, tired and troubled both in mind and body.[98] Rumour in London spoke of him being sent to the Tower to join Penn and Venables,[99] freshly returned from the fiasco at Hispaniola. But Cromwell was too great a man to blame the man on the spot for not fighting. He had judgment and strength enough to trust them enough to estimate men. Through Blake the Commonwealth had affronted and overcome the naval power of France, Spain and the Moor.

On 12 October the Admiralty Commissioners drew attention to the fact that Blake's men had received no pay during their twenty months' service at sea. Nor had a penny of the money due to them been made over to their wives and families. The wages bill for the fleet was £120,000 towards which they had £20,000 which they used to pay off the great ships. The rest was raised by stopping the money due for contracts, bills, wages and dockyards, while ships at sea were kept out to avoid paying the seamen's wages.[100] Cromwell was in the same position as Charles I had been: he had splendid ships, magnificent seamen, but no money with which to pay them.

His financial poverty stood in strong contrast to the wealth of reputation which Blake and his fleet had won. The Royalist, Clarendon, summed up what Blake had done. 'He was the first man that declined the old track, and made it manifest that that science might be obtained in less time than it was imagined; and despised those rules which had long been in practice, to keep his ships and his men out of danger, which had been held in former times a point of great ability and circumspection, as if the principal art requisite in the captain of a ship had been to be sure to come home safe again. He was the first man who brought the ships to contend castles on shore, which had been thought ever very formidable, and were discovered by him to make a noise only, and to fright those who could rarely be hurt by them. He was the first that infused that proportion of courage into the seamen by making them see by experience what mighty things they could do if they were resolved, and taught them to fight in fire as well as upon water, and though he hath been very well imitated and followed, he was the first that gave the example of that kind of naval courage and bold and resolute achievements.'[101]

CHAPTER 20

The Expedition of Blake and Mountagu in 1656

*

BLAKE had shown Cromwell that the Straits of Gibraltar cut in half the naval power of both France and Spain. Whoever held that narrow defile held the control of the Mediterranean itself. This fact had enormous possibilities. A port on the Straits would allow England to dominate that sea and with it the mercantile trade. To possess such was the conception that was to grow in Cromwell's fertile brain.

Yet for the moment the capture of the expected Spanish Plate Fleet dominated Cromwell's mind above all else. It would go a long way towards paying the heavy debts of the Commonwealth, and it would help to restore the prestige lost by the failure of Penn in the West Indies. So, with these objects in view, the fleet was preparing all through the winter of 1655 for service on the coast of Spain. The chief difficulty was, as usual, to man the ships. As Wilbur Abbott wrote, 'the financial difficulties of the Government had prevented the payment of the sailors, though the Army – which of course was more essential to the maintenance of the party in power – had been paid as fully and as promptly as possible'.[1] Small wonder was it that Blake's crews had received no pay for 20 months. Small wonder that the press-gangs had to seize men ashore, and that the outward-bound merchantmen were compelled to surrender their most efficient seamen. The Mayor and Jurats of Rye, for instance, were ordered to find sixty able men above the age of fifteen, and under that of sixty.[2] The horrors of a tropical climate, as related by Penn's returned crews, made the mariners 'so afraid of being sent to the West Indies that they say they would rather be hanged'. So much so that they ran away and hid themselves from the press-gangs.[3]

Blake remained the only man capable of commanding the fleet, sick though he was, for his previous experience of Spain and Portugal made his selection inevitable. Now, as he knew himself to be in ill health, he seems to have asked for a colleague to assist him, and to take over command should he die.[4] On 2 January,

Edward Mountagu was appointed. According to the Royalists, Blake is said to have complained of 'being joined to such a worthless fellow'.[5] But they were only too anxious to stir up trouble, as they had done in April 1649. Cromwell was no fool, and it was not likely that he would have forced upon Blake a man with whom he could not get on.

Mountagu, not yet thirty, had served in the army in the Civil War, though without any particular distinction. He was a faithful adherent of Cromwell, who had made him a member of the Council of State in 1654, and a Commissioner of the Treasury in the same year. Of the sea he had no experience whatever, yet he was to prove himself as a man of natural ability, with a great capacity to learn. He had a forcefulness of character and an instinctive love of action, that was the very opposite of Blake's careful weighing up of a situation in all its various aspects. His appointment may have been prompted by the fact that he was heavily in debt. But the real reason was a political one. Not that the loyalty of Blake was suspect, for he was above all political intrigue. His sole object was his work and the harassing of the Spaniard. But there were others under him who were not so loyal. Spanish gold had alienated some of the seamen, and Royalist intrigue was at work among men higher up. Mountagu was an active member of the council and in the closest touch with current political trends: especially with John Thurloe, Secretary of the Council, who had his agents everywhere, even in the inner circles of the Royalists both at home and abroad. Thurloe's attention was focused upon Sexby, an agitator, who had joined Cromwell's opponents. As he had a strong hold upon the Levellers in the army, he was a dangerous person. In September, 1654, agents reported that he had met at several times Major-General Overton, Colonels Alured and Saunders and Vice-Admiral Lawson.[6] They were mostly Levellers, with Sexby at their head. In Cromwell they saw the tyranny of the army personified. However they contented themselves with a petition demanding a free Parliament. The Colonels were arrested and Overton was sent to the Tower, but Sexby escaped.[7]

At Antwerp Sexby tried to persuade the Royalists to try to restore the Monarchy with the aid of the Levellers, but they would have nothing to do with him. He went on to Spain where he offered the King, in return for financial aid, that when the expected revolt in England took place, Irish troops would hold the fortified towns until Spanish troops arrived. For this purpose part of the fleet, under Lawson, would go over and anchor at Dunkirk. He was an eloquent, unscrupulous and plausible liar, but the King saw through him. For he was well informed of the state of affairs in England. All he would undertake was that the money would only be provided after the revolt was in full swing. Sexby, however, managed to extract £800 from the Grand Duke of Austria.[8]

Cromwell, through Thurloe, was well aware of what was afoot. Though he knew of Lawson's plotting, he was wise enough not to dismiss him as his popularity among the seamen was immense. Instead, on 21 January, 1656, Lawson was appointed Vice-Admiral, in the *Resolution*, of the Spanish-bound fleet, now lying in Stokes Bay, Portsmouth. In his old post, as commander of the Channel Fleet, he was potentially dangerous. On the coast of Spain, under Mountagu's eye, he would be practically harmless. Suddenly Lawson threw up his commission on the ground that he would not go to sea until he knew the purpose of the voyage.[9] But the real reason seems to have been that no money had reached him with which to suborn the seamen. For Sexby, now in Flanders, had sent the £800 over to England by Richard Overton (not to be confused with the Major-General). Unfortunately for Sexby, Overton had been Thurloe's agent since December, 1655. It seems that he revealed the plot to Thurloe and handed the money over to him.[10] Its non-arrival probably made Lawson suspect that the plot had been discovered and that, under Mountagu's eye, he could no longer fulfil the hopes he had tried to raise among the Royalists abroad, of bringing the fleet over to them.

Yet it was soon clear that Lawson had suborned some of the captains. For, on 29 February, Lyons of the *Resolution* interviewed Blake and declared his 'aversion to this employment'. Next day he resigned and the Generals sent for him. He now complained of the lack of care for the captains and their families, in case of death. He was not satisfied with the design; neither against whom he should go, or where. Mountagu replied 'that the sole enemy in view was the Spaniard, and to infest him was our work: but in what place concerned him not, who was to obey orders, and not to weigh designs, of which he was not properly cognisant'.[11] From this saying probably sprang the famous words, attributed to Blake, 'It is not for us to mind State Affairs, but to stop the foreigner from fooling us'. They certainly fit the occasion, but have been fathered, in another form, on to Blake. Then Captain Hill of the *Speaker* was sent for. He was more explicit still. He would not fight the Spaniard either in the West Indies or to the Southward. England had suffered no injury from Spain, but the English at Providence Island had used warships to prey on Spanish shipping, so that in self-defence the Spaniards had to root them out. He would, however, be willing to fight in the Channel for his own country's defence. He ended, a little feebly, by pleading that his health would not stand service in hot countries. He and Lyons were confined on the *Naseby* till they were sent to London.[12] On 7 March Captain Abelson, of the *Mermaid*, a close associate of Lawson, came to resign his commission. He thought the design lawful but pleaded that his wife's health would not stand his long absence at sea. The 'last of this gang', the lieutenant of the *Resolution*, declared that had he been in Lawson's place, he would have done what he did. He was coldly told that he would be no longer employed and was sent ashore.[13]

Badiley was now appointed Vice-Admiral, but the plotters made one last desperate effort. They got him arrested for debt, but a special committee of the council had him released at once.[14] On 4 March Thurloe acknowledged Mountagu's report. He saw the 'finger of Job, viz Spain in this business'. For he had seen letters that other captains were to resign, and that money had been sent over to seduce men and officers from their duty. He suspected 'the design laid further in the fleet than these two Captains, but the prudence you have shown in dealing with them may, I hope, at least discourage the others'.[15] On the 23rd he told Mountagu that Spain had got ready its fleet, which would sail shortly from Cadiz for the West Indies.[16] On the same day Blake, as if he had a presentiment that this was to be his last voyage, made his Will.* His property was divided among his relatives, but his two seamen servants were not forgotten, while £50 was entrusted to Captains Adams and Robert Blake, to bring up his Negro servant, Domingo, as a Christian.[17] Next day the Generals sailed and reached Plymouth on the 17th. Here it was decided, on the 19th, that if the fleet got scattered on the voyage, it should rendezvous off Cape St Vincent.[18] The fleet was divided into three squadrons, composed as follows:[19]

* see Appendix 1.

SHIP	CAPTAIN	GUNS
Naseby (flagship)	R. Cuttance	74
Unicorn	R. Clarke	56
Fairfax	Edw. Blagg	56
Lyme	Eus. Smith	52
Newbury	Rob. Blake	52
Entrance	Jno. Hayward	46
Bristol	Tho. Penrose	40
Maidstone	Tho. Adams	40
Taunton	Nath. Brown	40
Nantwich	J. Jeffries	40
Centurion	Anth. Spatchurst	40
Ruby	Rob. Kirby	40
Mermaid	Peter Foote	26
Resolution (flagship)	R. Badiley	84
Rainbow	R. Stoakes	54
Speaker	R. Stayner	52
Plymouth	Jno. Littlejohn	50
Tredagh	R. Harman	50
Newcastle	Edm. Curtis	50
Kentish	W. Hannan	40
Foresight	Peter Mootham	40
Dragon	H. Haddock	40
Amity	Hen. Pack	34
Guinea	Giles Shelley	32
Colchester	Sam. Blake	26
Swiftsure (flagship)	J. Bourne	56
Andrew	Ant. Young	56
Bridgwater	Anth. Earning	52
Langport	J. Coppin	52
Worcester	Rob. Nixon	48
Winsby	Jos. Ames	40
Diamond	Jno. Lloyd	40
Hampshire	Rob. Storey	36
Jersey	Symons	40
Phoenix	R. Whetstone	40
Providence	Mackey	32
Assurance	Phillip Holland	34
Beaver (fireship)	Ric. Penhallow	

| *Fox* (fireship) | Wm. Pickering | |

Other ships named later

Convert	R. Bevans	26
Hope	Jas. Strutt	12
Merlin	G. Ford	12
Marigold	Geo. Kendall	22
Nonsuch	Jno. Woolters	36
Old Warwick	Matt. Browne	22
Griffin	Jno. Taylor	12
Old President	Val. Tatnell	20
Sapphire	R. Clay	36
George	R. Clarke	50
James	—	48

After various delays the fleet at last sailed from Plymouth on 28 March.[19] In the interval two galleons and two smaller vessels of last year's belated Plate Fleet had got into Cadiz, though their consorts had been wrecked in the Indies.[20] By 10 April Blake was off Cape St Mary, too late to make a capture. Next day, after a Council of War, the *Amity* and the *Foresight* were sent off to get intelligence of the state of affairs at Cadiz. They were ordered to 'use their eyes as to what was to be done in that harbour'. On the 13th they returned. A fleet of about thirty sail had gone for San Domingo, Carthagena and Havana, to bring back the Plate Fleet. In Cadiz were twenty galleons, waiting for Flemish ships to bring them rigging.[21] Next day the Generals sent the Protector's letter to Meadowe, who had recently arrived back at Lisbon, bidding him ask for a speedy reply to his demand that the Portuguese King should ratify the Treaty of 1654.[22] This done, they sailed and reached Cadiz on the 20th.

After sending out frigates to intercept the Flemish ships, they debated their next course of action. They had the option of chasing the enemy fleet to the West Indies. Mountagu, writing to Thurloe, regretted that this suggestion had not been discussed when he was in London, especially 'as there was a general dread of the Indian voyage'. In turn they discussed the possibility of an attack upon Cadiz. Though they knew Cromwell was anxious for them to strike a vigorous blow, the prospect was not promising. For, on 9 May, some Dutch vessels leaving Cadiz, had told them of the state of the defences. Some thirty ships were tucked away

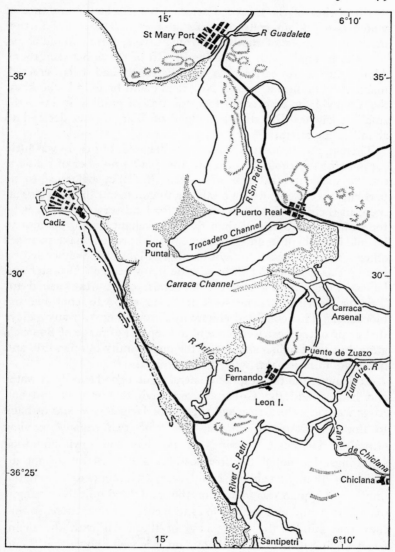

Cadiz Harbour, 1625

in the shelter of the narrow Carraca Channel, at the entrance of which two 60-gun galleons were anchored. Two miles further in, at the entrance of another narrow passage, were two old ships, ready to be sunk, with a chain and a raft of masts between them. Along the shore earthworks and batteries had been erected, manned by bodies of troops. No pilots could be found who knew the Channel, or who could take the risk of guiding in even the smallest frigates. So, after a Council of War, it was decided to abandon the attempt.[22]

Then an attack upon Gibraltar was debated, but there was little support for the project. On board they had a number of soldiers, sent to make up the lack of seamen. But they belonged to no particular regiment, with no officers to command them. The seamen, in their opinion, were useless 'for land service, unless it be for sudden plunder, and then they are valiant much, but not to be ruled and kept in any government on shore: nor have your sea officers much stomach to fight on shore'. However they ended by saying 'this work is not thrown aside upon debate'. As water and ballast were running low the Generals, on 7 May, sailed for Tangier, leaving Bourne with fourteen ships to continue the blockade.[23] This consisted chiefly in skirmishing with any galleys that came out. These were careful to keep out of range of Bourne's guns, but the English ships took the opportunity to open fire, and much ammunition was wasted to no purpose.[24]

At Tangier, on the 8th, the Generals 'got a good supply of water and ballast, and the Governor very civil to our men and us'. After watering, the *Lyme*, and three other frigates, were sent back to Bourne. Mountagu crossed over with two frigates to view Gibraltar. He made drawings of the bay and town and took soundings. He noted the fortifications and fixed on a spot up which he thought soldiers could creep. He concluded that the only possible plan was to land on the sand, 'and quickly cutting it off between land and sea: or, so as to secure our men there, so that they may hinder the intercourse of the town with the main frigates lying near to assist them; and it is well known that Spain never victualleth any place for one month. This will require 4,000 or 5,000 men well formed and officered'.[25] What Blake thought is unknown, but he probably agreed with Mountagu. So too did Cromwell, for, on getting the report, he observed that 'nothing

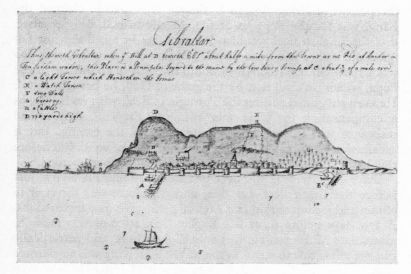

Gibraltar 1676

was feasible without a good body of landsmen'. But the idea still simmered at the back of his mind.[26]

The *Nantwich* and the *Ruby* took the new agent, Browne, to Algiers. He handed the Dey Cromwell's letter, congratulating him on his faithful observance of the peace, and with his friendly reception for English ships. He promised that Captain Griffith, of the *Acorn*, who had carried off a Flemish slave, should be dealt with and that, in future, neither Flemish nor French slaves were to be carried off.[27] The frigates then left to range the Spanish coast for pirates.

At Tangier, on the 15th, the captain with three officers of the *Old Warwick*, had foolishly landed to get wood. They were pounced upon by ten Moorish horse and killed. Three of their bodies were recovered. As there was nothing else to be done the fleet sailed for Cadiz, where it arrived on the 17th.[28] Letters from England were brought by three victuallers, with two from Meadowe at Lisbon. He reported that the Portuguese King was unwilling to ratify the Treaty as long as it contained clauses conceding the right of the English merchants to worship in their own houses, and requiring the return of runaway seamen who deserted under the pretext of being Roman Catholic. This matter, claimed the King, was for the Pope to decide. Meadowe had also promised that the English fleet would neither engage in hostilities nor fall upon the Plate Fleet from Brazil.[29] Mountagu was furious: so too was Cromwell. 'He (the King) would bring us to an owning of the Pope, which we shall not, by the grace of God, be brought unto'. He even suggested seizing the Portuguese fleet, with its lading, as a compensation for what was owing to England. Any armed resistance was to be met by destruction of the enemy. But if satisfaction was obtained this instruction 'shall be void'. But before this letter, dated 6 May, arrived the matter had been settled.[30]

Blake cleverly took the fleet to Lisbon, timing his arrival just before the Brazil fleet was due, and Meadowe was directed to obtain ratification within five days of getting his new instructions. A few days before these left England, an attempt was made to assassinate Meadowe. He was only slightly hurt, and patriotically did not allow this to stand in the way.[31] The King was so alarmed that he sent all the royal doctors to attend him. He was even more alarmed when Blake, on 27 May, appeared off Cape St Vincent. Though the five days' grace had expired the King ratified the Treaty on the 31st.[32]

Mountagu had been all for instant action. Blake wisely took a longer view. Hostilities would have aroused the enmity of the King, with the consequent loss of Lisbon as a base to careen and water. Without it it would be impossible to carry on the war with Spain. Moreover from personal experience he understood the Portuguese, and their sensitivity about their national dignity. Patience and a peaceful demonstration of the power of his fleet could better achieve his object.

On 4 June Meadowe boarded the *Naseby*. He got a mixed reception; Blake expressed himself as satisfied with the peace he had brought about, but Mountagu with approving memories of the Protector's instructions of 6 May, told Meadowe that 'I (Meadowe) should have received more thanks at Whitehall, if I had not concluded'. First, because the Treaty had not been ratified within the time limit: secondly because the Protector had been dishonoured by the attempt upon Meadowe's life. However Meadowe quietly and effectively justified himself. Blake himself had pointed out that if an attempt to seize the Brazil fleet had been made, it would have scattered in twenty directions, while the King would have seized £6,000 or £7,000 worth of the English estates within his realm.[33]

This incident may have caused the rumour in London that the two Generals had quarrelled. The Venetian Ambassador there, on 20 June, reported it: 'Only the Protector knew if it was true; one, who takes part in Affairs of State, had been heard to speak of Blake unfavourably, and to make accusations against him'.[34] Mountagu was an impatient young man, but Blake was always averse to the shedding of blood, if his end could be won peaceably. So he taught his colleague patience and the longer view. Both men learned to respect and trust one another. Nowhere in Mountagu's letters to Thurloe is there any sign of bad relations with Blake, while in Blake's letters to Mountagu there is instead a note of personal regard, trust and affection.

On 22 May, Captain Lloyd, briefed with Cromwell's ideas, brought the Protector's letter of 28 April, in the *Sapphire*. Cromwell desired 'to give no rule to you but building much more upon . . . your judgements on the place than on our own'. He had heard that the fleet in Cadiz was not likely to come out, owing to the lack of seamen. He thought that the Spaniards' 'object might be to delay you upon the coast, until your victuals are spent, and you are forced to come home'. Was there a possibility of burning or destroying the Cadiz Fleet, though the forts at Puntal might be so strong as to discourage them? If so, could not the island upon which Cadiz stood, be cut off from the mainland by destroying the bridge which joined them? Might not Gibraltar be taken? . . . 'which, if possessed and made tenable by us . . . would be an advantage to our trade, and an annoyance to the Spaniard: and enable us, without keeping so great a fleet on that coast, with six nimble frigates lodged there, do the Spaniard more harm than by a fleet, and ease our own charge'.[35]

Thurloe had ordered Lloyd to tell the Generals that the *Cullen* was bringing them sixty dozen sand baskets, 3,000 tools, with pick-axes, shovels and spades. If any design was agreed upon that needed three or four thousand foot, they would be sent, together with the *George*, *James*, *Triumph* and *Victory*, which were now in reserve. But only if they were needed, as such extra charge was, if possible, to be avoided.[36]

On 11 June the *Sapphire* and the *Phoenix*, with £50,000 paid by the Portuguese King on board, also took Lloyd home. Letters were sent to Cromwell, reporting that attacks, either upon Cadiz or Gibraltar, were impossible. Both had been strongly reinforced with troops, while Cadiz alone would require a force capable of meeting 40,000 men. Moreover the loss of the *Cullen* precluded any attack.[37] She had been captured, on 18 May, five leagues off Lisbon by the *Jesus*, *Maria* and *Joseph* of Ostend, and taken into Vigo.[38] Blake complained to Cromwell that the *Ruby* and *Nantwich* had returned with news from the agent at Algiers. As the Protector had not confirmed his appointment, the Dey would not ratify the Treaty. Instead 'they beginning very much to slight him, and were in a great aptness to break the peace. The vicinity of our fleet was the only restraint upon them'. They had already thirty warships, and were building more.[39]

So, on 12 June, Blagge, in the *Fairfax*, with seven frigates was sent to Vigo and Ponte Vedra to recover the *Cullen*, and to destroy any Ostenders and Dunkirkers, who rendezvoused there. Though they blew up the *Santa Teresa* and forced the *St Peter*, another Ostender, to fire his ship, the *Cullen* was under the shelter of a castle 'and too near fifty pieces of ordnance' to be recovered.[40]

On 22 June eight Portuguese warships came out. Both fleets saluted one another with guns and struck their flags. By this act of courtesy Blake removed any resentment the Portuguese still might have.[41] Next day he sailed for Cadiz, arriving there on the 28th. All was as before. On the 30th, the *Griffin* brought a letter from Cromwell dated 9 June. He had just got the Generals' letter of 9 May from Tangier. As the burning of Cadiz was impossible he proposed that some of the lesser ships should be sent home, to secure trade in the Channel, and to block up Dunkirk and Ostend. Nineteen of their privateers had taken twenty English merchantmen, while freebooters had even come into the Thames to seek their prey, which had raised the price of Newcastle coals in London. The choice of ships he left to the Generals, though if they had some new design they were to decide whether or not to send home the ships.[42] They decided, with twelve ships, to go to Tripoli and make a treaty and, if possible, with Tunis also. This was of great importance to English trade, as many rich ships were captured by these places. Bourne was left to continue the blockade of Cadiz. As Mountagu wrote to Thurloe on the 30th, it was 'a very bootless thing to lie here'. It made him angry to see the Dutch, Hamburg and Genoese trade with the Spaniard, which they could not hinder. Even if these ships were searched for contraband, it was always stored in the lowest part of the ship, and to search and find nothing bred much ill-will. He re-echoed Cromwell's words that 'twelve or fifteen nimble frigates would secure the Straits and annoy the Spaniard, and probably light upon his Plate Fleet than a greater number'. The cost would be less to the nation 'and they will have the benefit of Lisbon to careen and keep themselves always clean'. Mountagu had at last realised that Blake was right as to the importance of Lisbon.[43]

The *Unicorn*, *Kentish*, *Taunton*, *Guinea*, *Jersey*, *Mermaid*, *Dragon* and *Assurance* were picked to go home and it was suggested that the great ships, as they could not keep out safely in the winter, should accompany them. 'A good squadron of frigates would better answer any opportunity of service'. As the *Little President* was in danger of sinking in a heavy sea, she was also to go.[44]

Even as the Generals wrote, a violent gale of wind from the E.S.E. blew into the bay, and scattered most of the fleet out to sea; boats, cables and anchors were lost. At midnight the *Taunton* was driven upon the *Naseby*, which began to cut her two best cables. Just as a final 'chop' would have set her free, the *Taunton* managed to hoist her foresail, slip her cable and so missed the Flagship by a ship's length. 'Judge you,' wrote Mountagu, 'what this sea is to ride in winter time. This Providence hath occasioned our setting aside all thoughts of Tripoli for this summer.' By superb seamanship not a vessel was lost.[45]

On the 6th Blagge rejoined, and on the 8th Smith, in the *Lyme*, with three frigates and a fireship, were sent to Malaga, the headquarters of Balthazara, 'noted pirate', to try and catch him. He was not at home, but nine ships were burnt, the Spaniards driven from the mole, their guns spiked, and a storm of shot poured into the town. Blake had shown his captains, at Porto Farina, how to attack a fortified port. He had inspired them with the principle of attack, of seeking out the enemy and destroying him and, at the same time, not to attempt the impossible which might lead to the loss of their ship. By now he could trust to their initiative.[46]

'If a good place for watering and careening could be found' wrote Mountagu to Thurloe, 'it would be of unspeakable advantage to England to have a fort and possession thereof, to be always sure of it both for men-of-war and merchants' accommodation'. Such a place Buzema was said to be. There the Generals sailed, intending to go on to Sallee 'to see what might be done in the way of Amity'.[47] Some time about now Thurloe had told Mountagu that Mazarin had offered to invest Mardyke, if the Commonwealth would do so by sea. In return the place would be handed over to Cromwell. This secret Mountagu was to keep to himself, but it was another reason for the sending home of ships.[48]

Buzema proved to be useless for watering and careening, so by the end of July, they were back off Cadiz. Here they bought beverage wine from Lisbon and Faro which, with the wine from the Madeiras, gave them a good supply. Smith's squadron had returned so, on 20 July, they sent the *Newbury*, *Maidstone* and *Colchester* to ply before Sallee, prior to their coming in a day or so.[49]

On 3 August, they joined their frigates at Sallee. Next day the

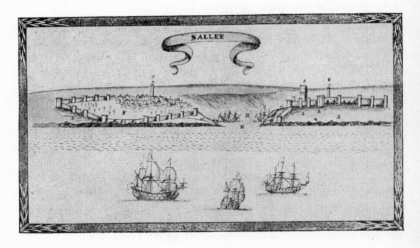

Sallee 1676

Governor agreed to send Commissioners aboard to discuss peace terms. But before they came two ships were sighted, which at once stood in close to the shore. When they saw they could not escape capture, they ran ashore and became complete wrecks. They proved to be the Governor's property. Nevertheless the Commissioners arrived, but they refused to hand over twenty-four captives without ransom. This the Generals insisted upon, 'as dishonourable to us, that appear before their port with the English Standard'. The Commissioners then went ashore, and Mountagu wanted to attack their ships which were about to come in from the sea, if agreement was not made before they appeared. But Blake refused to be diverted from his main objective by hostilities off North Africa, while the Spanish Plate Fleet was his true target. On the return of the Commissioners, negotiations broke down over the handing over of two English children. Neither side would budge. So on the 20th, the Generals sailed for Cadiz, leaving two ships and a ketch to blockade the port. As no news from England awaited them, they sailed for Lisbon on 2 September, leaving Stayner on watch with eight ships.[50]

After debate it was decided to keep the great ships, as Spain had eighteen galleons and twelve other vessels, which would be ready at the end of January. Three merchantmen came in from England with thousands of letters for the fleet. In most of them a paper had been inserted, connected probably with the attempt of the Fifth Monarchy men and Lawson to overthrow the Government by stirring up trouble in the fleet. The Generals wisely ignored them, merely confiscating the papers from undistributed letters.[51]

Suddenly, on 19 September, glorious news came from Stayner. On the 8th he had been forced from off Cadiz out to sea, by a strong westerly gale. In the evening he sighted eight sail five or six leagues west of Cadiz, part of the Plate Fleet from Havana. As there was no escort for them there they had resolved to sail alone. After twenty-eight days Cadiz was sighted. They were safe home. With them were two galleons, two armed store ships, three merchantmen and a Portuguese prize they had captured. They had anxiously questioned its crew as to Blake's whereabouts, and were told that the Spaniards had beaten him off the coast a month before. Reassured they sailed on, merely shifting the Admiral's flag from a galleon to a smaller vessel, so as to deceive any possible enemy. When Stayner stood with them, they took his ships for fishing vessels. Unperturbed they hung out lights as usual, and fired guns all night, for they were home.

At dawn next morning they were horrified to see Stayner in the *Speaker*, with the *Plymouth* and the *Bridgwater*, as the rest of his ships were far astern, bearing down to engage them. There was no escape. To an onlooker ashore his ships looked tiny compared with the tall and bulky galleons, and they seemed 'all sail and fire'.

Stayner was not taken in by the shift of flag, and merely 'slighted' her, so that she and the prize got away into Cadiz. After giving the Vice-Admiral several broadsides, he left her to the *Bridgwater*, and tackled the Rear-Admiral, which he suspected was really the Admiral. After a stout fight she surrendered, both ships being badly damaged in their hulls and masts. The captain told Stayner he had two million pieces of eight aboard. After a six hour fight the Vice-Admiral's crew fired her and she sank. The *Plymouth* engaged Captain Calderon's ship, of thirty guns, and captured her but she caught fire accidentally and sank with 600,000 pieces of eight. The *Tredagh* took a straggler, richly laden. In the end two ships were taken, three were sunk or burnt and three escaped. Stayner took his two prizes into Lagos. The Spanish Rear-Admiral had aboard forty-five tons of silver, 700 chests of indigo, 700 chests of sugar, with drugs and other goods, By the advice of his captains, Stayner took out of her, as she was badly damaged, seven or eight hundred bars of silver. He then put his prisoners ashore. The *Diamond* was sent to report the news to the Generals and Stayner, after leaving three of his 'best sailing ships' off Cape St Vincent, sailed for Lisbon, where he arrived on 15 September.[52]

Aboard the Spanish Vice-Admiral had been the Governor of Peru and his family. When his wife and daughter swooned, he chose to perish in the flames with them. His younger children were rescued and the eldest, the Marquis of Baydex, and his younger brother, found themselves without parents or means. All their possessions had gone to the bottom. The Marquis, aged sixteen, was described by Mountagu as 'a most ingenious and intelligent youth'. He conversed with the Generals, probably in Latin, and gave them much valuable information about Peru. Finding himself in the unusual position of imparting knowledge, instead of receiving it, in all innocence he revealed that the Plate Fleet, of ten galleons, with several millions of plate aboard, was at Havana. It would arrive home early in December, by way of the Canaries. Here it was to receive instructions from Spain as to where to sail, probably to Galicia.[53]

On 19 September Captain Storey, of the *Hampshire*, took home the Generals' dispatch, announcing the victory to the Protector, and enclosing Stayner's account. He arrived on 1 October, and got to the House three hours after it had risen. Next day Thurloe gave the great news, and a Day of Thanksgiving was fixed for 5

November. In great optimism the House decided not to vote new taxes until the value of the capture was known. It hoped that this might amount to £600,000, so that the war might pay for itself. But the answer was still in Lisbon.[54]

On 29 September the Generals got two letters, dated 28 August. One was from Cromwell. He recognised that an attack on Gibraltar was impossible without a great force of landsmen. So he recommended that the great ships should be sent home, as a good force of frigates could do all that was essential. As he wished to discuss the matter with one of them, he directed that Mountagu should come home, and that Blake should remain. The Spaniard, he thought, would concentrate upon his West India trade, and would not care 'much for what else is done to him'. His fleets therefore were to be intercepted either from going to, or coming from, these parts. All materials for shipping, or other contraband goods, were to be prevented from reaching Cadiz or any other ports. Twenty smaller vessels should suffice for this purpose and also preserve English trade, both in the Straits and with Portugal.[55]

The other letter was from Thurloe to Mountagu. In England there had been a strong combination of the Levellers and the Fifth Monarchy men 'to put us into blood'. Lawson, Lyons and others had been arrested. The Dutch had seized the opportunity to make trouble at Torbay. There fifty of their merchantmen had behaved themselves so insolently that there was 'a little less than a fight between our and their men-of-war'.[56]

These considerations, with the possibility that Lawson had again hoped to stir up trouble among the seamen, decided Cromwell that a strong force of ships was necessary in the Channel, commanded by a man he could trust, namely Mountagu. As it was known that Spain was fitting out thirty ships in Cadiz, ready to come out in January, the Generals decided, now that Lisbon was again available as a base, to keep out some of the great ships and Mountagu was to take home the *Naseby*, *Andrew*, *Resolution* and *Rainbow*, with seven other ships badly in need of repair, together with various prizes, including Stayner's captures. Blake therefore transferred his flag to the *Swiftsure*.[57]

Great trouble was taken to prevent embezzlement of the treasure, but it was too late. A great deal must have been taken by the seamen in the fight. 'As honest a commander as I could pick' wrote Mountagu, was put aboard the galleons. No boat was to board them without special permission from Mountagu, and selected persons were to search the ships for concealed hoards. The silver, he estimated, was worth £200,000.[58]

A revealing letter of Stayner to Mountagu, dated 17 May, 1658, says: 'I believe you have been informed, as well as divers other men, that I got a great estate by those ships, but on the word of a man I never got above £2,000 . . . I confess lamentably if I had not more regard to my reputation than I had to money: for had I taken £100, other men would have taken advantage to have taken ten'. Like Clive, later on, he seems to have been astonished at his own moderation. Yet in his modesty he omitted to explain how a pearl and emerald necklace, once the property of the Empress of Peru, came into his possession, so that he was able to bequeath it to his daughter.* This may explain why seven or eight hundred bars of silver were taken out by the advice of Stayner's captains.[59]

Mountagu arrived at Portsmouth about 24 October and a week later he received the thanks of the House.[60] The treasure, packed in ammunition wagons, went by road to the Tower, amid great public rejoicings, for the Protector knew full well the uses of publicity. On 11 November Colonel White, in charge of it, reported to the House that there were 225 chests of silver worth about as many pounds, and cochineal to the value of another £20,000. As Thurloe had estimated the treasure at a million, the nation was in a state of stunned disappointment. All, except a quarter or a third, had been embezzled by its captors. As Thurloe wrote, 'a private Captain they say had got to his share £60,000 and many private mariners £10,000 a man, and this is so universal amongst seamen, and taken in the heat of fight, that it is not possible to get it again nor any part of it'.[61] Thurloe may have used this wildly exaggerated gossip to account for his own optimistic estimate.

The Mayor of Plymouth arrested Joseph Harrison, when he was found in possession of silver on entering harbour.[62] Badiley was awarded £300 for discovering another man with two concealed pigs of silver.[63] These were the only two culprits unlucky enough to be found out. With their wages and prize money months and even years in arrear, solid pieces of eight were preferable to deferred promises to pay. With old Omar they preferred to 'take

---

* I owe this information to Mr Oliver Warner, who had it from a member of the Stayner family.

the cash and let the credit go'. And who shall blame them? The Government had brought the situation upon its own head.

The orphaned boys came with Mountagu, and Parliament allowed them £300 for their upkeep. Soon they were sent back to Spain in a proposed exchange for Captain Shadrack Blake, which however did not take place.[64] Nor did Mountagu forget his old colleague. Almost as soon as he landed he discovered that the victuals for Blake had not been sent off. He pointed out that Blake had only six weeks' provisions left, and even that on the basis of six men receiving four men's allowance. Nor was any beer provided so that ships and time had to be wasted, in getting water and wine to make beverage. He severely reprimanded Commissioner Willoughby, and insisted that iron-bound cask must be sent out with the beer. Next he was appalled to find that only eight bales of canvas had been ordered, and he insisted that each ship must be provided with two topsails at the least. Thereupon Willoughby said he could send out thirty bales, if so he was ordered.[65]

'My hopes do very much depend upon your noble self' wrote Blake to Mountagu on 10 October, '. . . to use your utmost endeavour to set all wheels at work'. He stressed how hard it was to keep the squadron together. 'Our troubles will be exceeding great if the victualling ships be not hastened, whereof we have no small cause to be very apprehensive because, as you know, the letter sent unto us touching it was so very indefinite in all the circumstances'. He asked Mountagu to assure the Protector 'of my faithful and utmost endeavours to discharge the trust reposed in me'.[66] Blake was so sick a man that he had entrusted Mountagu with much of their correspondence. Jointly they wrote nineteen letters, twelve of which were to Thurloe. Blake wrote personally two to Cromwell and one to Thurloe, while Mountagu wrote twenty to Thurloe, giving a full account of their proceedings.

In view of the difference of their ages, their relationship must have been difficult. Their temperaments, too, were opposed. Mountagu was impatient and all for instant action. But Blake saw his qualities. With his keen attention to detail he must have approved Mountagu's action in procuring a seaman, David Anderson, who devoted his spare time to building ship models, to build and rig for him a model, so that he might learn her working and navigation.[67] By sending Mountagu to view and sketch Gibraltar, Blake let his colleague learn the practical problems of an attack upon the place. When Buzema failed to provide a base, Lisbon was essential as such. Without it the war with Spain was impossible. To seize the Portuguese Brazil Fleet, as both Mountagu and Cromwell urged, could only result in the loss of it as a base. The main task, the capture of the Spanish Plate Fleet, must come first. Though Stayner had made the actual capture, behind him stood the tactic and strategy of Blake. He taught Mountagu the importance of the long view.

In the stress of blockade, storm and tempest the two men learned to trust and respect each other. Mountagu had come to Blake wholly ignorant of the sea. He left him a competent sailor, well versed in command and the requirements of a fleet. Through his training with Blake he was, in the future, to take a high place among the Admirals of his day.

After Mountagu's departure an undated letter came from Cromwell. It was obviously written after Storey's arrival, but before Mountagu's return, somewhere between 1 and 3 October, as it was addressed to both Generals. The order to send home the great ships was rescinded, and left to their discretion. If they had been sent off, as was the case, Cromwell was sending out, in view of the naval preparations in Cadiz, two second-rates, the *George* and the *Unicorn*, with four fourth-rates, the frigates *Bristol*, *Taunton*, *Phoenix* and *Jersey*. Cromwell summed up the situation as he saw it. 'There can be nothing of more consequence than to intercept the Spanish Fleet going to, and coming from, the West Indies, for which our purpose is to keep a fleet in those seas, which may be able to fight with any fleet the Spaniards can set forth, as the most effectual means to prosecute that war'.[68] But Blake had already interpreted it as such, for by the use of Lisbon as a base, he held the key to the capture of the Spanish Plate Fleet, the blockade of Cadiz.

Now sick, weary and almost worn out, but still indomitable, he was left in loneliness to keep his faithful and ceaseless vigil before Cadiz amid the tempests of the turbulent winter seas. But with the spring his last and most famous victory was to come.

CHAPTER 21

Blake's Final Victory

*

BLAKE'S lonely task was, in Cromwell's words, 'to prevent the Spanish fleet going to or coming from the West Indies.' This was emphasised by the information of the young De Baydex that a Plate Fleet from the Canaries was expected in Spanish waters in December. Blake left Lisbon and joined the fleet watching off Cape St Vincent on 14 November. He took the opportunity of good weather to water at Lagos, as he had got 'the best intelligence from Cadiz' that thirty-six warships and ten fireships were being fitted out there.

His chief concern was food and drink. It was almost impossible to get these locally. So the men had to be put on short rations, as he had only ten days' bread. His crews had been cast into 'flux' which he quaintly attributed to an offshore wind. Nor could Lisbon provide him with beer or wine for making beverage. He was offered 800 pipes of wine from the Madeiras, but it would take two months to reach him. He sardonically observed, 'where to find us, and how to get it on board at sea, and how to mix it without going into port, is a riddle to those of experience, though to others it may seem easy'. He dared not send ships to get drink as he expected 'the enemy to come forth with considerable strength'. He must therefore keep the fleet together. He complained of want of beer, and of defective victuals, for which he held the dishonesty of the pursers and the victuallers responsible.[1]

The lack of supplies forced him back to Lisbon. At last fortune favoured him. As he entered, on 4 November, he met two victuallers escorted by the *Guinea* and the *Jersey*, on board of which was Weale. Weale records that 'many Captains come this day aboard us to drink English beer'. They must have slaked a long deferred thirst.[2] On 4 December the *Taunton* brought in the *John and Abigail*. His provisions had come, as Blake thankfully recorded, 'in the nick of time'. All possible diligence was used to clear the victuals 'that we may go to sea'. But the news sent him by Thurloe 'of a right understanding between his Highness and the Parliament – the success of our friends abroad . . . the timely check given . . . unto the proud hopes of our old enemies at home and their accomplices in Flanders hath not a little revived our sad spirits in the midst of so many difficulties here'. The capture by Stayner of the Plate Fleet had prevented Spain from sending financial help to the Royalists so that they could venture on an invasion of England. Blake and his weary men must have felt that their labours had not been in vain.

Revived in spirit Blake was at sea again on 20 December, and by the 30th he was off Cadiz once more. But misfortune struck him. On 8 January a severe gale drove him with twelve or thirteen ships to the Straits' mouth. On the 9th he was forced to anchor at Tetuan. Here the *Maidstone* brought in a rich prize, taken on her way from Lisbon. She was a Dutch ship laden with tobacco and hides. Next day Blake made for the Straits, only to be forced back again.[3] Weale records that a seaman was hanged on the *Newcastle*. This ends a popular belief that Blake never inflicted the death penalty. On the 20th there was another violent gale, and the *Jersey* lost a man who was taking in the reefs.[4] Not until 1 February did the squadron reach Lagos. On its way it met the *Andrew* and the *Phoenix*, with the *Worcester*[5] and the *Diamond*, with the *George* and the *Unicorn*, which were escorting the supply ships *Anne and Joyce* and the *Champion*.[6] On the 9th Bourne was made Vice-Admiral in place of Badiley, while Stayner replaced him as Rear-Admiral. The supplies were taken aboard, and on the 11th, in true Puritan spirit, a Thanksgiving Service was held, 'for the deliverance we had in the Straits, when most of us were forced to anchor in a lee shore'.[7]

This reinforcement of ships came at an opportune moment. For on 10 January De Ruyter arrived at Cadiz with six warships escorting a convoy of eighty merchantmen. He had orders to resist any attempt by the English to search them, but he was to make sure that the convoy carried no Spanish goods, and took in no contraband in Spanish ports. Yet rumour popularly believed that his real purpose was to convoy the Spanish Plate Fleet safely home. This was due to an assertion by the Duke of Medina-Celi that such an agreement had been made with the Dutch. But De Ruyter declared that he had no such instructions. Instead he made his way into the Mediterranean to exact reprisals, from the French and Barbary privateers. Yet the possibility of Dutch intervention must have remained as a niggling possible danger at the back of Blake's mind.[8]

On 9 February Blake wrote to Mountagu, acknowledging two letters, dated the 13th and 15th of December. He opened his mind frankly to his old comrade and friend. Together they had experienced the difficulties of a blockade by sea, amid the tempestuous waters off Cadiz. They could only be appreciated by a man who had been upon the spot. Mountagu, he knew, had the ear of Cromwell, and would urge upon him Blake's wants and necessities. Yet his indomitable spirit showed itself. 'The Lord hath been pleased in great mercy to provide for our safety, and in particular for myself in supporting me against the great indispositions of my body, so that by His blessing I doubt not to be enabled to continue out in the service the ensuing summer.' How great the strain was is revealed in the next sentence. He could not believe the Admiralty Commissioners to be 'so insensible of my condition as to condemn me to the durance of another winter'. He had had to shift his flag from the *Swiftsure*, as she was so foul and unwieldy through the defects in her sheathing as to be unserviceable, to the *George*. 'A ship much unfit to bear the Standard of England'. If the Protector was 'throughly acquainted with these things he would be offended at them'. The rest of the fleet was in as bad a condition, and unfit to be kept out another winter. He lacked men, 'which cannot be recruited here', and he had no means for dealing with the sick and wounded. Yet despite all discouragements he could write, 'we are all together and behold one another's face with comfort'. A sentence which belongs with Henry the Fifth's words before Agincourt: 'we few, we happy few, we band of brothers'. He spoke of the *Maidstone*'s haul of tobacco, 'which men say is very good, and I would willingly transmit it in safe hands because possibly it may be rare in London' [does this imply that Blake was a non-smoker?]. He ended, 'Sir, the indispositions of my body permit me not to be more tedious . . . so I desire to end, wishing you all the health and happiness in the Lord'.[9]

From Lisbon Maynard sent conflicting reports, gathered from his agents in Cadiz. One stated that there were twenty-five ships there, of which ten were galleons, and the rest merchantmen, but they were in no condition to fight as they lacked masts and cables, which they hoped to get from the Dutch. They hoped to elude Blake, go to the Canaries, and bring back the treasure ships, which were to make for ports in Biscay or Galicia. Later on in February, he reported that only eight ships were to go out, evade Blake, and to make their way to America.[10]

On 19 February, as Blake was under sail off Cadiz with nineteen ships, a vessel came speeding in to him. She was the *Catherine*, commanded by David Young, who had served in the *Amity* in the Dutch War, and had lost his hand. He had broken off his voyage from the Barbados to Genoa, to tell his old commander that on his way he had sighted twelve galleons, which he kept in sight for many days, and had left them steering for the Canaries. Blake greeted this splendid news with a salvo of four guns, and instantly summoned Bourne and Stayner aboard him. They advised him to pick six or eight of the best frigates, provision them for six weeks, and send them to meet the Spaniards. A council of the captains eagerly supported the suggestion, doubtless with the memory of Stayner's rich haul off Cadiz. They, too, might get loot and plunder. But, writes Stayner, 'the General was very angry with us, charging us to speak no more of it'. For he would not divide the fleet. On enquiry it was found that there was not one month's victuals, even at six to four men's allowance. To this no one could make any reply.[11]

A letter to the Admiralty Commissioners, of 8 March, sums up his position. Maynard had reported the great preparations of the enemy in Cadiz. His own fleet was so foul from long service 'that if a fleet outward bound should deign to avoid us, few of our ships will be able to follow them up'. Many had been damaged by recent storms so that their masts and sails had been swept away. The *Fairfax* was so short of men that her whole company had to be called on deck when she tacked. Foul weather had forced him to abandon cruising off Cadiz as unsafe. Men, too, were dying from sickness, long service and bad victuals. He had often reminded them of the peril of keeping the fleet out so long that it might become unserviceable. With his common-sense religion he observed caustically, 'the Lord hath most wonderfully preserved us hitherto, but I know of no rule to tempt Him'. He trembled to think what another great storm might do, before they had the time and opportunity to effect repairs. He ended by speaking of 'my particular infirmities, the condition of my body growing every day weaker, but I hope the Lord will support me till the appointed time'.[12] Indeed he is said to have been living only 'on broths, jellies and cordials'.[13] Only by reading these letters concerning the perils and difficulties of blockade, which were his chief concern, can his greatness and utter devotion to duty, despite daily illness, be adequately assessed.

He weighed up the situation carefully. He felt sure that the Spaniards had heard of the arrival of the galleons. It was probable that the fleet in Cadiz might put to sea to protect their approach. To destroy this fleet was more important than intercepting the Plate Fleet, for it would be impossible for the treasure ships to reach Spain without its protection. Above all, until the long-delayed supplies reached him, all he could do was to remain upon his station. Maynard had warned him that the eight Spanish ships had been increased to thirty, and he suggested to Blake that 'eight to ten frigates, lying off Galicia, would do you great service'.[14] Blake therefore spread out his ships between Cape St Mary and Cape Spartel, with Bourne to the north, himself in the centre, and Stayner to the south.[15] At the end of March it became imperative to go to Lagos to water.

At last, on 23 March, Captain Baskett came in with a few victuallers, followed on the 26th by Captain Massey, in the *Yarmouth*, with the *Rainbow* in company, with nineteen victuallers from Oeiras, where they had touched on the 20th. They were taken to Tavira Road, fifty miles north of Cadiz. Prompted by Mountagu, Cromwell had insisted that beer must be sent, and Weale records that twenty tons were taken out.[16] Six months' provisions had come and by 7 April they were cleared. 'No man living remembereth so much goods taken out in so short a time, without the least damage either to the provisions or the ships, which were board by board'.[17] The enthusiasm was due to a report that the Spaniards were now at the Canaries, and had unloaded their plate at Santa Cruz. The impatient commanders, at a council, were all for going there direct, but Blake determined to visit Cadiz first, and sailed for St Lucar.[18] Here message after message came from agents ashore confirming that the Plate Fleet was at Santa Cruz, which was now strongly fortified. Stayner records that he had a letter brought out by a Dutch ship, telling of the Spaniards' arrival, and that he showed it to Blake, who thereupon sent for Bourne. They both advised him to sail for Santa Cruz, but he would not agree. Next day, 10 April, they urged him to do so again, saying that as they were now so well fitted, there could be no excuse for delay. 'The General said little, and we stayed aboard all night'. Stayner then says that on the afternoon of the 11th (Weale, who is the more accurate, says the 12th) William Saddleton, captain of an English privateer, brought the news that he had seen the galleons lying in Santa Cruz Bay, and had marked their positions.[19] For this he was later paid £100,[20] whereas the unfortunate Young, after being dismissed by his owners for disobedience, was merely recommended for a command in the Swedish navy.[21] Weale records that Blake sent in the *Lyme* and the *Colchester* to Cadiz, 'to discern the shipping', on the 12th and that on the 13th he called a Council of War.[22]

From the frigate's report he had assured himself that the fleet in Cadiz would not venture out. Accordingly he told his eager captains that he would go to the Canaries and attack the galleons in harbour, but that he would not divide the fleet.[23] For he had got information, which was however incorrect, that De Ruyter with sixteen or seventeen warships, 'is gone to those islands to bring that money into Flanders'. This had determined him to sail with the whole fleet.[24]

So leaving Stoakes, in the *Rainbow*, with the *Providence* and the *Yarmouth*, to watch off the North Cape, he sailed. With him were the *George, Swiftsure, Speaker, Bridgwater, Lyme, Centurion, Fairfax, Nantwich, Ruby, Hampshire, Langport, Maidstone, Newbury, Newcastle, Foresight, Plymouth, Worcester, Winsby, Jersey* and *Bristol* and probably the *Colchester, Convert* and *Unicorn*, some twenty-three ships in all. With a steady north-east wind the excited and eager fleet swept out upon their voyage.[25]

On Saturday evening, the 18th, Punto de Anaga, the north-west point of Teneriffe, was sighted and a Council of War was called. Stayner proposed that twelve of the best frigates should go in, while the rest stayed behind.[26] Blake, according to Stayner, refused because the next day was the Sabbath. This was probably a dig at Blake's Puritanism, written for the benefit of Charles the Second between 1660 and 1663. The real reason was very different. For the official account says the weather was thick and hazy, so that it would be impossible to make Teneriffe before noon the next day: 'whereby the enemy had longer notice of our being on the coast than we designed he should'.[27] The captains as usual supported Stayner. Blake however led the fleet southward until dawn on the 19th. The *Nantwich* and the *Plymouth* were sent in to scout, while the fleet lay some four leagues out.

At dawn the scouts signalled that the enemy were still in the harbour, though the shadow of the hills made them invisible to the fleet. So, at 6 a.m. Blake called his captains aboard to confer with him, and with Bourne and Stayner who were already on the flagship.[28]

Though the Spaniards had sighted the fleet, they felt themselves secure beneath their fortifications. They told a Fleming, who had asked leave to put to sea, that he might, for if the English fleet dared to come in, they would be served as Penn had been at Hispaniola. But the Fleming had served in the Dutch War, and knew both the English and the character and determination of the man who led them. 'Begone' said Don Diego Diagues, the Spanish Admiral, 'if you will and let Blake come in if he dares'. A prisoner from Hispaniola reported afterwards that the Spaniards 'derided us among themselves, laughed our intentions to scorn and were, for Spaniards, very jolly'.[29]

Their confidence was based upon their defences. Santa Cruz was a sheltered roadstead, with a coast line of a shallow crescent shape, open to the sea to the east. The shore extended about a mile and a half north and south. At the south-west end stood St Philip's Castle, a strong stone fort of forty guns. A line of seven stone forts ran northwards, connected with each other by a triple line of breastworks, manned by musketeers. Should any enemy attempt to approach the roadstead, a converging fire would meet them. Nine of the smaller galleons, of 300 to 800 tons, lay close inshore in the centre of the bay, under cover of the forts. Seven great galleons, of 1,000 tons and more, were anchored to the south further out, broadside on to the sea.[30]

Worn out with scurvy, dropsy and his old wound, Blake was short and brusque with his commanders. As they had displeased him so much the Saturday before, 'they said never a word till he earnestly desired them'. Stayner broke the sullen silence by saying he had already delivered his opinion 'and would say no more until I know better'. The captains supported him and asked Blake to name the twelve frigates. Blake accepted their decision and selected four out of each squadron. The captains then asked that Stayner should command them. When Blake asked him if he

would, he replied 'with all my heart'. Blake then added that he,
with the rest of the fleet, would come in and batter the forts, while
the galleons were being destroyed. He had determined to follow
his successful tactics at Porto Farina, and to apply the Blake
'touch'. Stayner's orders were simple. The frigates were to follow
him in line, and to lay themselves alongside the galleons at three
or four cables' length from the shore, so as to have room to veer
their ships, if necessary, during the fight, and then to veer them
off after they had done their work. Not a gun was to be fired until
they had anchored.[31]

Then, after the crews had assembled to invoke the blessing of

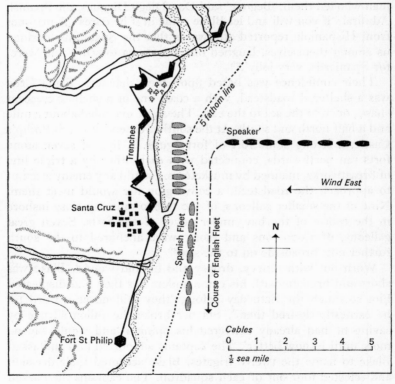

The Santa Cruz Raid

the Almighty,[32] Stayner in the *Speaker*, led in the *Lyme*, *Langport*, *Newport*, *Bridgwater*, *Plymouth*, *Worcester*, *Newcastle*, *Foresight*, *Centurion*, *Winsby* and *Maidstone*. This left Blake with eleven vessels. The time was 8 a.m.

With the exception of the two shots, fired probably by the *Plymouth* who had not heard Stayner's orders, the frigates anchored in the face of a heavy fire from the towering galleons. 'I stood' said Stayner, 'upon the forecastle to seek a good berth for the better doing of our work: I perceived I could get in between the Admiral and the Vice-Admiral, to our great advantage, which I did – we went as near as we could with safety, and were within pistol-shot of the Admiral and the Vice-Admiral, and a little more of the Rear: they were all great ships that rode near the Castle – the Spaniards firing so thick from the ships and shore put us into some confusion for want of due care in the commanders to prevent it'. The tall bulky galleons, by the irony of fate, served to shelter Stayner. 'The Admiral and Vice-Admiral, whom I could have first sent going, but they were my barricades for the Castle'.[33] The intrepid Smith had taken the *Lyme* into the thickest of the fight, and 'first began the dispute – and did much to further the victory'.[34] But the stoutly built galleons were capable of enduring a prolonged battering. It was not until the superior gunnery of the frigates had either silenced them, or forced them to strike, that Blake, anticipating the danger to Stayner of becoming an open target for the land batteries, decided to come into action himself. Through rifts in the smoke he saw that some of the frigates, having no immediate foe, were already warping themselves off, while others were trying either to secure prizes or to set them on fire. So between 11 and 12 o'clock, he entered with the rest of the fleet and posted himself to seaward of Stayner's division. Stayner had got his warps ready to tow his ship out, and then fired, according to his own account, three or four broadsides into the Vice-Admiral, which at once caught fire and blew up. He then hove a little further and fired into the Admiral and she too blew up. All that could be seen of her was the carved work upon her stern, floating upon the sea. Stayner then hove away as fast as he could 'apeak upon our anchor'.[35]

At this point there comes a serious conflict of evidence, not noticed by previous writers. Thomas Lurting, boatswain of the *Bristol*, in a tract entitled 'The fighting sailor turned peaceable

Christian' (he afterwards became a Quaker) writes thus: 'the wind
blew very right upon the shore, and we coming in, in a later squadron, went under our General's stern, to know where we should
be, and were answered where we could get room; so we ran in,
but could get no room to bring up our ship: so we went astern all
our ships, and the smoke being somewhat abated, we found ourselves to be within half a cable's length of the Vice-Admiral . . .
and not a cable's length of the Admiral, . . . and within musket-
shot of some forts and breastworks: when we had brought up
our ship, we were about half a cable's length from the Vice-
Admiral'. The captain ordered him to make all ready, or to veer
nearer the galleons; 'for I will' said he, 'be on board the Vice-
Admiral'. As Lurting veered, so did the foe until he was within
musket-shot of the shore. A hawser was got out, a spring put on
the cable, then the *Bristol* lay across the enemy hawse, at a musket-
shot distance. All the guns were run out on the side opposite the
enemy, twenty-eight in number. With the second broadside a shot
fell into his powder room, and she blew up, 'not a man escaping'.
The Spanish Admiral was 'about to serve us, as we had served his
Vice-Admiral' but, with the *Bristol*'s third broadside, all the crew
jumped overboard, and instantly she too blew up. This was at
2 p.m. The *Bristol* then dealt with a small castle, now unmasked,
'and in a short time made them weary of it'. She was now so far
into the bay that St Philip's Castle could only bring two or three
guns to bear upon her, but did little damage.[36]

It would seem that it was the *Bristol*, and not the *Speaker*,
that sank the Admirals. Stayner had probably hoped to repeat his
former exploit and secure prizes. He admits that he could have
sunk the Spaniards first, but excused himself by saying they protected him from the castle. In his letter to Mountagu of May,
1658, he admitted that he secured £2,000 from his prizes in 1656.
This may be why, in his account to the King, in 1660, he tried
to conceal his real intention by claiming to have sunk the Admirals
himself. This is, of course, mere conjecture to try and explain
the conflict of evidence. But Lurting's account seems, however,
to be more circumstantial, and there appears to be no reason why
he should have invented it.

Stayner now became the target of the increasingly unmasked
fire of the defences. He suffered severely from their concentrated
shot. Not only did his damaged ships need all his attention, but

he had also lost control of his squadron. His captains were busily engaged in securing the five unsunk galleons. The *Plymouth*, *Worcester* and *Maidstone* each had one at her stern, while Bourne, in the *Swiftsure*, had one that the *Bridgwater* had left to him, while she took another, 'all full of goods' as Stayner bewailed.[37] Blake at once asserted his authority. He sent orders to burn the galleons. Three times he had to repeat them before the reluctant captains would obey. One prize was already in flames, fired by her crew.[38] He realised that to bring out his ships with an inshore wind would be difficult enough, but to have flaming galleons amidst them was a danger to be prevented at all costs. The heavier metal of his guns had silenced most of the defences. He resolved therefore to complete the action by destroying the smaller galleons. Under cover of the great ships' guns, with their smoke blowing in thick clouds into the face of the enemy, driven on by the inshore wind, Blake sent off his ships' boats to burn them. Lurting gives a stirring account of how this was done. In a long-boat he went to board a galleon lying inshore, hoping that her crew had deserted her. Within a cable's length of her, her crew suddenly jumped up and fired several guns at him, but the shots went overhead. After burning her he returned, pursued by small and great shot, which came close, but did him no harm.

After the smoke had cleared, he saw three galleons within musket-shot of the *Bristol*, fifty yards from the shore. He took a pinnace with seven or eight men, and under cover of smoke from the *Bristol*'s guns, he boarded a galleon whose crew had fled. He fired her, and the flames set alight the other two. Beaten back by the heat of the roaring fires, Lurting had to retreat. In the excitement the *Bristol* forgot to give him covering smoke. 'The breast-works then having full sight of us, discharged a volley of fifty or sixty small shot, and killed two of our men, shot a third in the back, and I sat close to him that was shot in the back between him and shore, and received no harm'.[39] Weale, too, thirsting for 'a desperate enterprise, as in landing or firing ships' gratified his desire by taking a five-oared yawl, and firing a galleon that was aground. He had one man wounded, and another in a pinnace that was sent to his aid.[40]

Between three and four o'clock the task was completed. Only two of the galleons showed their masts above water, and Blake gave the order to withdraw. Stayner was severely mauled, for the

Speaker had holes between wind and water, four feet long and three feet wide. Hides were nailed over them, with butts along the sides to keep her from sinking. She had eight feet of water in her, and the pumps and bailing barely kept her afloat. Her masts threatened to fall, her main yard was shot away, and her top main-mast was shot by the board. She had not a whole rope or sail overhead, only a sprit sail and a spritsail topsail. Ships riding near the shore, sorely maimed, needed to be warped off, while others were driven into the bay by the wind, and one of the best frigates struck.[41] 'The enemy meanwhile had put fresh men into the forts, and from them and the Castle continually playing upon us, till about seven of the clock at night, every ship and vessel be-longing to the fleet were, by the hand of God, got safe out of command'.[42]

The *Bristol* came within three of four lengths of St Philip's Castle, which opened fire on her, but she was so near that the shot went overhead 'and did us little harm, only in our rigging: and I' wrote Lurting, 'was on the clue of the main-tack, getting the main-tack on board, and a shot cut the bolt-rope a little above my head'. Small wonder that he described it 'as the fourth deliver-ance in six hours time'.[43]

Blake now sent the *Swiftsure* to tow out the *Speaker*, but 'they being in such a hurry, the shot flying thick, they cut loose, and we rid by ourselves'. Every gun was brought to bear on her. 'They paid us extremely' wrote Stayner, 'so we rid till the sun went down: then the wind came off shore, and we set those pieces of sail we had, and cut away the anchor'. With her guns still defiantly blazing, the *Speaker* drifted out of the bay. 'Just as we passed by the great Castle, either by our shot or some accident among them-selves, there was a great quantity of powder blown up. After that they never fired one gun more at us'. Hardly had the *Speaker* got out than all her masts crashed down one after another. The *Plymouth*, standing in to her aid, took her in tow, while the fleet's boats brought carpenters and seamen to repair her.[44]

But the weary Blake did not spare himself. Instead he drew up a letter to Cromwell, which unfortunately is not complete. 'We resolved to attack them, though they were close along the shore, which was lined with musketeers and commanded by a Castle and six or seven forts. Yet in four hours time they were beaten, and all the ships driven on shore, except the Admiral and Vice-

Admiral, which resisted most: but by 2 p.m. one was fired and
the other blew up, and by evening all the rest were fired, except
two that were sunk ... to complete the mercy, our own ships got
off well, though some were maimed, and had to be warped off:
and the wind blew right into the Bay, and the forts and Castle
continued to play upon us. We had only fifty slain and 120
wounded ... to God be all the glory.'[45]

So miraculous seemed the withdrawal that legend at once got
to work. 'The wind blew so strong into the bay, that many
despaired of getting out again: but God's Providence was miracu-
lously seen in causing the wind upon the sudden to veer about to
the S.W. (a thing not known in years before),' which brought
Blake and his fleet safe to sea again.[46] Clarendon repeated the story[47]
and even Nelson adopted it.[48] Since the Armada Englishmen had
come to believe that theologically the wind was stoutly Protestant.
Yet this article of faith denied to Blake and his seamen their skill
and seamanship. For the truth is otherwise. Two days were spent
in repairing the damaged vessels, some ten of them. 'Indifferently
well', says the official account, 'for present security, which we had
no sooner done, but the wind veered to the S.W. (which is rare
among those islands) and lasted long enough to bring us to our
former station near Cape St Mary, where we arrived the 2 May
following'.[49] A careless reader, wrote Sir Charles Firth, 'transferred
the incident from the voyage to the battle, and it became one of
the consecrated fictions of history'.[50]

Blake reached Lagos on 6 May, and Captain Storey in the
Hampshire was sent off with Blake's letter of 20 April to Cromwell.
In the evening the *Speaker* and the *Fairfax* followed him. By the
11th Blake was back at Lisbon, and after refitting the fleet again
was cruising off Cadiz.[51]

On 28 May Thurloe read the relation of the battle to Parliament.
'The Captain that brought the news' he said, 'was in the action
and said that it was the hardest service that ever was. The enemy
thought themselves so secure that they wished the whole cause
between us and Spain had depended upon this. The silver was all
unladen and on shore, but some of the goods were taken. Not a
ship was left but all were burnt or sunk. Though we received no
benefit from it, yet certainly the enemy never had a greater loss.
It is the Lord's doing and the glory be His.'[52]

This surprising and overwhelming success, unexpected and

undreamed of, left the members silent for a moment. Then Strickland moved for a Day of Thanksgiving, which was fixed for Wednesday 3 June. Blake was voted a jewel, worth £500, as a token of national gratitude. Some wished to add a sum of money, as a member had heard from Blake's kinsmen that the Admiral had saved nothing by the service, but had spent of his own estate in it. But the Speaker reminded the House that Fairfax had only received a jewel of like worth for his victory at Naseby. Storey was then voted £100 for bringing the news, and it was proposed that every captain should get a medal worth £10, but this was not approved. Another wished Stayner to have a jewel worth £200, but it was objected that this would slight the other officers, and would lead to trouble in the fleet. Cromwell had no such scruples and knighted Stayner as soon as he arrived.[53]

On 10 June Cromwell wrote to Blake. 'We cannot but take notice also how eminently it hath pleased God to make use of you in this service: assisting you with wisdom in the conduct and carriage in the execution, and have sent you a small jewel, as a testimony of our own and the Parliament's good acceptance of your carriage in this action. We are also informed that the officers and men of the fleet, carried themselves with much honesty and courage: and we are considering of a way to show our acceptance thereof'.[54] The jewel consisted of a portrait of Cromwell, set in crystal and gold, surrounded with forty-six diamonds.[55] In view of the State's finances, it is probable that 'chill penury repressed his noble rage' and that the officers and men got nothing.

With the letter were sent instructions. Blake was to bring home the fleet 'before the winter season', and Stoakes, with fourteen ships, was to continue to ply off Cadiz, while five frigates were to be sent into the Straits 'to ply up and down, for the preservation of trade, and also for offending the enemy'. The commander of this squadron was to treat with Tunis, or other places on the Barbary coast, 'for the settling of enmity and commerce between then and this Commonwealth'. Blake was to provide these ships with such provisions as he could spare. The letter was probably prompted by the arrival, on 20 May, of a special ship that brought the news that Blake was only expected to live for a few days.[56]

But Blake had recovered from what was probably a reaction after the strain of Santa Cruz. He was tough and resilient. For on 8 June he arranged with the Duke of Medina-Celi for an exchange of prisoners. One had been sent ashore, and on board were 'others of a somewhat better quality'. The Duke however detained two English prisoners on the ground that they were 'incapable' prisoners of war. Blake nevertheless insisted upon their release.[57] Two days later he sailed, after a Council of War, for Sallee, leaving Bourne to watch before Cadiz; for Cromwell's letter of 10 June naturally had not reached him. Here the mere appearance of his squadron induced the Moors to resume the negotiations broken off in August 1656. All the English prisoners were redeemed and a treaty of peace was signed. Blake had concluded his last task, and by 26 June he was again before Cadiz.[58]

In his absence, four frigates, the *Providence, Centurion, Foresight* and *Nantwich*, somewhere about 19 June, had chased ashore the *Flying Fame* of Amsterdam. She was making for Cadiz from the Canaries. With the aid of an ebb tide they got her off again. In her company had been two other Dutchmen, which escaped into St Lucar. She had managed to land most of her silver in boats, while twelve of her crew had leaped overboard and got ashore at Huelva.[59] The Venetian Ambassador says there were 300 aboard, nearly all officers, who were coming to Spain to take up new commissions. Most of the money remaining on board was looted by the English seamen. Blake released the ship, but detained the passengers as prisoners.[60] Thurloe, writing to Henry Cromwell, on 8 July, enclosed a letter from Blake, saying there were 300 men aboard, and 60,000 pieces of eight.[61]

His reputation now stood at its highest. Maynard, writing to Thurloe, on 8 June, gave a vivid picture of the effects of the Santa Cruz victory. The loss of the treasure had dealt a mortal blow to the Spanish military operations. In May their troops had invaded Portugal on two fronts, and the conquest of that country seemed certain. But by July it was impossible either to pay the troops or to feed them. The infantry simply melted away, not 3,000 men remaining with the colours. With only the Queen as regent for the infant King, Portugal could hardly have kept its independence. 'Tis God's great good to these people' wrote Maynard, 'that preserved them from the fury of the Spaniards, for they have hitherto taken no course to oppose them: for there hath been nothing but emulations among the nobility, thwarting and contradicting one another'. His contempt for them was great. 'A petty people, who could not have subsisted, but would all have been trampled under their enemies feet this summer, if his Highness's fleet had not kept them from invasion by sea'.[62]

On 29 June the *Nonsuch* brought Cromwell's letter of 10 June to Blake, and the fleet sailed for Travila. Blake thus had his last dim view of the city before which he had so long and so wearily kept his vigil. On 9 July the fleet sailed northwards. In the evening Stoakes took leave of his old commander with a salute of thirteen guns, to which Blake replied with one, while Bourne was given a farewell salute of eleven, which Blake cut short with one gun, probably as a reminder to preserve powder. As night began to fall the fleet parted. Blake in the sea-worn *George*, with the *Swiftsure*, *Newbury*, *Worcester*, *Bridgwater*, *Newcastle*, *Foresight*, *Maidstone*, *Colchester*, *Marigold* and *Nonsuch* ketch, left for England, while Stoakes returned to Travila to take over his command.[63]

On 11 July Blake was at Lisbon, where Maynard was alarmed at his condition. 'The General is very weak: I beseech God to strengthen him'.[64] Daily he grew weaker. On 6 August he was off the Lizard where his failing sight for the last time saw the country he had served so long and faithfully. Feeling his end to be near he summoned Bourne and Creed, his secretary, with Clarke his ship's captain. He bade them with the *George*, *Newbury* and *Colchester*, to bear up for Plymouth, while the rest went on. He was 'very desirous to be ashore – for the settling of his estate'.[65] Always his thoughts were for his men, never for himself. So he charged them to remind the Commissioners 'of the sad condition of the fleet we left behind'. Then he gave verbal order to the Purser to make six seamen, among whom were his two servants, James Knowles and Nicholas Bartlett, midshipmen.[66]

Next morning, 7 August, 'as we came to the entering of the Sound, death seized him, and he departed this life about 10 o'clock in the morning'.[67] 'He had his memory even to the last moment and he continued faithful to his death.'[68] It was as if the sea had claimed him as belonging to her by dedication, and would not relinquish him to the land. But his body was not committed to the deep. Instead it was taken ashore, where it was embalmed by his old surgeon and comrade, Matthew Lynde, for which he received a fee of £30.[69] The bowels were buried before the Chancel of St Andrew's Church, under a stone bearing the inscription, 'Admiral Blake, died 7 August, 1657.'[70] The body was then encased in a sheet of lead and taken back to the *George*. The three ships then sailed for the Thames where, as Commissioner Hatsell supposed, 'he will have a very honourable interment, befitting a person of his worth, who indeed setting some human frailties aside (from which the best of men are not free) may be ranked with most that have gone before him in our age'. If only Cromwell could have whispered in his ear, 'warts and all', he might have done much to complete Blake's portrait.[71]

On arrival at Gravesend, on the 17th, Mountagu with a kindly thought of sympathy for the bereaved kinsfolk, ordered the body to be transferred to the *Colchester*, commanded by Samuel Blake, Robert's nephew, to be taken to Greenwich on the 19th. Here it lay in State in the Great Hall of the Queen's House.[72]

The council ordered that he should be buried in Westminster Abbey, and the funeral was fixed for 4 September, according to the arrangements for that of Deane.[73] A great procession of barges was formed on the Thames, led by trumpeters, guidons and banners, and followed by the Lords of the council, the Lord Mayor and the city companies. The corpse, with its trappings of jaumbes, gauntlets, target, mantle, helmet, crest and sword, was solemnly borne up the river. In the van was the barge from which floated the Great Standard of the Admiralty; and in the rear was a barge with Blake's own regiment of foot. To the watchers on the river side the trumpeters proclaimed the advent of Blake's last journey. The body was landed and borne to the Abbey between two ranks of soldiers, behind whom stood the vast silent mourning crowds. To the sound of volleys fired by all the regiments in London, Blake was buried in Henry the Seventh's Chapel.[73] Here he lay until 9 September, 1661, when together with the bodies of Cromwell, Deane, Pym and others his was disinterred[74] and thrown into a pit, somewhere on the north side of the Abbey towards the West End. On the same day that Blake died, so did Richard Badiley, comrades in death as in life.[75]

The nation thus honoured Blake, who surely stands second only to Cromwell among the great men of the Commonwealth and, as an Admiral, only to be surpassed by Nelson. For he is in a very real sense one of the founders of the navy, and an inspiration to the silent service. Before himself he ever set the 'service of this Commonwealth'. A deeply religious man he saw himself as called of God, a humble servant raised up for great purposes. His fleet proved to be Cromwell's most powerful Ambassador for peace. He was ever against the unnecessary shedding of blood. At Dunster he had learned from the 'extraordinary clemency' of Sir Thomas Fairfax that the 'price of time and blood' could be avoided by generous negotiation. This he accompanied by a due respect for the feelings of those who had yielded, so that their self-respect was not offended. By carefully observing all the correctness of diplomacy he left them without any feeling of resentment, for he acknowledged their national sovereignty and pride. 'Peace hath its victories no less renowned than war'. Those who rejected his terms soon learned the power of his fleet, held unobtrusively in reserve. Against them he used the weapon of surprise. They were left guessing as to when, where, and how he could attack. For surprise is one of the marks of genius in battle.

England was fortunate in having his flexible and adaptable mind to grapple with the new problem which confronted the navy. He had trained up a brilliant galaxy of Captains and Admirals, Jordan, Bourne, Lawson, Penn, Stayner, Myngs and Mountagu himself who were to share in working it out. The broadside had made obsolete the old tactic of line abreast. For the problem was now how to manoeuvre the fleet so as to make full use of its enormous gun power. Deane had taught his gunners to fire more accurately and faster than the Dutch. The answer, slowly and gradually evolved, was that of line ahead, or, to put it more accurately, to come into action on a line of bearing parallel to the line of the enemy. This was to take time and understanding before the more conservative captains could grasp and adapt themselves to it. At the Gabbard some of them neither understood nor obeyed the new fighting instructions, so that Monck wisely reverted to the old method of fighting in groups, led by the Admiral. But at Scheveningen he boldly used the new tactic to defeat Tromp in the battle in which the gallant Dutchman met his death. The new tactic, pioneered by Blake and his Admirals, was to revolutionise the fighting technique of the navy. This priceless gift they handed on to future generations of English seamen.

'One who desired no greater worldly happiness than to be accounted honest and faithful in his employment'. So runs his memorial tablet in Westminster Abbey. For 'the service of this Commonwealth' was the guiding star of Blake's life. So in seven years of almost continual employment at sea he wore himself to death. Though suffering constant pain from his old wound, and afflicted with scurvy and dropsy, his indomitable spirit overcame the weakness of his body. So he turned a blind eye to the beckoning signal of, as Sir Henry Newbolt puts it, 'the senior flag of all that floats, and his name is Admiral Death'. Instead by sheer determination of will he completed his allotted task. At Sallee the sight of his squadron was sufficient to decide the Dey, mindful of Blake's exploit at Porto Farina, to sign a Treaty of peace, and to allow Blake to redeem all the English prisoners which he held.

Most of the work of this great seaman was done in distant waters, so that the magnitude of his achievement was hidden from his countrymen, so Sir Henry Newbolt rightly places him among those great Admirals who

> 'Fought to build England above the tide
>   Of war and windy fate,
> And passed content: leaving to us the pride
>   Of lives obscurely great.'

Blake's Will

*

THE last will and testament of me, Robert Blake, written with my own hand as followeth: First, I bequeath my soul unto the hands of my most merciful Redeemer, the Lord Jesus Christ, by Him to be presented to His heavenly Father, pure and spotless, through the washing of His blood which He shed for the remission of my sins, and, after a short separation from the body to be again united with the same by the power of his Eternal Spirit, and so to be for ever with the Lord.

Item, unto the town of Bridgwater I give £100 to be distributed amongst the poor thereof at the discretion of Humphrey Blake, my brother, and of the Mayor for the time being.

Item, unto the town of Taunton I give £100 to be distributed amongst the poor of both parishes at the discretion of Samuel Perry, once my Lieutenant-Colonel, and Mr George Newton, minister of the gospel there, and of the Mayor for the time being.

Item, I give unto Humphrey Blake, my brother, the manor of Crandon-cum-Puriton, with all the rights thereto appertaining, to him and his heirs for ever.

Item, I give unto my brother, Dr Wm Blake £300.

Item, unto my brother George Blake I give £300, also to my brother Nicholas I give £300.

Item, unto my brother Benjamin I give my dwelling-house, situate in St Mary's Street, Bridgwater, with the garden and appurtenances, as also my other house, thereunto adjoining, purchased of the widow Coxe; likewise I give unto him all the claims I have in eleven acres of meadow or pasture (more or less) lying in the village of Hamp, in the Parish of Bridgwater, lately in the possession of the widow Vincombe, deceased.

Item, unto my sister Bridget Bowdich, of Chard Stock, I give £100, and to her children, of the body of Henry Bowdich aforesaid, I give the sum of £900, to be disposed of among them according to the discretion of Humphrey, William, George, Nicholas and Benjamin Blake, aforesaid, my brothers, or any three of them.

Item, unto my brother Smythes,* goldsmith, in Cheapside, I give the sum of £100.

Item, unto my nephew, Robert Blake, son to Samuel Blake, my brother, deceased, I give the gold chain bestowed on me by the late Parliament of England, also all claims I have in an annuity of £20, payable out of the farm at Pawlett.

Item, unto my nephew, Samuel Blake, younger son to Samuel, my brother, deceased, I give £200.

Item, unto Sarah Quarrell, daughter of my late niece, Sarah Quarrell, by her husband Peter Quarrell, now dwelling in Taunton, I give the sum of £200 to be disposed of for the benefit of the said Sarah Quarrell, according to the discretion of Humphrey, Nicholas and Benjamin Blake, my brothers aforesaid.

Item, unto my cousin, John Blake, son unto my brother Nicholas, I give £100 (Note cousin should be nephew).

Item, unto my cousin John Avery of Pawlett, once a soldier with me in Taunton Castle, I give £50.

Item, unto Thomas Blake, son of my cousin William Blake, once commander of the *Tresco* frigate, deceased, now aboard of the *Centurion* frigate in the service, I give £50.

Item, all my plate, linen, bedding, with all my provisions, aboard the ship *Naseby*, I give unto my nephews, Robt and Samuel Blake, aforesaid, and unto my nephew John Blake, aforesaid, to be divided by them by even and equal parts.

Item, unto the Negro, called Domingo, my servant, I give £50, to be disposed of by my aforesaid nephew, Capt Robt Blake and Capt Thomas Adams, for his better education in the knowledge and fear of God.

Item, unto my servants James Knowles and Nicholas Bartlett, I give to each of them £10.

Item, unto the widow Owen, the relict of Mr Owen, Minister, I give £10.

Item, unto Eleanor Potter, widow, I give £10.

All the rest of my goods and chattels I do give and bequeath unto George, Nicholas and Benjamin Blake, my brothers aforesaid, and also to Alexander Blake, my brother, to be equally divided amongst them, whom I do appoint and ordain to be the executors of this my last Will and Testament.

Signed and sealed aboard the *Naseby*, 13 March, 1655, in Ellens

* Step-brother.

Road in the presence of Roger Cuttance, M. Lynde, John Bourne, Antho Earning.

Note: Lynde was the ship's doctor on the *George*. He embalmed Blake's body, for which he received a fee of £30. Add. Mss 9300.359. Nicholas Bartlett, his servant, was one of the six seamen who the General, before he died, gave verbal order to the Purser to be made midshipmen. S.P.D.18. 170, 65.

APPENDIX 2

Ship Lists of Blake's Fleets

*

Ship Lists of Blake's Fleets printed in the *Mariner's Mirror* Volume 24, Number 4. October 1938. Compiled by Dr R. C. Anderson. Pages 429-433.

Action off Dover 19 May 1652. p. 430.

SHIPS	GUNS	CAPTAIN
James	60	Blake, General
		John Gilson Capt.
Victory	55	Lionel Lane
Garland	44	John Gibbs
Speaker	52	John Coppin
Ruby	42	Anthony Houlding
Sapphire	38	Robert Moulton Jun.
Worcester	42	Chas. Thorrowgood
Star	24	Robt. Saunders
Portsmouth	36	Wm. Brandley
Martin	12	
Mermaid	24	Rich. Stayner
Reuben		
Three small craft.		
Andrew	56	Nehemiah Bourne
		Rear-Admiral
Triumph	62	Wm. Penn (ashore)
Fairfax	52	John Lawson
Entrance	44	
Centurion	36	
Adventure	36	Andrew Ball
Assurance	40	Ben. Blake
Greyhound	20	Henry Southwood
Seven Brothers (m)*	26	Robt. Land

The Kentish Knock

Sovereign	100	Nicholas Reed
Resolution	88	Robt. Blake Gen.

James	66	Wm. Penn
		Vice-Admiral
Triumph	62	Ben. Blake
Andrew	56	Nehemiah Bourne
		Rear-Admiral
Vanguard	56	Wm. Haddock
Speaker	54	John Coppin
Lion	50	Chas. Saltonstall
Garland	44	Robt. Batten
Convertine	44	
Ruby	42	Anth. Houlding
Foresight	42	Sam Howett
Diamond	42	Roger Martin
Advice	42	Geo. Deakins
President	40	Wm. Graves
Pelican	40	Joseph Jordan
Nonsuch	40	John Mildmay
Assistance	40	John Bourne
Portsmouth	38	Wm. Brandley
Dragon	38	John Stoakes
Assurance	33	Robt. Saunders
Hound	36	John Golding
Guinea	34	Edmund Curtis
Convert	32	Ricd. Johnson?
Sampson	26	Edmund Button?
Advantage	26	Wm. Beck
Falmouth	26	John Jeffries?
Mary Flyboat	24	Wm. Younger
Nightingale	22	John Humphreys
Warwick	22	Wm. Godfrey
Little President	22	Thos. Sparling
Pearl	22	John Cadman?
Cignet	22	Phil. Holland
Paradox	12	
Renown	10	Nath. Mead
London (m)	40	John Stevens
Richard and Martha (m)	40	Eustace Smith
Anthony Bonaventure (m)	36	Walter Hoxon
Lisbon Merchant (m)	34	Simon Bailey?
Hercules (m)	34	Zach. Browne
Culpepper (m)	30	
Prudent Mary (m)	26	Ben. Salmon
Cullen (m)	26	Tho. Gilbert?
Exchange (m)	26	Hen. Tiddiman?

Martha (m)	25	Stephen Jay
Golden Dove (m)	24	Henry Toope?
Acorn (m)	22	
Gift Pink (m)	—	
11 Merchantmen		

Dungeness 30 November 1652

Triumph	60	Robert Blake, Gen.
Victory	60	Lionel Lane
Vanguard	58	John Mildmay
Fairfax	56	John Lawson
Speaker	54	John Gilson
Laurel	50	John Taylor
Worcester	44	Anthony Young
Garland	44	Robert Batten
Entrance	43	Edmund Chapman
Lion	42	Charles Saltonstall
Convertine	42	
Foresight	42	Samuel Howett
Dragon	40	John Stoakes
Fortune	36	
Hound	35	
Sapphire	34	William Hill
Princess Maria	33	
Mary flyboat	32	William Younger
Waterhound	30	John Goulding
Dolphin	30	William Badiley
Advantage	26	William Beck
Swan	22	Richard Newberry
Greyhound	20	Henry Southwood
Hannibal (m)	44	Francis Barham
Anthony Bonaventure (m)	36	Walter Hoxton
Lisbon Merchant (m)	34	Simon Bailey?
Loyalty (m)	34	John Limbery
Culpepper (m)	30	
Cullen (m)	28	Thomas Gilbert?
Prudent Mary (m)	26	Ben. Salmon
Samuel (m)	26	
Martha (m)	25	Stephen Jay
Katherine (m)	24	William Redgacke
Exchange (m)	24	Henry Tiddiman
Acorn (m)	22	

Possibly some more merchantmen.

Portland 18-20 February, 1653

Ship	Guns	Commander
Triumph	62	Blake & Deane. Ads. Red.
Fairfax	56	Andrew Ball Capt.
		John Lawson V.A. Red.
Laurel	48	Samuel Howett R.A. Red.
Vanguard	56	Monck (Gen.) White
		John Mildmay Capt.
Rainbow	58	James Peacocke. V.A. White
Diamond	42	Roger Martin R.A. White
Speaker	56	William Penn Ad. Blue
Victory	60	Lionel Lane V.A. Blue
Assistance	40	John Bourne R.A. Blue
Lion	50	John Lambert?
Worcester	50	George Dakins
Kentish	46	James Reynolds
Sussex	46	Roger Cuttance
Convertine	44	Anthony Zoyne?
Entrance	44	William Goodson
Foresight	44	Richard Stayner?
Ruby	42	Anthony Houlding
Advice	44	John Day
Centurion	42	Walter Wood
Nonsuch	40	Thomas Penrose
Tiger	40	Gabriel Saunders?
Pelican	40	John Stoakes
President	40	Thomas Graves
Success	38	William Kendall
Adventure	38	Robert Nixon
Sapphire	38	William Hill
Mary prize	37	William Tunick
Amity	36	Henry Packe
Dragon	36	John Seaman
Assurance	36	Phillip Holland?
Providence	30	John Pearce
Guinea	30	Edmund Curtis
Pearl	26	James Cadman
Nightingale	26	John Humphrey
Cignet	20	Robert Fuller
Discovery	20	Thomas Marriott
Paradox	14	
Martin	14	John Vesey?
Merlin	12	
Nicodemus	10	William Ledgant

Raven	38	Robert Taylor
Hound	36	Jonathan Hide
Gift	34	Thomas Salmon
Fortune	32	William Tatnell
Waterhound	32	Giles Shelley
Sampson	32	Edmund Button
Tulip	32	Joseph Cubitt
Oak	32	John Edwin
Convert	32	Phillip Gething?
Dolphin	30	
Plover	26	Robert Robinson?
Advantage	26	William Beck?
Falmouth	26	
Duchess	24	Richard Suffield
Prosperous (m)	44	John Barker
Richard and Martha (m)	44	Eustace Smith
Reformation (m)	40	Anthony Earning
Lisbon Merchant (m)	38	Simon Bailey
Thomas and William (m)	36	John Jefferson
Angel (m)		
Thomas and Lucy (m)	34	Andrew Rand
Ann and Joyce (m)	34	William Pile
Charles (m)	33	Robert Knox
Ann Percy (m)	32	Thomas Hare
Brazil Frigate (m)	30	Thomas Heath
Exchange (m)	30	Henry Tiddiman
Giles (m)	30	Henry Toope
Elizabeth and Anne (m)	30	Richard Langford
Ruth (m)	30	Edward Thompson?
Cullen (m)	26	Thomas Gilbert
Roebuck		John Rawlins?
Katherine (m)	24	Wm. Redgacke
Providence (m)	24	
Chase (m)	22	Ben. Gunston?
Eagle (m)		
Mary ketch		Corbet

* (m) denotes merchantman

The list of the thirteen ships that Blake took with him to the Gabbard is omitted here but may be found in *Letters*, p. 216

Abbreviations

A.B.B.	A. H. Powell, *The Ancient Borough of Bridgwater*, Bridgwater, [1907]
Abbott	Wilbur C. Abbott, *The Writings and Speeches of Oliver Cromwell*, Harvard U.P., [1937–47]
Add. MSS.	Additional Manuscripts, British Museum
A.H.R.	*Army Historical Review*, Journal of the Army Historical Research Society, December, [1925]
Bath MSS.	Manuscripts of the Marquis of Bath at Longleat
Bayley	A. R. Bayley, *The Great Civil War in Dorset 1642–1660*, Taunton, [1910]
Brandt	Geeraert Brandt the Elder, *Het Leven en bedryf van den Heere Michiel de Ruiter* . . , Amsterdam, [1687]
Burnet	Bishop Burnet, *History of my own Time*, 2 vols., London, [1724]
Carte MSS.	Carte Manuscripts. Bodleian Library, Oxford
Carte	Thomas Carte, *A collection of Original Letters and Papers concerning the Affairs of England 1641–1660 found among the Duke of Ormonde's Papers*, 2 vols., London, [1739]
C.A.M.	Committee for the Advancement of Money [1642–1656: 3 vols. H.M.S.O. 1888]
Chevalier	*Journal de Jean Chevalier*, ed. J. A. Messervy, St Helier, [1914] (Société Jersiaise)
C.J.	House of Commons Journals
Clarendon	Edward Hyde, Earl of Clarendon, *The History of the Rebellion*, re-edited W. D. Macray, 6 vols., [1888 etc.]
Clarendon S.P.	*Calendar of Clarendon State Papers* etc. (vol. 2 ed. by W. D. Macray), 6 vols., [1872 etc]
Clarke Papers	*The Clarke Papers*, ed. C. H. Firth, Camden Society, 4 vols., [1891–1901]
Coate	Mary Coate, *Cornwall in the Great Civil War and Interregnum, 1642–1660*, Oxford, [1933]
Colliber	Samuel Colliber, *Columna Rostrata*, London, [1727]
Corbett	Sir Julian Corbett, *England in the Mediterranean*, 1603–1713, 2 vols., London, [1904]
C.S.P.D.	Calendar of State Papers Domestic, England

C.S.P.D. Scotland — Calendar of State Papers Domestic, Scotland

Curtis — C. D. Curtis, *Robert Blake, General at Sea*, Taunton, [1934]

Deane — J. B. Deane, *The Life of Richard Deane*, London, [1870]

D.S.A. — *Defeat of the Spanish Armada*, Navy Records Society, 2 vols., [1894]

Documents — *Documents relating to the Civil War*, ed. J. R. Powell and E. K. Timings, Navy Records Society, [1963]

D.W. — *The First Dutch War*, Navy Records Society, 6 vols., [1899–1930]

Fanshawe — *Memoirs of Lady Fanshawe, wife of Sir Richard Fanshawe 1600–72*, ed. Herbert C. Fanshawe, London, [1907]

Firth — Sir Charles Firth, *The Last Years of the Protectorate, 1656–58*, 2 vols., London, [1909]

Gardiner C.W. — S. R. Gardiner, *History of the Civil War*, 4 vols, New Edition, London, [1893]

Gardiner C.P. — S. R. Gardiner, *History of the Commonwealth and Protectorate*, 3 vols., London, [1894–1903]

G.R.O. — Glamorgan Records Office, Cardiff

Guizot — F. P. G. Guizot, *Life of Oliver Cromwell*, tr. A. R. Scoble, New Edition, London, [1860]

Gumble — Thomas Gumble, *The Life of General Moncke*, London, [1671]

H.C.A. — *High Court of Admiralty, Documents relating to the Law and Customs of the Sea*, ed. R. G. Marsden, Navy Records Society, [1915 etc]

Heath — Heath J. *Chronicle* [1676]

Jal — Auguste Jal, *A. du Quesne et la Marine de son temps*, 2 tom. Paris, [1873]

J.R.U.S. — *Journal of the Royal United Services Institution*, vol. 62, [1917]

Letters — *The Letters of Robert Blake*, ed. J. R. Powell, Navy Records Society, [1937]

Lewis — Michael Lewis, *History of the British Navy*, Penguin Books, [1957]

L.P. — Leyborne-Popham Papers, Hist. Mss. Commission, [1899]

Ludlow — *The Memoirs of Edmund Ludlow*, ed. C. H. Firth, 2 vols, Oxford, [1894]

Lurting — Thomas Lurting, *The Fighting Sailor turned Peaceable Christian*, Leeds, [1816]

Mahan — A. T. Mahan, *The Influence of Seapower upon History*, London, [1890]

R.B.–X

M.M.	*Mariner's Mirror*, Journal of the Nautical Research Society.
Mountagu MSS.	Mountagu Manuscripts, Bodleian Library, Oxford
N.M.M. MSS.	National Maritime Museum, Greenwich, Manuscripts
Nickolls	J. Nickolls, *Original Letters and Papers of State . . . found among the Political Collections of Mr John Milton*, London, [1743]
N. H.	Nicolas, *Despatches and Letters of Lord Nelson 7 Vols.*, [1844]
N.R.S.	Navy Records Society.
Oldmixon	John Oldmixon, *The History and Life of Robert Blake*, [1740]
Oppenheim	M. Oppenheim, *The Administration of the Royal Navy*, London, [1896]
Penn	Granville Penn, *Memorial of the Professional Life and Times of Sir William Penn*, 2 vols, London, [1833]
P.R.L.	*Prince Rupert at Lisbon*, ed. S. R. Gardiner, Camden Society, [1902]
Rawlinson	Rawlinson Manuscripts, Bodleian Library, Oxford.
Rowe	Violet A. Rowe, *Sir Henry Vane the Younger*, London, [1970]
S.A.P.	Somerset Archaeological Proceedings, [1887]
Sloane MSS.	Sloane Manuscripts, 1431, British Museum.
S.N.R.	Society for Nautical Research
Spalding	T. A. Spalding, *The Life of Richard Badiley*, Westminster, [1899]
Sprigge	Joshua Sprigge, *Anglia Rediviva*, London, [1647]
S.P. Barbary	State Papers, Barbary
S.P.D.	State Papers Domestic
S.P. Ven.	State Papers Venetian
State Trials	*A Complete Collection of State Trials*, ed. William Cobbett M.P., vol. 4., [1809]
Stayner	Naval Miscellany 2, Navy Records Society, vol. 40, [1912]
Tanner	Tanner Manuscripts, Bodleian Library, Oxford
Thurloe	State Papers of John Thurloe, Ed. T. Birch 4 vols., [1942]
T.T.E.	*Catalogue of Books and Pamphlets etc. relating to the Civil War, Commonwealth and Restoration, collected by G. Thomason, 1640–1661*, British Museum, [1908]
U.S.M.	United Services Magazine
Vicars	John Vicars, *Jehovah-Jireh, God in the Mount . . . or England's Parliamentary Chronicle*, 4 parts, London, [1644–6]

Warburton	B. E. G. Warburton, *Memoirs of Prince Rupert and the Cavaliers*, 3 vols., London, [1849]
Weale	*Journal of John Weale*, ed. J. R. Powell in Naval Miscellany, vol. 4, Navy Records Society, [1952]
Wedgwood K.P.	C. V. Wedgwood, *The King's Peace*, London, [1955]
Wedgwood K.W.	C. V. Wedgwood, *The King's War*, London, [1958]
Whitelocke	Bulstrode Whitelocke the Elder, *Memorials of the English Affairs*, A new Edition, London, [1732]
Wood	Anthony Wood, *Athenae Oxonienses* to which are added the *Fasti*, a new edition with continuation by Philip Bliss, 4 vols., London, [1813–20]
Yonge	James Yonge, *The Journal of James Yonge, 1647–1721, Plymouth surgeon*, ed. F. N. L. Poynter, London, [1963]

Notes and References

CHAPTER 1 *The Appearance of the Blakes*

1. Curtis, 175
2. *ibid.*, 1
3. C.S.P.D. Scotland 5., 668
4. Curtis, 176
5. Letters, 19
6. Bridgwater Port Books
7. A.B.B., 210
8. D.S.A., 329
9. A.B.B., 210
10. Oldmixon, 4
11. Wood Fasti, 2., 329
12. Clarendon C.W. 6., 371
13. Oldmixon, 5
14. Letters, 376
15. Curtis, 6
16. *ibid.*, 175
17. Lewis, 74
18. C.S.P.D. 1640, 320
19. Lewis, 74
20. Oldmixon, 6, 8
21. Weale, 108
22. *ibid.*, 121
23. D.W.I., 402
24. Letters, 162
25. M.M. 17., 208
26. Curtis, 13
27. J.R.U.S. Feb., 256
28. M.M. 17., 256

CHAPTER 2 *Blake makes his Appearance at Bristol*

1. Wood, Fasti 2., 367
2. Oldmixon, 8
3. *ibid.*, 9
4. A.H.R. Vol. 4., 183
5. *ibid.*, 183
6. *ibid.*, 184
7. *ibid.*, 187
8. *ibid.*, 188
9. *ibid.*, 189
10. *ibid.*, 189
11. *ibid.*, 190
12. *ibid.*, 192
13. *ibid.*, 192
14. *ibid.*, 190
15. *ibid.*, 196
16. *ibid.*, 194
17. *ibid.*, 197
18. Clarendon 6., 218
19. Documents, 84
20. Wedgwood. K.W., 234
    Coate, 100
21. State Trials vol. 4, 4
22. Oldmixon, 12, 13
23. Letters, 2
24. Wood, 2., 367

CHAPTER 3 *Blake defies Maurice at Lyme*

1. Bayley, 153
2. *ibid.*, 137
3. *ibid.*, 136
4. *ibid.*, 142
5. *ibid.*, 143
6. *ibid.*, 146
7. *ibid.*, 147
8. C.S.P.D. 1644, 137

9. Bayley, 149
10. C.S.P.D. 1644, 147
11. Bayley, 150
12. *ibid.*, 152
13. *ibid.*, 155
14. *ibid.*, 156
15. *ibid.*, 157
16. *ibid.*, 163
17. Documents, 145
18. Bayley, 166
19. Documents, 146
20. *ibid.*, 146
21. Bayley, 168
    E. 51, 9
22. Bayley, 171
    Documents, 155

23. *ibid.*, 148
24. Letters, 22
    Bayley, 177
25. Documents, 150
26. C.S.P.D. 1644, 227, 232
27. Bayley, 185
    Documents, 155
28. Bayley, 185
29. *ibid.*, 187
30. *ibid.*, 187
31. *ibid.*, 187
32. Documents, 153
33. *ibid.*, 186
34. *ibid.*, 154
35. *ibid.*, 157

CHAPTER 4 *Blake holds Taunton*

1. T.T.E. 21, 34
2. Vicars. 3., 285
3. T.T.E. 186, 65
4. C.S.P.D. 1644, 301
5. T.T.E. 284, 34
6. Clarendon 3., 426
7. T.T.E. 256, 24
8. T.T.E. 285, 4
9. *ibid.*, 22, 8
10. *ibid.*, 256, 44
11. Letters, 1
12. T.T.E. 258, 4
13. Vicars 3., 82
14. T.T.E. 258, 7
15. *ibid.*, 158, 11
16. Clarendon 4., 11
17. T.T.E. 288, 34
18. *ibid.*, 277, 14
19. Clarendon S.P. Vol. 1, 1833
20. *ibid.*, 1834
21. Clarendon 4., 15
22. *ibid.*, 17
23. *ibid.*, 15
24. T.T.E. 258, 46
25. *ibid.*, 268, 26

26. *ibid.*, 260, 25
27. Gardiner, C.W. 2., 204
28. Sprigge, 13
29. T.T.E. 281, 10
30. *ibid.*, 258, 6
31. *ibid.*, 281, 10
32. C.S.P.D. 1645, 479
33. Sprigge, 16
34. T.T.E. 285, 10
35. *ibid.*, 284, 10
36. *ibid.*, 284, 9
37. C.S.P.D. 1645, 479
38. T.T.E. 285, 10
39. C.S.P.D. 1645, 479
40. T.T.B. 285, 10
41. *ibid.*, 285, 10
42. Carte 2., 85
43. T.T.E. 285, 11
44. *ibid.*, 285, 10
45. *ibid.*, 260, 39
    ibid., 285, 33
46. C.S.P.D. 1645, 499
    T.T.E. 205, 10
47. Vicars 3., 148
48. T.T.E. 258, 10

49. Vicars 3., 148
50. T.T.E. 258, 40
51. *ibid.*, 284, 11
52. Vicars 3., 146
53. T.T.B. 282, 11
    ibid., 360, 39
54. C.S.P.D. 1645, 499
55. *ibid.*, 506
56. Clarendon 4., 50
57. T.T.E. 662, 4
58. *ibid.*, 287, 5
59. *ibid.*, 285, 3, 19
60. *ibid.*, 262, 10
61. *ibid.*, 262, 10

62. Clarendon 4., 51
63. *ibid.*, 4., 16
64. T.T.E. 292, 10
65. Sprigge, 67
66. *ibid.*, 57
67. *ibid.*, 60–4
68. Abbott. 1., 300
69. Documents, C.W., 207
70. A.B.B., 258
71. T.T.E. 100, 18
72. Abbott, 1., 368
73. Sprigge, 90–6
74. Curtis, 59

CHAPTER 5 *Dunster and After*

1. T.T.E. 315, 25
2. *ibid.*, 266, 19
3. *ibid.*, 266, 22
4. *ibid.*, 315, 4
5. *ibid.*, 266, 32
6. *ibid.*, 366, 34
7. Carte. 1., 16
8. T.T.E. 266, 34
9. *ibid.*, 315, 4
10. Carte. 1., 110
11. T.T.E. 332, 15, 19
12. *ibid.*, 316, 9
13. *ibid.*, 332, 33
14. Letters, 5
15. C.A.M. 2., 815
16. A.B.B., 255
17. Ludlow 1., 133
18. Documents, 260
19. *ibid.*, 284
20. *ibid.*, 288
21. *ibid.*, 289
22. *ibid.*, 291
23. *ibid.*, 296
24. *ibid.*, 297
25. *ibid.*, 311

26. *ibid.*, 316
27. *ibid.*, 330
28. *ibid.*, 334
29. *ibid.*, 336
30. *ibid.*, 337
31. *ibid.*, 340
32. T.T.E. 453, 17
33. Documents, 342
34. *ibid.*, 392
35. *ibid.*, 348
36. Letters, 4
37. Oldmixon, 27
38. Documents, 358
39. *ibid.*, 379
40. T.T.E. 459, 2, 3, 4
41. Documents, 381
42. *ibid.*, 384
43. *ibid.*, 389
44. Clarendon 4., 423
45. Documents, 392
46. *ibid.*, 395
47. Documents, 402
48. *ibid.*, 390
49. *ibid.*, 406

CHAPTER 6 *The Pursuit of Rupert*

1. Tanner 57., 45
   Add. MSS. 3048, 5058
2. Lewis, 88
3. Letters, 48
4. Deane, 38, 40
5. Documents, 406
6. Letters, 20
7. L.P., 11
8. *ibid.*, 12
9. Letters, 20
10. *ibid.*, 29
11. *ibid.*, 22
12. *ibid.*, 22
13. C.S.P.D. 1649–50, 50, 98
14. T.T.E. 527, 104
    ibid., 529, 21
15. *ibid.*, 529, 21
16. Letters, 39
17. L.P., 12
18. Letters, 40
19. Warburton 3., 290
20. G.M.O.,
    Stradling D/Dtd., 13
21. H.C.A. 2., 5
22. Tanner 56., 16
23. M.M. Vol. 14., 327
24. Letters, 72
25. L.P., 17
26. Letters, 72
27. *ibid.*, 43
28. *ibid.*, 44
29. Tanner 56., 66
30. Letters, 44

31. L.P., 24
32. Letters, 73
33. *ibid.*, 73
34. L.P., 40
35. Letters, 49
36. L.P., 41
37. *ibid.*, 35
38. T.T.E. 533, 4
39. Letters, 40
40. L.P., 35
41. Letters, 46
42. C.S.P.D. 1649–50, 326
43. Letters, 46
44. *ibid.*, 47
45. L.P., 47
46. Deane, 412–14
47. C.S.P.D. 1649–50, 379
48. Fanshawe, 398
49. Abbott. 2., 166
50. *ibid.*, 2., 370
51. C.S.P.D. 1649–50, 393
52. *ibid.*, 393
53. *ibid.*, 412
54. *ibid.*, 417
55. *ibid.*, 471
56. Letters, 51
57. *ibid.*, 53
58. Thurloe 1., 134
59. Letters, 51
60. *ibid.*, 50
61. *ibid.*, 53
62. Thurloe 1., 134
63. Letters, 71

CHAPTER 7 *The Pursuit moves to Portugal*

1. Letters, 78
2. *ibid.*, 85
3. P.R.L., 12
4. Letters, 54
5. *ibid.*, 82
6. *ibid.*, 57, 82

7. *ibid.*, 76
8. *ibid.*, 57
9. *ibid.*, 84
10. *ibid.*, 74
11. *ibid.*, 55
12. Warburton, 3., 303

13. Thurloe 1., 143
14. P.R.L. & D.W. 1., 3., 7
    Warburton 3., 304
15. Letters, 58
16. Letters, 85
    Warburton 3., 304
17. Thurloe 1., 145
18. Clarendon 41., 117
19. L.P., 664
20. Letters, 84
21. Sloane Mss. 1039, 115
22. L.P., 65
23. Thurloe 1., 142
24. Letters, 86
25. L.P., 66
26. N.M.M., 9876
27. L.P., 67
28. N.M.M., 9876
29. L.P., 69
30. Dutch War 1., 3
31. Letters 60,
32. M.M. Vol. 17., 151
33. Letters, 60
34. *ibid.*, 88
35. N.M.M., 9876
36. Warburton 3., 309
37. N.M.M., 9876
38. M.M., 17., 148
39. Letters, 61
40. Warburton 3., 309
41. Letters, 61, 88
42. *ibid.*, 61, 88

43. N.M.M., 9876
44. Letters, 62
45. *ibid.*, 89
46. *ibid.*, 62
47. *ibid.*, 62
48. T.T.E. 780, 17
49. M.M. vol. 17, 149
50. Letters, 63
51. D.W. 1., 13
52. Letters, 64
53. *ibid.*, 64
54. *ibid.*, 64
55. *ibid.*, 65
56. Warburton 3., 313
57. Letters, 65
    D.W. 1. 7.,
58. Letters, 90
59. *ibid.*, 69, 94
60. *ibid.*, 67
61. *ibid.*, 90
62. *ibid.*, 69
63. Warburton 3., 323
64. Letters, 70
65. C.S.P.D. 1651, 44
66. Letters, 69
67. *ibid.*, 91
68. Corbett 1., 233
69. Thurloe 1., 100
70. Penn 1., 322
71. Nickolls, 41
72. C.J. 6., 534

CHAPTER 8 *Amphibious Operations: I Scilly*

1. T.T.E. 384, 34
2. C.S.P.D. 1651, 86, 108
3. D.W. 1., 67
4. T.T.E. 785, 1
5. C.S.P.D. 1651 123
6. Thurloe 1., 177
7. T.T.E. 385, 12
8. M.M. Vol. 20, 62
9. M.M. 20, 58

10. *ibid.*, 785, 10
11. M.M. Vol. 20, 62
12. M.M. 20, 64
13. Letters, 113
14. Letters, 113
15. D.W. 1., 217
16. T.T.E. 875, 24
17. Letters, 113
18. *ibid.*, 119

19. *ibid.*, 128
20. *ibid.*, 113
21. T.T.E. 192, 25
22. Letters, 165
23. *ibid.*, 119
24. T.T.E. 292, 25
25. Letters, 120
26. *ibid.*, 129
27. *ibid.*, 121
28. *ibid.*, 129
29. *ibid.*, 122
30. *ibid.*, 123
31. *ibid.*, 113
32. *ibid.*, 123
33. *ibid.*, 97
34. T.T.E. 785, 27
35. *ibid.*, 385, 21
36. *ibid.*, 385, 4

37. Letters, 114
38. *ibid.*, 134
39. *ibid.*, 535
40. T.T.B. 385, 20
41. C.S.P.D. 1651, 187
42. T.T.E. 629, 7
43. Letters, 115
44. *ibid.*, 117
    T.T.E. 629, 7
45. Letters, 99
46. T.T.E. 344, 11
47. T.T.E. 785, 10
48. T.T.E. 786, 7
49. M.M. 20, 63
50. C.S.P.D. 1651, 342
51. *ibid.*, 357
52. Letters, 107
53. *ibid.*, 108

CHAPTER 9 *Amphibious Operations: II Jersey*

1. C.S.P.D. 1651, 441
2. *ibid.*, 451
3. Add. Mss. 22546, 43
4. T.T.E. 791, 3
5. Letters, 136
6. Clarendon S.P. Vol. 2 1652 1
7. Chevalier 2., 945
8. Clarendon S.P., 2
9. Letters, 136
10. Chevalier 2., 945
11. Letters, 136
12. *ibid.*, 140
13. *ibid.*, 142
14. *ibid.*, 140
15. Clarendon S.P., 1
16. Letters, 141
17. Chevalier 2., 947
18. Clarendon S.P., 2
19. Letters, 137
20. T.T.E. 791, 3
21. Clarendon S.P., 3
22. Letters, 141
23. Clarendon S.P., 3

24. Letters, 141
25. *ibid.*, 142
26. Clarendon S. P., 4
    Chevalier 2., 947
    T.T.E. 791, 33
27. Clarendon S.P., 4
    T.T.E. 791, 3
28. Letters, 137
29. Chevalier 2., 954
    Add. Mss. 22546, 42
    Letters, 344
30. Chevalier 2., 956
31. Letters, 111
32. Chevalier 2., 963
33. Letters, 139
34. Clarendon S.P., 4
35. Chevalier 2., 957
    T.T.E. 691, 3
36. Clarendon S.P., 4
37. C.S.P.D. 1652, 579
38. Clarendon S.P., 4
39. Chevalier 2., 959
40. Clarendon S.P., 4

41. T.T.E. 791, 16
42. Clarendon, 4
43. T.T.E. 651, 9
44. *ibid.*, 791, 10

45. *ibid.*, 651, 9
46. C.S.P.D. 1652, 94
47. *ibid.*, XL viii
48. D.W. 1., 130

CHAPTER 10 *The Approach of War with the Dutch*

1. Thurloe 1., 130
2. Gardiner C.P. 2., 359
3. *ibid.*, 362
4. Thurloe 1., 82
5. *ibid.*, 193
6. Gardiner C.P. 2., 83
7. *ibid.*, 101
8. D.W. 1., 134
9. *ibid.*, 81
10. *ibid.*, 88
11. *ibid.*, 129

12. *ibid.*, 130
13. *ibid.*, 155
14. Oppenheim, 341
15. *ibid.*, 347
16. *ibid.*, 348
17 *ibid.*, 317
18. D.W. 1., 55
19. *ibid.*, 55
20. *ibid.*, 57
21. *ibid.*, 64–66
22. *ibid.*, 142

CHAPTER 11 *The War with the Dutch breaks out*

1. D.W. 1., 164
2. *ibid.*, 178
3. *ibid.*, 181
4. *ibid.*, 183
5. *ibid.*, 201
6. *ibid.*, 251
7. *ibid.*, 417
8. D.W. 1., 251
9. *ibid.*, 252
10. Letters, 159
11. D.W. 1., 192
12. *ibid.*, 296
13. *ibid.*, 219
14. *ibid.*, 282
15. *ibid.*, 173
16. *ibid.*, 220
17. *ibid.*, 9
18. Letters, 158
19. D.W. 1., 109
20. *ibid.*, 420
21. *ibid.*, 420
22. *ibid.*, 277
23. *ibid.*, 193
24. *ibid.*, 254

25. *ibid.*, 198
26. Letters, 195
27. D.W. 1., 191
28. *ibid.*, 201
29. *ibid.*, 203
30. D.W. 1., 210
31. *ibid.*, 212
32. *ibid.*, 189
33. *ibid.*, 201
34. *ibid.*, 216
35. *ibid.*, 228
36. *ibid.*, 238
37. *ibid.*, 191
38. *ibid.*, 228
39. *ibid.*, 225
40. *ibid.*, 241
41. *ibid.*, 249
42. *ibid.*, 257
43. *ibid.*, 241
44. Letters, 161
45. *ibid.*, 162
46. D.W. 1., 246
47. *ibid.*, 268
48. *ibid.*, 270

49. *ibid.*, 278
50. Gardiner. C.P. 2., 119
51. D.W. 1., 276
52. *ibid.*, 283
53. *ibid.*, 292
54. Whitlocke 3., 429
55. D.W. 1., 292
56. *ibid.*, 293
57. Letters, 163
58. D.W. 1., 301
59. Letters, 167
60. D.W. 1., 315
61. *ibid.*, 304

62. *ibid.*, 305
63. *ibid.*, 309
64. *ibid.*, 311
65. *ibid.*, 312
66. *ibid.*, 312
67. *ibid.*, 316
68. Gardiner C.P. 2., 119
69. D.W. 1., 322
70. Penn 1., 432
71. D.W. 1., 325
72. *ibid.*, 329
73. Gardiner C.P. 2., 119
74. D.W. 1., 332

CHAPTER 12 *Blake's Northern Voyage*

1. D.W. 1., 325
2. Letters, 167
3. D.W. 1., 339
4. *ibid.*, 341
5. *ibid.*, 345, 347
6. *ibid.*, 247
7. *ibid.*, 350
8. *ibid.*, 337
9. *ibid.*, 352
10. *ibid.*, 353
11. *ibid.*, 346
12. *ibid.*, 369
13. *ibid.*, 365
14. *ibid.*, 372
15. *ibid.*, 376
16. *ibid.*, 360
17. *ibid.*, 366
18. *ibid.*, 363
19. *ibid.*, 371
20. *ibid.*, 385
    D.W. 1., 17
21. *ibid.*, 386
22. *ibid.*, 402
23. Letters, 168
24. D.W. 1., 383
25. *ibid.*, 378, 381
26. *ibid.*, 400
27. *ibid.*, 395

28. *ibid.*, 403
29. *ibid.*, 404
30. *ibid.*, 398
31. *ibid.*, 392
32. D.W. 1., 411
33. *ibid.*, 406
    D.W. 1., 14
34. *ibid.*, 405
35. *ibid.*, 406
36. Letters, 170
37. D.W. 2., 103, 113
38. *ibid.*, 17
39. *ibid.*, 39
40. *ibid.*, 59
41. *ibid.*, 57
42. *ibid.*, 68
43. *ibid.*, 99
44. *ibid.*, 100
45. *ibid.*, 93
46. *ibid.*, 55
47. *ibid.*, 76
48. *ibid.*, 107
49. *ibid.*, 120
50. *ibid.*, 142
51. *ibid.*, 197
52. *ibid.*, 181
53. *ibid.*, 202
54. *ibid.*, 117

55. Letters, 172
56. *ibid.*, 173
57. *ibid.*, 174
58. Corbett 1., 256
59. Gardiner C. P.2., 103
60. Jal, 202
61. Corbett 1., 256
62. Cal. S.P.D. 1652, 383
63. T.T.E. 675, 3
64. *ibid.*, 4

65. *ibid.*, 3
66. T.T.E. 697, 8
67. Jal, 203
68. Cal. S.P.D. 1652, 400
69. Jal, 204
70. Guizot Appendix 20, 460
71. Jal, 204
72. Guizot. Appendix 20, 463
73. *ibid.*, 462

CHAPTER 13 *Blake, De With and De Ruyter*

1. D.W. 3., 236
2. T.T.E. 675, 11
3. *ibid.*, 674, 32
4. D.W. 2., 208
5. D.W. 2., 185
6. T.T.E. 675, 11
7. D.W. 2., 238
8. *ibid.*, 207
9. *ibid.*, 239
10. *ibid.*, 240
11. *ibid.*, 241
12. *ibid.*, 242
13. *ibid.*, 210
14. T.T.E. 799, 3
15. H.C.A. 2., 15
16. D.W. 3., 37
17. D.W. 2., 243
18. *ibid.*, 235, 259
19. *ibid.*, 172
20. *ibid.*, 245
21. *ibid.*, 294, 301
22. *ibid.*, 357
23. *ibid.*, 266
24. *ibid.*, 269
25. *ibid.*, 257
26. *ibid.*, 269
27. *ibid.*, 274
28. D.W. 3., 54
    Letters, 176
29. D.W. 2., 269
30. Gardiner C.P. 2., 136

31. D.W. 2., 277
32. *ibid.*, 283
33. *ibid.*, 277
34. Letters, 176
35. D.W. 2., 270
36. *ibid.*, 282
37. *ibid.*, 357
38. D.W. 3., 54
39. *ibid.*, 2., 357
40. *ibid.*, 330, 360
41. *ibid.*, 278
42. *ibid.*, 358
43. Letters, 177
44. D.W. 2., 278
45. *ibid.*, 271
46. *ibid.*, 358
47. *ibid.*, 307
48. *ibid.*, 307
49. *ibid.*, 359
50. *ibid.*, 308
51. *ibid.*, 360
52. *ibid.*, 309
53. Letters, 177
54. D.W. 2., 313
55. *ibid.*, 329
56. *ibid.*, 367
57. *ibid.*, 303
58. *ibid.*, 373
59. D.W. 3., 112
60. Letters, 179

CHAPTER 14 *With Tromp's Recall a Dutch Victory*

1. D.W. 3., 21
2. *ibid.*, 11, 15, 26, 102
3. *ibid.*, 23, 24
4. *ibid.*, 10
5. *ibid.*, 44
6. *ibid.*, 62
7. *ibid.*, 78
8. *ibid.*, 186
9. *ibid.*, 40
10. Gardiner C.P. 2., 220
11. C.J. 7., 210
12. Penn 1., 426
13. D.W. 3., 120
14. *ibid.*, 32
15. *ibid.*, 30
16. *ibid.*, 73
17. *ibid.*, 10
18. *ibid.*, 26
19. *ibid.*, 71
20. Gardiner C.P. 2., 119
21. D.W. 3., 78
22. Letters, 182
23. *ibid.*, 183
24. D.W. 3., 84
25. *ibid.*, 78
26. *ibid.*, 81
27. *ibid.*, 116
28. *ibid.*, 90
29. *ibid.*, 107
30. *ibid.*, 116
31. Letters, 184
32. D.W. 3., 116
33. *ibid.*, 116
34. *ibid.*, 107
35. Letters, 184
36. *ibid.*, 184
37. D.W. 3., 117
38. *ibid.*, 117
39. *ibid.*, 230
40. *ibid.*, 117, 230
    Letters, 184
41. D.W. 3., 137
42. D.W. 3., 117, 230
43. *ibid.*, 94
44. *ibid.*, 130
45. Letters, 184
46. D.W. 3., 167
47. *ibid.*, 130
48. T.T.E. 683, 19
49. D.W. 3., 95
50. Letters, 185
51. D.W. 3., 101, 118
52. Letters, 184
53. D.W. 3., 113
54. *ibid.*, 196, 112, 135
55. *ibid.*, 119
56. *ibid.*, 97
57. Letters., 186
58. D.W. 3., 122
59. Letters, 188
60. D.W. 3., 139, 155, 160
61. *ibid.*, 165
62. *ibid.*, 167
63. *ibid.*, 418
64. *ibid.*, 364, 406, 437
    Oppenheim, 353
65. D.W. 3., 445
66. *ibid.*, 390
67. *ibid.*, 418

CHAPTER 15 *Blake and Vane Reorganise the Navy*

1. Rowe, 177
2. *ibid.*, 178
3. D.W. 3., 121
4. *ibid.*, 147
5. Gardiner C.P. 2., 153
6. D.W. 3., 283
7. *ibid.*, 288
8. *ibid.*, 373

9. *ibid.*, 409
10. *ibid.*, 293
11. Rowe, 181
12. D.W. 3., 363
13. *ibid.*, 319
14. *ibid.*, 324
15. *ibid.*, 318
16. *ibid.*, 340
17. *ibid.*, 289
18. *ibid.*, 385
19. *ibid.*, 342
20. *ibid.*, 231
21. D.W. 3., 366
22. *ibid.*, 350
23. *ibid.*, 182
24. N.M.M.,
     A.G.C. B., 2
25. D.W. 3., 110
26. *ibid.*, 367
27. *ibid.*, 381
28. *ibid.*, 374
29. Rowe, 182

30. D.W. 3., 393
31. Letters, 194
32. *ibid.*, 197
33. Mountagu Mss. 123. D., 11
34. Letters, 197
35. N.M.M. A.G.C. B., 2
36. D.W. 3., 407
37. Rowe, 182
38. D.W. 3., 414
39. Rowe, 183
40. *ibid.*, 184
41. Letters, 197
42. *ibid.*, 195
43. D.W. 3., 418
44. *ibid.*, 428
45. Letters, 198
46. *ibid.*, 198
47. D.W. 3., 451
48. Letters, 199
49. *ibid.*, 200
50. *ibid.*, 203

CHAPTER 16 *Portland: the Balaclava of the Sea*

1 D.W. 4., 23
2. *ibid.*, 27
3. *ibid.*, 48
4. *ibid.*, 177
5. *ibid.*, 187
6. *ibid.*, 180
7. *ibid.*, 188
8. D.W. 1., 15
9 D.W. 4., 184
10. *ibid.*, 188
11. *ibid.*, 160
12. *ibid.*, 126
13. *ibid.*, 33
14. *ibid.*, 100
15. *ibid.*, 64
16. Letters, 206
17. D.W. 4., 90
18. Gardiner C.P. 2., 156
19. D.W. 4., 62

20. *ibid.*, 63
21. Letters, 206
22. D.W. 4., 280
23. *ibid.*, 180
24. Letters, 204
25. D.W. 1., 14
     Penn 2., 615
26. D.W. 4., 118
27. Letters, 207
28. D.W. 1., 14
29. D.W. 4., 118
30. *ibid.*, 194
31. *ibid.*, 180
32. *ibid.*, 121
33. *ibid.*, 79
34. *ibid.*, 68
35. *ibid.*, 79
36. D.W. 1., 15
37. Penn 2., 416

38. D.W. 4., 194
39. ibid., 79
40. ibid., 188
41. ibid., 80
42. ibid., 95
43. ibid., 80
44. Brandt, 90
45. Letters, 207
46. D.W. 4., 101
47. ibid., 118
48. ibid., 80
49. ibid., 118
50. ibid., 80
51. ibid., 188
52. ibid., 68
53. ibid., 73, 80
54. Tromp's Life, 92
55. D.W. 4., 123
56. ibid., 81
57. ibid., 69
58. ibid., 118
59. Letters, 207
60. D.W. 4., 138
61. ibid., 84
62. Letters, 208
63. ibid., 208
64. D.W. 4., 183
65. ibid., 195
66. ibid., 182
67. ibid., 81
68. ibid., 119
69. Letters, 208
70. D.W. 4., 195
71. ibid., 70
72. D.W. 1., 16

73. D.W. 4., 190
74. Tromp's Life, 96
75. D.W. 4., 120
76. Letters, 208
77. D.W. 4., 70
78. Letters, 208
79. D.W. 4., 120
80. Letters, 208
81. D.W. 4., 90
82. Tromp's Life, 91
83. Letters, 208
84. D.W. 4., 71
85. ibid., 91
86. ibid., 94
87. ibid., 111
88. ibid., 183
89. ibid., 122
90. Letters, 209
91. D.W. 4., 121
92. Letters, 208
93. ibid., 204
94. D.W. 4., 121
95. ibid., 170
96. ibid., 111
97. Letters, 209
98. D.W. 4., 152
99. Letters, 206
100. D.W. 4., 14
101. ibid., 116
102. ibid., 145
103. ibid., 149
104. ibid., 174
      T.T.E. 689, 13
105. Gardiner, C.P. 2., 151

CHAPTER 17 *From a Sick Bed to the Gabbard*

1. Letters, 210
2. D.W. 4., 223
3. ibid., 104
4. ibid., 223
5. ibid., 231
6. C.S.P.D. 1653, 199

7. D.W. 4., 241
8. ibid., 325
9. ibid., 51
10. ibid , 255
11 D.W. 4., 262
12. ibid., 264

13. *ibid.*, 265
14. *ibid.*, 266-72
15. *ibid.*, 234
16. *ibid.*, 233
17. *ibid.*, 255
18. *ibid.*, 259
19. *ibid.*, 282
20. *ibid.*, 290
21. *ibid.*, 299
22. *ibid.*, 305
23. *ibid.*, 252
24. *ibid.*, 247
25. *ibid.*, 257
26. *ibid.*, 281
27. *ibid.*, 334
28. *ibid.*, 317
29. *ibid.*, 335
30. *ibid.*, 333
31. *ibid.*, 348
32. *ibid.*, 379
33. Rowe, 189
34.
35.
36. T.T.E. 693, 12
37. D.W. 4., 358
38. Letters, 212
39. D.W. 4., 358
40. *ibid.*, 377
41. D.W. 5., 39
42. *ibid.*, 40
43. *ibid.*, 43
44. *ibid.*, 42
45. *ibid.*, 43
46. *ibid.*, 47
47. *ibid.*, 26
48. *ibid.*, 139
49. *ibid.*, 53
50. *ibid.*, 141
51. *ibid.*, 57
52. *ibid.*, 65
53. *ibid.*, 75

54. *ibid.*, 50
55. *ibid.*, 49
56. *ibid.*, 60
57. *ibid.*, 64
58. Letters, 214
59. D.W. 5., 143
60. *ibid.*, 10
61. *ibid.*, 143
62. *ibid.*, 83
63. D.W. 5., 72
64. Letters, 214
65. D.W. 5., 264
66. *ibid.*, 287
67. *ibid.*, 20
68. *ibid.*, 56
69. *ibid.*, 72
70. *ibid.*, 100
71. *ibid.*, 21
72. *ibid.*, 83, 144
73. *ibid.*, 98
74. Penn 1, 493
75. Colliber, 124
76. D.W. 5., 144
77. *ibid.*, 73
78. *ibid.*, 81
79. Gumble, 64
80. D.W. 5., 70
81. Letters, 216
    Penn 1., 495
82. D.W. 5., 101
83. *ibid.*, 87
84. Penn 1., 498
85. D.W. 5., 81
86. *ibid.*, 92
87. *ibid.*, 94
88. Letters, 215
89. *ibid.*, 218
90. D.W. 5., 105
91. *ibid.*, 107
92. *ibid.*, 147

CHAPTER 18 *Victory Over the Dutch*

1. D.W. 5., 213
2. *ibid.*, 197
3. *ibid.*, 208
4. Letters, 224
5. D.W. 5., 193
6. Letters, 218
7. *ibid.*, 218, 221
8. D.W. 5., 215
9. *ibid.*, 228
10. *ibid.*, 195
11. Letters, 229
12. *ibid.*, 233
13. *ibid.*, 230
14. *ibid.*, 233, 235
15. D.W. 5., 206
16. *ibid.*, 256
17. Letters, 241
18. D.W. 5., 291
19. *ibid.*, 258
20. *ibid.*, 263
21. *ibid.*, 271
22. *ibid.*, 274
23. *ibid.*, 291
24. *ibid.*, 259
25. *ibid.*, 276
26. *ibid.*, 295
27. *ibid.*, 247
28. *ibid.*, 270
29. *ibid.*, 190
30. *ibid.*, 198
31. *ibid.*, 193
32. *ibid.*, 201
33. *ibid.*, 286
34. *ibid.*, 290
35. *ibid.*, 304
36. *ibid.*, 313
37. *ibid.*, 312
38. *ibid.*, 224
39. *ibid.*, 289
40. *ibid.*, 350
41. Brandt, 142
42. D.W. 5., 367
43. Penn 1., 504
44. D.W. 5., 372
45. *ibid.*, 352
46. *ibid.*, 398
47. D.W. 6., 31
48. D.W. 5., 291
49. *ibid.*, 310
50. *ibid.*, 340
51. *ibid.*, 381
52. Letters, 243
53. *ibid.*, 244
54. C.J. 7., 332
55. D.W. 5., 398
56. D.W. 6., 60
57. *ibid.*, 53
58. *ibid.*, 107
59. *ibid.*, 128
60. Gardiner C.P. 3., 75
61. D.W. 6., 133
62. *ibid.*, 172
63. Oppenheim, 307
64. D.W. 6., 189
65. Letters, 245
66. *ibid.*, 248
67. *ibid.*, 249
68. Letters, 263
69. D.W. 1., 25
70. Letters, 263
71. N.M.M., A.G.C., 1
72. D.W. 6., 64
73. Gardiner, C.P. 3.,
74. Lewis, 93
75. Mahan, 37
76. D.W. 1., 12, 13

CHAPTER 19 *Return to the Mediterranean*

1. C.S.P.D. 1654, 100
2. Spalding, 54
3. T.T.E. 286, 122
4. Gardiner C.P. 3., 373

5. Corbett, 1., 276
6. Letters, 292
7. Thurloe 2., 252
8. *ibid.*, 1., 437
9. *ibid.*, 456
10. S.P. Venetian 1654, 228
11. Thurloe 1., 656
12. *ibid.*, 2., 432
13. *ibid.*, 2., 447
14. Penn 2., 157
15. Letters, 280
16. *ibid.*, 281
17. C.S.P.D. 1644, 68, 85
18. Gardiner C.P. 3., 285
19. Weale 92
20. T.T.E. 820, 5
21. Corbett 1., 286
22. T.T.E. 840, 2
23. Letters, 315
24. Weale 93
25. *ibid.*, 94
26. *ibid.*, 94
27. *ibid.*, 95
28. Letters, 316
29. Weale, 96
30. Thurloe 3., 12
31. Weale, 96
32. Letters, 283
33. C.S.P.D. Venetian 1654, 10
34. Letters, 285
35. S.P. Venetian 1654, 10
36. Letters, 287
37. Letters, 288
38. Corbett 1., 299
39. S.P. Venetian 1654, 29
40. Letters, 288
41. Weale, 101
42. Letters, 291
43. Gardiner C.P. 3., 377
44. Letters, 292
45. Weale, 101
46. *ibid.*, 103
47. Letters, 291
48. *ibid.*, 312

49. Weale, 102
50. Letters, 289, 310
51. *ibid.*, 290
52. *ibid.*, 291
53. Weale, 106
54. Letters, 294
55. T.T.E. 1954, 3
56. Letters, 320
57. T.T.E. 1954, 3
58. Letters, 292
59. Weale, 108
60. T.T.E. 1954, 3
61. Letters, 294
62. S.P.D. 184, 86
63. Weale, 109
64. T.T.E. 787, 8
65. Weale, 109
66. Letters, 195
67. *ibid.*, 319
68. *ibid.*, 294
69. *ibid.*, 296
70. S.P. Barbary. A. 2., 252
71. Letters, 314
72. *ibid.*, 297
73. Burnet, 1., 86
74. Abbott, 3., 721
75. Weale, 96, 123
76. T.T.E. 826, 16
77. Ludlow 1., 408
78. Thurloe 3., 342
79. Letters, 298
80. Abbott 3., 745
81. Letters, 299
82. *ibid.*, 300
83. *ibid.*, 302
84. *ibid.*, 303
85. *ibid.*, 305
86. Thurloe 4., 694
87. Letters, 307
88. Abbott 3., 390
89. Letters, 307
90. Weale, 121
91. *ibid.*, 122
92. Letters, 307

93. *ibid.*, 308
94. *ibid*, 310
95. *ibid.*, 312
96. *ibid.*, 313
97. Abbott 3., 311
98. Weale, 123
99. S.P. Venetian 1655, 196
100. Thurloe 4., 79
101. Clarendon 6., 33

CHAPTER 20 *The Expedition of Blake and Mountagu in 1656*

1. Abbott 3., 721
2. Letters, 355
3. S.P.D. 1656, 124, 18
4. C.S.P.D. 1656, 178
5. S.P.D. 129, 32
6. Thurloe 3., 147
7. Gardiner C.P. 3., 460
8. *ibid.*, 458–462
9. S.P.D. 125, 75
10. Thurloe 2., 590
11. Letters, 393
12. *ibid.*, 339, 394
13. *ibid.*, 396
14. T.T.E. 492, 6
15. Carte 2., 88
16. *ibid.*, 88
17. Letters, 342
18. *ibid.*, 346
19. S.P. Venetian 1656, 220
    S.P.D. 1656, 138, 81
20. T.T.E. 493, 8, 12
21. Letters, 399
    Weale, 131
22. Letters, 347
23. *ibid.*, 348
24. *ibid.*, 433
25. *ibid.*, 404
26. Abbott 4., 239
27. *ibid.*, 149
28. Letters, 405
29. *ibid.*, 402
30. Thurloe 4., 758
31. T.T.E. 494, 11
    S.P. Venetian 1656, 242
32. Thurloe 5., 79
33. *ibid.*, 113
34. S.P. Venetian 1656, 208
35. Abbott 4., 148
36. *ibid.*, 148
37. Letters, 364
38. S.P.D. 1656, 141, 29
39. Letters, 362
40. *ibid.*, 440
41. *ibid.*, 441
42. Abbott 4., 183
43. Letters, 412
44. *ibid.*, 368
45. *ibid.*, 369
46. *ibid.*, 445, 416
47. *ibid.*, 415
48. Carte Mss. 73, 20
49. Letters, 416
50. *ibid.*, 418
51. *ibid.*, 420
52. *ibid.*, 447, 450
    Bath Papers, Longleat,
    41, 97-f
53. Letters, 448
54. Thurloe 5., 472
    C.J. 7., 432
55. Abbott 4., 239
56. Carte 2., 111
57. Letters, 374, 430
58. *ibid.*, 426
59. Carte Mss. 73, 197
60. C.J. 7., 456
61. Thurloe 5., 569
62. C.S.P.D. 1656, 415
63. *ibid.*, 517
64. Rawlinson Mss. 62, 1
65. Letters, 428
66. *ibid.*, 357
67. C.S.P.D. 1657–1658, 494
68. Abbott 4., 301

CHAPTER 21 *Blake's Final Victory*

1. Letters, 377
2. Weale, 144
3. Letters, 379
4. Weale, 142
5. Letters, 381
6. C.S.P.D. 1656, 482
7. Letters, 453
8. Brandt, 73
9. Letters, 381
10. Thurloe 6., 48
11. Letters, 453
    Weale, 143
12. Letters, 383
13. Clarke. Papers 3., 115
14. Thurloe 6., 401
15. Stayner, 2
16. Weale, 143
17. Letters, 455
18. Stayner, 129
19. *ibid.*, 139
20. C.S.P.D. 1657, 74
21. *ibid.*, 545
22. Weale, 146
23. Stayner, 130
24. Letters, 385
25. U.S.M. May 1911
26. Stayner, 31
27. Letters, 386
28. Stayner, 131
29. Letters, 457
30. *ibid.*, 386
31. Stayner, 131
32. Letters, 386
33. Stayner, 133
34. Letters, 459
35. Stayner, 133
36. Lurting, 7
37. Stayner, 134
38. *ibid.*, 134

39. Lurting, 10
40. Weale, 146
41. Stayner, 134
42. Letters, 387
43. Lurting, 9
44. Stayner, 134
45. S.A.P., 60
46. Heath, 648
47. Clarendon 6., 36
48. N.H.N. 2. 379
49. Letters, 387
50. Firth 1., 259
51. Stayner, 136
    Weale, 147
52. C.J. 7., 41
53. Thurloe 6., 342
54. Abbott 4., 548
55. C.S.P.D. 1657, 368
56. S.P. Ven. 1657, 63
57. Letters, 392
58. Weale, 149
59. Weale, 149
60. S.P. Ven. 1657, 95
61. Thurloe 6., 364
62. *ibid.*, 314, 366
63. Weale, 150
64. Clarke Papers 3., 115
65. Letters, 463
66. S.P.P. 170, 65
67. Letters, 463
68. C.S.P.D. 1657, 170
69. Add. Mss. 9300, 359
70. Yonge,
71. S.P.D. 156, 20
72. C.S.P.D. 1657, 126
73. Add. Mss. 9394, 126
74. Clarke Papers 3., 118
75. Spalding, 621

Index

Compiled by the Rev. S. B-R. Poole

List of Ships referred to in the text

NOTE: (m) after an entry denotes 'merchantman'

2. FOREIGN SHIPS